Captain Cook's World

Captain Cook's World

Maps of the Life and Voyages of James Cook R.N.

Maps and Text by
John Robson

CHATHAM PUBLISHING
LONDON

To Troy and Oscar

First published in Great Britain in 2001 by
Chatham Publishing, 99 High Street,
Rochester, Kent ME1 1LX

Chatham Publishing is an imprint of Gerald Duckworth & Co Ltd,
61 Frith Street, London W1D 3JL

ISBN 1 86176 181 3

First published in 2000 by Random House New Zealand

Cover and text design: Christine Hansen
Cover illustrations: Captain Cook's sextant and Captain James Cook (portrait)
    © National Maritime Museum Picture Library, London
Editor: Jane Parkin
Text layout: Kate Greenaway
Cartographer: Max Oulton
Map design: Timon Maxey
Map production: Elin Termannsen

Printed in Hong Kong

Contents

List of Maps

Preface

When I was a boy growing up in Stockton-on-Tees, England, my mother used to tell me that we were related to Captain James Cook, who came from nearby Marton. His presence was still strong in the area, and the concept was developing of it being known as Captain Cook country. According to my mother, our connection to Cook, albeit remote, was through relations of hers at Redcar, and there were further connections to farmers in the Cleveland area (alas, later research has not confirmed this). At the time, though, it gave us a special link to Cook. We could clearly see the Captain Cook Monument on Easby Moor from Stockton, and we often visited family friends at Great Ayton, where Cook grew up. With this early inspiration, I began a lifelong interest in Cook. Later, that interest developed further, especially as our paths kept crossing when I began to travel. I spent time in Canada and Australia before I ended up in New Zealand with all its Cook connections.

Another of my lifelong interests has been maps. I can spend hours looking at and poring over them. Any sort of map, old or new, will do, and over the years I have built up a collection of both maps and atlases. From a very early age, when asked what I wanted for Christmas, I would answer, *The Times Atlas of the World*. Eventually I treated myself to a copy of that magnificent book, and it is one of my most used and treasured possessions. Much of my enjoyment of travelling lies in the fact that it gives me an excuse to obtain more maps for my collection.

I also enjoy drawing maps, and I have often produced maps of walks, excursions and other activities for my friends. A long-time admirer of Alfred Wainwright and his guides of the English Lake District, I have tried to draw maps that also incorporate lots of extra information.

Captain Cook and maps sit very easily together, for much of his life was involved with the use and production of maps. However, while hundreds of books have been written about Cook and his life, a universal failing has been their lack of good, detailed maps. When trying to follow his voyages, detailed maps or a good atlas are a necessity, but most readers do not have collections of such maps and most atlases probably do not have the detail required.

So an opportunity presented itself for me to bring my interests together. I have, therefore, produced in this book a sequence of maps attempting to depict all stages in Cook's life and all the places associated with him.

I have received much encouragement throughout the long process, and would like to thank many people for their support. Firstly, Mona, my mother, and George, my father, who, though both dead for several years, gave me the initial impetus and always said I should produce a book. Rosanne Jatania, the Map Librarian at the University of Waikato Library (but also a close personal friend), has helped me find many of the base maps from which I have produced my final versions. Sally Sleigh, another close friend, has given much support and contributed the photograph for the book's back cover flap. She also helped proofread the manuscript with Megan Symes.

Ian Boreham, Alwyn Peel and Cliff Thornton from the Captain Cook Study Unit have offered encouragement and advice, for which I am very grateful.

I would like to thank Jane Connor of Random House New Zealand for all her help in bringing the book to publication. A special thank you to Max Oulton and Elin Termannsen for computerising my drafts of the maps and turning them into the professional and attractive versions reproduced here.

Finally a very special thanks to my two corgis, Troy (who sadly died in May 1999) and Oscar, who sat patiently for hours and hours while I worked on the book, without ever complaining. They kept me going and ensured that I finished what I had started. For that reason the book is dedicated to Troy and Oscar, 'the boys'.

Introduction

James Cook, the eighteenth-century British explorer, travelled the world and reached nearly every corner of it. He sailed into every ocean and was one of the first, if not the first British explorer, to set foot on the continents of Europe, Asia, Africa, Australia, and North and South America. He even came very close to being the first to land on Antarctica. He was the first to cross the Antarctic Circle and also to cross both it and the Arctic Circle.

During his voyages, Cook drew many maps and bestowed more names on places and geographical features than probably any other person. Many of his choices have since been replaced by local names, but a very large number of them are still in common usage in many parts of the world, among them New Caledonia, South Georgia, the Whitsunday Islands and Christmas Island. After his death, other people began to give Cook's name to places and features, so that now there is Cook Bay, Cook Strait, Cook Stream, Mount Cook and even Cook Glacier. The Cook Islands were named for James Cook and, interestingly, a recent referendum there resulted in the name being retained in preference to a local Polynesian name.

Cook's name and exploits are known worldwide. His is an international fame in the same way as that of Christopher Columbus and Marco Polo, with all three known for their journeys of exploration. In the 200 years since Cook's death his journals have been translated into many languages, and books about him and his voyages continue to be published in countries around the world. In the last few years books have been published in countries as varied as Estonia, Iran, Mexico and New Zealand.

Where are the places Cook sailed to and that are mentioned in his journals? The hundreds of books that have been written and continue to be written about Cook and his voyages rarely provide the answers. A reader of those books would find it difficult to establish where events took place, because the accompanying maps are so poor and lack so much detail. Even an atlas of the quality of *The Times Atlas of the World* struggles to show in detail many of the 'out-of-the-way' places that Cook visited, such as some of the smaller islands in the Pacific or Southern Oceans.

Cook, himself, would have endorsed readers' access to these maps which were so important to him and his work. The collection of maps and charts that he drew himself, or that members of his crew drew, in the course of his voyages is a huge testament to his life. They are some of the best maps ever drawn, especially considering the conditions and times in which they were researched and compiled. They are instantly recognisable when examined, and stand comparison with their modern equivalents. In many cases, they could still be used today (indeed, part of Cook's chart of Dusky Sound in New Zealand was being replaced by a modern survey as late as 1996). All of the maps and charts drawn on Cook's three voyages have been assembled and published in three volumes as *The Charts and Coastal Views of Captain Cook's Voyages* by the Hakluyt Society in London from 1988 to 1998. These wonderful books, compiled and edited by Andrew David, are a magnificent addition to the library of works devoted to James Cook.

Unfortunately only a few people have easy access to the Hakluyt volumes and, even with them, it can be difficult to locate a place mentioned in the descriptive text of Cook's voyages. While Cook usually showed a good representation of the overall shapes, the details were sometimes lacking. Cook did not always record the names correctly and, often, names that he used have been replaced by local names. Cook's maps were often compiled very quickly and therefore were selective in what they recorded. Not all the places and features of a locality were included, especially if adverse weather conditions such as thick fog prevented their being sighted.

The initial aim for this work was that it comprise a set of maps which would serve as a complement to other books about Cook. However, with time the maps began to assume an entity of their own so that, with the addition of accompanying text, the book can now be read as a biography or chronology of James Cook in its own right.

Another potential use came to mind as the book developed. As well as recording the events of the eighteenth century, the maps show, among other things, the locations of monuments and statues of Cook, of museums with collections of material associated with Cook's voyages, and of libraries holding Cook's logs, journals, and so on.

The maps

The 128 maps give a detailed overview of Cook's life from his father's arrival in Cleveland in 1720 through to 1780 when Gore brought the *Resolution* and the *Discovery* back to Britain after Cook's death. The maps are sketch maps and aim to provide as true a representation as possible. However, the originals were hand-drawn and copied from published atlases, maps and charts, so small errors may occur. I have used a huge number of sources in creating these maps, often combining information from several originals to build up the finished product.

The process of creating these maps started by sketching a rough draft and then adding relevant information. Gradually a sequence of related maps would develop, depicting aspects of Cook's life. Most of the maps then underwent several modifications to reach the versions that appear here. When the final version had been reached, a tracing of the outline of the geographical features, together with the tracks of ships, was made. The tracing was then scanned into the computer. The headings, names of features and the pieces of text were loaded separately on to the computer and were later combined with the map outlines to produce the final versions. These last actions were performed most professionally for me by Max Oulton.

Map organisation and numbering

The maps have been brought together in four sections and, with only a few exceptions, they are in chronological order. The exceptions occur where available space (or lack of it) dictated that a change be made. For example, the map showing the separation of the *Resolution* and the *Adventure* at the end of the first island sweep during the Second Voyage fitted more easily into the map showing that island sweep than it did in its true position after the visit to Tonga. Similarly, where Cook doubled back and revisited a location, both visits are shown on one map. An example of this occurs on the Third Voyage at Unalaska, which Cook visited in both July and October 1778.

Each voyage has a section devoted to it, and the maps have been numbered in such a way as to provide a link between that voyage and its maps. Maps from the First Voyage are, therefore, numbered 1.01, 1.02, etc.; the Second Voyage 2.01, 2.02, etc. This has resulted in maps from Cook's early life and his time in Canada carrying numbers 0.01, 0.02, etc. Since most interest will be in the maps of the voyages, I trust the use of this form of numbering will not prove too confusing.

North points and scales

I apologise to cartographers and map purists for the fact that none of the maps has a scale or a north point. Lack of space prevented those pieces of information being included, but nearly all of the maps have been drawn with north at the top of the map, or close to it. Occasionally the map has been manoeuvred so as to fit into the space available and north may be a little away from the top of the map. The map of Poverty Bay is one of these.

With regards to scale, virtually all of the maps have been reduced or enlarged by photocopy, sometimes on more than one occasion, to fit into the space available. What might have started as having a scale of 1: 500,000 has, therefore, probably been modified to 1: 467,672 or a figure too difficult to compute.

Tracks

The representations of the tracks of Cook's vessels and the movement of people on land are only approximate. The intention has been to show, as closely as can be determined, where the ships passed, but the scales of the maps and gaps in the source information sometimes prevent exact details being shown. The navigational equipment that Cook used was limited, so that he often recorded positions in his logs and journals with minor errors. His charts suffered accordingly, and the absolute positions of the ships at any time are open to question. Moreover, in many places it has been impossible to show all the detail of the ships tacking and plying back and forth, so the tracks depicted are smoothed-out versions. For some events the information available is too vague. For instance, we cannot be sure which path Cook took across the mountains in Moorea when attempting to retrieve the goat that had been stolen.

Nomenclature

Wherever possible, Cook tried to obtain the local name of a place or a feature, but often the translation, transliteration or transcription lost something. As a result, what Cook recorded in his journal or on his charts bore little resemblance to the name by which the feature was known locally. Somehow, for example, Uawa on the east coast of Te Ika a Maui, the North Island of New Zealand, became Tolaga Bay!

Similarly, Cook often sailed through an area without making contact with local people, and ascribed names without knowing the local name. Many of his names have survived, but many have lapsed in favour of the original name. In some cases later names have eclipsed those of Cook. The maps in this atlas normally show the current, commonly used name, with Cook's name or his attempt at the local name either alongside or somewhere on the map.

Text on maps

Some text has been included on each map so that it may be understood and stand alone, out of sequence, if required. Information relevant to that part of Cook's life has also been incorporated. Like nature abhorring a vacuum, I have tried to insert details in what would otherwise have been blank spaces. However, not all maps had large areas of blank space, so for those maps it may be necessary to consult the accompanying text to gain a better understanding of what was happening.

Gazetteer

A gazetteer in which all geographical features such as towns, seas, capes, and so on are listed has been included following the maps. For each location, the map or maps on which they can be found are given. Space did not allow co-ordinates to be given for each location, so the designated map will need to be searched to find the required item. The gazetteer does not include the names of people.

Accompanying text

As stated elsewhere, the original intention of this work was that the maps would stand alone as a record of Cook's life and travels. Unfortunately, some maps did not have sufficient space for very much text so it became necessary to provide a separate text. This text has been inserted in such a way as to form breaks between the sets of maps. In these pieces I have given a very brief version of Cook's life and travels, which may help place the maps in context. It does not pretend to be a detailed or definitive version of Cook's life; that has been done more than adequately by others, especially J.C. Beaglehole.

J.C. Beaglehole's work on Cook will, I am sure, never be surpassed. I refer everyone who wishes to read about Cook in detail to his biography of Cook and to his editions of Cook's *Journals.*

Beaglehole's books are not so good when dealing with Cook's early life. Accurate information about Cook's childhood has always been in short supply. Cliff Thornton has done much research in recent years to remedy this situation and his book *Captain Cook in Cleveland* helps fill some of the gaps. Similarly, Julia Rae has researched Cook's time in the East End of London, and her book *Captain James Cook Endeavours* covers this period of the explorer's life.

Cook's early time in the Royal Navy remains poorly served, especially the years spent in Canada. William Whiteley has written a short book called *James Cook in Newfoundland, 1762–1767*, and this work, together with *James Cook: Surveyor of Newfoundland*, edited by Skelton, provide a background to that part of the story. There is an opportunity, however, for a Canadian historian to produce a proper history of Cook in Canada from Halifax and Louisbourg through to Newfoundland.

Select bibliography

Details of the books mentioned above, together with several other essential titles, have been included in a short but select bibliography. Hundreds of books have been published about many aspects of Cook's life in recent years, but most only rework the information found in the titles listed here.

Acknowledgements

I would like to thank the Guildhall Library in the City of London for providing information that confirmed that Cook had taken his Masters' examination through Trinity House in Water Lane, near the Tower of London, and not in Deptford. Also thanks to Andrew David for helping me locate a copy of Alexander Dalrymple's map of the South Atlantic Ocean, and to the UK Hydrographic Office for providing a copy of the map.

Conclusion

Captain James Cook's reputation has suffered somewhat in the 1990s as academic historians rewrite history ascribing present-day interpretations, morals and attitudes to eighteenth-century events. Cook may not have deserved some of the adulation and praise that earlier generations lavished upon him, but he certainly does not deserve the negative twists currently being placed on his actions of 200 years ago.

However, it is for exploring that Cook will be remembered: for all the places he visited; for the journals and records he and his colleagues kept; and, especially, for the maps he produced. I hope this atlas helps in the understanding and appreciation of James Cook.

I believe him to have been one of the greatest seafaring explorers of all time; he also possessed huge talents in seamanship, surveying, navigation, astronomy and cartography. Importantly, he was a born leader and his handling of the ships' crews on the three long and arduous voyages in cramped and appalling conditions is testimony to his ability. Part of the criticism of Cook in recent years has centred on the deaths of Pacific people during contact with the British ships. Nobody was more saddened than Cook by such deaths, and it is a measure of Cook's leadership and respect for other people that so few deaths actually took place. The coming together of two vastly different cultures was bound to lead to some friction, and on Cook's voyages there was, thanks largely to him, much less than on other European voyages.

Early Life

Background

James Cook, the sailor, surveyor, cartographer and explorer, was born in 1728 in Cleveland, in the North Riding of Yorkshire in Northeast England [0.01]. Cleveland is a district bounded to the north by the River Tees, to the south by the North Yorkshire Moors and to the east by the North Sea. This low-lying area was rich agricultural land which supported many farms, but further south the land rose and gave way to the Cleveland Hills, which stretch eastwards to the coast where they form some of England's highest cliffs (hence the name Cleveland) [0.02].

In the early eighteenth century, when Cook was born, the Industrial Revolution had not yet begun; the nearby Durham Coalfield was still in its infancy; the Stockton and Darlington Railway was not thought of; and Middlesbrough, which now dominates the area, was only two or three buildings. Yarm, Stockton and Guisborough were the local market towns, while York and Newcastle were a day's journey away. London was a very distant 400 kilometres to the south, and in many ways Edinburgh and Scotland were more accessible and influential. The whole area from Yorkshire to Edinburgh had once been part of the ancient Kingdom of Northumbria and, even now, its legacy remains.

Cook's parents

It was not so surprising, therefore, for a farm labourer from near Kelso in Roxburghshire in Scotland to move south to Cleveland some time in the 1720s. This labourer was James Cook senior. Church records in Ednam, near Kelso, show that he was born (in 1694) and raised in Ednam, the son of John Cook, a tailor. There are very few details of this James Cook's life before he appeared in Cleveland. Quite why and when he moved south remains unknown and open to speculation.

In 1715 there had been an uprising, the Jacobite rebellion for the Old Pretender, and there had been much support for it in South Scotland and Northumbria. Kelso had been a rallying point for the rebellion and Cook senior may have played a role, in which case he would have needed to avoid repercussions. Or he may simply have needed to move to find work, and the prosperous farms of Cleveland offered prospects of a good job.

The church records for Stainton-in-Cleveland Parish Church show that James Cook and Grace Pace were married on 10 October 1725, when the groom was 31 and the bride was 23 [0.01]. Grace had grown up with her family in Thornaby-on-Tees, nearby to the northwest and across the River Tees from Stockton.

Around this time, farm work was seasonal and temporary, so labourers moved wherever they could get work, attending hirings which were held in the market towns. The Cooks became part of this system and over the next few years they regularly moved round the Cleveland district, albeit a few kilometres on each occasion [0.02]. In 1727 they were living in Morton when their first child, John, was born and baptised in nearby Ormesby. Soon after, they moved 3 kilometres northwest to Marton where Cook senior had secured work with George Mewburn [0.03].

Cook's childhood

On Sunday 27 October 1728 the Cooks' second son was born. He was baptised a week later, on 3 November, in St. Cuthbert's, Marton Parish Church. This was James Cook. Cook's early life is a mixture of fact, hearsay and legend blended together over the years by various biographers, many of whom did little or no research and simply perpetuated the existing stories. Clifford Thornton has done the most to verify the true details.

James Cook senior was still not secure in his employment and the family soon moved again. Their third child, Christiana, was born in 1731 and baptised in Ormesby. By 1733 the family had returned to Marton, and James and Grace's fourth child, Mary, was born (she was to die in 1737). The Cooks were still poor, and pressures would dictate that all the children would work as soon as they were able. It is believed, therefore, that young James was already tending stock, watering horses and running errands for the Walker family by the age of five. In return, Dame Walker taught him his alphabet and how to read.

It is thought that the Cooks lived in two separate homes in Marton, but nothing remains of either of them. In 1736 the family left Marton to live at Aireyholme Farm on the slopes of Roseberry Topping near Great Ayton, 6 kilometres to the southeast [0.04]. Aireyholme was owned by Thomas Skottowe, the lord of the manor of Great Ayton. The move represented promotion for Cook senior who was the new hind or foreman on the farm. It also represented security for the family, as it meant their travelling days were over and they would stay at the farm until 1755, a period of 19 years. At Ayton four more children were born: Jane, born 1738 (died 1742); Mary (no. 2), born 1740 (died 1741); Margaret, born 1742; and William, born 1745 (died 1748).

James, by now eight years old, went to the Postgate School in the village as well as working on the farm. It is thought that he was an average student, though proficient in mathematics. He was a loner and obstinate but deserving of respect from other boys. He attended the school until he was 12, then he began full-time work, probably for the Skottowe family. This brought him to the attention of Thomas Skottowe, who would prove to have a considerable influence on his life.

Skottowe was also a Justice of the Peace for the North Riding of Yorkshire, and would have attended sessions at Guisborough where it is probable he met William Sanderson. Sanderson was a shopkeeper from Staithes, who acted as a constable in the district. The two men became friends and later even became related when their sons married sisters named Gill. In 1745, when James Cook was ready to leave home and get a job, it was arranged that he should work for Sanderson in his haberdashery and grocery shop at Staithes on the coast between Redcar and Whitby [0.05].

Staithes is a small, cramped fishing village nestled at the foot of cliffs where Roxby Beck enters the sea. It was always a very close community, and newcomers took a long time to be accepted; and for a young boy like Cook, away from home for the first time, it would have been a strange and lonely place. Sanderson, realising Cook was unsettled, used his connections and influence to introduce the boy to the Walker family in Whitby.

The North Sea coal trade

In 1746, Whitby, 12 kilometres to the east of Staithes at the mouth of the River Esk, was a port town of over 5000 people. This presented a new experience for the 17-year-old Cook [0.06]. The town already had a long history, mostly associated with the abbey which dominated the town from high on East Cliff. The town's prosperity came from its involvement in the North Sea coal trade, and Whitby families owned and operated more than 200 ships on the North and

Baltic Seas. The Walkers, John and Henry, operated several ships and were always in need of crew, so James Cook was a welcome addition. He was taken on either as an apprentice or as a servant and lived in John Walker's house in Grape Lane when not at sea.

It is not known in which ships he sailed during his first year, but in 1747 a new Act of Parliament was passed that decreed that all ships must keep muster rolls. From that time, therefore, there is a near complete record of the Whitby (and other) vessels on which Cook sailed. Cook is known to have sailed on the *Freelove* (1747–48), the *Three Brothers* (1748–51) and the *Friendship* (1751–55), all owned by the Walkers. After his apprenticeship finished in 1749, he also spent some months on the *Mary* and the *Hopewell*.

The North Sea coal trade had developed to meet London's ever-expanding need for coal [0.07]. The South Northumberland coalfield, close to the coast and with good port facilities at the mouth of the River Tyne, had been best able to satisfy that need, and fleets of ships sprang up to transport the coal down the east coast to the capital. Whitby, along this trade route, became a major factor. Each round-trip could take over a month: a week to load the coal at North Shields, a week to unload at Wapping on the Thames, and a week each way sailing along the east coast. As the weather and conditions in the North Sea could be treacherous, the crew would be given a break of two to three months over the winter.

While the majority of Cook's experience was on the Tyne–Thames coal route, he also visited Norway on the *Three Brothers* and he sailed into the Baltic Sea on the *Mary*. He may even have reached St. Petersburg. Cook was also on board the *Three Brothers* when it was commandeered to take British troops and horses from Middelburg in Zeeland to Dublin and Liverpool [0.07].

This period was crucial in Cook's life, as it was now that he learned the skills in seamanship that would serve him well in the future. Cook was prepared to study and learn, and this obviously impressed Walker so that a lasting friendship developed between the two men. Cook's abilities singled him out and enabled him to progress from seaman to mate, and he would have become a master of one of Walker's ships had he not surprised everyone by volunteering for the Royal Navy in 1755.

Cook's legacy in Cleveland

Cook's legacy is very strong in Cleveland. The local Tourist Authority promotes the area as Captain Cook Country, and has a Captain Cook Heritage Trail linking most of the places involved with Cook, his early life and his family [0.02]. At Marton, the Captain Cook Birthplace Museum is situated close to the supposed site of the cottage where he was born, while Great Ayton, Staithes and Whitby all have small museums remembering Cook's involvement with those places. There are statues of Cook, memorials to him and replicas of his vessels. St. Cuthbert's Church at Marton contains the register recording Cook's birth.

Cook's mother, Grace, died in 1765 and was buried at All Saints Church, Great Ayton, where five of Cook's brothers and sisters were already buried [0.04]. In 1771 his father left Great Ayton and moved to live with Cook's sister Margaret, who had married a Redcar fisherman called Fleck [0.02]. Cook senior died in 1779 and was buried at St. Germain's Church at Marske, near Redcar. Margaret lived until 1804 and it is from her that anyone claiming a family connection to James Cook must be descended (another sister, Christiana, did marry a Mr Cocker, but it is not known whether they had any children).

Cook and London

Cook is most closely connected with the area of London north of the River Thames and east of Tower Bridge [0.09]. The North Sea colliers discharged their coal at wharves in Wapping and Shadwell, and Cook is believed to have had lodgings at the Bell Alehouse near Execution Dock in Wapping. The Batts Family who owned the Bell had a daughter, Elizabeth, born in 1741 and baptised in St. John's Church, Wapping.

When Cook returned from Newfoundland in December 1762 he married Elizabeth Batts at St. Margaret's Church in Barking [0.08]. The couple made their first home at 126 Upper Shadwell and their first child was baptised in St. Paul's Church in Shadwell [0.09]. When James Cook returned from Newfoundland the next year, in 1763, the family moved a kilometre north to a new home at 7 Assembly Row on Mile End, between the London Hospital and Stepney Green.

Assembly Row remained the Cook home until Elizabeth Cook moved to Clapham in 1788, but James Cook spent only short periods there between voyages. Later Cook children were baptised at St. Dunstan's Church in Stepney. The houses occupied by Cook have disappeared, but plaques mark their locations.

When Cook was on HMS *Eagle* he came to Trinity House in Water Lane near Tower Bridge to sit his Master's examination [0.09]. The Royal Naval Dockyard at Deptford, downriver from Tower Bridge, fitted out all of Cook's ships and they all sailed from here [0.08]. Further east is Greenwich, where Cook spent a short period between his Second and Third Voyages as a captain at Greenwich Hospital. Cook is remembered in Greenwich by a permanent display at the National Maritime Museum and a statue near the Queen's House. There is another statue of Cook in Central London in the Mall outside The Admiralty, to which he would have been a regular visitor after his First and Second Voyages [0.08]. At the other end of Whitehall, Cook is one of three Navigators remembered by a Memorial in Westminster Abbey.

Cook submitted several papers to the Royal Society and in March 1776 he was elected a Fellow of the Society. Cook attended their meetings at Crane Court, off Fleet Street, and their dinners in The Mitre Tavern nearby [0.08]. The president of the Royal Society for many years was Sir Joseph Banks, who had sailed with Cook on the *Endeavour* voyage, and Cook visited Banks' house in New Burlington Street in Mayfair. He may have also visited the Banks' family home on Paradise Row in Chelsea. Banks later lived in Soho Square.

After Cook's death, Elizabeth Cook left Mile End in 1788 to live in Clapham High Street, just north of the Common [0.08]. She stayed here until her death in 1835, sharing it for most of the time with her cousin Isaac Smith.

The Royal Navy

The rivalry between European nations in the eighteenth century, and especially between Britain and France, meant that for long periods the countries were at war, punctuated by short breaks of peace. Coinciding with these countries' colonial expansion, the fighting often took place in Asia and North America as well as in Europe. One peace, begun by the Treaty of Aix-la-Chapelle in 1748,

collapsed in 1754 when fighting started again in North America. While France was stronger on land, the Royal Navy gave Britain a marked superiority at sea and, through patrols and blockades, they controlled the English Channel and the North Atlantic.

With this background, in 1755 Cook, aged 26, surprised everyone when he left the *Friendship* at Wapping and enlisted as an able seaman in the Royal Navy. His reasons for this move and its timing remain unknown. It may have been to avoid the press-gang, or he may have been ready for a change and a new challenge. His first posting was HMS *Eagle* under the command of Captain Joseph Hamar at Spithead off Portsmouth [0.10]. Cook's ability was once again quickly identified when in July he was appointed master's mate. The *Eagle* sailed out to patrol St. George's Channel between the Scilly Isles and Cape Clear in Ireland, before returning to port at Plymouth in September 1755.

In late 1755 Hamar was replaced as captain of HMS *Eagle* by Hugh Palliser. Palliser, who would feature often in Cook's life, took the *Eagle* out to resume patrolling, this time in the Channel's Western Approaches and the Bay of Biscay. In early March 1756 the *Eagle*, needing repairs, was back in Plymouth, but later in the month it set out again to patrol off Cherbourg, the Channel Islands and near the Isle de Batz off the Brittany coast. In early April, Cook was transferred to a cutter and took part in actions near Morlaix and Les Triagoz. He was then taken on board HMS *Falmouth* and returned to Plymouth.

After six days in port, HMS *St. Albans* ferried Cook back out to the *Eagle*, which he rejoined on 3 May. For several weeks they patrolled in the Bay of Biscay. Cook then helped take a captured prize, the *Triton*, back to London via Plymouth. He was back on board the *Eagle* in Plymouth in early July [1.11]. The *Eagle* helped accompany several merchant ships down the Channel before joining the blockade off Ushant in August. Another return to Plymouth in November preceded a sortie out to the Isle of Wight at the end of December. A gale forced the *Eagle* into Spithead and back once more to Plymouth. In late January 1757 Captain Palliser took the *Eagle* out to join the patrol of the Bay of Biscay before returning to port in April.

At the end of May the *Eagle* sailed in company with HMS *Medway*. They attacked and captured a French East Indiaman, the *Duc d'Aquitaine*, and took the prize back to Plymouth. Later in the year the *Eagle* sailed for North America, but Cook was not aboard. His days with the *Eagle* were over. Events were happening that would take him elsewhere.

Captain Palliser received a letter from William Osbaldestone, MP for Scarborough, written at John Walker's behest, suggesting that Cook be commissioned as an officer. Unfortunately a master's mate needed to have six years' service before he could be considered for preferment, so Cook was well short and Palliser did not himself have sufficient influence to hasten Cook's cause. Instead, Palliser recommended Cook for a master's warrant, and Cook left HMS *Eagle* for London, where he passed the master's examination in June 1757.

Cook was then assigned to HMS *Solebay*, a 24-gun frigate commanded by Captain Robert Craig and currently in harbour at Leith near Edinburgh in Scotland [0.12]. It was 30 July when Cook joined his new ship, so it is probable that he made a visit to his family and friends on the way north. HMS *Solebay* sailed from Leith on 2 August on a patrol up the Scottish east coast to Orkney and Shetland. The voyage kept close to the coast and the ship put in at Stonehaven and Peterhead on the mainland, Copinsay in Orkney, and Fair Isle before reaching Lerwick in Shetland on 9 August. After a few days in Lerwick the *Solebay* returned via Stromness in Orkney to reach Leith in September.

Cook did not sail again with the *Solebay*, as he received a warrant transferring him to HMS *Pembroke* as Master. But his short stay in Scotland, the country of his father, made an impression, for he later used the name New Caledonia (Caledonia being an ancient name for part of Scotland) for an island in the Pacific.

Cook travelled south to Portsmouth to join HMS *Pembroke*, 1250 tons and 64 guns, under the command of Captain John Simcoe in October 1757 [0.13]. The *Pembroke*, a new ship, sailed in December on a patrol through the Bay of Biscay to Cape Finisterre. This lasted until February 1758, when the ship returned to Plymouth. Cook's own ability and ambition undoubtedly contributed to his success, but on board the *Pembroke* was another of the people who recognised Cook's talents and helped him develop further. John Simcoe, following in the line of Skottowe, Sanderson, Walker and Palliser, gave Cook the opportunity and much encouragement to learn navigation, surveying, cartography and astronomy to add to his seamanship skills.

In North America

In 1756, the Seven Years War had broken out in Europe, widening the conflict from North America and committing French troops to events on the European continent. Britain, already in command of the North Atlantic Ocean through the Royal Navy, saw its opportunity to capture isolated French Canada. The French strongholds of Louisbourg on Ile Royale (later Cape Breton Island) and Quebec were deemed the key to taking Canada, and in early 1758 a fleet was assembled to transport the British Army across the Atlantic to North America [0.13].

The *Pembroke*, with Cook on board, was part of the fleet under Admiral Boscawen that in February 1758 sailed from Plymouth via Tenerife in the Canary Islands and Bermuda to reach Halifax in Nova Scotia on 9 May. Despite being a new ship, the *Pembroke* had a rough crossing and needed repairs, so it remained in port at Halifax for a month.

On 12 June 1758 the *Pembroke* reached Louisbourg to join the blockade of the fortress, which lasted until 27 July when the French finally surrendered [0.14]. The next day Cook met Samuel Holland, an Army surveyor-engineer, who was surveying on the beach at Kennington Cove near Louisbourg. Cook was curious and, with Simcoe's permission, Holland began to teach Cook how to survey and draw charts. The British hesitated about pressing on to attack Quebec and, instead, made forays into the Gulf of St. Lawrence to attack other French positions [0.15]. Cook and Holland were present during General Wolfe's attack on Gaspe, and they surveyed the harbour and bay afterwards. This was James Cook's first known chart.

The British then returned to Halifax to spend the winter away from the ice and cold of the St. Lawrence. Cook would spend several of his next winters and all of 1761 in Halifax, and he made charts of the harbour [0.14]. Ice detained the British early in 1759, but in May the fleet set off up the St. Lawrence for Quebec, under the command of Admiral Saunders. Tragedy struck on 16 May off Anticosti Island when Captain Simcoe died suddenly. He was replaced by Captain John Wheelock. The St. Lawrence was largely unknown to the British, except through captured charts. It was thought to be difficult to navigate, so a vanguard of ships, including the *Pembroke*, was sent ahead to establish a route.

Progress proved surprisingly quick and the British fleet anchored in The Bason just below Quebec in June [0.16].

Dislodging the French from Quebec was a much more difficult task and, over the next 11 weeks, the British tried many times and using many methods. Cook helped in a back-up role by ferrying troops and charting the river. Finally, on 13 September, the British made an audacious ascent to the Plains of Abraham and successfully attacked the French from the rear. (Louise Antoine de Bougainville, the future French explorer of the Pacific, was aide-de-camp to the French General Montcalm throughout the campaign.)

Cook meanwhile had come to the attention of Admiral Saunders and he was soon transferred, on Saunders' orders, to the 70-gun HMS *Northumberland*, captained by Lord Colville. Saunders took most of the fleet back to Britain, where he arranged for Cook's charts to be published, and Colville was left in charge of a small detachment, which spent the winter of 1759–60 in Halifax. In April 1760 the *Northumberland* sailed back to Quebec and stayed up the St. Lawrence until October. It then returned to Halifax, where it remained for 21 quiet and uneventful months until news arrived of a French attack on Newfoundland [0.17].

Newfoundland, off the coast of Canada, was an important location for controlling the rich cod fishery on the nearby Grand Banks. Basque, French and British fishermen had been crossing the Atlantic for over 150 years to fish the cod, and they had established settlements and fish factories around the coast. The British had nominal control of the southeast of the island but had shown little interest in creating a permanent colony. As a final effort of the Seven Years War, and to ensure their continued interest in the cod fishery, the French captured St. John's in July 1762. Laperouse, who would become the greatest of French Pacific explorers, was in the French fleet that took St. John's. He escaped just before the British recaptured the town. News of the attack reached Nova Scotia, and Colville immediately set off from Halifax in the *Northumberland*, with Cook aboard, to recapture Newfoundland.

In Newfoundland

Cook was about to begin an acquaintance with Newfoundland that would last until 1767 [0.17]. In August 1762, HMS *Northumberland*, under Captain Lord Colville, sailed to Placentia on the west side of the Avalon Peninsula and then continued round to rendezvous with other British forces off Cape Spear. St. John's was quickly retaken, and Cook began making surveys and charts around the southeast of the island at Placentia, St. Mary's, Trinity, Carbonnear and around St. John's. In October 1762, the *Northumberland* returned to London, where Cook was discharged in December. He soon married Elizabeth Batts in Barking and the couple settled in Shadwell [0.09].

The Seven Years War finished, France, under the Treaty of Paris signed in February 1763, retained the islands of St. Pierre and Miquelon off the south coast of Newfoundland, but gave up all other claims to Canada. The governor of Newfoundland, Thomas Graves, realised the need to have good charts of the coast, including the islands about to be passed back to France. Cook was the ideal choice to carry out the surveys and so, in May 1763, he accompanied Graves back to Newfoundland aboard the *Antelope*.

On 14 June they reached Trepassey, where Cook transferred to HMS *Tweed* under Captain Douglas [0.18]. He had less than two months to complete the task of surveying St. Pierre and Miquelon before they were handed over and, though he kept the French governor waiting, Cook finished by late July. Afterwards, the *Tweed* sailed to St. John's where Governor Graves had a schooner, the *Grenville*, ready for Cook to begin his surveys of Newfoundland's coasts.

Graves was aware of a strong French presence around Petit-Nord (the Northern Peninsula), part of an area known as the French Shore, and Cook was dispatched to make surveys [0.19]. In September and October 1763 Cook charted the harbours of Croque, Noddy and Quirpon as well as Chateau Bay on the nearby Labrador coast. He then headed back to St. John's and on to London, which he reached on 29 November. Cook saw his first child, James, for the first time, and the family moved to Mile End Road [0.09]. Here Cook spent the winter drawing up his charts and plans.

Cook had begun what would be a regular schedule for the next few years: sail to Newfoundland in April; spend until October surveying; and return to London for the winter to produce final versions of the charts and associated sailing instructions and descriptions.

Hugh Palliser, Cook's captain on the *Eagle*, replaced Graves as Governor of Newfoundland, and he and Cook sailed together for St. John's on the *Lark* in May 1764. This would be Cook's first full summer in Newfoundland. There, having collected the *Grenville*, he sailed back up to Petit-Nord to begin surveying at Quirpon [0.19]. He worked his way meticulously along the coast past Cape Onion, Pistolet Bay and Cape Norman as far as Pointe Ferolle before turning back in October. In August Cook had an accident at Unfortunate Cove when a powderhorn exploded and damaged his hand (it was the scars from this injury that helped identify his remains after his death in Hawaii in 1779); he was rushed to Noddy Bay for treatment. But Cook sailed the *Grenville* back to London, and arrived on the same day his second son, Nathaniel, was born. The *Grenville* was changed from a schooner to a brig during that winter.

Instead of continuing where he left off at Pointe Ferolle, Cook was directed to the south of Newfoundland when he returned in April 1765 [0.20]. The British had fears of renewed French activity out of their base at St. Pierre and Miquelon, so Governor Palliser wanted the south coast investigated first. In June, Cook began surveying at St. Lawrence on the Burin Peninsula and proceeded round the peninsula past Lawn Bay, Lamaline, Fortune and Garnish into Fortune Bay. The *Grenville* ran aground in Long Harbour at the head of Fortune Bay and needed repairs, so Cook carefully sailed the boat through Belle Bay, past Harbour Breton into Bay d'Espoir (Despair Bay), where repairs were carried out in Ship Cove (present-day St. Albans). The season was over, so Cook sailed for London, reaching the Thames on 17 December.

Cook sailed west again in April 1766 and was off Cape Race on 29 May [0.21]. He proceeded to Bonne Bay, next to Bay d'Espoir where he had finished the previous year. From Bonne Bay, Cook surveyed west along the south coast to Cape Ray and Cape Anguille, the southwest points of the island. Numerous bays including La Poile, Connoire, Facheux and White Bear were investigated, as were the island groups of Penguin, Ramea and Burgeo.

At the Burgeo Islands an auspicious event took place. There was fog when they arrived at the islands, but it cleared just in time for Cook to observe a solar eclipse, the details of which he wrote up as a paper that Dr John Bevis read to the Royal Society in London in April 1767. In this way Cook's name was brought to the attention of the Royal Society, the body that would be involved with sending the expedition to the South Pacific in 1768. On his way back to London, Cook called in at St. John's where the frigate *Niger* was in port. Joseph Banks, Cook's *Endeavour* passenger, was on board, but it is not certain whether the two men met at this time. Cook sailed on and was in London on 30 November 1766.

Cook was back in Newfoundland by May 1767, but the crossing was not without incident, as the *Grenville* collided with a collier, the *Three Sisters*, while still in the Thames. Cook began at Cape Anguille in the southwest and worked up the west coast towards Pointe Ferolle (previously charted in 1764), thus filling in the gap on this coast [0.22]. Pointe Ferolle was reached in August, and Cook made his way back to the Bay of Islands, where he stayed for a month. He even made a rare trip inland, rowing up the Humber River to Deer Lake. Leaving the bay in September, he sailed via St. John's and, having nearly run aground in the Thames near Sheerness, he was in London on 15 November 1767.

Cook did not return to Newfoundland, and his assistant, Matthew Lane, completed what remained to be surveyed. Their combined charts were published in 1770. Cook had started his surveying career in a careful and correct fashion. As well as the charts themselves, he recorded detailed sailing instructions in and out of every harbour, recommended new harbours and new fishing grounds, and provided much other useful information. He used, wherever possible, local knowledge, employing local pilots or sailors to show channels, sandbanks, and so on, and to learn existing local names for places and features. He was also able to develop his leadership skills and recognised the need for a healthy and happy crew — the brewing of spruce beer was a regular activity. His encounters with local Beothuk and Micmac people gave him his first experiences of communicating with non-European peoples.

Cook in Eastern Canada

Considering Cook was in Eastern Canada from 1758 until 1767 and took part in a crucial stage of the formative history of Canada, there are only a few monuments and names of features to commemorate him. Cook is remembered on mainland Canada only by a memorial in Halifax and the name Cook's Bay for the southern arm of Lake Simcoe in Ontario [0.13].

On Newfoundland there are many features and localities with Cook in the title, but by no means all can be linked with James Cook. Cook's Harbour at the top of Petit-Nord, and Cook's Brook and the Cook Ponds in the Bay of Islands are named for him. It is not so certain for Cook's Lookout at Burin and Cook Hill near Bonne Bay. There is a memorial to Cook on Crow Hill overlooking the Humber River in the Bay of Islands. A Captain Cook's Trail runs west along the south side of the Humber as far as Bottle Cove near Lark Harbour. A small memorial to Cook marks the end of the trail.

Lead-up to the First Voyage

Astronomers had observed a Transit of Venus in 1761 in various localities around the world but not satisfactorily. Another opportunity was to occur in 1769, and astronomers did not want to fail again [0.24]: such observations were needed to help calculate the distance from the Earth to the Sun. Thomas Hornsby, an Oxford University astronomer who had observed the 1761 Transit, made representations to the Royal Society that this time Britain should play a significant role, and by late 1767 it was committed to the scheme. The Royal Society nominated Alexander Dalrymple to lead an expedition to the Pacific, where, it had been determined, the best sightings of the Transit would occur. Dalrymple had worked for the East India Company in Madras and Sulu, had written about exploration in the South Seas, and had become proficient in astronomy.

Since the acceptance of the Earth as a sphere, there had been a theory that there had to be as much landmass in the southern hemisphere as was known in the north, otherwise the world was unbalanced. People in Europe postulated that there was a southern continent waiting to be discovered, and minerals, spices and other resources waiting to be exploited. This *Terra australis incognita* was thought to stretch across most of the southern Pacific and to include New Holland (Australia).

The Royal Society had no ships of its own to send to the Pacific, so the Admiralty was approached to provide a vessel. The Admiralty agreed to participate in the voyage but would not agree to a non-Royal Navy person such as Dalrymple being in charge of one of its ships. In April 1768 a Whitby-built cat, previously a collier, was purchased as the ship for the voyage and renamed the *Endeavour*. James Cook was appointed by the Admiralty to command the venture later in April and was presented to the Royal Society for approval on 5 May. The Society had little choice, but Cook's experience and ability, and his having presented a paper to the Society, helped to ease members' acceptance of him. Dalrymple, though, was not so easily placated, and remained convinced that only he could and should have commanded the expedition.

In May 1768 Captain Samuel Wallis returned to Britain from a voyage to the Pacific and reported favourably about the island of Tahiti, which lay in the ideal location for observing the Transit of Venus. Cook was promoted to lieutenant on 25 May and took charge of HMB *Endeavour* the following day. The *Endeavour* was prepared for the voyage at the Royal Naval Dockyard at Deptford. As well as its naval crew, the ship had to accommodate extra persons, including Charles Green from the Royal Observatory who would be the astronomer aboard. Joseph Banks, a rich and enthusiastic botanist, had gained permission and was paying for himself and a retinue to sail.

On 30 July 1768 Cook received his secret instructions from the Admiralty and made ready to sail to the Pacific to observe the Transit of Venus and to search for *Terra australis incognita*, the Great Southern Continent.

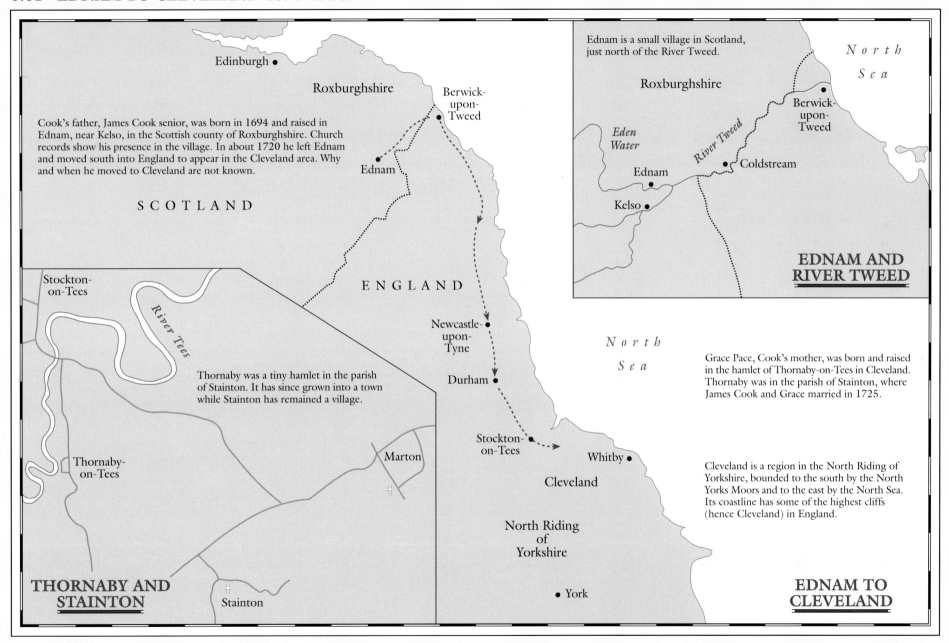

Cook's father, James Cook senior, was born in 1694 and raised in Ednam, near Kelso, in the Scottish county of Roxburghshire. Church records show his presence in the village. In about 1720 he left Ednam and moved south into England to appear in the Cleveland area. Why and when he moved to Cleveland are not known.

SCOTLAND

Edinburgh •

Roxburghshire

Berwick-upon-Tweed •

Ednam •

ENGLAND

Newcastle-upon-Tyne •

Durham •

Stockton-on-Tees •

Whitby •

Cleveland

North Riding of Yorkshire

• York

North Sea

Ednam is a small village in Scotland, just north of the River Tweed.

North Sea

Roxburghshire

Eden Water

River Tweed

Berwick-upon-Tweed •

Ednam •   • Coldstream

Kelso •

EDNAM AND RIVER TWEED

Grace Pace, Cook's mother, was born and raised in the hamlet of Thornaby-on-Tees in Cleveland. Thornaby was in the parish of Stainton, where James Cook and Grace married in 1725.

Cleveland is a region in the North Riding of Yorkshire, bounded to the south by the North Yorks Moors and to the east by the North Sea. Its coastline has some of the highest cliffs (hence Cleveland) in England.

EDNAM TO CLEVELAND

Stockton-on-Tees

River Tees

Thornaby was a tiny hamlet in the parish of Stainton. It has since grown into a town while Stainton has remained a village.

Thornaby-on-Tees

Marton

THORNABY AND STAINTON

Stainton

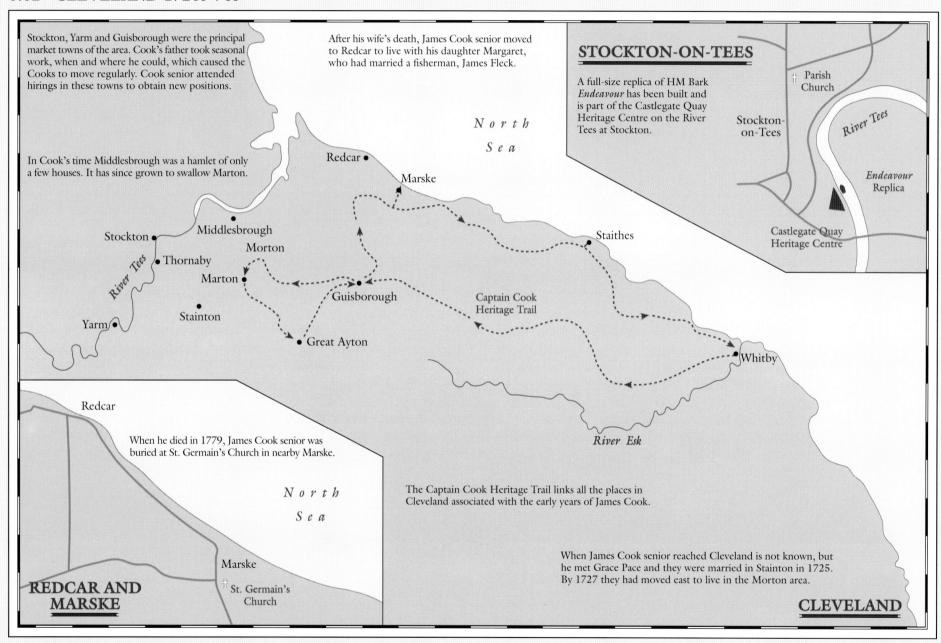

Stockton, Yarm and Guisborough were the principal market towns of the area. Cook's father took seasonal work, when and where he could, which caused the Cooks to move regularly. Cook senior attended hirings in these towns to obtain new positions.

After his wife's death, James Cook senior moved to Redcar to live with his daughter Margaret, who had married a fisherman, James Fleck.

In Cook's time Middlesbrough was a hamlet of only a few houses. It has since grown to swallow Marton.

STOCKTON-ON-TEES

A full-size replica of HM Bark *Endeavour* has been built and is part of the Castlegate Quay Heritage Centre on the River Tees at Stockton.

Parish Church

Stockton-on-Tees

River Tees

Endeavour Replica

Castlegate Quay Heritage Centre

North Sea

Redcar

Marske

Staithes

Stockton

Middlesbrough

Morton

Thornaby

Marton

Guisborough

Captain Cook Heritage Trail

Stainton

Yarm

Great Ayton

Whitby

River Esk

REDCAR AND MARSKE

Redcar

When he died in 1779, James Cook senior was buried at St. Germain's Church in nearby Marske.

North Sea

Marske

St. Germain's Church

The Captain Cook Heritage Trail links all the places in Cleveland associated with the early years of James Cook.

When James Cook senior reached Cleveland is not known, but he met Grace Pace and they were married in Stainton in 1725. By 1727 they had moved east to live in the Morton area.

CLEVELAND

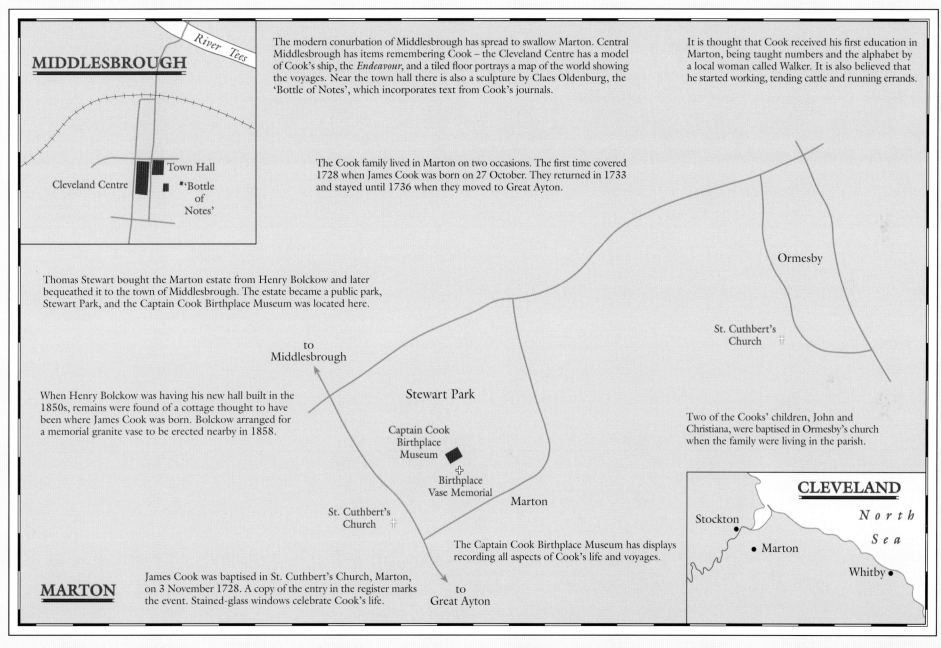

MIDDLESBROUGH

River Tees

Town Hall

Cleveland Centre

'Bottle of Notes'

The modern conurbation of Middlesbrough has spread to swallow Marton. Central Middlesbrough has items remembering Cook – the Cleveland Centre has a model of Cook's ship, the *Endeavour*, and a tiled floor portrays a map of the world showing the voyages. Near the town hall there is also a sculpture by Claes Oldenburg, the 'Bottle of Notes', which incorporates text from Cook's journals.

It is thought that Cook received his first education in Marton, being taught numbers and the alphabet by a local woman called Walker. It is also believed that he started working, tending cattle and running errands.

The Cook family lived in Marton on two occasions. The first time covered 1728 when James Cook was born on 27 October. They returned in 1733 and stayed until 1736 when they moved to Great Ayton.

Ormesby

Thomas Stewart bought the Marton estate from Henry Bolckow and later bequeathed it to the town of Middlesbrough. The estate became a public park, Stewart Park, and the Captain Cook Birthplace Museum was located here.

St. Cuthbert's Church

to Middlesbrough

Stewart Park

When Henry Bolckow was having his new hall built in the 1850s, remains were found of a cottage thought to have been where James Cook was born. Bolckow arranged for a memorial granite vase to be erected nearby in 1858.

Captain Cook Birthplace Museum

Birthplace Vase Memorial

Marton

Two of the Cooks' children, John and Christiana, were baptised in Ormesby's church when the family were living in the parish.

St. Cuthbert's Church

The Captain Cook Birthplace Museum has displays recording all aspects of Cook's life and voyages.

CLEVELAND

North Sea

Stockton

• Marton

Whitby •

MARTON

James Cook was baptised in St. Cuthbert's Church, Marton, on 3 November 1728. A copy of the entry in the register marks the event. Stained-glass windows celebrate Cook's life.

to Great Ayton

GREAT AYTON

Great Ayton is still a peaceful place where a series of village greens straddle the River Leven.

Cook began his formal education by attending the local Postgate School, built in 1704. It had been paid for by a local yeoman, Michael Postgate. In recent times it has become the Captain Cook Schoolroom Museum.

Cook's mother died in 1765 and is buried at All Saints Church with five of Cook's sisters and brothers.

Roseberry Topping (Ounesbury Hill) is a conical hill, 320m high and clearly visible from all points on the lower Tees plain. From Marton the Cooks would have seen it easily. They would have also seen neighbouring Easby Moor. This hill became a most suitable location for the Captain Cook Monument that was erected in 1827.

Cook's brothers and sisters were: John (1727–50), Christiana (1731–?), Mary I (1733–37), Jane (1738–42), Mary II (1740–41), Margaret (1742–1804) and William (1745–48).

Thomas Skottowe's son John later became the governor of St. Helena and received Cook and his crew when the *Resolution* called at the island in 1774. They were briefly able to renew their boyhood friendship.

In 1736 the Cooks came to live at Aireyholme Farm. This was owned by Thomas Skottowe, lord of the manor of Great Ayton. James Cook's father was the hind or foreman. Cook junior worked on the farm when not attending school. It is still a working farm.

The statue of 'James Cook as a boy' by Nicholas Dimbleby was unveiled in 1997 by Chris Blake, captain of the *Endeavour* replica.

Cook's father's cottage in Bridge Street was dismantled and removed in 1934 to Fitzroy Gardens in Melbourne, where it is known as Cook's Cottage. A memorial marks the site in Bridge Street.

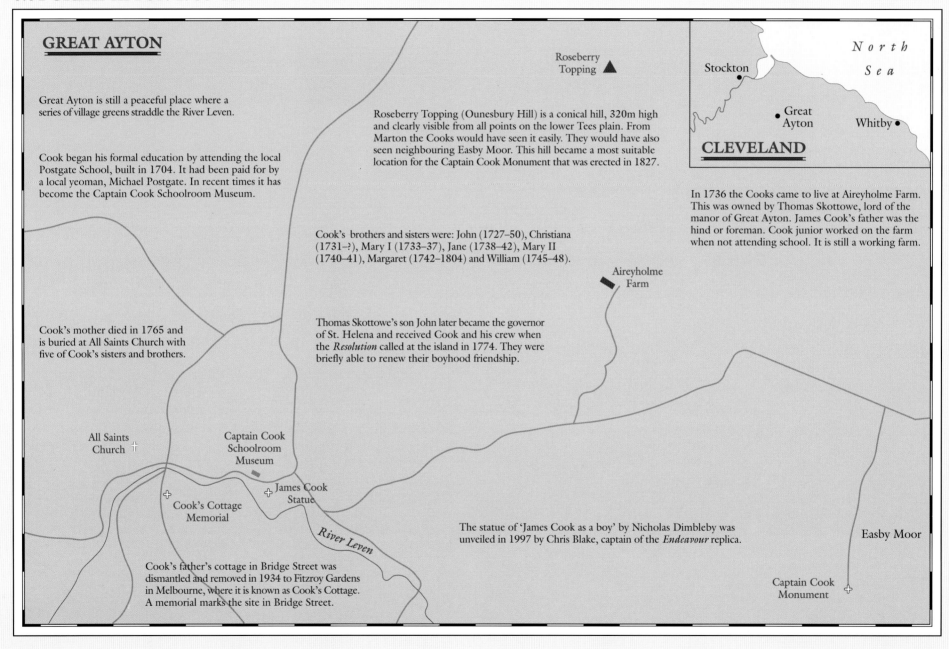

Roseberry Topping

CLEVELAND

North Sea

Stockton

Great Ayton

Whitby

All Saints Church

Captain Cook Schoolroom Museum

James Cook Statue

Cook's Cottage Memorial

River Leven

Aireyholme Farm

Easby Moor

Captain Cook Monument

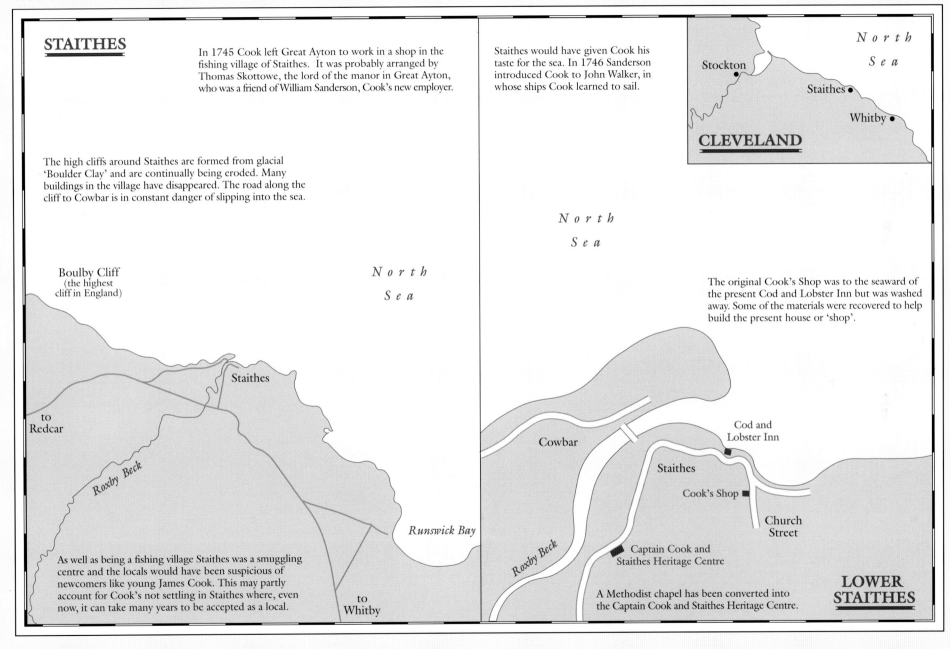

STAITHES

In 1745 Cook left Great Ayton to work in a shop in the fishing village of Staithes. It was probably arranged by Thomas Skottowe, the lord of the manor in Great Ayton, who was a friend of William Sanderson, Cook's new employer.

Staithes would have given Cook his taste for the sea. In 1746 Sanderson introduced Cook to John Walker, in whose ships Cook learned to sail.

North Sea

Stockton

Staithes •

Whitby •

CLEVELAND

The high cliffs around Staithes are formed from glacial 'Boulder Clay' and are continually being eroded. Many buildings in the village have disappeared. The road along the cliff to Cowbar is in constant danger of slipping into the sea.

North Sea

Boulby Cliff
(the highest cliff in England)

The original Cook's Shop was to the seaward of the present Cod and Lobster Inn but was washed away. Some of the materials were recovered to help build the present house or 'shop'.

to Redcar

Staithes

Cod and Lobster Inn

Cowbar

Staithes

Cook's Shop

Roxby Beck

Church Street

Runswick Bay

Roxby Beck

Captain Cook and Staithes Heritage Centre

As well as being a fishing village Staithes was a smuggling centre and the locals would have been suspicious of newcomers like young James Cook. This may partly account for Cook's not settling in Staithes where, even now, it can take many years to be accepted as a local.

to Whitby

A Methodist chapel has been converted into the Captain Cook and Staithes Heritage Centre.

LOWER STAITHES

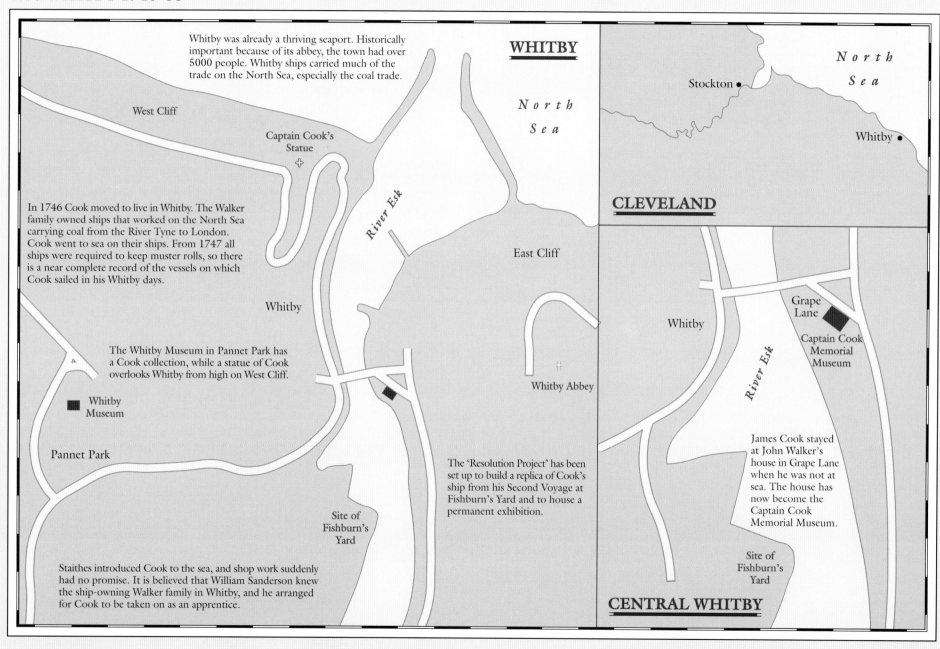

Whitby was already a thriving seaport. Historically important because of its abbey, the town had over 5000 people. Whitby ships carried much of the trade on the North Sea, especially the coal trade.

WHITBY

North Sea

West Cliff

Captain Cook's Statue

River Esk

In 1746 Cook moved to live in Whitby. The Walker family owned ships that worked on the North Sea carrying coal from the River Tyne to London. Cook went to sea on their ships. From 1747 all ships were required to keep muster rolls, so there is a near complete record of the vessels on which Cook sailed in his Whitby days.

East Cliff

Whitby

The Whitby Museum in Pannet Park has a Cook collection, while a statue of Cook overlooks Whitby from high on West Cliff.

Whitby Museum

Whitby Abbey

Pannet Park

The 'Resolution Project' has been set up to build a replica of Cook's ship from his Second Voyage at Fishburn's Yard and to house a permanent exhibition.

Site of Fishburn's Yard

Staithes introduced Cook to the sea, and shop work suddenly had no promise. It is believed that William Sanderson knew the ship-owning Walker family in Whitby, and he arranged for Cook to be taken on as an apprentice.

Stockton ·

North Sea

Whitby ·

CLEVELAND

Grape Lane

Whitby

Captain Cook Memorial Museum

River Esk

James Cook stayed at John Walker's house in Grape Lane when he was not at sea. The house has now become the Captain Cook Memorial Museum.

Site of Fishburn's Yard

CENTRAL WHITBY

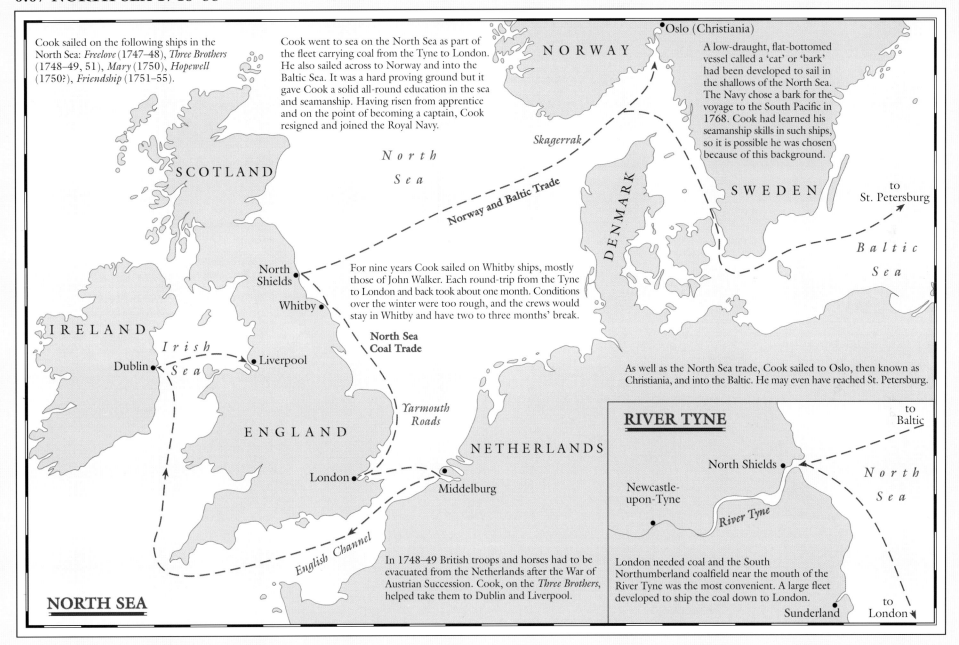

Cook sailed on the following ships in the North Sea: *Freelove* (1747–48), *Three Brothers* (1748–49, 51), *Mary* (1750), *Hopewell* (1750?), *Friendship* (1751–55).

Cook went to sea on the North Sea as part of the fleet carrying coal from the Tyne to London. He also sailed across to Norway and into the Baltic Sea. It was a hard proving ground but it gave Cook a solid all-round education in the sea and seamanship. Having risen from apprentice and on the point of becoming a captain, Cook resigned and joined the Royal Navy.

A low-draught, flat-bottomed vessel called a 'cat' or 'bark' had been developed to sail in the shallows of the North Sea. The Navy chose a bark for the voyage to the South Pacific in 1768. Cook had learned his seamanship skills in such ships, so it is possible he was chosen because of this background.

For nine years Cook sailed on Whitby ships, mostly those of John Walker. Each round-trip from the Tyne to London and back took about one month. Conditions over the winter were too rough, and the crews would stay in Whitby and have two to three months' break.

As well as the North Sea trade, Cook sailed to Oslo, then known as Christiania, and into the Baltic. He may even have reached St. Petersburg.

In 1748–49 British troops and horses had to be evacuated from the Netherlands after the War of Austrian Succession. Cook, on the *Three Brothers*, helped take them to Dublin and Liverpool.

London needed coal and the South Northumberland coalfield near the mouth of the River Tyne was the most convenient. A large fleet developed to ship the coal down to London.

Oslo (Christiania)

NORWAY

Skagerrak

North Sea

SCOTLAND

DENMARK

SWEDEN

to St. Petersburg

Norway and Baltic Trade

Baltic Sea

North Shields

Whitby

IRELAND

Irish Sea

Dublin

Liverpool

North Sea Coal Trade

Yarmouth Roads

ENGLAND

NETHERLANDS

London

Middelburg

English Channel

RIVER TYNE

to Baltic

North Shields

Newcastle-upon-Tyne

River Tyne

North Sea

Sunderland

to London

NORTH SEA

0.08 LONDON. THE COOKS AND BANKS 1740–1835

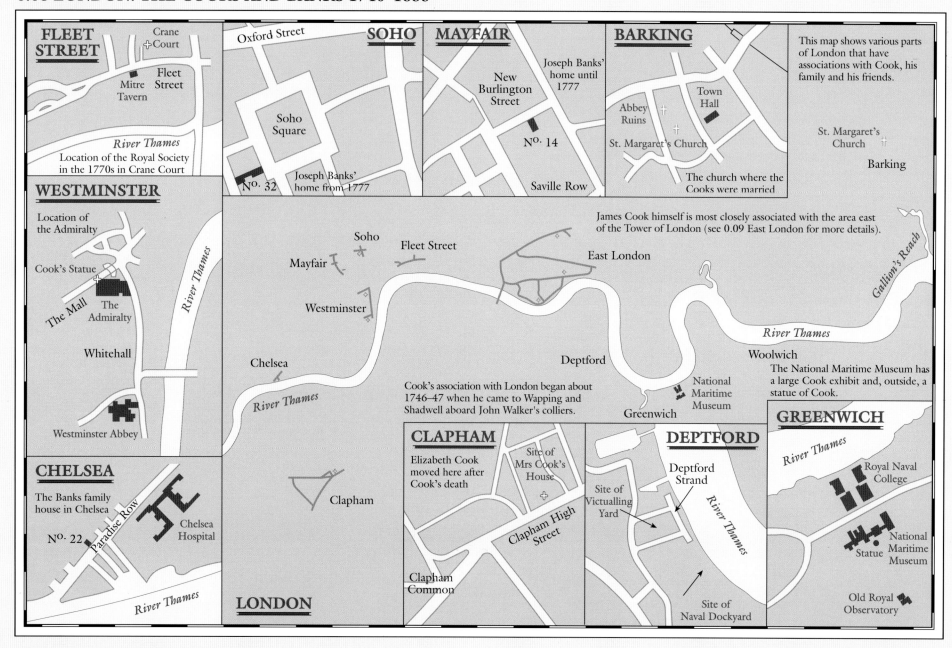

FLEET STREET

Crane Court

Fleet Street

Mitre Tavern

River Thames

Location of the Royal Society in the 1770s in Crane Court

WESTMINSTER

Location of the Admiralty

Cook's Statue

The Mall

The Admiralty

Whitehall

River Thames

Westminster Abbey

CHELSEA

The Banks family house in Chelsea

No. 22

Paradise Row

Chelsea Hospital

River Thames

SOHO

Oxford Street

Soho Square

No. 32   Joseph Banks' home from 1777

MAYFAIR

New Burlington Street

Joseph Banks' home until 1777

No. 14

Saville Row

BARKING

Town Hall

Abbey Ruins

St. Margaret's Church

The church where the Cooks were married

This map shows various parts of London that have associations with Cook, his family and his friends.

St. Margaret's Church

Barking

James Cook himself is most closely associated with the area east of the Tower of London (see 0.09 East London for more details).

Soho

Fleet Street

Mayfair

East London

Westminster

River Thames

Gallion's Reach

Chelsea

River Thames

Deptford

Woolwich

The National Maritime Museum has a large Cook exhibit and, outside, a statue of Cook.

Cook's association with London began about 1746–47 when he came to Wapping and Shadwell aboard John Walker's colliers.

National Maritime Museum

Greenwich

CLAPHAM

Elizabeth Cook moved here after Cook's death

Site of Mrs Cook's House

Clapham

Clapham High Street

Clapham Common

LONDON

DEPTFORD

Deptford Strand

Site of Victualling Yard

River Thames

Site of Naval Dockyard

GREENWICH

River Thames

Royal Naval College

Statue

National Maritime Museum

Old Royal Observatory

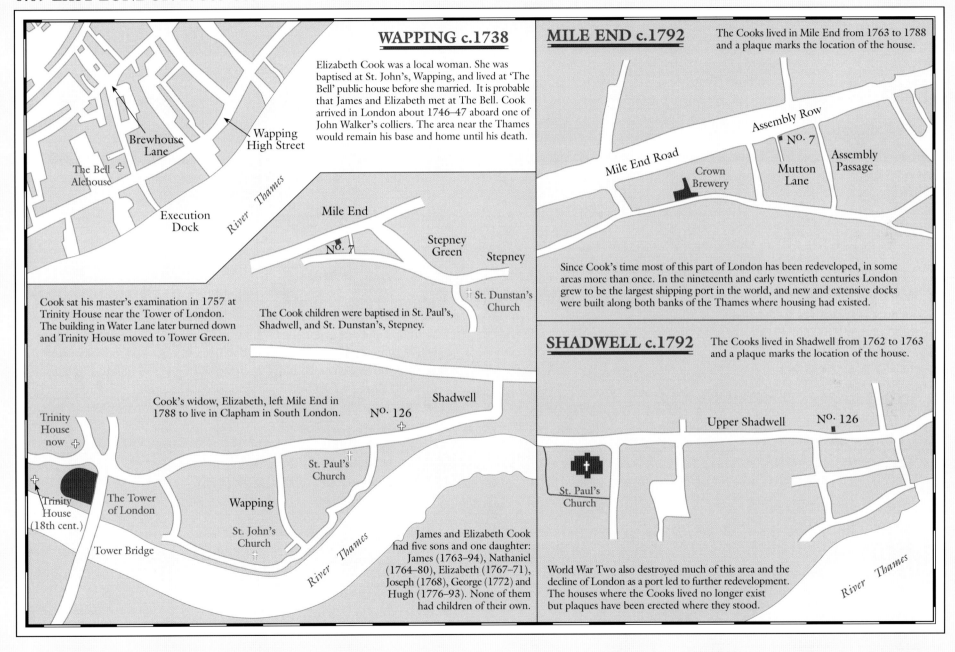

WAPPING c.1738

Elizabeth Cook was a local woman. She was baptised at St. John's, Wapping, and lived at 'The Bell' public house before she married. It is probable that James and Elizabeth met at The Bell. Cook arrived in London about 1746–47 aboard one of John Walker's colliers. The area near the Thames would remain his base and home until his death.

Brewhouse Lane

Wapping High Street

The Bell Alehouse

Execution Dock

River Thames

Mile End

Stepney Green

Stepney

St. Dunstan's Church

Cook sat his master's examination in 1757 at Trinity House near the Tower of London. The building in Water Lane later burned down and Trinity House moved to Tower Green.

The Cook children were baptised in St. Paul's, Shadwell, and St. Dunstan's, Stepney.

Cook's widow, Elizabeth, left Mile End in 1788 to live in Clapham in South London.

Shadwell

Nº 126

Trinity House now

Trinity House (18th cent.)

The Tower of London

Wapping

St. Paul's Church

St. John's Church

Tower Bridge

River Thames

James and Elizabeth Cook had five sons and one daughter: James (1763–94), Nathaniel (1764–80), Elizabeth (1767–71), Joseph (1768), George (1772) and Hugh (1776–93). None of them had children of their own.

MILE END c.1792

The Cooks lived in Mile End from 1763 to 1788 and a plaque marks the location of the house.

Assembly Row

Nº 7

Mile End Road

Crown Brewery

Mutton Lane

Assembly Passage

Since Cook's time most of this part of London has been redeveloped, in some areas more than once. In the nineteenth and early twentieth centuries London grew to be the largest shipping port in the world, and new and extensive docks were built along both banks of the Thames where housing had existed.

SHADWELL c.1792

The Cooks lived in Shadwell from 1762 to 1763 and a plaque marks the location of the house.

Upper Shadwell

Nº 126

St. Paul's Church

River Thames

World War Two also destroyed much of this area and the decline of London as a port led to further redevelopment. The houses where the Cooks lived no longer exist but plaques have been erected where they stood.

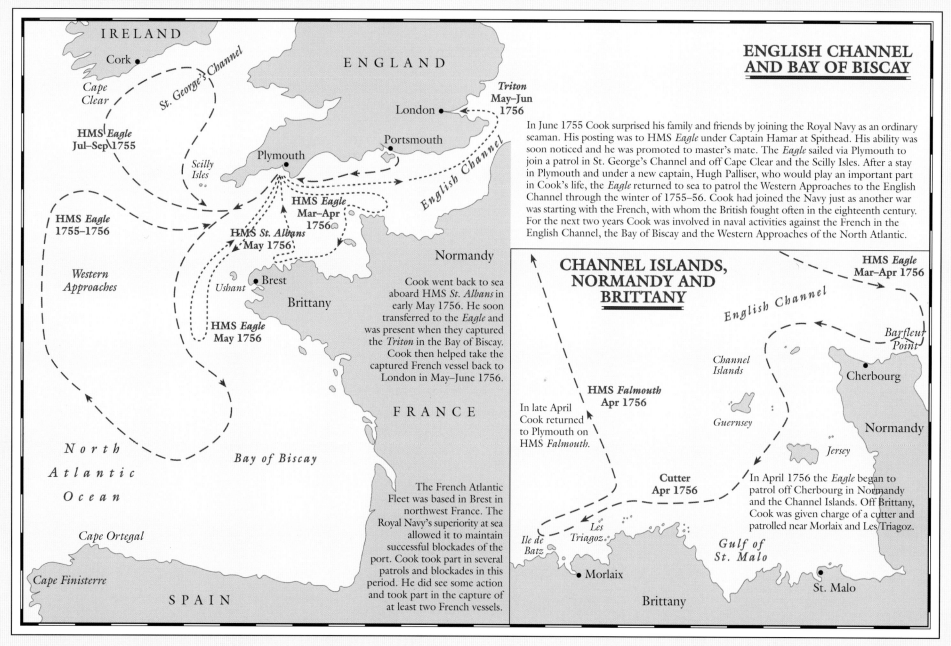

ENGLISH CHANNEL AND BAY OF BISCAY

IRELAND

Cork

Cape Clear

St. George's Channel

ENGLAND

London

Portsmouth

Triton May–Jun 1756

HMS *Eagle* Jul–Sep 1755

Scilly Isles

Plymouth

English Channel

HMS *Eagle* 1755–1756

HMS *Eagle* Mar–Apr 1756

HMS *St. Albans* May 1756

Western Approaches

Ushant • Brest

Brittany

Normandy

HMS *Eagle* May 1756

In June 1755 Cook surprised his family and friends by joining the Royal Navy as an ordinary seaman. His posting was to HMS *Eagle* under Captain Hamar at Spithead. His ability was soon noticed and he was promoted to master's mate. The *Eagle* sailed via Plymouth to join a patrol in St. George's Channel and off Cape Clear and the Scilly Isles. After a stay in Plymouth and under a new captain, Hugh Palliser, who would play an important part in Cook's life, the *Eagle* returned to sea to patrol the Western Approaches to the English Channel through the winter of 1755–56. Cook had joined the Navy just as another war was starting with the French, with whom the British fought often in the eighteenth century. For the next two years Cook was involved in naval activities against the French in the English Channel, the Bay of Biscay and the Western Approaches of the North Atlantic.

Cook went back to sea aboard HMS *St. Albans* in early May 1756. He soon transferred to the *Eagle* and was present when they captured the *Triton* in the Bay of Biscay. Cook then helped take the captured French vessel back to London in May–June 1756.

FRANCE

North Atlantic Ocean

Bay of Biscay

Cape Ortegal

Cape Finisterre

SPAIN

The French Atlantic Fleet was based in Brest in northwest France. The Royal Navy's superiority at sea allowed it to maintain successful blockades of the port. Cook took part in several patrols and blockades in this period. He did see some action and took part in the capture of at least two French vessels.

CHANNEL ISLANDS, NORMANDY AND BRITTANY

HMS *Eagle* Mar–Apr 1756

English Channel

Barfleur Point

Channel Islands

Cherbourg

Guernsey

Normandy

Jersey

HMS *Falmouth* Apr 1756

In late April Cook returned to Plymouth on HMS *Falmouth*.

Cutter Apr 1756

In April 1756 the *Eagle* began to patrol off Cherbourg in Normandy and the Channel Islands. Off Brittany, Cook was given charge of a cutter and patrolled near Morlaix and Les Triagoz.

Ile de Batz

Les Triagoz

Morlaix

Gulf of St. Malo

St. Malo

Brittany

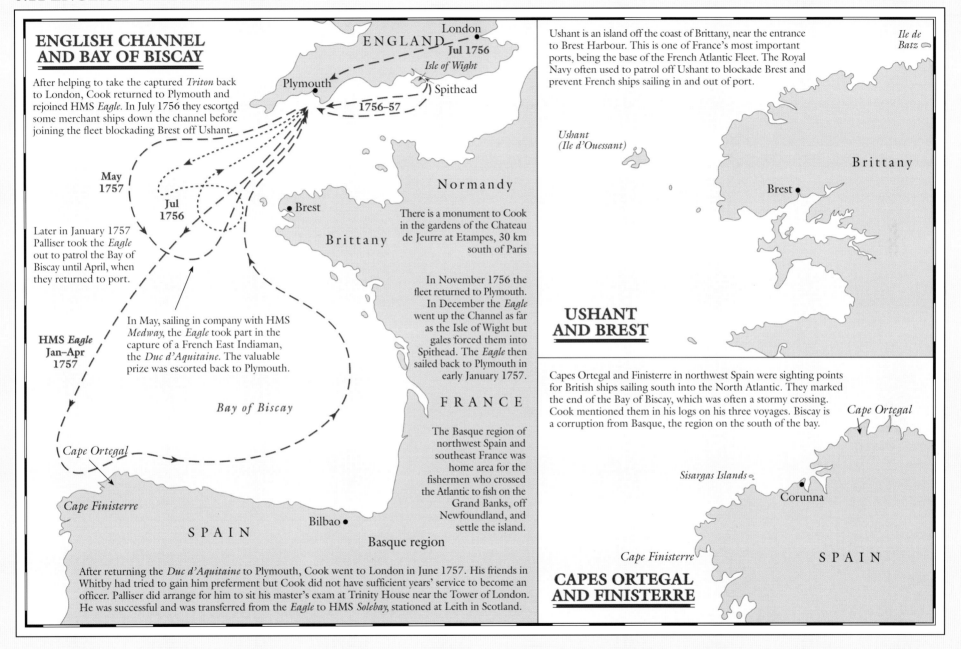

ENGLISH CHANNEL AND BAY OF BISCAY

After helping to take the captured *Triton* back to London, Cook returned to Plymouth and rejoined HMS *Eagle*. In July 1756 they escorted some merchant ships down the channel before joining the fleet blockading Brest off Ushant.

Later in January 1757 Palliser took the *Eagle* out to patrol the Bay of Biscay until April, when they returned to port.

HMS Eagle Jan–Apr 1757

In May, sailing in company with HMS *Medway*, the *Eagle* took part in the capture of a French East Indiaman, the *Duc d'Aquitaine*. The valuable prize was escorted back to Plymouth.

May 1757

Jul 1756

1756–57

London

ENGLAND

Jul 1756

Isle of Wight

Plymouth

Spithead

Normandy

• Brest

Brittany

There is a monument to Cook in the gardens of the Chateau de Jeurre at Etampes, 30 km south of Paris

In November 1756 the fleet returned to Plymouth. In December the *Eagle* went up the Channel as far as the Isle of Wight but gales forced them into Spithead. The *Eagle* then sailed back to Plymouth in early January 1757.

F R A N C E

The Basque region of northwest Spain and southeast France was home area for the fishermen who crossed the Atlantic to fish on the Grand Banks, off Newfoundland, and settle the island.

Bay of Biscay

Cape Ortegal

Cape Finisterre

S P A I N

Bilbao •

Basque region

After returning the *Duc d'Aquitaine* to Plymouth, Cook went to London in June 1757. His friends in Whitby had tried to gain him preferment but Cook did not have sufficient years' service to become an officer. Palliser did arrange for him to sit his master's exam at Trinity House near the Tower of London. He was successful and was transferred from the *Eagle* to HMS *Solebay*, stationed at Leith in Scotland.

Ushant is an island off the coast of Brittany, near the entrance to Brest Harbour. This is one of France's most important ports, being the base of the French Atlantic Fleet. The Royal Navy often used to patrol off Ushant to blockade Brest and prevent French ships sailing in and out of port.

Ile de Batz

Ushant (Ile d'Ouessant)

Brittany

Brest •

USHANT AND BREST

Capes Ortegal and Finisterre in northwest Spain were sighting points for British ships sailing south into the North Atlantic. They marked the end of the Bay of Biscay, which was often a stormy crossing. Cook mentioned them in his logs on his three voyages. Biscay is a corruption from Basque, the region on the south of the bay.

Cape Ortegal

Sisargas Islands

Corunna

Cape Finisterre

S P A I N

CAPES ORTEGAL AND FINISTERRE

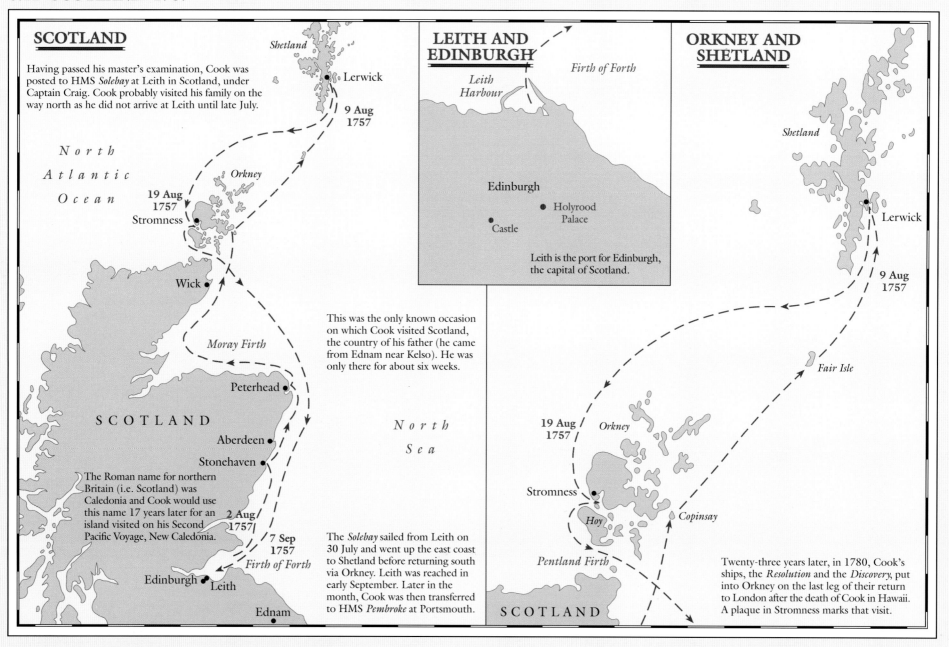

SCOTLAND

Having passed his master's examination, Cook was posted to HMS *Solebay* at Leith in Scotland, under Captain Craig. Cook probably visited his family on the way north as he did not arrive at Leith until late July.

Shetland

Lerwick

9 Aug 1757

North Atlantic Ocean

Orkney

19 Aug 1757

Stromness

Wick

Moray Firth

S C O T L A N D

Peterhead

Aberdeen

Stonehaven

The Roman name for northern Britain (i.e. Scotland) was Caledonia and Cook would use this name 17 years later for an island visited on his Second Pacific Voyage, New Caledonia.

2 Aug 1757

7 Sep 1757

Firth of Forth

Edinburgh   Leith

Ednam

This was the only known occasion on which Cook visited Scotland, the country of his father (he came from Ednam near Kelso). He was only there for about six weeks.

North Sea

The *Solebay* sailed from Leith on 30 July and went up the east coast to Shetland before returning south via Orkney. Leith was reached in early September. Later in the month, Cook was then transferred to HMS *Pembroke* at Portsmouth.

LEITH AND EDINBURGH

Firth of Forth

Leith Harbour

Edinburgh

● Holyrood Palace

● Castle

Leith is the port for Edinburgh, the capital of Scotland.

ORKNEY AND SHETLAND

Shetland

Lerwick

9 Aug 1757

19 Aug 1757   *Orkney*

Fair Isle

Stromness

Hoy

Copinsay

Pentland Firth

S C O T L A N D

Twenty-three years later, in 1780, Cook's ships, the *Resolution* and the *Discovery*, put into Orkney on the last leg of their return to London after the death of Cook in Hawaii. A plaque in Stromness marks that visit.

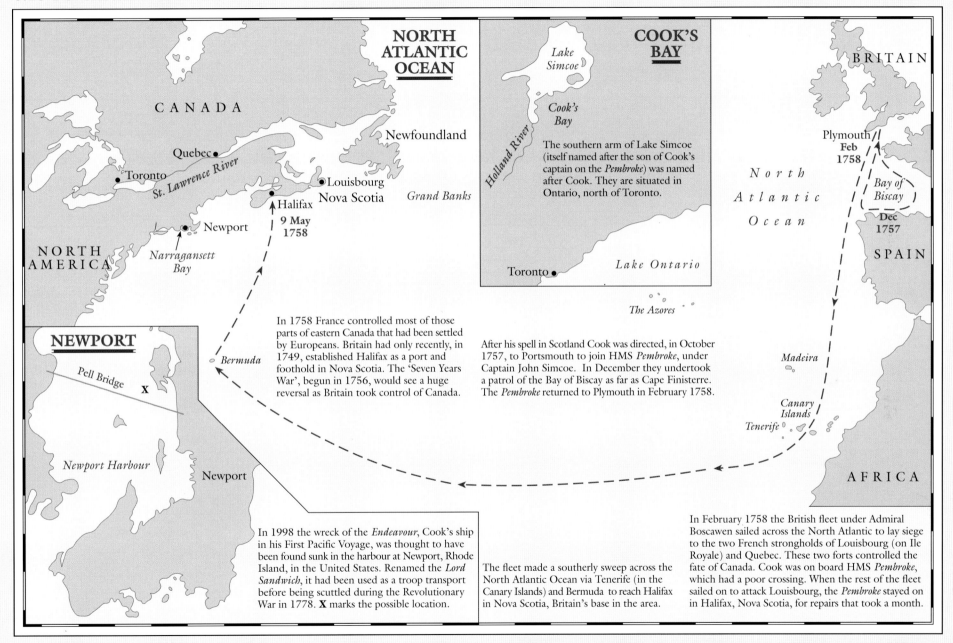

NORTH ATLANTIC OCEAN

CANADA

Newfoundland

Quebec

Toronto

St. Lawrence River

Louisbourg

Halifax
Nova Scotia

9 May 1758

Grand Banks

Newport

NORTH AMERICA

Narragansett Bay

Bermuda

COOK'S BAY

Lake Simcoe

Cook's Bay

Holland River

The southern arm of Lake Simcoe (itself named after the son of Cook's captain on the *Pembroke*) was named after Cook. They are situated in Ontario, north of Toronto.

Toronto

Lake Ontario

The Azores

BRITAIN

Plymouth
Feb 1758

North Atlantic Ocean

Bay of Biscay

Dec 1757

SPAIN

Madeira

Canary Islands

Tenerife

AFRICA

NEWPORT

Pell Bridge

X

Newport Harbour

Newport

In 1758 France controlled most of those parts of eastern Canada that had been settled by Europeans. Britain had only recently, in 1749, established Halifax as a port and foothold in Nova Scotia. The 'Seven Years War', begun in 1756, would see a huge reversal as Britain took control of Canada.

After his spell in Scotland Cook was directed, in October 1757, to Portsmouth to join HMS *Pembroke*, under Captain John Simcoe. In December they undertook a patrol of the Bay of Biscay as far as Cape Finisterre. The *Pembroke* returned to Plymouth in February 1758.

In 1998 the wreck of the *Endeavour*, Cook's ship in his First Pacific Voyage, was thought to have been found sunk in the harbour at Newport, Rhode Island, in the United States. Renamed the *Lord Sandwich*, it had been used as a troop transport before being scuttled during the Revolutionary War in 1778. **X** marks the possible location.

The fleet made a southerly sweep across the North Atlantic Ocean via Tenerife (in the Canary Islands) and Bermuda to reach Halifax in Nova Scotia, Britain's base in the area.

In February 1758 the British fleet under Admiral Boscawen sailed across the North Atlantic to lay siege to the two French strongholds of Louisbourg (on Ile Royale) and Quebec. These two forts controlled the fate of Canada. Cook was on board HMS *Pembroke*, which had a poor crossing. When the rest of the fleet sailed on to attack Louisbourg, the *Pembroke* stayed on in Halifax, Nova Scotia, for repairs that took a month.

0.14 HALIFAX AND LOUISBOURG 1758

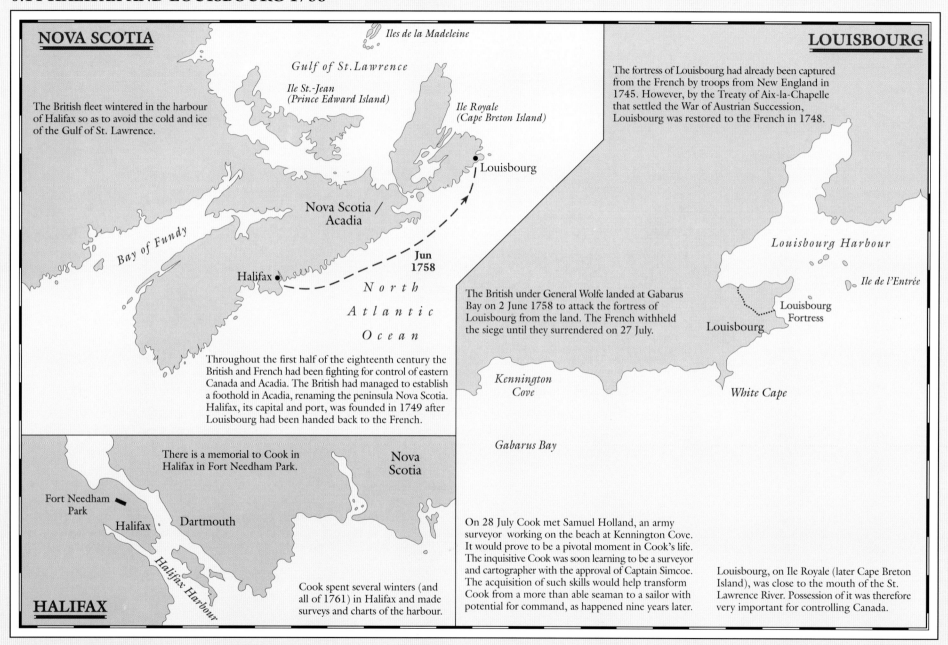

NOVA SCOTIA

Iles de la Madeleine

Gulf of St. Lawrence

Ile St.-Jean (Prince Edward Island)

Ile Royale (Cape Breton Island)

The British fleet wintered in the harbour of Halifax so as to avoid the cold and ice of the Gulf of St. Lawrence.

Louisbourg

Nova Scotia / Acadia

Bay of Fundy

Jun 1758

Halifax

North Atlantic Ocean

Throughout the first half of the eighteenth century the British and French had been fighting for control of eastern Canada and Acadia. The British had managed to establish a foothold in Acadia, renaming the peninsula Nova Scotia. Halifax, its capital and port, was founded in 1749 after Louisbourg had been handed back to the French.

LOUISBOURG

The fortress of Louisbourg had already been captured from the French by troops from New England in 1745. However, by the Treaty of Aix-la-Chapelle that settled the War of Austrian Succession, Louisbourg was restored to the French in 1748.

Louisbourg Harbour

Ile de l'Entrée

Louisbourg Fortress

The British under General Wolfe landed at Gabarus Bay on 2 June 1758 to attack the fortress of Louisbourg from the land. The French withheld the siege until they surrendered on 27 July.

Louisbourg

Kennington Cove

White Cape

Gabarus Bay

On 28 July Cook met Samuel Holland, an army surveyor working on the beach at Kennington Cove. It would prove to be a pivotal moment in Cook's life. The inquisitive Cook was soon learning to be a surveyor and cartographer with the approval of Captain Simcoe. The acquisition of such skills would help transform Cook from a more than able seaman to a sailor with potential for command, as happened nine years later.

Louisbourg, on Ile Royale (later Cape Breton Island), was close to the mouth of the St. Lawrence River. Possession of it was therefore very important for controlling Canada.

There is a memorial to Cook in Halifax in Fort Needham Park.

Nova Scotia

Fort Needham Park

Halifax

Dartmouth

Halifax Harbour

Cook spent several winters (and all of 1761) in Halifax and made surveys and charts of the harbour.

HALIFAX

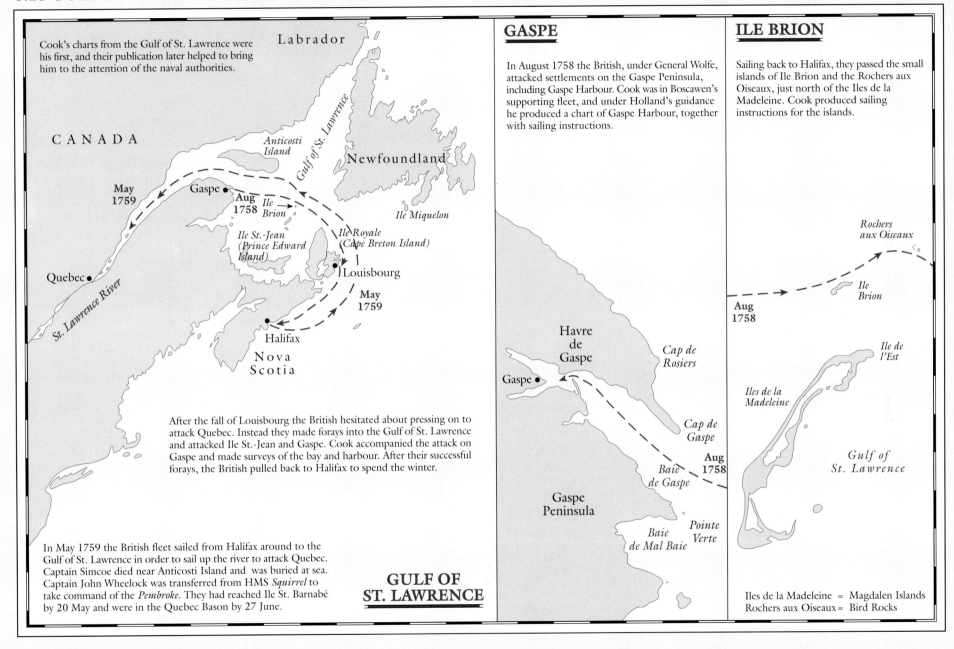

Cook's charts from the Gulf of St. Lawrence were his first, and their publication later helped to bring him to the attention of the naval authorities.

Labrador

CANADA

Anticosti Island

Gulf of St. Lawrence

Newfoundland

May 1759

Gaspe

Aug 1758 *Ile Brion*

Ile Miquelon

Ile St.-Jean (Prince Edward Island)

Ile Royale (Cape Breton Island)

Quebec

St. Lawrence River

Louisbourg

May 1759

Halifax

N o v a S c o t i a

After the fall of Louisbourg the British hesitated about pressing on to attack Quebec. Instead they made forays into the Gulf of St. Lawrence and attacked Ile St.-Jean and Gaspe. Cook accompanied the attack on Gaspe and made surveys of the bay and harbour. After their successful forays, the British pulled back to Halifax to spend the winter.

In May 1759 the British fleet sailed from Halifax around to the Gulf of St. Lawrence in order to sail up the river to attack Quebec. Captain Simcoe died near Anticosti Island and was buried at sea. Captain John Wheelock was transferred from HMS *Squirrel* to take command of the *Pembroke*. They had reached Ile St. Barnabé by 20 May and were in the Quebec Bason by 27 June.

GULF OF ST. LAWRENCE

GASPE

In August 1758 the British, under General Wolfe, attacked settlements on the Gaspe Peninsula, including Gaspe Harbour. Cook was in Boscawen's supporting fleet, and under Holland's guidance he produced a chart of Gaspe Harbour, together with sailing instructions.

Havre de Gaspe

Cap de Rosiers

Gaspe

Cap de Gaspe

Aug 1758

Baie de Gaspe

Gaspe Peninsula

Baie de Mal Baie

Pointe Verte

ILE BRION

Sailing back to Halifax, they passed the small islands of Ile Brion and the Rochers aux Oiseaux, just north of the Iles de la Madeleine. Cook produced sailing instructions for the islands.

Rochers aux Oiseaux

Ile Brion

Aug 1758

Ile de l'Est

Iles de la Madeleine

Gulf of St. Lawrence

Iles de la Madeleine = Magdalen Islands
Rochers aux Oiseaux = Bird Rocks

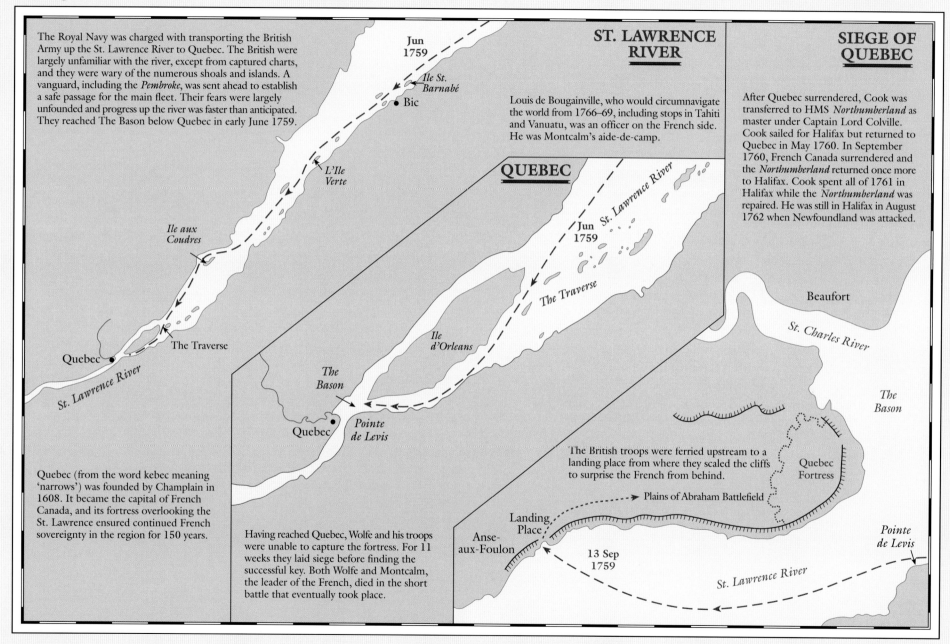

The Royal Navy was charged with transporting the British Army up the St. Lawrence River to Quebec. The British were largely unfamiliar with the river, except from captured charts, and they were wary of the numerous shoals and islands. A vanguard, including the *Pembroke*, was sent ahead to establish a safe passage for the main fleet. Their fears were largely unfounded and progress up the river was faster than anticipated. They reached The Bason below Quebec in early June 1759.

Jun 1759

Ile St. Barnabé

Bic

L'Ile Verte

Ile aux Coudres

Quebec

St. Lawrence River

The Traverse

ST. LAWRENCE RIVER

Louis de Bougainville, who would circumnavigate the world from 1766–69, including stops in Tahiti and Vanuatu, was an officer on the French side. He was Montcalm's aide-de-camp.

QUEBEC

Jun 1759

St. Lawrence River

The Traverse

Ile d'Orleans

The Bason

Quebec

Pointe de Levis

SIEGE OF QUEBEC

After Quebec surrendered, Cook was transferred to HMS *Northumberland* as master under Captain Lord Colville. Cook sailed for Halifax but returned to Quebec in May 1760. In September 1760, French Canada surrendered and the *Northumberland* returned once more to Halifax. Cook spent all of 1761 in Halifax while the *Northumberland* was repaired. He was still in Halifax in August 1762 when Newfoundland was attacked.

Beaufort

St. Charles River

The Bason

Quebec Fortress

The British troops were ferried upstream to a landing place from where they scaled the cliffs to surprise the French from behind.

Plains of Abraham Battlefield

Landing Place

Anse-aux-Foulon

13 Sep 1759

St. Lawrence River

Pointe de Levis

Quebec (from the word kebec meaning 'narrows') was founded by Champlain in 1608. It became the capital of French Canada, and its fortress overlooking the St. Lawrence ensured continued French sovereignty in the region for 150 years.

Having reached Quebec, Wolfe and his troops were unable to capture the fortress. For 11 weeks they laid siege before finding the successful key. Both Wolfe and Montcalm, the leader of the French, died in the short battle that eventually took place.

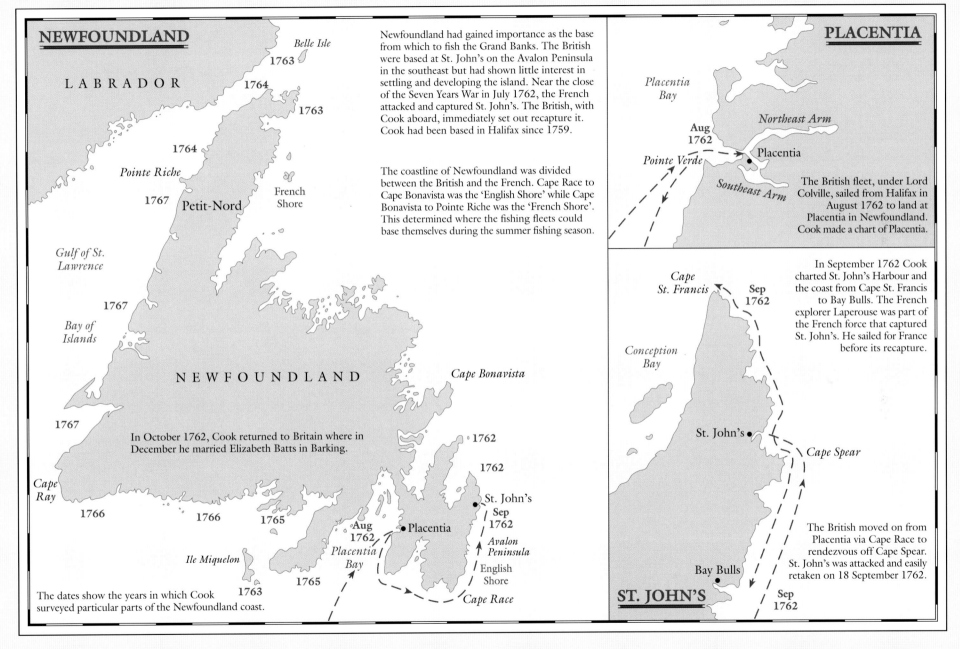

NEWFOUNDLAND

Belle Isle
1763

LABRADOR

1764

1763

1764

Pointe Riche

1767

Petit-Nord

French
Shore

Gulf of St.
Lawrence

1767

Bay of
Islands

NEWFOUNDLAND

Cape Bonavista

1767

In October 1762, Cook returned to Britain where in December he married Elizabeth Batts in Barking.

1762

1762

Cape
Ray

St. John's
Sep
1762

1766

1766

1765

Aug
1762

Placentia

Avalon
Peninsula

Ile Miquelon

Placentia
Bay

English
Shore

1765

1763

Cape Race

The dates show the years in which Cook surveyed particular parts of the Newfoundland coast.

Newfoundland had gained importance as the base from which to fish the Grand Banks. The British were based at St. John's on the Avalon Peninsula in the southeast but had shown little interest in settling and developing the island. Near the close of the Seven Years War in July 1762, the French attacked and captured St. John's. The British, with Cook aboard, immediately set out recapture it. Cook had been based in Halifax since 1759.

The coastline of Newfoundland was divided between the British and the French. Cape Race to Cape Bonavista was the 'English Shore' while Cape Bonavista to Pointe Riche was the 'French Shore'. This determined where the fishing fleets could base themselves during the summer fishing season.

PLACENTIA

Placentia
Bay

Northeast Arm

Aug
1762

Pointe Verde

Placentia

Southeast Arm

The British fleet, under Lord Colville, sailed from Halifax in August 1762 to land at Placentia in Newfoundland. Cook made a chart of Placentia.

In September 1762 Cook charted St. John's Harbour and the coast from Cape St. Francis to Bay Bulls. The French explorer Laperouse was part of the French force that captured St. John's. He sailed for France before its recapture.

Cape
St. Francis

Sep
1762

Conception
Bay

St. John's

Cape Spear

The British moved on from Placentia via Cape Race to rendezvous off Cape Spear. St. John's was attacked and easily retaken on 18 September 1762.

Bay Bulls

ST. JOHN'S

Sep
1762

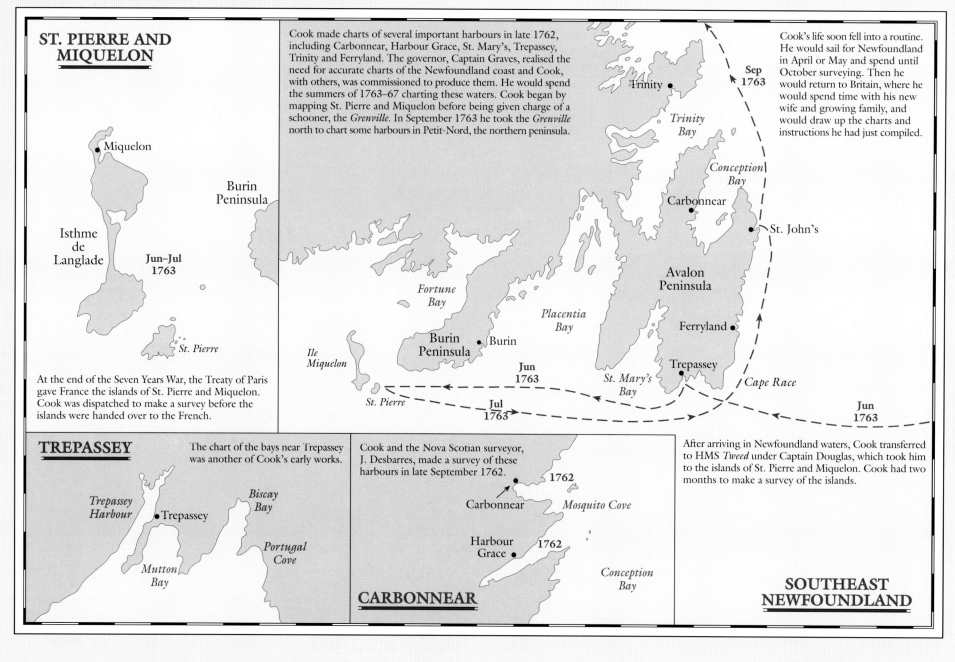

ST. PIERRE AND MIQUELON

Cook made charts of several important harbours in late 1762, including Carbonnear, Harbour Grace, St. Mary's, Trepassey, Trinity and Ferryland. The governor, Captain Graves, realised the need for accurate charts of the Newfoundland coast and Cook, with others, was commissioned to produce them. He would spend the summers of 1763–67 charting these waters. Cook began by mapping St. Pierre and Miquelon before being given charge of a schooner, the *Grenville*. In September 1763 he took the *Grenville* north to chart some harbours in Petit-Nord, the northern peninsula.

Cook's life soon fell into a routine. He would sail for Newfoundland in April or May and spend until October surveying. Then he would return to Britain, where he would spend time with his new wife and growing family, and would draw up the charts and instructions he had just compiled.

Miquelon

Burin
Peninsula

Isthme
de
Langlade

**Jun–Jul
1763**

St. Pierre

Trinity

*Trinity
Bay*

*Conception
Bay*

Carbonnear

**Sep
1763**

St. John's

Avalon
Peninsula

*Fortune
Bay*

*Placentia
Bay*

Ferryland

*Ile
Miquelon*

Burin
Peninsula • Burin

Trepassey

St. Pierre

**Jun
1763**

*St. Mary's
Bay*

Cape Race

**Jul
1763**

**Jun
1763**

At the end of the Seven Years War, the Treaty of Paris gave France the islands of St. Pierre and Miquelon. Cook was dispatched to make a survey before the islands were handed over to the French.

TREPASSEY

The chart of the bays near Trepassey was another of Cook's early works.

*Trepassey
Harbour* • Trepassey

*Biscay
Bay*

*Mutton
Bay*

*Portugal
Cove*

Cook and the Nova Scotian surveyor, J. Desbarres, made a survey of these harbours in late September 1762.

Carbonnear **1762**

Mosquito Cove

Harbour
Grace **1762**

*Conception
Bay*

CARBONNEAR

After arriving in Newfoundland waters, Cook transferred to HMS *Tweed* under Captain Douglas, which took him to the islands of St. Pierre and Miquelon. Cook had two months to make a survey of the islands.

SOUTHEAST
NEWFOUNDLAND

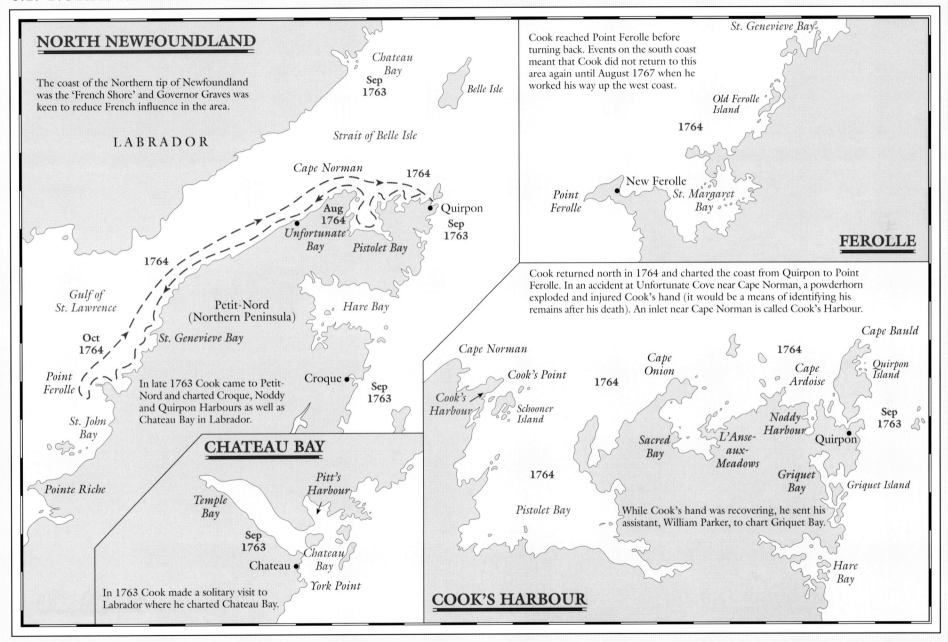

NORTH NEWFOUNDLAND

The coast of the Northern tip of Newfoundland was the 'French Shore' and Governor Graves was keen to reduce French influence in the area.

LABRADOR

Chateau Bay
Sep 1763

Belle Isle

Strait of Belle Isle

Cape Norman

1764

Aug 1764

Unfortunate Bay

Pistolet Bay

Quirpon
Sep 1763

1764

Gulf of St. Lawrence

Petit-Nord (Northern Peninsula)

Hare Bay

Oct 1764

St. Genevieve Bay

Croque
Sep 1763

Point Ferolle

St. John Bay

Pointe Riche

In late 1763 Cook came to Petit-Nord and charted Croque, Noddy and Quirpon Harbours as well as Chateau Bay in Labrador.

CHATEAU BAY

Pitt's Harbour

Temple Bay

Sep 1763

Chateau
Chateau Bay

York Point

In 1763 Cook made a solitary visit to Labrador where he charted Chateau Bay.

Cook reached Point Ferolle before turning back. Events on the south coast meant that Cook did not return to this area again until August 1767 when he worked his way up the west coast.

St. Genevieve Bay

Old Ferolle Island

1764

New Ferolle
Point Ferolle
St. Margaret Bay

FEROLLE

Cook returned north in 1764 and charted the coast from Quirpon to Point Ferolle. In an accident at Unfortunate Cove near Cape Norman, a powderhorn exploded and injured Cook's hand (it would be a means of identifying his remains after his death). An inlet near Cape Norman is called Cook's Harbour.

Cape Norman

Cook's Point

1764

Cook's Harbour

Schooner Island

Cape Onion

1764

Cape Bauld

Quirpon Island

Cape Ardoise

Sacred Bay

L'Anse-aux-Meadows

Noddy Harbour

Quirpon
Sep 1763

1764

Pistolet Bay

Griquet Bay

Griquet Island

While Cook's hand was recovering, he sent his assistant, William Parker, to chart Griquet Bay.

Hare Bay

COOK'S HARBOUR

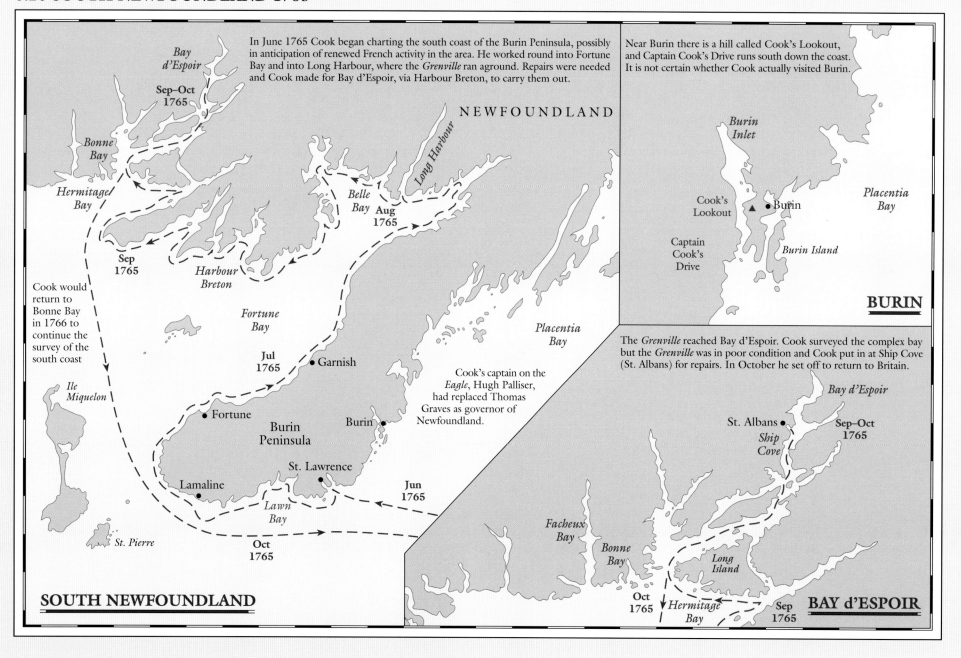

In June 1765 Cook began charting the south coast of the Burin Peninsula, possibly in anticipation of renewed French activity in the area. He worked round into Fortune Bay and into Long Harbour, where the *Grenville* ran aground. Repairs were needed and Cook made for Bay d'Espoir, via Harbour Breton, to carry them out.

Near Burin there is a hill called Cook's Lookout, and Captain Cook's Drive runs south down the coast. It is not certain whether Cook actually visited Burin.

NEWFOUNDLAND

Bay d'Espoir

Sep–Oct 1765

Bonne Bay

Hermitage Bay

Sep 1765

Harbour Breton

Belle Bay

Aug 1765

Long Harbour

Cook would return to Bonne Bay in 1766 to continue the survey of the south coast

Fortune Bay

Jul 1765

Garnish

Placentia Bay

Cook's captain on the *Eagle*, Hugh Palliser, had replaced Thomas Graves as governor of Newfoundland.

Ile Miquelon

Fortune

Burin Peninsula

Burin

St. Lawrence

Jun 1765

Lamaline

Lawn Bay

St. Pierre

Oct 1765

SOUTH NEWFOUNDLAND

BURIN

Burin Inlet

Cook's Lookout

Burin

Placentia Bay

Captain Cook's Drive

Burin Island

The *Grenville* reached Bay d'Espoir. Cook surveyed the complex bay but the *Grenville* was in poor condition and Cook put in at Ship Cove (St. Albans) for repairs. In October he set off to return to Britain.

Bay d'Espoir

St. Albans

Ship Cove

Sep–Oct 1765

Facheux Bay

Bonne Bay

Long Island

Oct 1765

Hermitage Bay

Sep 1765

BAY d'ESPOIR

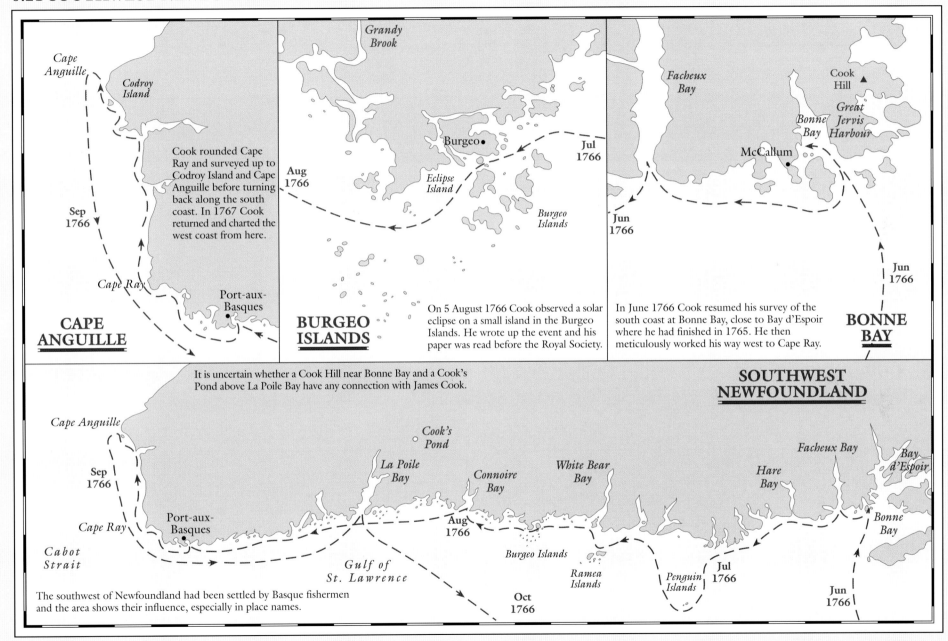

Cape Anguille

Codroy Island

Cook rounded Cape Ray and surveyed up to Codroy Island and Cape Anguille before turning back along the south coast. In 1767 Cook returned and charted the west coast from here.

Sep 1766

Cape Ray

Port-aux-Basques

CAPE ANGUILLE

Grandy Brook

Jul 1766

Aug 1766

Burgeo●

Eclipse Island

Burgeo Islands

BURGEO ISLANDS

On 5 August 1766 Cook observed a solar eclipse on a small island in the Burgeo Islands. He wrote up the event and his paper was read before the Royal Society.

Facheux Bay

Cook Hill ▲

Great Jervis Harbour

Bonne Bay

McCallum●

Jun 1766

Jun 1766

In June 1766 Cook resumed his survey of the south coast at Bonne Bay, close to Bay d'Espoir where he had finished in 1765. He then meticulously worked his way west to Cape Ray.

BONNE BAY

It is uncertain whether a Cook Hill near Bonne Bay and a Cook's Pond above La Poile Bay have any connection with James Cook.

SOUTHWEST NEWFOUNDLAND

Cape Anguille

Sep 1766

Cape Ray

Cabot Strait

Port-aux-Basques

Cook's Pond

La Poile Bay

Connoire Bay

White Bear Bay

Aug 1766

Burgeo Islands

Ramea Islands

Facheux Bay

Hare Bay

Bay d'Espoir

Bonne Bay

Penguin Islands

Jul 1766

Jun 1766

Gulf of St. Lawrence

Oct 1766

The southwest of Newfoundland had been settled by Basque fishermen and the area shows their influence, especially in place names.

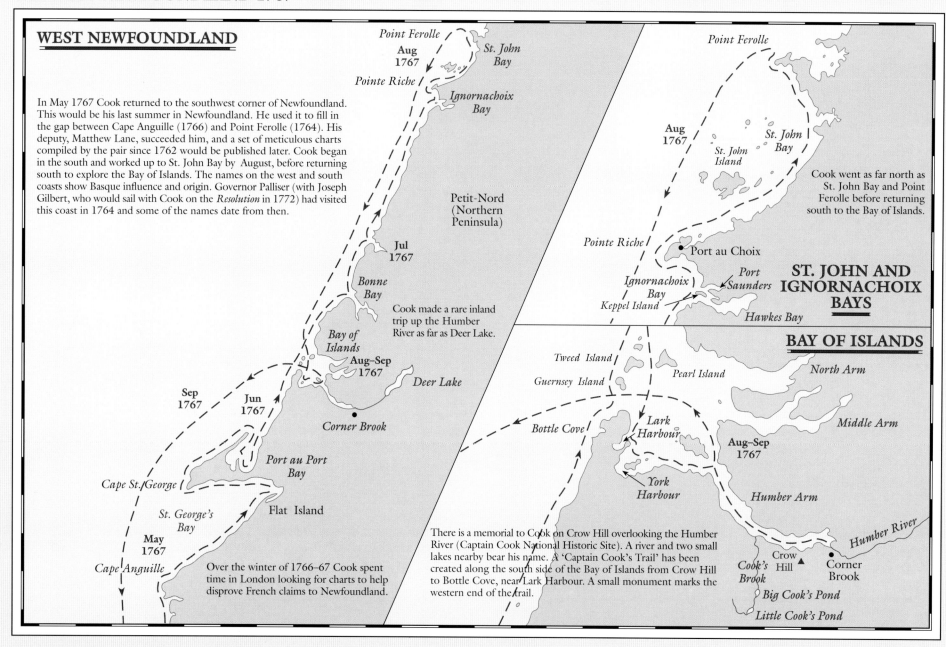

WEST NEWFOUNDLAND

In May 1767 Cook returned to the southwest corner of Newfoundland. This would be his last summer in Newfoundland. He used it to fill in the gap between Cape Anguille (1766) and Point Ferolle (1764). His deputy, Matthew Lane, succeeded him, and a set of meticulous charts compiled by the pair since 1762 would be published later. Cook began in the south and worked up to St. John Bay by August, before returning south to explore the Bay of Islands. The names on the west and south coasts show Basque influence and origin. Governor Palliser (with Joseph Gilbert, who would sail with Cook on the *Resolution* in 1772) had visited this coast in 1764 and some of the names date from then.

Cook made a rare inland trip up the Humber River as far as Deer Lake.

Over the winter of 1766–67 Cook spent time in London looking for charts to help disprove French claims to Newfoundland.

Point Ferolle

Aug 1767

St. John Bay

Pointe Riche

Ignornachoix Bay

Aug 1767

Petit-Nord (Northern Peninsula)

Jul 1767

Bonne Bay

Bay of Islands
Aug–Sep 1767

Deer Lake

Sep 1767

Jun 1767

Corner Brook

Port au Port Bay

Cape St. George

St. George's Bay

Flat Island

May 1767

Cape Anguille

ST. JOHN AND IGNORNACHOIX BAYS

Point Ferolle

Aug 1767

St. John Island

St. John Bay

Cook went as far north as St. John Bay and Point Ferolle before returning south to the Bay of Islands.

Pointe Riche

Port au Choix

Ignornachoix Bay

Keppel Island

Port Saunders

Hawkes Bay

BAY OF ISLANDS

Tweed Island

Guernsey Island

Pearl Island

North Arm

Middle Arm

Bottle Cove

Lark Harbour

Aug–Sep 1767

York Harbour

Humber Arm

Humber River

There is a memorial to Cook on Crow Hill overlooking the Humber River (Captain Cook National Historic Site). A river and two small lakes nearby bear his name. A 'Captain Cook's Trail' has been created along the south side of the Bay of Islands from Crow Hill to Bottle Cove, near Lark Harbour. A small monument marks the western end of the trail.

Cook's Brook

Crow Hill

Corner Brook

Big Cook's Pond

Little Cook's Pond

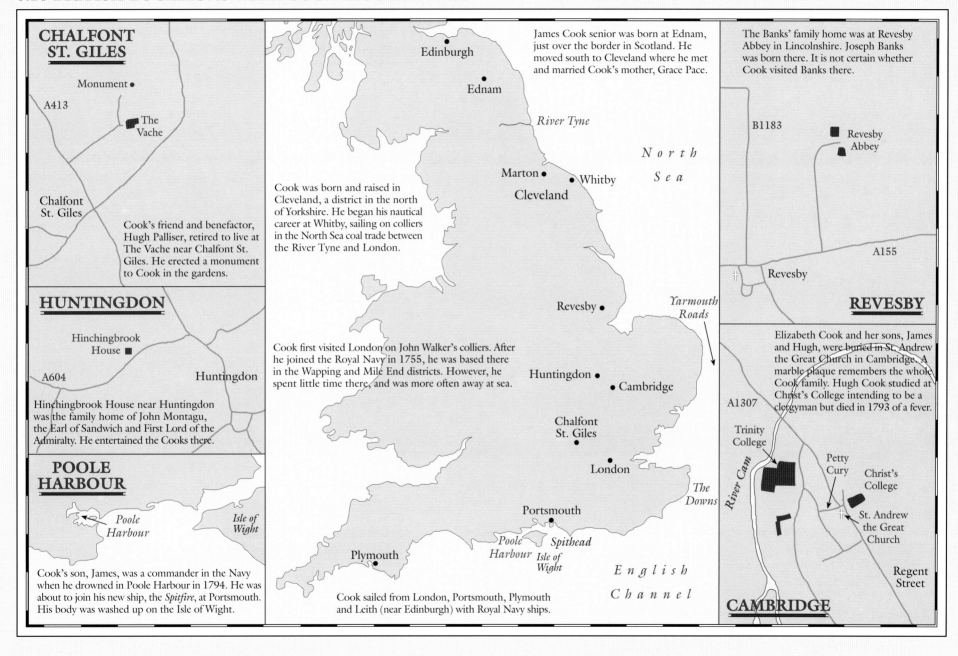

CHALFONT ST. GILES

Monument •

A413

Chalfont St. Giles

■ The Vache

Cook's friend and benefactor, Hugh Palliser, retired to live at The Vache near Chalfont St. Giles. He erected a monument to Cook in the gardens.

HUNTINGDON

Hinchingbrook House ■

A604

Huntingdon

Hinchingbrook House near Huntingdon was the family home of John Montagu, the Earl of Sandwich and First Lord of the Admiralty. He entertained the Cooks there.

POOLE HARBOUR

Poole Harbour

Isle of Wight

Cook's son, James, was a commander in the Navy when he drowned in Poole Harbour in 1794. He was about to join his new ship, the *Spitfire*, at Portsmouth. His body was washed up on the Isle of Wight.

Edinburgh

Ednam

James Cook senior was born at Ednam, just over the border in Scotland. He moved south to Cleveland where he met and married Cook's mother, Grace Pace.

River Tyne

North Sea

Marton •   • Whitby

Cleveland

Cook was born and raised in Cleveland, a district in the north of Yorkshire. He began his nautical career at Whitby, sailing on colliers in the North Sea coal trade between the River Tyne and London.

Revesby •

Yarmouth Roads

Cook first visited London on John Walker's colliers. After he joined the Royal Navy in 1755, he was based there in the Wapping and Mile End districts. However, he spent little time there, and was more often away at sea.

Huntingdon •

• Cambridge

Chalfont St. Giles •

• London

The Downs

Portsmouth •

Plymouth •

Poole Harbour   *Spithead*
Isle of Wight

English Channel

Cook sailed from London, Portsmouth, Plymouth and Leith (near Edinburgh) with Royal Navy ships.

The Banks' family home was at Revesby Abbey in Lincolnshire. Joseph Banks was born there. It is not certain whether Cook visited Banks there.

B1183

■ Revesby
■ Abbey

A155

✝ Revesby

REVESBY

Elizabeth Cook and her sons, James and Hugh, were buried in St. Andrew the Great Church in Cambridge. A marble plaque remembers the whole Cook family. Hugh Cook studied at Christ's College intending to be a clergyman but died in 1793 of a fever.

A1307

River Cam

Trinity College

Petty Cury

Christ's College

✝ St. Andrew the Great Church

Regent Street

CAMBRIDGE

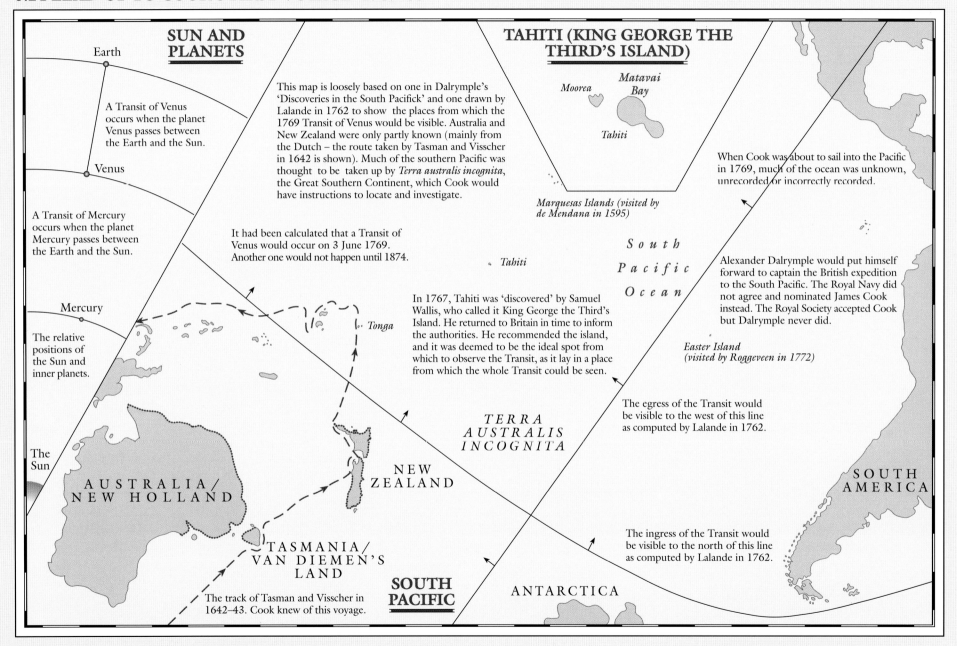

SUN AND PLANETS

Earth

A Transit of Venus occurs when the planet Venus passes between the Earth and the Sun.

Venus

A Transit of Mercury occurs when the planet Mercury passes between the Earth and the Sun.

Mercury

The relative positions of the Sun and inner planets.

The Sun

This map is loosely based on one in Dalrymple's 'Discoveries in the South Pacifick' and one drawn by Lalande in 1762 to show the places from which the 1769 Transit of Venus would be visible. Australia and New Zealand were only partly known (mainly from the Dutch – the route taken by Tasman and Visscher in 1642 is shown). Much of the southern Pacific was thought to be taken up by *Terra australis incognita*, the Great Southern Continent, which Cook would have instructions to locate and investigate.

It had been calculated that a Transit of Venus would occur on 3 June 1769. Another one would not happen until 1874.

In 1767, Tahiti was 'discovered' by Samuel Wallis, who called it King George the Third's Island. He returned to Britain in time to inform the authorities. He recommended the island, and it was deemed to be the ideal spot from which to observe the Transit, as it lay in a place from which the whole Transit could be seen.

TAHITI (KING GEORGE THE THIRD'S ISLAND)

Moorea

Matavai Bay

Tahiti

Marquesas Islands (visited by de Mendana in 1595)

When Cook was about to sail into the Pacific in 1769, much of the ocean was unknown, unrecorded or incorrectly recorded.

South Pacific Ocean

. Tahiti

Alexander Dalrymple would put himself forward to captain the British expedition to the South Pacific. The Royal Navy did not agree and nominated James Cook instead. The Royal Society accepted Cook but Dalrymple never did.

Easter Island (visited by Roggeveen in 1772)

The egress of the Transit would be visible to the west of this line as computed by Lalande in 1762.

|o Tonga

TERRA AUSTRALIS INCOGNITA

NEW ZEALAND

AUSTRALIA/ NEW HOLLAND

TASMANIA/ VAN DIEMEN'S LAND

The track of Tasman and Visscher in 1642–43. Cook knew of this voyage.

SOUTH PACIFIC

ANTARCTICA

SOUTH AMERICA

The ingress of the Transit would be visible to the north of this line as computed by Lalande in 1762.

The First Voyage

Preparations

The Royal Society and the Admiralty had come together in 1767 to organise a voyage to the Pacific to observe a Transit of Venus across the Sun and to search for the Great Southern Continent. The British naval Captain Samuel Wallis had returned to London in 1768 having visited Tahiti on a voyage round the world and recommended Tahiti, or King George the Third's Island as he called it, as a suitable location from which to observe the Transit.

The *Earl of Pembroke*, a North Sea collier, had been purchased by the Royal Navy, renamed HMB *Endeavour* and made ready for the voyage. James Cook, a sailor who had been working as a naval surveyor and cartographer on the Newfoundland station, was snatched from relative obscurity to command the voyage in preference to the Royal Society's choice, Alexander Dalrymple. Cook was not even an officer, and was promoted to lieutenant before the voyage, but he was a sailor of considerable experience (he was already 39) and proven skill and ability. One of his skills was a knowledge of astronomy, and he was therefore chosen to act also as assistant astronomer to Charles Green, from the Royal Observatory, who would be the principal astronomer. A member of the Royal Society, Joseph Banks, gained permission for himself, several scientists and artists and some servants to sail on the voyage at Banks' own expense.

The *Endeavour* was three years and nine months old when purchased from Thomas Milner for £2200. The Navy Board registered it as a bark, the term for a three-masted, flat-bottomed ship. It was 29.8 metres long, 8.9 metres beam width, had a depth in the hold of 3 metres and 368 tons burden. While not a warship, it carried 10 four-pounder cannons and 12 small swivel guns. When it sailed there were 94 persons on board, 71 of whom were Navy, 12 were marines and 11 were civilians, mainly from Joseph Banks' party, whose late inclusion required further rearrangements to what were already very cramped living conditions. Eighteen months' provisions had been provided, and there were also four pigs, three cats, two dogs, one goat and several dozen fowl on board. For getting ashore and other duties there were a longboat, a pinnace, a yawl, a barge and two small boats.

In early August the *Endeavour* sailed from the Thames round to Plymouth, where Banks' party joined the ship. With Joseph Banks were two artists, Alexander Buchan and Sydney Parkinson, whose work was to prove a most valuable and lasting visual record of the Pacific. A Swedish naturalist, Daniel Solander, was also in the party, and he and Banks created a huge botanical, zoological and ethnological record of the places they visited and the people they met. Herman Sporing, another Swede, acted as secretary and contributed many fine sketches.

Before sailing, Cook, Banks and Solander were entertained by William Cookworthy at his home in Plymouth.

To Tahiti

On 25 August 1768 the *Endeavour* left Plymouth and sailed south across the Bay of Biscay [1.01]. The passage through the Bay was very stormy and some of the deck cargo, including many hens, was washed overboard. Passing Cape Finisterre on 4 September, the *Endeavour* came to Madeira, a popular stopping-off point for British vessels [1.02]. Cook brought the ship into the port of Funchal, where it stayed for six days. During the stay Banks and his party went off botanising and socialising while Cook was left to deal with practical matters such as obtaining supplies and checking on the state of the ship. Madeira was famous for its wine, and Cook took on board 3000 gallons. It was also famous for fruit and vegetables, and Cook obtained plenty, including quantities of onions. The onions were to form part of Cook's diet regimen aimed at keeping a healthy crew. Cook was aware of the health problems of long voyages and intended to feed his crew with fresh vegetables as often as possible and sauerkraut at other times. In Newfoundland he had also learned the value to good health of brewing beer to give to his men. Cook's efforts were to prove immensely successful, even though some of his methods achieved little and delayed the application of better methods for several years. Cook insisted that all on board, including the officers, ate the same food, and this helped to overcome reluctance on the part of some men.

Before they left Madeira on 18 September the master's mate, Alexander Weir, was dragged by the anchor chain into the harbour and drowned. Thereafter, the *Endeavour* sailed on down the Atlantic past the Canary and Cape Verde Islands without incident to its next port of call. This was Rio de Janeiro in Brazil, reached on 13 November [1.02].

Brazil, like Madeira, was a Portuguese colony, and though Portugal was nominally an ally of Britain, Cook received a very cold and wary welcome. Portugal was competing with Spain for land on the South American continent and had just expelled the Jesuits, another problem, from the country. The Viceroy had moved the capital from Salvador de Bahia to Rio only five years earlier, and the arrival of Cook's ship there was regarded as suspicious; Cook himself was suspected of being a spy or a smuggler. Such a reception was unexpected and incomprehensible to Cook, who was still very inexperienced in diplomacy. The British were required to stay on board, and a tense period ensued while written communications passed between ship and shore. Eventually limited shore access was agreed to allow Banks to collect some plants and Cook to replenish supplies. Cook, though, was not idle, and he made a chart of the magnificent harbour and compiled sailing instructions.

Cook was more than ready to leave Rio de Janeiro and began to do so on 2 December. But even then there were problems. Peter Flower, who had sailed with Cook in Newfoundland, was lost overboard in the harbour, and adverse conditions meant it was the 7th before they made the open sea. They sailed south to pass between Patagonia and the Falkland Islands [1.03]. The first Christmas of the voyage was celebrated with most on board becoming drunk; Cook apparently turned a blind eye. Temperatures began to drop, even in the southern summer, and 'Fearnought' woollen jackets and trousers were issued to the crew. The *Endeavour* impressed the previously sceptical Banks when it came through strong gales with flying colours. Green, the astronomer, had given several of the crew instructions in how to make astronomical observations on this passage down the South Atlantic.

Tierra del Fuego was sighted on 11 January 1769 and Cook, having decided not to sail through the Strait of Magellan, approached the Strait of Le Maire two days later. It proved difficult to sail through the strait, and Cook stood the *Endeavour* off Thetis Bay, allowing Banks to go ashore. There he collected over 100 new plant species [1.04]. Two days later they successfully negotiated the strait and anchored in the Bay of Good Success on 15 January. Their stay of five days there was very eventful. On the 17th Cook, ashore looking for water, met local Fuegan people. Banks was more ambitious and organised an expedition to go inland to collect botanical specimens, but things soon went wrong. Buchan, the artist, suffered an epileptic fit, and while he was being tended, the temperature dropped and snow fell. Efforts were made to return to the ship, but some of the party were in no state to do so and spent the night in the open. Search parties the next day found Banks' two servants dead, either from the cold or from the rum they had drunk to keep warm.

Meanwhile Cook had surveyed the bay and replenished the fresh water supplies, so on 21 January they were ready to sail. Ahead was the daunting prospect of rounding Cape Horn in a westerly direction against prevailing currents and winds. They passed the Cape on the 25th, heading southwesterly through Drake Passage to latitude 60°10'S on 30 January. Cook then turned north into a new ocean, the Pacific [1.05].

The Transit of Venus was scheduled for 3 June and Cook was intent on reaching Tahiti in plenty of time to prepare for the observation. He therefore gave little priority at this stage to looking for the Southern Continent and steered a direct course for Tahiti. At first helpful winds enabled the ship to make good progress north and then northwest, and on some days 130 miles were being covered. In late February and March warmer but calmer conditions prevailed, and daily distances dropped to 13 miles. No land or signs of land were seen.

By the end of March they had reached the latitude of Tahiti, and Cook headed west to find the island. On 4 April the *Endeavour* encountered Vahitahi (Cook called it Lagoon Island), the first of the Tuamotu Archipelago, a group of many small islands scattered over this part of the Pacific. They had no contact with the few people they saw on the islands. Over the next few days they sailed past several other islands in the group, including Akiaki, Hao and Anaa, before they reached Mehetia, an outlier of the Tahiti group on the 10th. Wallis had seen Mehetia, and he had called it Osnaburg Island. Cook's goal, Tahiti itself, was sighted the next day.

Tahiti

On 13 April 1769 Cook anchored the *Endeavour* in Matavai Bay on the north coast of Tahiti, having been greeted and made welcome by the local people [1.06,1.07]. The crew was in good health and nobody had died from sickness, especially from scurvy (though Buchan, the artist, had another epileptic fit and died on the 16th). The *Endeavour* had proven eminently suitable for the task, and they had seven weeks to prepare for the Transit of Venus.

Tahiti is the largest of a group of islands to which Cook gave the name the Society Islands [1.06]. The name may have been a pun to describe the friendly and sociable welcome received, and to honour the Royal Society which had sponsored the voyage. The people on Tahiti are Polynesians, who are thought to have originated in South East Asia and spread through Fiji and Samoa to reach the Society Islands. From here they spread further to occupy most of the islands in the Pacific, including Hawaii, New Zealand and Easter Island. In noting the similarity between the language and culture of the people he met on distant islands, Cook was one of the first outsiders to recognise the diaspora of Polynesian people. Tupaia, a Raiatean, who later sailed on the *Endeavour*, demonstrated the sailing and navigational skills of the Polynesians that enabled them to make these huge migrations.

Matavai Bay is one of the few places on Tahiti where there is a large enough gap in the fringing coral reef to allow a ship through to anchor [1.07]. A small, low, sandy promontory juts out northwards to form and protect a beautiful and safe bay. The Vaipopoo River entered the sea nearby, furnishing fresh drinking water. Cook and Green decided to build the observatory for the Transit on the promontory, which acquired the name Point Venus. Several tents were erected on the point to house observation equipment and to provide living quarters ashore for Green, Banks and others. A wooden stockade termed Fort Venus was constructed around the tents but did not prevent the astronomical quadrant being stolen. A panic ensued, as the instrument was crucial for the observation, but after much searching and threats the quadrant was returned and all was in readiness to observe the Transit.

In case of cloud cover it was decided to supplement the observation at Matavai Bay by sending two groups to other locations [1.08]. Lieutenant Hicks, Cook's second-in-command, took a party in the pinnace east to an islet, Motu Taaupiri, while Lieutenant Gore's group rowed west across to Moorea, to a rock named Motu Irioa. The day of the Transit, 3 June, was clear, bright and very hot, and Green and the two other groups had a good sighting of it. Cook had distinct reservations about his own readings.

Cook was not yet ready to leave Tahiti, probably realising it was too soon in the year to venture to the colder climates of high latitudes in search of the Southern Continent. Instead, he decided to make a tour of the island, and he, Banks and a small party set out in the pinnace on 26 June [1.08]. They alternated rowing and walking on the tour, which was made in a clockwise direction in six days.

At Hitiaa on the first day they were shown where Bougainville, the French explorer, had landed the previous year. At Taravao they realised Tahiti was two sections linked by a narrow isthmus, and proceeded from Tahiti Nui, the larger part of the island, to Tahiti Iti, the smaller part. At Tautira on Tahiti Iti they met the local chief and his son, Te Arii, who accompanied the tour as far as Pare, where they spent the second night. Another chief, Matahiapo, travelled with them on the third day to Vairao. Back on Tahiti Nui, they saw near Papara the marae at Mahaiatea, which impressed Banks greatly. Then the party made its way up the west coast to Faaa and Pare, and finally back to Matavai Bay.

The restocked and repaired *Endeavour* sailed from Matavai Bay on 13 July 1769. Tahiti had had a considerable effect on Cook and all others on board. The drawings of Parkinson and the descriptions by Cook, Banks and others all contributed to the idyllic picture of the South Seas that soon developed in Europe. The concept of the 'noble savage' as a description for the Polynesians stemmed from Bougainville's and Banks' writings. Cook, though, was more practical and saw Tahiti as an ideal base from which to explore the Pacific. It was central, possessed an equitable climate, and afforded fruit, vegetables, water and other supplies that Cook might need.

Banks persuaded Cook to take Tupaia on board, and this proved to be a beneficial move as Tupaia's navigational, translating and diplomatic skills were used often. He helped draw a map, 'Tupaia's chart', that showed that the Polynesians possessed a great knowledge of the geography of the Pacific and had obviously sailed to much of it. Cook still showed no inclination to head south, but instead decided to investigate the other islands in the Society group [1.06].

Strangely, Cook did not cross to Moorea but sailed north to inspect Tetiaroa, where they did not land, and then headed west to Huahine [1.09]. Skirting the north of the island, Cook anchored at Fare, where they stayed for three days, entertained by Chief Ori. On 19 July they made the short hop to Raiatea, Tupaia's home island, to anchor at Opoa at the southeast corner. Raiatea is believed to have been the religious, cultural and political centre of the Polynesian islands, and it is said that it was from here that the canoes left to colonise the Pacific. Marae Taputapuatea near Opoa is one of the most sacred places in Polynesia.

On 25 July Cook headed north to the adjacent island of Tahaa but could not land, so he rounded the north of the island and carried on towards Bora Bora, a few kilometres to the northwest. He could not land there either, so sailed south to the west coast of Raiatea and anchored inside Passe Rautoanui. They repaired a leak there and took on rocks for ballast, and fresh water. Bora Bora controlled the other islands at this time and its chief, Puni, was on Raiatea, so Cook went to pay his respects. Tupaia was of great value as he led the British through Polynesian protocol. Cook also made shorts trips to Baie Hurepiti on Tahaa and south down the west coast of Raiatea as far as Pointe Pautu. After a week on Raiatea, Cook was ready to head south to explore the Southern Ocean.

Terra australis incognita, the Great Southern Continent

Cook sailed south from Raiatea on 9 August 1769 to begin searching for the Great Southern Continent [1.10]. Dalrymple was later to chide Cook for not having spent more effort looking for the continent on the beat up from Tierra del Fuego to Tahiti, but Cook's priority then had been to reach Tahiti. Now he could appease Dalrymple, who had produced a chart on which was indicated a land mass to the south seen by the Spanish 150 years earlier. Cook also possessed a chart by De Vaugondy that showed parts of New Holland (Australia) and New Zealand known to the Dutch.

Tupaia was immediately able to demonstrate his geographical knowledge when he predicted the *Endeavour* would encounter a small island, and on 14 August they arrived at Rurutu. Cook circled the island, a member of the Austral

Group, while Banks and Tupaia unsuccessfully tried to land from the pinnace. Sailing on southwards they sighted a comet on 29 August and experienced gales and high seas at 40°S. No land had been seen. Cook changed course northwest and had returned to 29°S by 19 September. He then changed course again and steered towards the southwest, where he knew Tasman had found land in 1642. The *Endeavour* was by now in poor condition and Cook knew he had to find land so he could repair the ship. The crew was put on alert to sight land, and on 6 October Nicholas Young, the cabin boy, saw the east coast of the North Island of New Zealand, Aotearoa [1.11].

New Zealand/Aotearoa

New Zealand was one of the last places to be inhabited by humans, having been colonised by Polynesian people approximately 1000 years ago. By the time Cook and the Europeans arrived, these people, the Maori, had spread to occupy all corners of the islands they call Aotearoa. Tupaia could follow their language, but it had developed differences from that of Raiatea, as had their culture.

The *Endeavour* was not the first European ship to visit. The Dutch sailors Tasman and Visscher had sailed up the west coast in 1642, and Cook possessed a copy of their narratives and charts. The Dutch had called it Staten Land but this name was soon changed to New Zealand. It is possible Spanish, Portuguese, Chinese and Malay ships had also visited New Zealand before Cook.

New Zealand comprises two large islands, Te Ika a Maui (North Island) and Te Wai Pounamu (South Island), together with many smaller islands. In the next five months Cook would circumnavigate the islands and, after carrying out a running survey with only a few landings, produce a chart of exceptional quality.

Te Ika a Maui

Cook and the *Endeavour* made landfall in the northeast corner of Te Ika a Maui on 8 October 1769 at Turanga Nui, a location now also called Poverty Bay (a name given by Cook, as the bay offered him little in terms of supplies) [1.12]. Cook, Banks, Solander and some marines landed near the mouth of Turanganui River (the site of Gisborne). They saw people across the river and crossed to meet them. However, the people quickly disappeared and only empty huts were found. In the meantime the coxswain and three young seamen had met four Maori, and in the encounter one Maori had been shot dead. The next day Cook took another party ashore and this time about 100 Maori performed a haka (fierce rhythmical dance) on the opposite bank of the river. It was realised that Tupaia could converse with them and, after he had made an initial breakthrough, a Maori and Cook waded into the water to meet on a sand bank in the middle of the river. They greeted each other, which encouraged more Maori to come forward, and exchanges were made. However, Green's sword was taken and Surgeon Monkhouse shot the thief, so the British retired back on board the *Endeavour* for safety.

Cook still needed fresh water so he tried to land further round the bay, but surf stopped them reaching the shore. They met more Maori in canoes near the mouth of the Kohututea River, and another skirmish occurred; three young Maori were taken captive. The next day, 10 October, they landed again and, as the botanists collected plants, 200 Maori assembled, including the uncle of one of the captive boys. Negotiations were held but, surprisingly, the boys preferred to stay on board. Cook, though, was ready to leave and the boys were put ashore.

These events highlighted the problems of two peoples with completely different cultures coming together. The nervousness and suspicions of both parties led to actions and gestures being misinterpreted, with tragic results. In his journal Cook expressed sadness at the shootings and deaths.

Leaving Poverty Bay, Cook took the *Endeavour* south, rounding the Mahia Peninsula, to enter a large bay that Cook called Hawke's Bay [1.13]. At the southern end of the bay Maori approached them in canoes and trading took place. Suddenly, though, Taiata, Tupaia's servant, was snatched by the Maori but released after gunfire scared his captors away. Cook called the nearby headland Cape Kidnappers after this incident. Cook continued south as far as 40°S, where he reversed course near another headland, Cape Turnagain, and headed north.

They sailed north past Poverty Bay, but they needed water and the botanists wanted to get ashore, so they put into the northern of two promising bays. Here Cook's ability to record local names failed him completely, as he recorded 'Tegadoo' and 'Tolaga' for Anaura and Uawa, the local names of the two bays. At Anaura they obtained some provisions but local Maori suggested the other bay as a better source of water. On 23 October Cook anchored near a small cove (later renamed Cook's Cove) on the southern edge of 'Tolaga' Bay. They stayed here for five profitable days, as relations with the Maori were most friendly and much trading took place. Water, wood and vegetables were obtained in plenty; numerous botanical specimens were found; drawings of people, canoes and landscapes made; and surveys carried out.

The *Endeavour* left Tolaga Bay on 29 October 1769 and headed north, rounding East Cape and Cape Runaway, so named after Maori in canoes approached the ship and scurried off after a shot was fired. Now, heading westwards, they skirted the shoreline of a very large bay that from the ship appeared fertile and well populated; it earned from Cook the name Bay of Plenty. An active offshore volcano was called White Island. Further west, another island was called Mayor Island and a nearby group the Court of Aldermen.

Cook was aware that a Transit of Mercury was approaching and needed to be ashore to observe it. On 4 November they reached an inlet suitable for this purpose, Te-Whanganui-a-Hei, where Cook anchored the *Endeavour* [1.14]. The observation of the Transit of Mercury would help in determining the longitude of the location, so an observatory was set up on the south shore, 150 metres west of the mouth of the Purangi River (Oyster River). Clear skies on 9 November allowed a good sighting of the event, which gave the bay its other name, Mercury Bay. The bay was charted carefully and trips were made to all corners, including deep into Whitianga Harbour (Mangrove River). Two pa (Maori fortified settlements) on the north shore, Te Puta o Paretauhinau (the site of Sporing's Grotto) and Wharetaewa, were visited, and relations with the local Maori, Ngati Hei, were very friendly. The visit was described by Te Horeta Te Taniwha from a Maori point of view many years later.

After leaving Mercury Bay on 15 November, the *Endeavour* had to skirt some islands, the Mercury Islands, before regaining the coast of what would prove to be the Coromandel Peninsula [1.15]. By the 18th, Cook had rounded the northern point of the peninsula, called Cape Colville after his old captain in Canada, and entered a large gulf. Now sailing south, Cook kept close to the eastern shore until he came to the head of the gulf and anchored. Cook, Banks, Solander and Tupaia then took the pinnace into the mouth of a large river that reminded Cook of the Thames, so he gave it that name. It has now reverted to its Maori name, Waihou River, but Thames is used for a town near its mouth and the lower end of the gulf the river flows into.

Rowing up the river, they were amazed at the tremendous height and girth of the trees, probably kauri and kahikatea. Their reports about the trees soon led to Europeans coming to the area to cut down huge numbers of them. Sadly, few now remain. Cook's party travelled nearly as far as Netherton before turning back to the *Endeavour*. On 23 November it raised anchor and began working its way north up the gulf now known as the Hauraki Gulf, noting but not exploring the islands and inlets it passed to the west [1.15]. Cook therefore missed Waitemata Harbour, the site of Auckland. He called islands protecting the Hauraki Gulf on the east the Barrier Islands.

Two days later, Cook called a bay where they caught some fish Bream Bay, and some islands just offshore the Hen and Chicken Islands [1.16]. They continued north, passing the Poor Knights Islands, to reach a headland on 27 November. An arch (Hole-in-the-rock) in one of two offshore rocks amused Cook, causing him to name the headland Cape Brett after Admiral Piercy Brett [1.17]. The headland signalled a large bay, but Cook pressed on to another small island group where they met Maori who sold them fish. The winds prevented them sailing on, so Cook returned from the Cavalli Islands to retreat to the large bay they had passed earlier.

Cook worked the *Endeavour* into the bay and anchored south of a small island near the southern shore on 29 November. Landing on the island they found it was called Motuarohia (from local Maori), and a skirmish ensued. Landing again, they were able to climb a hill which afforded a panorama of the bay. They took on fresh water and vegetables, and Cook tried to leave on the 30th, but was becalmed. Three sailors were punished for stealing sweet potatoes from gardens on the island. Cook and a party rowed south across Te Rawhiti

Inlet to the mainland, but it is uncertain where they landed; Te Hue Bay is the most likely. (A few years later Marion Dufresne and members of his crew were killed in Te Hue Bay.) The next day they made a trip to the neighbouring island of Moturua to replenish water supplies. They made a further visit south to the mainland, but again there is uncertainty. Cook was shown round a village and a pa that may have been Tangitu Pa.

On 5 December Cook set sail, but currents nearly carried the *Endeavour* onto Whale Rock. They survived and Cook left the Bay of Islands to resume his journey north. Conditions were very poor; progress was slow; and keeping close to the coast was difficult. A large bay, Doubtless Bay, was seen but could not be entered, and later the same day Mount Camel was sighted [1.16]. They were close to North Cape on 14 December when Cook nearly encountered the French explorer, Surville, who was sailing in the opposite direction around North Cape on the same day. Cook was forced away from land, which possibly prevented the meeting, and it was the 19th before he regained the coast briefly. Next they were swept far to the north before the *Endeavour* could attempt to sail south down the west coast of the country.

Cook had narrowly missed meeting a French explorer, but he realised he had reached the northern end of the land depicted on the chart of Dutch explorer Visscher [1.11]. On Christmas Day they sighted Tasman's Three Kings Islands and celebrated Christmas by eating gannet pie. However, hurricane-strength gales over the next few days cut short festivities for the New Year. On 1 January 1770 they were close to Cape Maria Van Diemen but soon learned the perils of sailing on the west coast when they were swept down as far as the mouth of Kaipara Harbour [1.16]. Cook sensed he should not get too close to the shore as he made his way north again to sight and fix Cape Maria Van Diemen. As he headed south once more he was not impressed by what he termed a 'desert coast'. Progress proved steady, and they passed Woody Head near Raglan, and Gannet Island and Albatross Point near Kawhia on 10 January.

The next day a high conical mountain was seen in the distance before them, and for several days Mount Taranaki/Egmont, a snow-capped dormant volcano, dominated the skyline [1.18]. The *Endeavour* rounded Cape Egmont (Tasman's Cape Pieter Boerel) on the 13th, and turned southeast into the Taranaki Bight.

This bight was shown on Visscher's chart as Zeehaen's Bight but the Dutch had not determined if it was only a bay or the entrance to a passage back to the Pacific. Cook sailed on to find out the answer, and on 14 January as he passed Kapiti, or Entry Island, he could see no end to the bay. However, the *Endeavour* was in need of repairs, and Cook chose to enter a large inlet to the southwest to find a safe harbour.

Te Wai Pounamu

The large inlet was Totaranui or, as Cook called it, Queen Charlotte Sound [1.19]. With Tahiti, it would become Cook's place of refuge in the Pacific, and he returned here several times. A possible anchorage was seen on the west shore but reaching it was difficult and the *Endeavour* had to be towed round an inhabited island, Motuara, to get there. This was Ship Cove (Meretoto), and Cook remained there for three weeks. The ship was immediately careened on the shore and repairs continued for many days. Water and wood were obtained in plentiful quantities from around the cove. Local Maori soon made contact, and relations were friendly.

A trip was made to a bay to the north, and here they saw bones which were confirmed as coming from humans who had been eaten. This earned the location the name Cannibal Cove. They made two more trips into bays on the west of the inlet, probably the bays now known as Endeavour Inlet and Resolution Bay; but here the dense wooded terrain restricted exploration ashore. On 22 January 1770 Cook took the pinnace up the inlet to a point near the entrance to what is now called Tory Channel, before turning back and going ashore on the southern shore. He climbed a hill, Cook's Lookout, and was rewarded by being able to see the 'Eastern Sea' (Pacific) and a strait linking it to the *Endeavour*'s present position. They returned via Pickersgill Island and East Bay. A few days later Cook returned to East Bay and climbed another hill, Bald Hill, for another view of the strait. Seeming to enjoy climbing, Cook then went up the hill behind Cannibal Cove, from where he could see Port Gore (not named after the *Endeavour*'s Lieutenant Gore!) and Cape Jackson.

The island guarding Ship Cove, Motuara, was visited several times, especially the pa precariously situated at the southern end (it was also called Hippa Island). Cook raised the British flag on the island and then, on 7 February, he set off to explore the strait that would carry his name. Leaving Queen Charlotte Sound, the *Endeavour* nearly ran aground on rocks, The Brothers, close to Cape Koamaru, but the breeze and ebb tide combined to save the ship and carry it through the strait [1.18] which Joseph Banks called Cook Strait. The *Endeavour* kept close to the western shore, so missing the entrance to Wellington Harbour. They passed Cloudy Bay and Cape Campbell, with the snow-capped Kaikoura Range (Snowy Mountains) forming a dramatic backcloth, before Cook agreed with his officers that they should attempt to revisit Cape Turnagain. This would establish that they had indeed sailed around an island.

The *Endeavour* headed northeast past Cape Palliser, named after Cook's captain on HMS *Eagle*, before they recognised Cape Turnagain, which proved that Te Ika a Maui (it was called North Island much later) was an island. With everyone satisfied, Cook turned south and passed Castle Point and Flat Point before regaining Cape Campbell to investigate what lay beyond. On 15 February 1770 the *Endeavour* was approached by Maori in canoes, but they would not talk or trade and returned to land from where they followed the ship's progress south [1.20]. This was Kaikoura, though Cook called it Lookers on. Two days later they saw land which seemed detached from the mainland and Cook gave it the name Banks' Island. This was a rare mistake for Cook, as the island is really a peninsula.

Lieutenant Gore thought he saw land to the southeast, and even though Cook was sure it was cloud, the *Endeavour* changed course to investigate. Nothing was found and Cook turned back towards the land, but a section of the coast went unobserved. Strong southerly winds slowed their progress, but on 25 February they came to the Otago Peninsula, the head of which Cook called Cape Saunders. The strong winds turned to gales and the *Endeavour* was driven 200 kilometres from shore. It was several days before they regained the coast, and they reached Ruapuke, Cook's Bench Island, on 6 March.

Cook could see land beyond Ruapuke but could not discern whether this was an island or part of the mainland. He took the cautious approach, and sailed south and around it. In doing so he made another mistake, because the land is in fact Stewart Island, separated from Te Wai Pounamu by the Foveaux Strait. Cook named some rocks west of Stewart Island after Daniel Solander, but the ship was then forced away from the coast again by gales. On 14 March Cook named the southwestern headland of Te Wai Pounamu West Cape and began sailing up the island's west coast.

Even Joseph Banks was now agreed that the two islands of New Zealand were just that, islands, and not part of the Great Southern Continent. The coast they now followed contained many fiords (it is now known as Fiordland) and Cook named two inlets as Dusky Sound, to which he would return on his second voyage, and Doubtful Sound. Banks, who had not been ashore for several weeks, tried to persuade Cook to enter one of the fiords but Cook refused because he was unsure whether they would be able to sail out again. As on Te Ika a Maui's west coast, conditions were not to Cook's liking, and he pressed on northwards past Cascade Point and Cape Foulwind to be off Rocks Point on 23 March.

The next day, the 24th, they rounded a long spit, Farewell Spit, looking for the bays shown on Visscher's chart where the Dutch had had contact with Maori in 1642 [1.11]. Some Dutch sailors had been killed, so Tasman called it Murderer's Bay (it is now known as Tasman Bay). The *Endeavour* could not make it into the bay, and Cook steered instead for a cape he had seen in the distance from Queen Charlotte Sound back in January [1.21]. Rounding the cape, Cook anchored the *Endeavour* just south of a promontory, Old Man's Head. While the crew stocked up with water, Cook took the pinnace south to another headland where he climbed a hill. The view was good, but not good enough to show him he was on an island, Rangitoto Ki Te Tonga. Before he left Cook bestowed some names: the bay to the east became Admiralty Bay, the cape to the north was Cape Stephens, and a small offshore island was Stephens Island. The unrealised island would later be called D'Urville Island, after the French explorer Dumont D'Urville; and the place where Cook climbed the hill became D'Urville Peninsula.

Cook convened a meeting to discuss which route would be followed to get them home to Britain. The choice was between going east via Cape Horn or going west via New Holland and the Dutch East Indies. The consensus was to go west, and so the *Endeavour* sailed on 31 March, passing Cape Farewell the next day and heading west into the Tasman Sea.

As Cook left New Zealand/Aotearoa he could feel reasonably pleased with his time in the country. He had shown in six months that it consisted of two large islands, Te Ika a Maui (North Island) and Te Wai Pounamu (South Island), as well as many smaller islands. He had circumnavigated them and, using running surveys, produced charts and maps of such quality that some would still be in use in the twentieth century. His own and his colleagues' journals provided records of the Maori people at the time of contact which would prove immensely valuable for future scholars. The contacts had not been without mistakes and problems (for example, Cook deeply regretted the deaths), but on the whole they had been good. Cook, himself, contributed a great deal to the harmony, but Tupaia's presence probably helped more than anything else.

Cook had been particularly impressed by Queen Charlotte Sound, which he saw as a base from which to explore the Pacific. The Southern Continent idea was, by now, largely accepted as a myth, but Cook was already formulating ideas for a second voyage that would disprove it finally. Before he could do that, though, he had to sail the *Endeavour* safely back to Britain.

Australia/New Holland

James Cook is often credited with discovering Australia. He never claimed this achievement for himself, knowing from charts in his possession that other Europeans had been there before him and, of course, Aboriginal people had been there for tens of thousands of years. When Cook approached the east coast of Australia in April 1770 it was, however, largely unknown to the outside world [1.10, 1.22].

The history of the east coast is full of theories and doubts as to who had sailed there before Cook. Malay, Chinese and even Arab ships may have ventured here. The Dutch had certainly visited the other three coasts and named the landmass New Holland, but there is no evidence of them having been on this coast. There are claims that the Spanish and Portuguese had visited earlier and

charted the coast. The Lisbon earthquake of 1755 destroyed most of Portugal's historical records, but a set of maps drawn in France from Portuguese originals and known as the Dieppe Maps show, it is claimed, proof of prior European visits. It is also claimed that Cook even used translations of existing place names from these maps, but it is not known which, if any, of these maps Cook carried on the *Endeavour*.

Cook left New Zealand on 31 March 1770 to return to Britain, having chosen to do so via New Holland and Batavia (Jakarta) in the Dutch East Indies. From charts in his possession he was steering for Van Diemen's Land (Tasmania) as he sailed across the Tasman Sea [1.10]. Cook, though, was too far north and when, on 19 April, his second-in-command Zachary Hicks sighted land, it was part of the mainland of New Holland that he saw. The exact position remains in doubt, but a headland in East Victoria is called Point Hicks to mark the event (on some maps it is called Cape Everard) [1.22].

The *Endeavour* then turned east and north past Cape Howe to begin what would be a long journey up the east coast of Australia. Because of conditions, including heavy surf, Cook kept the ship a safe distance from shore, and several good harbours were missed as a result. No landings were attempted until 28 April. Just north of Red Point and present-day Wollongong, Cook tried, first in the pinnace, and then in the yawl, to land at Bulli, but the surf swamped the boats and prevented them getting ashore [1.23].

Botany Bay

The next day, 29 April 1770, the *Endeavour* sailed into a large bay and anchored just off the inner shore of the bay's southern point [1.24]. People were seen onshore, but when a party landed (led by Isaac Smith, a cousin of Cook's wife) all but two of them ran away. The party tried to converse with the two who remained but no one, including Tupaia, could understand or be understood. The situation worsened, the British fired their guns and the Aboriginal men from the Gwiyyagal tribe threw their spears. For the rest of the stay no further contact took place. The Aborigines would watch from or follow at a distance, as happened when Lieutenant Gore made a journey up the bay to collect oysters.

Cook made several excursions around the bay, including one up a river on the north side where his party explored inland and commented on soils and vegetation (this river, near present-day Sydney Airport, is now called Cook's River). A crewman, Forby Sutherland, died on 1 May and was buried near the landing point (the inner point was named for him). Spores and tracks of animals were seen but actual sightings were uncertain (a small rat-like animal may have been a wombat). Banks and Solander collected many botanical specimens, occasioning the bay's eventual name, Botany Bay. At first it had been called Sting-ray Bay after the many fish they had caught there.

The east coast of New Holland

On 6 May Cook took the *Endeavour* out of the bay and headed north once more, soon passing an inlet he named Port Jackson that would become the site of Australia's first European settlement. This settlement eventually became Sydney [1.23]. By the 11th they had passed Port Stephens and Cape Hawke [1.25]. Cook was conducting a running survey and compiling a chart as he went along the coast, but he was more intent on reaching home so made little effort to land anywhere. He called three high hills he saw on 12 May the Three Brothers, while a point further north, where he could see fires alight, he called Smoky Cape [1.25].

The *Endeavour* sailed past the Solitary Islands to arrive at Cape Byron on the 15 May. Behind the cape Cook could see an inland mountain, and when dangerous rocks were encountered it later acquired the name Mount Warning. A cape near the dangerous rocks was called Point Danger, and a nearby small island later became Cook Island [1.26]. The point that Cook called Point Danger is now called Point Fingal, while the name Point Danger has been applied to another point just to the north at present-day Tweed Heads. Cook next sailed outside two large islands, but was not aware that this is what they were. He gave the name Point Lookout to the northern point of the first island (North Stradbroke Island) and the name Cape Morton to that of the second island (Moreton Island — Morton later gained the letter 'e'). Cook suspected but did not see the large bay behind the islands, now known as Moreton Bay, nor the river that flows into the bay (Brisbane stands on that river).

They saw more inland hills, and from their resemblance to glass kilns Cook called them The Glass Houses. They passed Double Island Point and Wide Bay on 18 May before they came to a very large sand island now known as Fraser Island [1.27]. Rounding Indian Head and Sandy Cape at the north of the island, the *Endeavour* was entering an interesting section of the voyage. They had reached latitude 25°S and, as the coast turned more to the northwest, were about to come to the Great Barrier Reef, the sequence of extensive coral reefs that fringe the coast all the way north.

Looking for water, Cook put the *Endeavour* into a bay on 23 May. Here he anchored and went ashore. He explored a channel that led to a lagoon surrounded by mangroves, but most of the area was very dry, sandy and uninviting. Still-smouldering fires were found along with the remains of a meal, but no people were encountered, though some were seen from the ship. Some large birds were caught and eaten, causing Cook to call the bay Bustard Bay. He left the next day. In a strange incident on board, Cook's clerk, Orton, had pieces of his ears chopped off while he was drunk and asleep. Suspicion fell on Midshipman Magra but later it was thought to be Midshipman Saunders who had done the deed.

Crossing the Tropic of Capricorn, Cook called the nearby point Cape Capricorn. He crossed Keppel Bay but, unsure of the way ahead, anchored by the Keppel Islands while he dispatched the ship's master in one of the small boats to locate a passage. This action would be repeated often among the reefs and small islands. The *Endeavour* then carefully negotiated a route past Cape Manifold, Island Head, Cape Townshend and across the mouth of Shoalwater Bay to anchor on 29 May at the mouth of an inlet. Cook was considering cleaning the *Endeavour*'s hull and needed more drinking water, but when no fresh water was found he pressed on. The inlet became Thirsty Sound.

The *Endeavour* was sailing north with numerous small islands — the Northumberland and Cumberland Islands — to seaward, and a dry coast to landward that did not entice Cook to go ashore. No contact with local people was made and indeed few signs of people were seen. On 3 June they approached another maze of small islands north of Repulse Bay [1.28]. On Whitsunday (Pentecost) a route was discovered to the east of the headland, Cape Conway, and through the network of islands now known as the Whitsundays. Having passed the Capes Gloucester, Upstart, Bowling Green and Cleveland, the ship's compass behaved irregularly near an island. Cook called the island Magnetic Island, and its highest point is now known as Mount Cook. Things by now had a tropical look and the next islands became the Palm Isles. Cook got in a muddle over the next two large bays and mixed up their names, Rockingham and Halifax. Dunk Island, the Family Islands, Frankland Islands and Fitzroy Island followed before Cook arrived at Cape Grafton.

Cook required water and attempted to land in a bay north of the cape, but mangroves lined the shore and Cook contented himself by landing on the cape itself, in Mission Bay. The larger bay is Trinity Bay, and Cairns is situated close to where Cook tried to land. A small cove in Cairns is called Cook Bay. Sailing on near Green Island, Cook passed the northern end of Trinity Bay, Cape Tribulation, on 10 June. He gave that cape its name later, after the events of the next day had unfurled, as he deemed it was a portent for what was to follow [1.29].

Endeavour Reef and Cooktown

The *Endeavour* had already navigated its way through hundreds of coral reefs, cays or sandbanks and small islands when, on 11 June 1770 at 10.30 p.m., disaster struck. The ship ran aground on the reef (later called Endeavour Reef). They tried everything to free the ship, including throwing cannons, stone ballast and stores overboard to lighten the load and allow it to float off. High water came but still the ship was stuck fast, and the three pumps that worked were losing the battle against the leaks. Midshipman Monkhouse was charged with preparing a fothering to cover the hole, and after 23 hours on the reef, the ship was finally freed and made for shore. The *Endeavour* limped toward a bay, Weary Bay (now called Walker Bay; another bay to the south is now called Weary Bay), but this did not prove satisfactory and the ship struggled on to an inlet which

the master had located just to the north. Even then gales and a sandbank prevented the *Endeavour* reaching safety until 18 June [1.29].

The inlet was a river mouth and Cook managed to beach the ship on the southern shore just inside the mouth [1.30]. Cook's relief at making land must have been considerable; even he had been forming contingency plans involving building a makeshift vessel to sail to Batavia (Jakarta). However, though the extent of the damage was soon appreciated, the fothering had been very successful, and big pieces of coral had broken off and plugged the holes to a large extent. It would take some time, but the damage was repairable. The carpenters set to work.

Relieved that the ship could be saved, Cook, his officers and the scientists began exploring the hinterland and collecting botanical and zoological specimens. Gore shot a kangaroo, the first of several. The local people, Gogo-Yimidirs, were indifferent to the visitors at first, and went about their normal activities such as fishing. Gradually, though, contact was established and by 19 July some of the locals went on board the *Endeavour*. Communication was difficult but they let it be known that they did not approve of the large number of turtles Cook's party had caught.

After seven weeks the repairs were completed and Cook was ready to sail on 4 August. A settlement called Cooktown later grew up at the mouth of the river, the Endeavour River.

Cook realised the *Endeavour* was in delicate condition and needed to be nursed through to Batavia. He sent the small boats ahead to plot a safe passage over and through the reef but they made slow progress [1.29]. He climbed a headland, Lookout Point, to gain a view of the reef's outer edge, having decided it would be safer to sail in the open sea than to stay on the reef. An island could be seen closer to the reef, so Cook took the pinnace out to it and climbed the island's hill. Views were hazy and they could see no obvious channel through the reef, even though they remained overnight to look again next morning. They did see many lizards, so the island became Lizard Island; later the hill became Cook's Look. Cook sailed the *Endeavour* past Lizard Island and the crew located a gap; Cook thankfully took the ship through the reef on 14 August and out into deep water.

To Torres Strait

Though he was now in deep water, Cook soon realised he was also out of sight of land and was unable to continue his chart of the coast [1.31]. The ship was leaking and Cook, needing the shortest route to Batavia for proper repairs, was on the lookout for Torres Strait between New Holland and New Guinea. He was uncertain whether the strait existed but knew he should regain the coast just in case it did. After two days outside the reef, he began searching for a way back inside. Approaching the reef from the open sea was dangerous, and the *Endeavour* was nearly driven onto the coral and destroyed. The small boats towed the ship, which, with ebb tides and good luck, was saved. They found a gap, named Providential Channel, and Cook, inside the reef once more on 17 August, decided to remain there. A section of the coast between Lookout Point and Cape Weymouth remained uncharted [1.31].

They anchored among the Forbes Islands off Bolt Head before continuing northwards to a headland, Cape Grenville, off which were numerous small islets. Many of these islets were later given names of men on board the *Endeavour*, among them Gore, Clerke, Buchan, Orton and Magra. Sailing on, they came on 21 August to the northernmost tip of the east coast, a point Cook called York Cape (the words were later reversed). Rounding the cape, Cook anchored and went ashore on a small island [1.32].

From the top of a small hill Cook was convinced he had reached the north of New Holland and that a strait did exist which would allow him to sail west. He then raised the flag and claimed the whole of the east coast of New Holland for Britain; in doing so he renamed the coast New South Wales. Cook returned to the ship and sailed it through a short strait, the Endeavour Strait, and out into the Arafura Sea. Cook was trying to determine the extent of Torres Strait, so he headed northwest towards New Guinea, passing Booby Island and encountering more shoals, Cook Reef and Cook Shoal.

Cook and Australia

Cook was rightly proud of his feat of sailing the *Endeavour* up the length of the east coast and of the charts drawn and information collected in the journey. He had taken only about eight weeks of sailing time to travel the 3500-kilometre journey. The ship had stopped only when Cook needed water or in emergency. Contact with local people had been minimal, and what there had been was difficult. Cook described the Aborigines and their simple lifestyle and, while commenting on their apparent wretchedness, felt that in reality they were far happier than Europeans. (Interestingly, for many Aborigines the words 'Captain Cook' have come to symbolise Europeans in general and all the bad things which have resulted from contact with the outside world.) Cook therefore had no local names to use, and his charts are full of names he coined for features and places, many of which survive today. His crew remained very healthy, even if his ship did not.

Cook described New South Wales in his journal, but he and Banks disagreed over the potential of the country. Banks, possibly because of the large amount of zoological and, especially, botanical specimens collected (virtually all new to European science), would extol the merits of the place. Cook was far less enthusiastic about the country and its potential, returning only once for a very brief stopover in Tasmania on his Third Voyage. He preferred New Zealand as a base.

As stated above, the east coast of Australia is full of names bestowed by Cook, from Cape Howe on the Victoria–New South Wales border to Cape York in the north. Many capes, islands and other features carry names dating from the *Endeavour* voyage, while a few others were named later to commemorate persons involved in it. Cook used the name Botany Bay, which has become one of the most famous in Australian history, but in 2000 its future is in doubt because of a recent Government decision to use an Aboriginal name instead.

In 1969 and 1970 many places in Australia marked the bicentenary of Cook's 1770 voyage by erecting monuments and plaques to record his passage along the east coast. In some cases these places were well away from the coast. The range in the form of the monuments is large, with parks, statues and even a

'Singing Ship' near Rockhampton. At other times Cook's name has been used for bridges, suburbs of large cities (and, of course, Cooktown), public houses, universities and schools, and companies, especially those with a maritime connection.

The most important memorial, though, is the Historic Landing Site at Kurnell on the south side of Botany Bay.

New Guinea and the Dutch East Indies

The *Endeavour* was returning to better-known waters that featured on European charts, including De Vaugondy's chart of 1756 that Cook carried on board [1.33]. By 29 August 1770 Cook had arrived at the New Guinea coast, and he followed it around False Cape to a small bay (Teluk Cook) where he went ashore in the pinnace. Four men attacked them, so they retreated to the ship and sailed off. Cook reported that there was huge relief among the crew that they were finally going home. They had been away for two years, and while their general health was good even the most adventurous among them would have been ready to be home in Britain.

Sailing west across the Arafura Sea, they passed to the south of the Aru and Tanimbar Islands. Cook was not happy about the accuracy of the charts he had on board and in his journal he made the case for proper charts to be produced by trained surveyors and maintained by an agency. This plea was eventually realised by the creation of the Hydrographic Board. The Dutch, through their Dutch East India Company and control of the spice trade, had had a strong presence in this area for over 100 years, and Cook knew that a British ship would be viewed with suspicion sailing through these waters. He was therefore making for Batavia on the island of Java with a minimum of stops. Cook would have liked to have called in at Timor for its associations with the explorer Dampier, but he sailed on to pass through the strait between Timor and Roti (Selat Roti) on 16 September.

On the 17th Cook was surprised to arrive at a small island, Savu, where he stayed for four days [1.34]. The Dutch resident official was predictably unhappy about the *Endeavour*'s presence and reluctant to allow any trade, but the local sultan and his people were more receptive. Eventually oxen and other stores were taken on board. Cook then sailed on past the neighbouring island of Raijua towards Java.

On 1 October they rounded Java Head and Princes Island to enter Sunda Strait, between Java and Sumatra [1.34]. Adverse winds, currents and the suspicions of Dutch Naval officials slowed their progress, and it took them until the 10th before they anchored in the Batavia Roads. The Dutch then insisted that any repairs be carried out in their yards, by their men and at exorbitant rates set by them, to all of which Cook most reluctantly had to agree. Even then bureaucracy slowed matters further, and it was the 18th before the *Endeavour* was transferred to Onrust Island and November before repairs began there.

Cook was proud of reaching Batavia with only three people suffering from minor ailments, but Batavia was to be his undoing. The city was low-lying, and its canals, built by the Dutch, were stagnant and a breeding ground for tropical diseases such as dysentery, cholera, malaria and typhoid. These diseases were rampant and seven men died here, including Tupaia and Surgeon Monkhouse. Everyone, including Cook, was ill at some time during the stay, and many who contracted the diseases died over the next few weeks. To everyone's great relief the *Endeavour* left Batavia on 26 December, but going back through the Sunda Strait was another slow ordeal. They anchored at Princes Island (Pulau Panaitan) on 6 January 1771 to take on drinking water, but afterwards this water was thought to be polluted and responsible for many of the subsequent deaths.

Indian Ocean and Cape Town

After 10 days at Princes Island the *Endeavour* set off on 16 January 1771 to cross the Indian Ocean for Cape Town [1.35]. Cook's journal for the crossing was a catalogue of deaths: 24 men succumbed. Among them were Green, the astronomer; Parkinson and Sporing who had contributed so many drawings and sketches; and Midshipman Monkhouse who had successfully fothered the ship on Endeavour Reef. Cook feared the voyage would be remembered for all this loss of life, but the *Endeavour*'s death toll was still relatively low. When he came to Cape Town, Cook saw other ships that had sailed from Bombay and Batavia, and most of them had much larger death tolls on voyages much shorter than his own.

They saw the coast of Africa on 5 March, probably near Port St. Johns between Durban and East London. The Agulhas coastal current then carried them down past the southernmost point of Africa, Cape Agulhas. The *Endeavour* was off the Cape of Good Hope on 13 March, ready to enter Cape Town the next day. A relieved Cook anchored in Table Bay and sought permission to take the sick, among them Solander, ashore [1.36]. Twenty-eight were dispatched to sick quarters, where all but two recovered.

Cook went to present his papers to the Dutch governor of the colony and to gain permission to trade, restock and repair the ship. All trade had to be handled by the Dutch East India Company on its terms, which did not impress Cook. Shore leave was granted, and while most of the party remained in the town, Gore climbed Table Mountain and collected specimens for Banks. Banks heard about Bougainville's expedition to the Pacific and French plans for more voyages. They left port on 15 April, and Cook put into Robben Island (Penguin Island) but was not allowed to land. The next day the master, Molyneux, died.

Back to Britain

The passage north through the South Atlantic was straightforward, and the *Endeavour* arrived at St. Helena on 1 May 1771 [1.37]. Already in port were HMS *Portland* and a fleet of 12 Indiamen en route for Britain. When this fleet left three days later, Cook sailed with them. (When Cook's journal, edited and rewritten by John Hawkesworth, was published, some of Cook's remarks about St. Helena would cause concern and make his second visit to the island in 1774 most awkward.) The *Endeavour* kept pace with the fleet as they passed Ascension Island on 10 May. Banks wanted to go ashore, but Cook wanted to stay with the other ships so they pressed on. They were still with the fleet as they crossed the Equator, but by the 24th they had lost contact [1.38].

On 26 May Zachary Hicks, Cook's second-in-command, died after a long illness. Cook held a course northwest until 11 June, when in latitude 40°N they turned and headed just north of east for Britain.

Cook and the ship had been away for nearly three years and he, like most on board, was keen to be home. He was concerned for his family and for how many of his children would still be alive. Would his father and his sisters be alive in Cleveland? Another concern for him was how the voyage and his role in it would be assessed. Unlike Banks, he was not a member of the establishment, so could not mix in influential circles to give his version of events.

They were by now in more crowded waters and saw and conversed with several other ships. They even briefly regained contact with the Indiamen fleet. On 10 July Nicholas Young, the boy who had first sighted New Zealand, was the first to see Land's End. They quickly sailed up the English Channel, passing Dover on the 12th, and anchored in the Downs off Kent on 13 July. Cook immediately set off for London to report to the Admiralty and to see his family on Mile End.

Post-mortem

When the *Endeavour* returned to Britain the voyage was hailed as a great success but, significantly, it was regarded as Joseph Banks' success. 'Society' and newspapers honoured Banks and, to a lesser extent, Daniel Solander, and the two men were presented to King George III. Cook had sailed as a nobody and, in most people's eyes, he remained one on his return. Nevertheless, he quietly set about discharging his duties to wrap up the voyage by writing up the journals, logs and charts for the Admiralty which, along with the Royal Society, recognised that the success of the voyage owed a great deal to Cook. Gradually, it became known to the wider population.

The *Endeavour* had gone to Tahiti to observe the Transit of Venus [1.39]. It had arrived in time and its men had made a reasonably successful sighting. Unfortunately, Green had not written up the records properly, and after his death on the Indian Ocean, Cook and others were left to complete them. Following the Transit, Cook had set off in search of *Terra australis incognita*, the Great Southern Continent, and had shown to most people's satisfaction that it did not exist. There were some, like Dalrymple, who felt Cook had not been diligent enough in looking and that a continent still waited to be located. Cook himself already had ideas for another voyage that would finally lay the myth to rest [1.40].

Cook's charts of New Zealand and the east coast of Australia remain very fine records of his prowess as a surveyor and cartographer. In his dealings with the people of the Pacific, Cook did make some mistakes, but generally the contacts went very well and many friendships were established. His treatment of his own crew and the fact that he lost so few men in nearly three years away (Batavia could not be helped) set new standards even for short journeys. The voyage can be regarded as one of the first scientific expeditions, thanks to the collecting work of Banks and Solander; the ethnographic observations of Banks, Solander and Cook; and the drawings of Parkinson and Sporing. Again, new standards were created for future voyages to emulate.

All in all, the *Endeavour* voyage had achieved its purposes, and for James Cook, its architect, manager and principal player, it marked the start of his rise to fame.

Cook in Britain, 1771–1772

Cook returned to his wife, Elizabeth, and the family in Mile End, London. Sadly two children had died in his absence. Joseph, who was born shortly after Cook's departure, lived only for a month. Daughter Elizabeth died just before Cook's return, aged four years. Only young James and Nathaniel survived.

At first he was absorbed with his family and with preparing the records of the voyage for the Admiralty. In August, though, the Admiralty thanked him for what he had achieved on the voyage. It confirmed the promotions that Cook had recommended for the crew of the *Endeavour* and told Cook he would be made a commander. Then, at the end of the month, Cook was presented to the King, who confirmed Cook's promotion. Linked to his promotion was an appointment to HMS *Scorpion*, a sloop commissioned to renew the charts of British waters, but Cook never sailed on this ship or in this capacity.

During this period Cook had been corresponding with people such as John Walker in Whitby. In December he applied for leave and travelled north to Cleveland with Elizabeth to see his family and friends, including the Walkers. When he returned to London in early January 1772, plans were already underway for a second voyage, and much of Cook's time from now on was spent on these preparations.

Cook was beginning to mix in other circles. He began meeting with members of the Royal Society and was a dinner guest at influential houses in London. The Earl of Sandwich invited him to his country house, Hinchingbrook, near Huntingdon.

On 21 June 1772 Cook said farewell to his family and went down the Thames to Sheerness to join the *Resolution* for the second voyage.

Cook's legacy in New Zealand

Cook occupies a strange position in New Zealand at the end of the twentieth century. Historians and other academics have deemed that he does not hold a sufficiently important place in the country's history for him to feature in a government-sponsored *Historical Atlas*. This attitude is mirrored by the major museums which, if they display him at all, relegate Cook-related exhibits to dark corners.

Conversely the replica of HMB *Endeavour* drew huge crowds when it visited the country. His visits are also remembered at:

Gisborne and East Cape: A monument marks the spot where Cook landed in New Zealand, while up on Kaiti Hill a statue (supposedly of Cook, but actually of a Spanish naval officer) looks out over Poverty Bay [1.12]. The Gisborne Museum has a small Cook display and a more authentic statue of Cook. There is also a statue representing Young Nick (Nicholas Young) pointing at the headland now named after him. Further north, at Tolaga Bay, the small inlet where Cook obtained fresh water is now called Cook's Cove and there is a tablet recording the visit [1.13]. Anaura Bay has a small cairn marking Cook's visit there.

Coromandel Peninsula: Mercury Bay has several mementoes of Cook's visit [1.14]. The place where the *Endeavour* anchored is now called Cook's Bay, and a settlement on its southern shore is Cook's Beach. A cairn in Cook's Beach marks the spot where the Transit of Mercury was observed, and another cairn on Shakespeare Cliff marks the visit in general. Whitianga Museum has a Cook exhibit. Across the peninsula there are two monuments to Cook [1.15]. One monument is by the roadside in Kopu while another, on the side of the Waihou River near Netherton, marks how far Cook's party rowed up the river.

Auckland: While Cook never called in at Auckland or the Waitemata Harbour, there is a statue of Cook next to the Lion Brewery on Khyber Pass Road. The Maritime Museum has a very tiny exhibit.

Bay of Islands: A plaque under the water marks the spot south of Motuarohia Island where the *Endeavour* was anchored [1.17]. Russell Museum has a model of the *Endeavour*.

Wellington: Cook missed Wellington Harbour but Wellington does have some Cook connections [1.18]. The Alexander Turnbull Library, part of the National Library, has one of the world's best collections of Cook material. There is the James Cook Centra Hotel and a suburb called Mount Cook. Wellington Harbour opens onto Cook Strait, which lies between the two main islands of New Zealand.

Queen Charlotte Sound: Ship Cove (Meretoto) has a large cairn near the beach which Cook visited on all his voyages to the Pacific [1.19]. Offshore, on Motuara Island, there is another cairn close to the spot where Cook claimed possession of the islands. The hill on Arapawa Island, where Cook sighted Cook Strait, is now called Cook's Lookout.

Te Wai Pounamu (South Island): The highest mountain in the Southern Alps was named after Cook by Captain Stokes in 1849 [1.20]. Now known as Mount Cook/Aoraki, a Cook River flows from its slopes to the Tasman Sea, while the settlement near the mountain is Mount Cook. Dusky Sound in Fiordland is associated with Cook's Second Voyage [2.05]. A plaque marks the visit to Pickersgill Harbour in the sound, while Cook is remembered by the names Cook Channel and Cook Stream, which flows into Pickersgill Harbour.

Many towns have streets named after Cook. There are schools, public houses and products, including wine, that have used his name. Many features named by Cook still carry those names (e.g. Bay of Islands, Cape Farewell), while other features carry the names of people who sailed with him (Banks Peninsula, Pickersgill Island) or of the ships (Resolution Island).

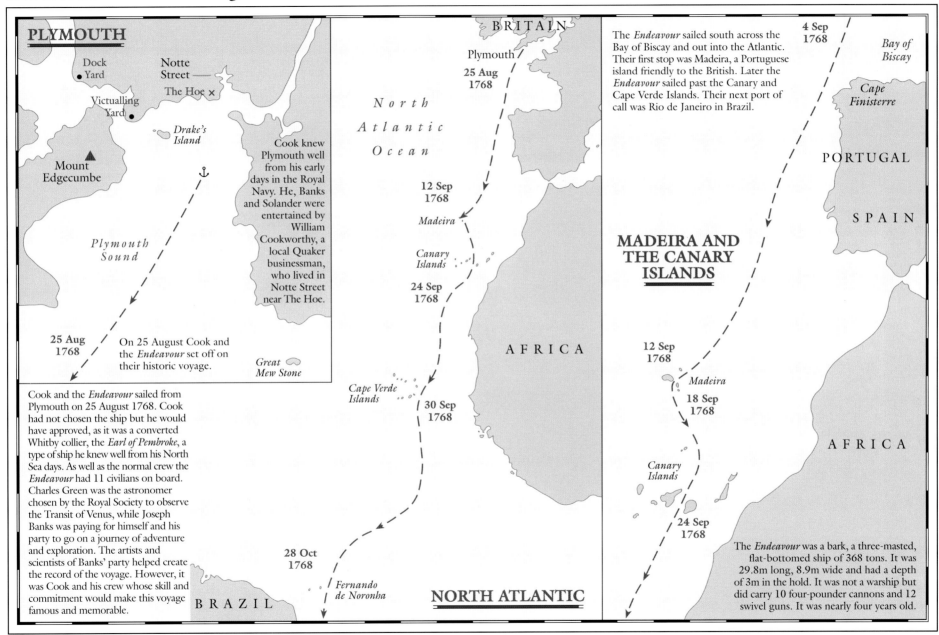

PLYMOUTH

Dock Yard

Notte Street

The Hoe ×

Victualling Yard

Drake's Island

Mount Edgecumbe

Plymouth Sound

Great Mew Stone

Cook knew Plymouth well from his early days in the Royal Navy. He, Banks and Solander were entertained by William Cookworthy, a local Quaker businessman, who lived in Notte Street near The Hoe.

25 Aug 1768

On 25 August Cook and the *Endeavour* set off on their historic voyage.

Cook and the *Endeavour* sailed from Plymouth on 25 August 1768. Cook had not chosen the ship but he would have approved, as it was a converted Whitby collier, the *Earl of Pembroke*, a type of ship he knew well from his North Sea days. As well as the normal crew the *Endeavour* had 11 civilians on board. Charles Green was the astronomer chosen by the Royal Society to observe the Transit of Venus, while Joseph Banks was paying for himself and his party to go on a journey of adventure and exploration. The artists and scientists of Banks' party helped create the record of the voyage. However, it was Cook and his crew whose skill and commitment would make this voyage famous and memorable.

BRITAIN

Plymouth

25 Aug 1768

North Atlantic Ocean

12 Sep 1768

Madeira

Canary Islands

24 Sep 1768

AFRICA

Cape Verde Islands

30 Sep 1768

28 Oct 1768

BRAZIL

Fernando de Noronha

NORTH ATLANTIC

The *Endeavour* sailed south across the Bay of Biscay and out into the Atlantic. Their first stop was Madeira, a Portuguese island friendly to the British. Later the *Endeavour* sailed past the Canary and Cape Verde Islands. Their next port of call was Rio de Janeiro in Brazil.

4 Sep 1768

Bay of Biscay

Cape Finisterre

PORTUGAL

SPAIN

MADEIRA AND THE CANARY ISLANDS

12 Sep 1768

Madeira

18 Sep 1768

Canary Islands

24 Sep 1768

AFRICA

The *Endeavour* was a bark, a three-masted, flat-bottomed ship of 368 tons. It was 29.8m long, 8.9m wide and had a depth of 3m in the hold. It was not a warship but did carry 10 four-pounder cannons and 12 swivel guns. It was nearly four years old.

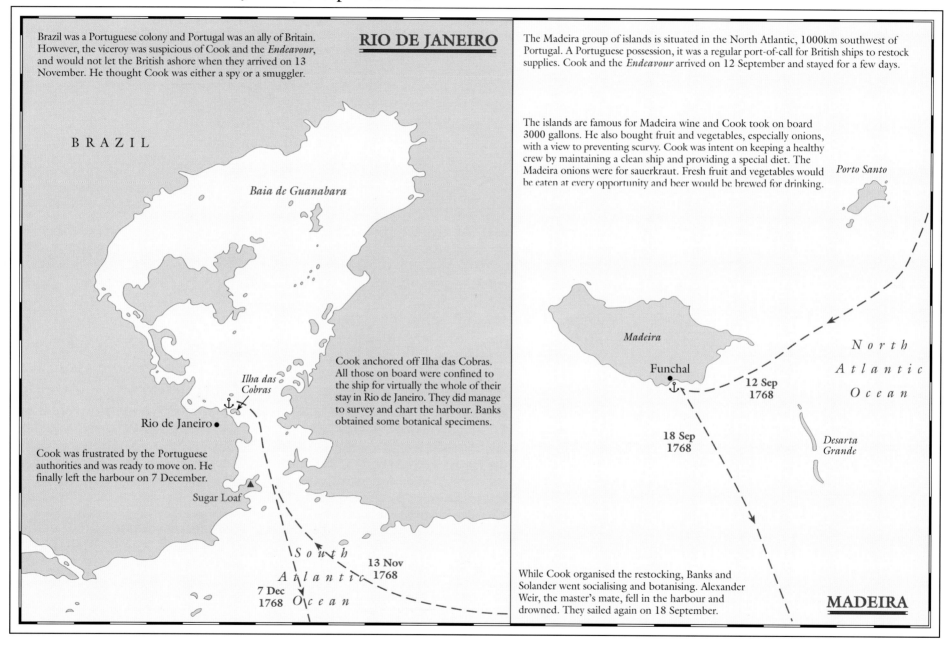

RIO DE JANEIRO

Brazil was a Portuguese colony and Portugal was an ally of Britain. However, the viceroy was suspicious of Cook and the *Endeavour*, and would not let the British ashore when they arrived on 13 November. He thought Cook was either a spy or a smuggler.

B R A Z I L

Baia de Guanabara

Ilha das Cobras

Cook anchored off Ilha das Cobras. All those on board were confined to the ship for virtually the whole of their stay in Rio de Janeiro. They did manage to survey and chart the harbour. Banks obtained some botanical specimens.

Rio de Janeiro ●

Cook was frustrated by the Portuguese authorities and was ready to move on. He finally left the harbour on 7 December.

Sugar Loaf

South Atlantic Ocean

13 Nov 1768

7 Dec 1768

The Madeira group of islands is situated in the North Atlantic, 1000km southwest of Portugal. A Portuguese possession, it was a regular port-of-call for British ships to restock supplies. Cook and the *Endeavour* arrived on 12 September and stayed for a few days.

The islands are famous for Madeira wine and Cook took on board 3000 gallons. He also bought fruit and vegetables, especially onions, with a view to preventing scurvy. Cook was intent on keeping a healthy crew by maintaining a clean ship and providing a special diet. The Madeira onions were for sauerkraut. Fresh fruit and vegetables would be eaten at every opportunity and beer would be brewed for drinking.

Porto Santo

Madeira

Funchal

12 Sep 1768

18 Sep 1768

North Atlantic Ocean

Desarta Grande

While Cook organised the restocking, Banks and Solander went socialising and botanising. Alexander Weir, the master's mate, fell in the harbour and drowned. They sailed again on 18 September.

MADEIRA

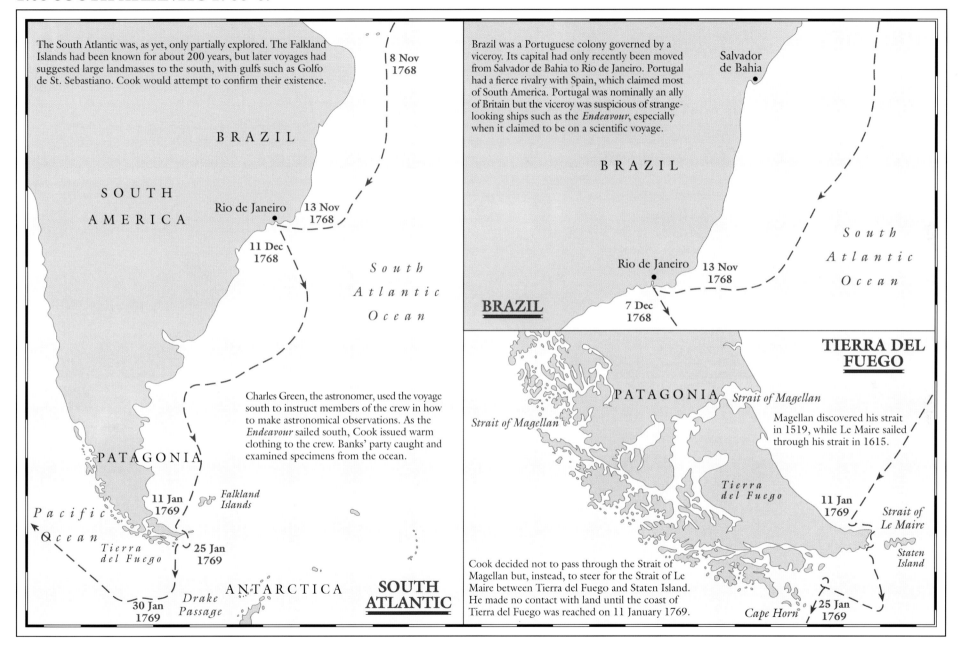

The South Atlantic was, as yet, only partially explored. The Falkland Islands had been known for about 200 years, but later voyages had suggested large landmasses to the south, with gulfs such as Golfo de St. Sebastiano. Cook would attempt to confirm their existence.

8 Nov 1768

BRAZIL

SOUTH AMERICA

Rio de Janeiro

13 Nov 1768

11 Dec 1768

South Atlantic Ocean

Charles Green, the astronomer, used the voyage south to instruct members of the crew in how to make astronomical observations. As the *Endeavour* sailed south, Cook issued warm clothing to the crew. Banks' party caught and examined specimens from the ocean.

PATAGONIA

11 Jan 1769

Falkland Islands

Pacific Ocean

Tierra del Fuego

25 Jan 1769

30 Jan 1769

Drake Passage

ANTARCTICA

SOUTH ATLANTIC

Brazil was a Portuguese colony governed by a viceroy. Its capital had only recently been moved from Salvador de Bahia to Rio de Janeiro. Portugal had a fierce rivalry with Spain, which claimed most of South America. Portugal was nominally an ally of Britain but the viceroy was suspicious of strange-looking ships such as the *Endeavour*, especially when it claimed to be on a scientific voyage.

Salvador de Bahia

BRAZIL

South Atlantic Ocean

Rio de Janeiro

13 Nov 1768

BRAZIL

7 Dec 1768

TIERRA DEL FUEGO

PATAGONIA

Strait of Magellan

Strait of Magellan

Magellan discovered his strait in 1519, while Le Maire sailed through his strait in 1615.

Tierra del Fuego

11 Jan 1769

Strait of Le Maire

Staten Island

Cook decided not to pass through the Strait of Magellan but, instead, to steer for the Strait of Le Maire between Tierra del Fuego and Staten Island. He made no contact with land until the coast of Tierra del Fuego was reached on 11 January 1769.

Cape Horn

25 Jan 1769

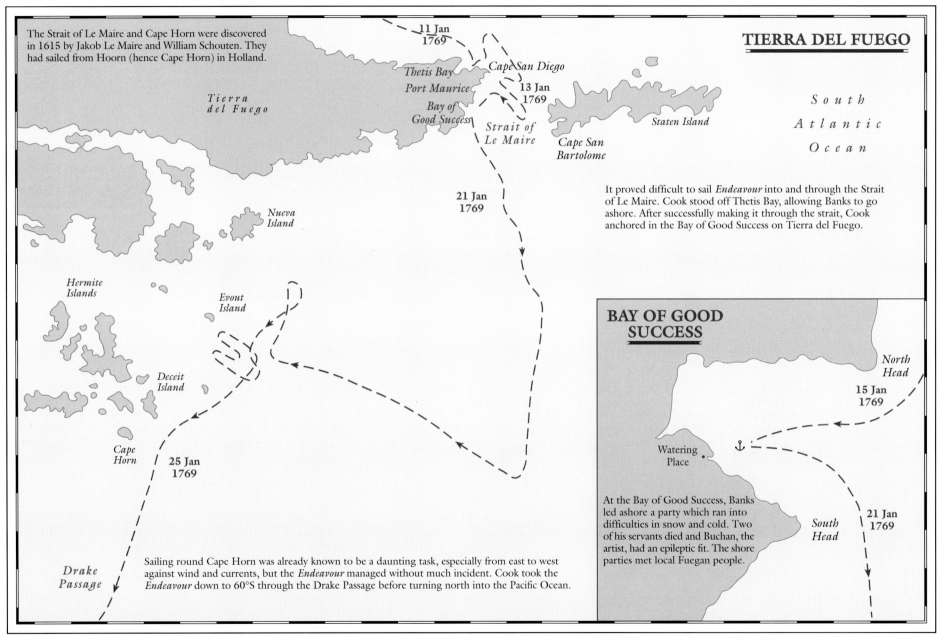

The Strait of Le Maire and Cape Horn were discovered in 1615 by Jakob Le Maire and William Schouten. They had sailed from Hoorn (hence Cape Horn) in Holland.

TIERRA DEL FUEGO

Tierra del Fuego

Thetis Bay
Port Maurice
Bay of Good Success

Cape San Diego

11 Jan 1769

13 Jan 1769

Strait of Le Maire

Cape San Bartolome

Staten Island

South Atlantic Ocean

Nueva Island

21 Jan 1769

It proved difficult to sail *Endeavour* into and through the Strait of Le Maire. Cook stood off Thetis Bay, allowing Banks to go ashore. After successfully making it through the strait, Cook anchored in the Bay of Good Success on Tierra del Fuego.

Hermite Islands

Evout Island

Deceit Island

BAY OF GOOD SUCCESS

North Head

15 Jan 1769

Watering Place

21 Jan 1769

South Head

Cape Horn

25 Jan 1769

At the Bay of Good Success, Banks led ashore a party which ran into difficulties in snow and cold. Two of his servants died and Buchan, the artist, had an epileptic fit. The shore parties met local Fuegan people.

Drake Passage

Sailing round Cape Horn was already known to be a daunting task, especially from east to west against wind and currents, but the *Endeavour* managed without much incident. Cook took the *Endeavour* down to 60°S through the Drake Passage before turning north into the Pacific Ocean.

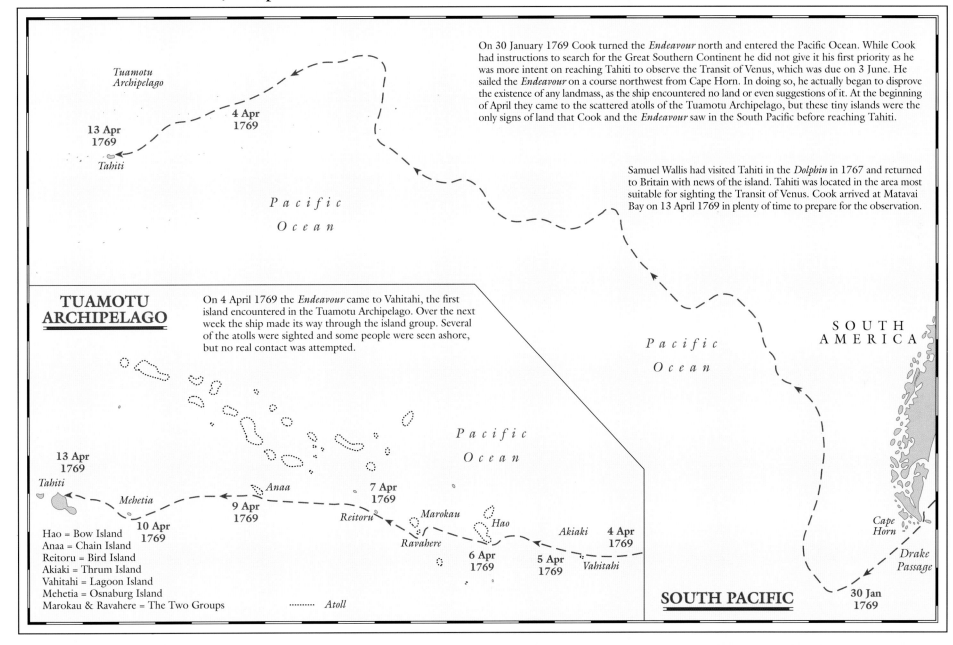

On 30 January 1769 Cook turned the *Endeavour* north and entered the Pacific Ocean. While Cook had instructions to search for the Great Southern Continent he did not give it his first priority as he was more intent on reaching Tahiti to observe the Transit of Venus, which was due on 3 June. He sailed the *Endeavour* on a course northwest from Cape Horn. In doing so, he actually began to disprove the existence of any landmass, as the ship encountered no land or even suggestions of it. At the beginning of April they came to the scattered atolls of the Tuamotu Archipelago, but these tiny islands were the only signs of land that Cook and the *Endeavour* saw in the South Pacific before reaching Tahiti.

Samuel Wallis had visited Tahiti in the *Dolphin* in 1767 and returned to Britain with news of the island. Tahiti was located in the area most suitable for sighting the Transit of Venus. Cook arrived at Matavai Bay on 13 April 1769 in plenty of time to prepare for the observation.

Tuamotu Archipelago

4 Apr 1769

13 Apr 1769

Tahiti

Pacific Ocean

SOUTH AMERICA

30 Jan 1769

Cape Horn

Drake Passage

TUAMOTU ARCHIPELAGO

On 4 April 1769 the *Endeavour* came to Vahitahi, the first island encountered in the Tuamotu Archipelago. Over the next week the ship made its way through the island group. Several of the atolls were sighted and some people were seen ashore, but no real contact was attempted.

Pacific Ocean

13 Apr 1769

Tahiti

Mehetia

Anaa

9 Apr 1769

10 Apr 1769

Reitoru

7 Apr 1769

Marokau

Ravahere

Hao

6 Apr 1769

5 Apr 1769

Vahitahi

Akiaki

4 Apr 1769

Hao = Bow Island
Anaa = Chain Island
Reitoru = Bird Island
Akiaki = Thrum Island
Vahitahi = Lagoon Island
Mehetia = Osnaburg Island
Marokau & Ravahere = The Two Groups

.... Atoll

SOUTH PACIFIC

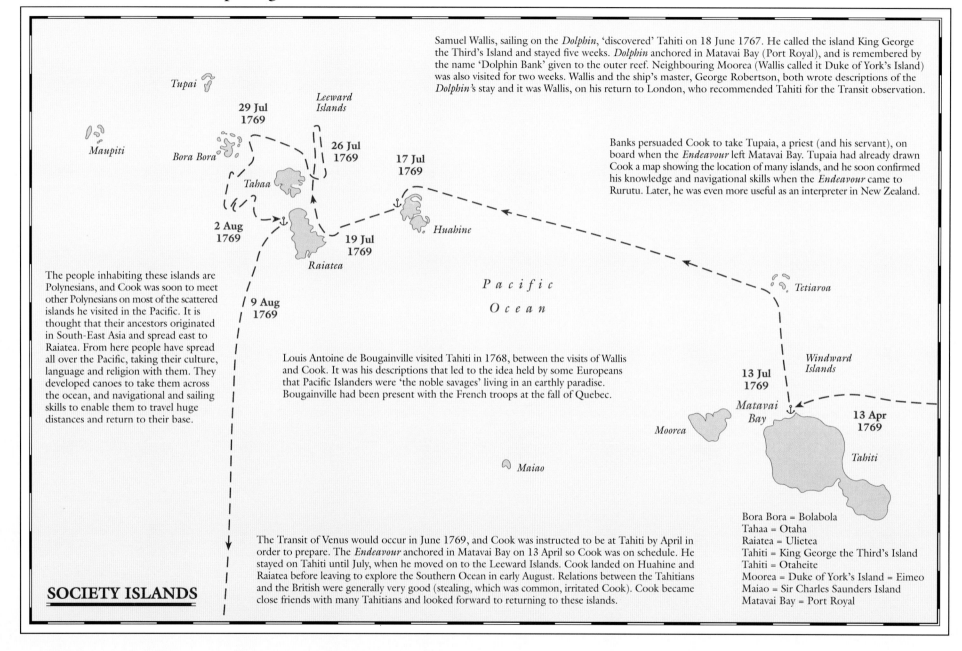

Samuel Wallis, sailing on the *Dolphin*, 'discovered' Tahiti on 18 June 1767. He called the island King George the Third's Island and stayed five weeks. *Dolphin* anchored in Matavai Bay (Port Royal), and is remembered by the name 'Dolphin Bank' given to the outer reef. Neighbouring Moorea (Wallis called it Duke of York's Island) was also visited for two weeks. Wallis and the ship's master, George Robertson, both wrote descriptions of the *Dolphin's* stay and it was Wallis, on his return to London, who recommended Tahiti for the Transit observation.

Banks persuaded Cook to take Tupaia, a priest (and his servant), on board when the *Endeavour* left Matavai Bay. Tupaia had already drawn Cook a map showing the location of many islands, and he soon confirmed his knowledge and navigational skills when the *Endeavour* came to Rurutu. Later, he was even more useful as an interpreter in New Zealand.

The people inhabiting these islands are Polynesians, and Cook was soon to meet other Polynesians on most of the scattered islands he visited in the Pacific. It is thought that their ancestors originated in South-East Asia and spread east to Raiatea. From here people have spread all over the Pacific, taking their culture, language and religion with them. They developed canoes to take them across the ocean, and navigational and sailing skills to enable them to travel huge distances and return to their base.

Louis Antoine de Bougainville visited Tahiti in 1768, between the visits of Wallis and Cook. It was his descriptions that led to the idea held by some Europeans that Pacific Islanders were 'the noble savages' living in an earthly paradise. Bougainville had been present with the French troops at the fall of Quebec.

Tupai

Maupiti

Bora Bora

29 Jul 1769

Leeward Islands

26 Jul 1769

17 Jul 1769

Tahaa

2 Aug 1769

19 Jul 1769

Raiatea

9 Aug 1769

Huahine

Pacific Ocean

Tetiaroa

Windward Islands

13 Jul 1769

Matavai Bay

13 Apr 1769

Moorea

Maiao

Tahiti

The Transit of Venus would occur in June 1769, and Cook was instructed to be at Tahiti by April in order to prepare. The *Endeavour* anchored in Matavai Bay on 13 April so Cook was on schedule. He stayed on Tahiti until July, when he moved on to the Leeward Islands. Cook landed on Huahine and Raiatea before leaving to explore the Southern Ocean in early August. Relations between the Tahitians and the British were generally very good (stealing, which was common, irritated Cook). Cook became close friends with many Tahitians and looked forward to returning to these islands.

SOCIETY ISLANDS

Bora Bora = Bolabola
Tahaa = Otaha
Raiatea = Ulietea
Tahiti = King George the Third's Island
Tahiti = Otaheite
Moorea = Duke of York's Island = Eimeo
Maiao = Sir Charles Saunders Island
Matavai Bay = Port Royal

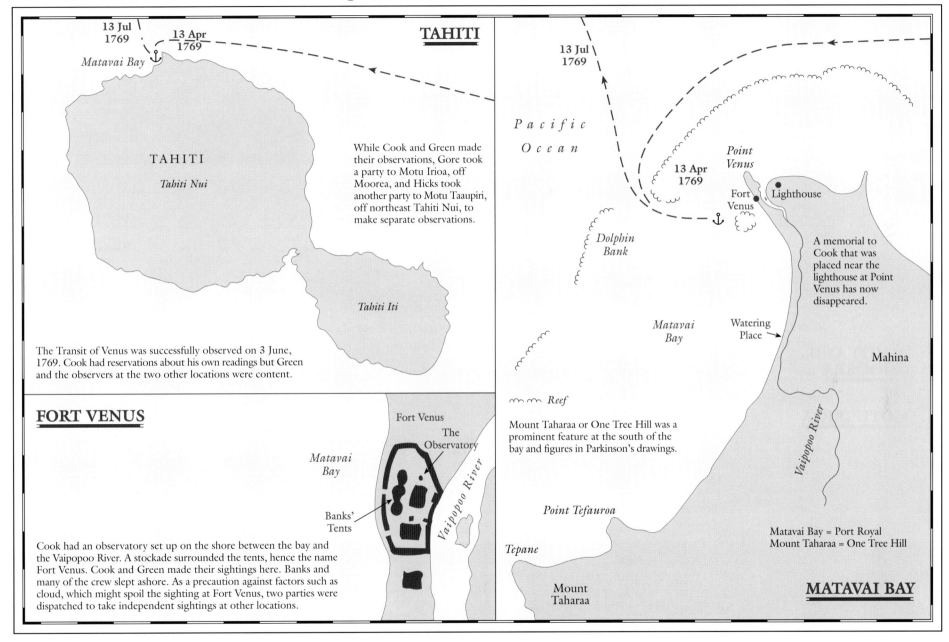

TAHITI

13 Jul 1769

13 Apr 1769

Matavai Bay

TAHITI

Tahiti Nui

Tahiti Iti

While Cook and Green made their observations, Gore took a party to Motu Irioa, off Moorea, and Hicks took another party to Motu Taaupiri, off northeast Tahiti Nui, to make separate observations.

The Transit of Venus was successfully observed on 3 June, 1769. Cook had reservations about his own readings but Green and the observers at the two other locations were content.

FORT VENUS

Matavai Bay

Fort Venus

The Observatory

Banks' Tents

Vaipopoo River

Cook had an observatory set up on the shore between the bay and the Vaipopoo River. A stockade surrounded the tents, hence the name Fort Venus. Cook and Green made their sightings here. Banks and many of the crew slept ashore. As a precaution against factors such as cloud, which might spoil the sighting at Fort Venus, two parties were dispatched to take independent sightings at other locations.

Pacific Ocean

13 Jul 1769

13 Apr 1769

Point Venus

Fort Venus

Lighthouse

A memorial to Cook that was placed near the lighthouse at Point Venus has now disappeared.

Dolphin Bank

Matavai Bay

Watering Place

Mahina

Reef

Mount Taharaa or One Tree Hill was a prominent feature at the south of the bay and figures in Parkinson's drawings.

Point Tefauroa

Vaipopoo River

Tepane

Mount Taharaa

Matavai Bay = Port Royal
Mount Taharaa = One Tree Hill

MATAVAI BAY

1.08 TOUR OF TAHITI Jun–Jul 1769

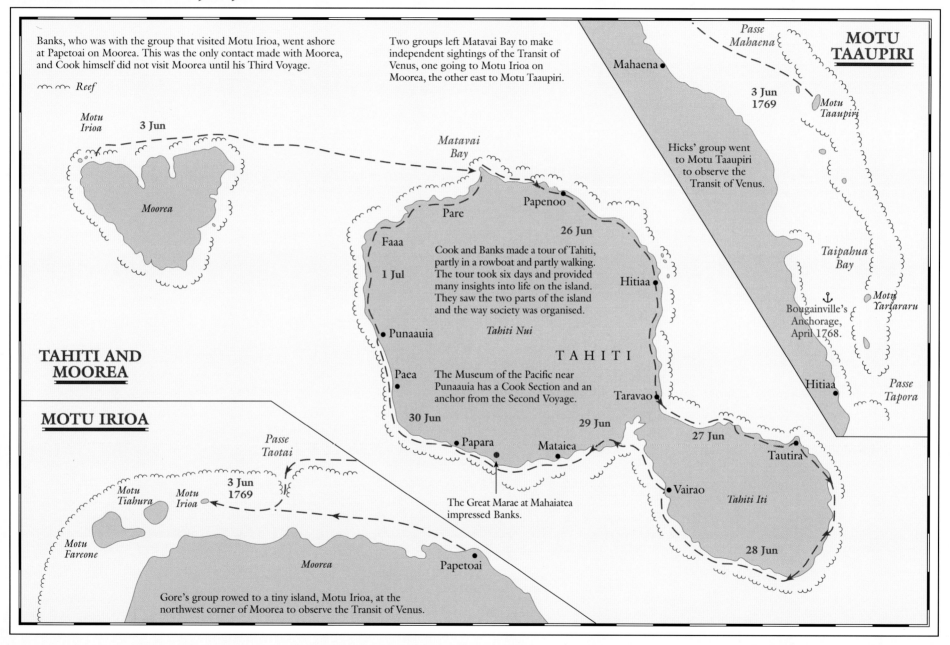

Banks, who was with the group that visited Motu Irioa, went ashore at Papetoai on Moorea. This was the only contact made with Moorea, and Cook himself did not visit Moorea until his Third Voyage.

〜〜 *Reef*

Motu Irioa

3 Jun

Moorea

Two groups left Matavai Bay to make independent sightings of the Transit of Venus, one going to Motu Irioa on Moorea, the other east to Motu Taaupiri.

Passe Mahaena

MOTU TAAUPIRI

Mahaena •

3 Jun 1769

Motu Taaupiri

Hicks' group went to Motu Taaupiri to observe the Transit of Venus.

Matavai Bay

Papenoo •

Pare

26 Jun

Faaa

1 Jul

Cook and Banks made a tour of Tahiti, partly in a rowboat and partly walking. The tour took six days and provided many insights into life on the island. They saw the two parts of the island and the way society was organised.

Hitiaa •

Taipahua Bay

⚓ Bougainville's Anchorage, April 1768.

Motu Yariararu

TAHITI AND MOOREA

• Punaauia

Tahiti Nui

TAHITI

The Museum of the Pacific near Punaauia has a Cook Section and an anchor from the Second Voyage.

Paea •

Hitiaa •

Taravao •

Passe Tapora

30 Jun

29 Jun

27 Jun

MOTU IRIOA

• Papara

Mataiea •

Tautira •

The Great Marae at Mahaiatea impressed Banks.

Passe Taotai

Motu Tiahura *Motu Irioa*

3 Jun 1769

• Vairao

Tahiti Iti

Motu Fareone

Moorea

28 Jun

Papetoai •

Gore's group rowed to a tiny island, Motu Irioa, at the northwest corner of Moorea to observe the Transit of Venus.

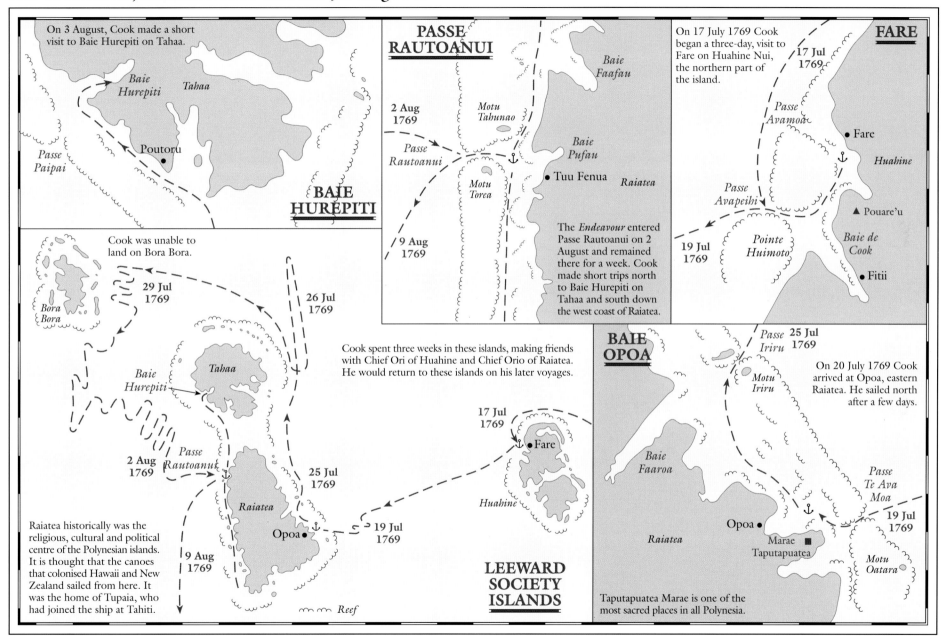

On 3 August, Cook made a short visit to Baie Hurepiti on Tahaa.

Baie Hurepiti

Tahaa

Passe Paipai

Poutoru

BAIE HUREPITI

PASSE RAUTOANUI

Baie Faafau

2 Aug 1769

Motu Tahunao

Passe Rautoanui

Baie Pufau

Tuu Fenua

Raiatea

Motu Torea

9 Aug 1769

The *Endeavour* entered Passe Rautoanui on 2 August and remained there for a week. Cook made short trips north to Baie Hurepiti on Tahaa and south down the west coast of Raiatea.

On 17 July 1769 Cook began a three-day, visit to Fare on Huahine Nui, the northern part of the island.

FARE

17 Jul 1769

Passe Avamoa

Fare

Huahine

Passe Avapeihi

▲ Pouare'u

19 Jul 1769

Pointe Huimoto

Baie de Cook

Fitii

Cook was unable to land on Bora Bora.

Bora Bora

29 Jul 1769

26 Jul 1769

Cook spent three weeks in these islands, making friends with Chief Ori of Huahine and Chief Orio of Raiatea. He would return to these islands on his later voyages.

Baie Hurepiti

Tahaa

17 Jul 1769

Fare

25 Jul 1769

Passe Rautoanui

2 Aug 1769

Raiatea

Opoa

19 Jul 1769

Huahine

Raiatea historically was the religious, cultural and political centre of the Polynesian islands. It is thought that the canoes that colonised Hawaii and New Zealand sailed from here. It was the home of Tupaia, who had joined the ship at Tahiti.

9 Aug 1769

Reef

LEEWARD SOCIETY ISLANDS

BAIE OPOA

Passe Iriru

25 Jul 1769

Motu Iriru

On 20 July 1769 Cook arrived at Opoa, eastern Raiatea. He sailed north after a few days.

Baie Faaroa

Passe Te Ava Moa

19 Jul 1769

Opoa

Raiatea

Marae Taputapuatea

Motu Oatara

Taputapuatea Marae is one of the most sacred places in all Polynesia.

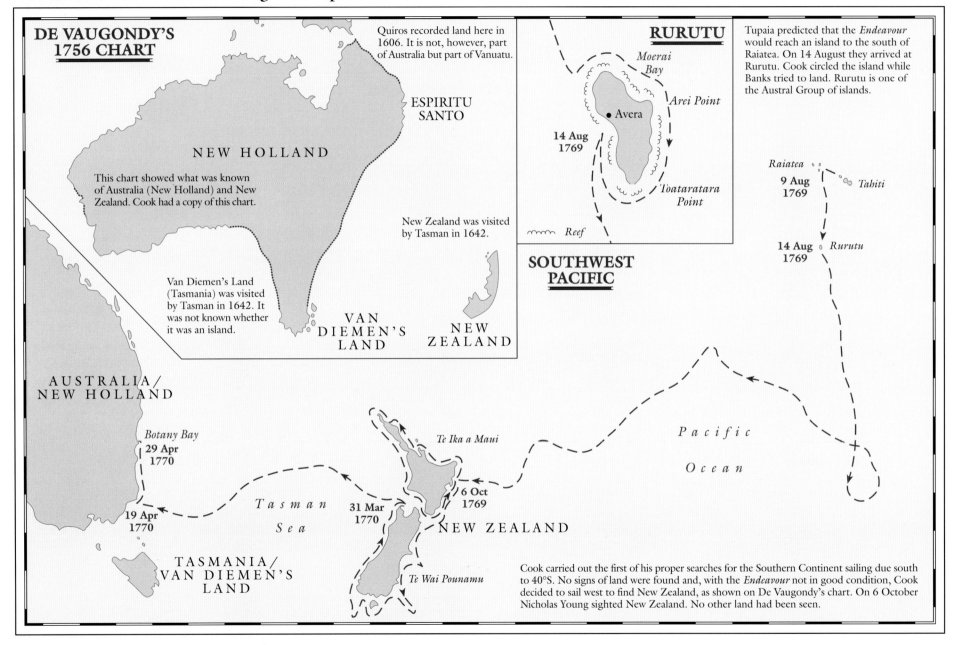

DE VAUGONDY'S 1756 CHART

NEW HOLLAND

This chart showed what was known of Australia (New Holland) and New Zealand. Cook had a copy of this chart.

Van Diemen's Land (Tasmania) was visited by Tasman in 1642. It was not known whether it was an island.

VAN DIEMEN'S LAND

NEW ZEALAND

Quiros recorded land here in 1606. It is not, however, part of Australia but part of Vanuatu.

ESPIRITU SANTO

New Zealand was visited by Tasman in 1642.

RURUTU

Moerai Bay

Arei Point

● Avera

14 Aug 1769

Toataratara Point

Reef

Tupaia predicted that the *Endeavour* would reach an island to the south of Raiatea. On 14 August they arrived at Rurutu. Cook circled the island while Banks tried to land. Rurutu is one of the Austral Group of islands.

SOUTHWEST PACIFIC

Raiatea
9 Aug 1769
Tahiti

14 Aug 1769
Rurutu

AUSTRALIA/ NEW HOLLAND

Botany Bay
29 Apr 1770

19 Apr 1770

Tasman Sea

31 Mar 1770

Te Ika a Maui

Pacific Ocean

6 Oct 1769

NEW ZEALAND

TASMANIA/ VAN DIEMEN'S LAND

Te Wai Pounamu

Cook carried out the first of his proper searches for the Southern Continent sailing due south to 40°S. No signs of land were found and, with the *Endeavour* not in good condition, Cook decided to sail west to find New Zealand, as shown on De Vaugondy's chart. On 6 October Nicholas Young sighted New Zealand. No other land had been seen.

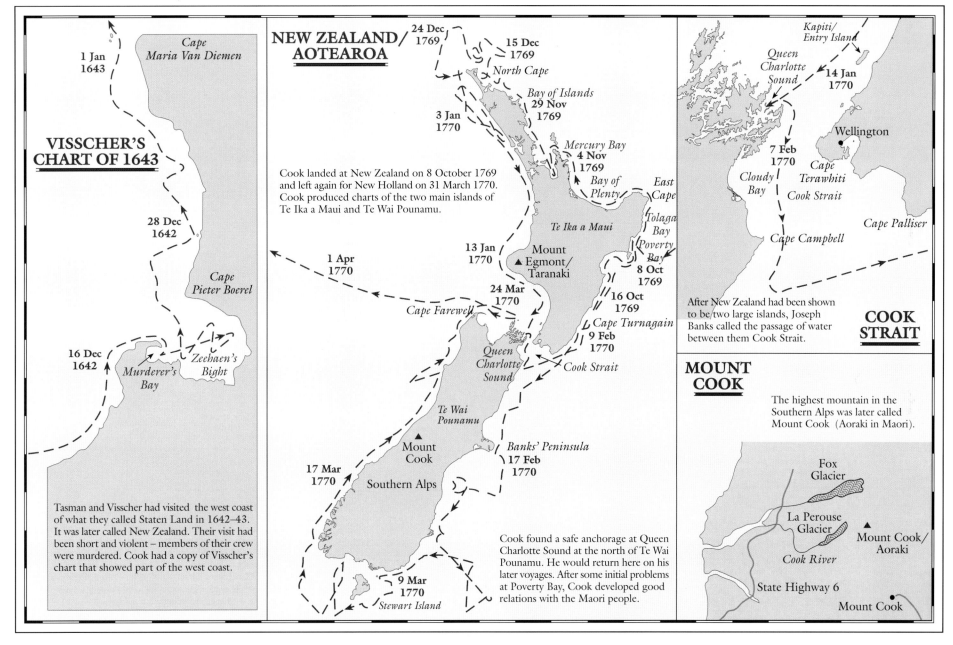

VISSCHER'S CHART OF 1643

1 Jan 1643

Cape Maria Van Diemen

28 Dec 1642

Cape Pieter Boerel

16 Dec 1642

Murderer's Bay

Zeehaen's Bight

Tasman and Visscher had visited the west coast of what they called Staten Land in 1642–43. It was later called New Zealand. Their visit had been short and violent – members of their crew were murdered. Cook had a copy of Visscher's chart that showed part of the west coast.

NEW ZEALAND/AOTEAROA

Cook landed at New Zealand on 8 October 1769 and left again for New Holland on 31 March 1770. Cook produced charts of the two main islands of Te Ika a Maui and Te Wai Pounamu.

24 Dec 1769

15 Dec 1769

North Cape

Bay of Islands
29 Nov 1769

3 Jan 1770

Mercury Bay
4 Nov 1769

Bay of Plenty

East Cape

Te Ika a Maui

Tolaga Bay

Poverty Bay

13 Jan 1770

Mount Egmont/ Taranaki

8 Oct 1769

16 Oct 1769

1 Apr 1770

24 Mar 1770

Cape Farewell

Cape Turnagain

9 Feb 1770

Queen Charlotte Sound

Cook Strait

Te Wai Pounamu

Mount Cook

Banks' Peninsula
17 Feb 1770

17 Mar 1770

Southern Alps

9 Mar 1770

Stewart Island

Cook found a safe anchorage at Queen Charlotte Sound at the north of Te Wai Pounamu. He would return here on his later voyages. After some initial problems at Poverty Bay, Cook developed good relations with the Maori people.

COOK STRAIT

Kapiti/ Entry Island

Queen Charlotte Sound

14 Jan 1770

Wellington

7 Feb 1770

Cloudy Bay

Cape Terawhiti

Cook Strait

Cape Campbell

Cape Palliser

After New Zealand had been shown to be two large islands, Joseph Banks called the passage of water between them Cook Strait.

MOUNT COOK

The highest mountain in the Southern Alps was later called Mount Cook (Aoraki in Maori).

Fox Glacier

La Perouse Glacier

Cook River

Mount Cook/ Aoraki

State Highway 6

Mount Cook

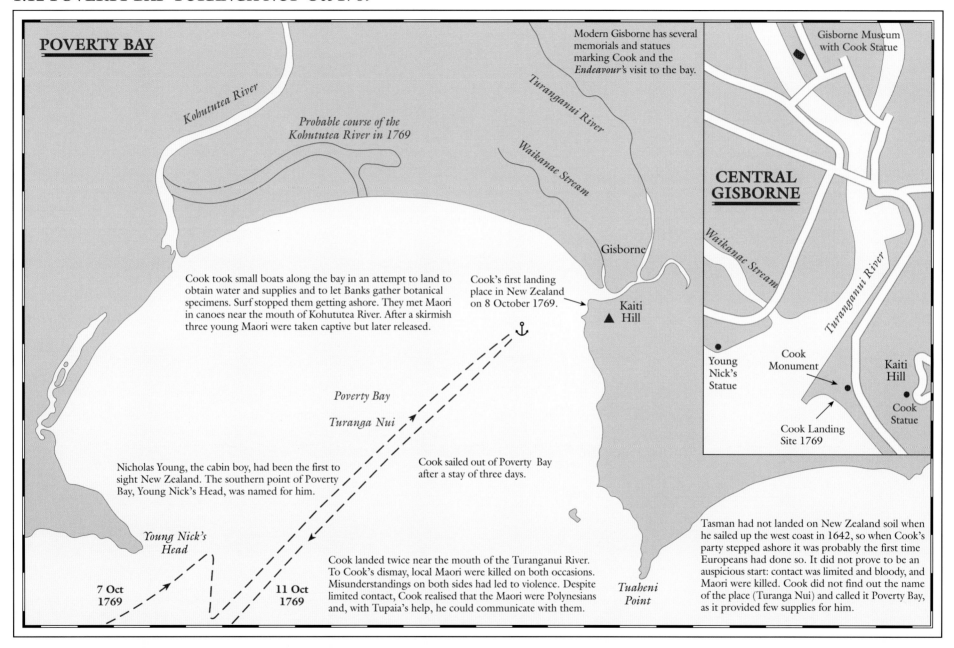

POVERTY BAY

Kohututea River

Probable course of the Kohututea River in 1769

Turanganui River

Waikanae Stream

Modern Gisborne has several memorials and statues marking Cook and the *Endeavour's* visit to the bay.

Gisborne

Kaiti
▲ Hill

Cook took small boats along the bay in an attempt to land to obtain water and supplies and to let Banks gather botanical specimens. Surf stopped them getting ashore. They met Maori in canoes near the mouth of Kohututea River. After a skirmish three young Maori were taken captive but later released.

Cook's first landing place in New Zealand on 8 October 1769.

⚓

Poverty Bay

Turanga Nui

Cook sailed out of Poverty Bay after a stay of three days.

Nicholas Young, the cabin boy, had been the first to sight New Zealand. The southern point of Poverty Bay, Young Nick's Head, was named for him.

Young Nick's Head

7 Oct
1769

11 Oct
1769

Cook landed twice near the mouth of the Turanganui River. To Cook's dismay, local Maori were killed on both occasions. Misunderstandings on both sides had led to violence. Despite limited contact, Cook realised that the Maori were Polynesians and, with Tupaia's help, he could communicate with them.

Tuaheni Point

Tasman had not landed on New Zealand soil when he sailed up the west coast in 1642, so when Cook's party stepped ashore it was probably the first time Europeans had done so. It did not prove to be an auspicious start: contact was limited and bloody, and Maori were killed. Cook did not find out the name of the place (Turanga Nui) and called it Poverty Bay, as it provided few supplies for him.

CENTRAL GISBORNE

Gisborne Museum with Cook Statue

Waikanae Stream

Turanganui River

Young Nick's Statue

Cook Monument

Kaiti Hill

Cook Landing Site 1769

Cook Statue

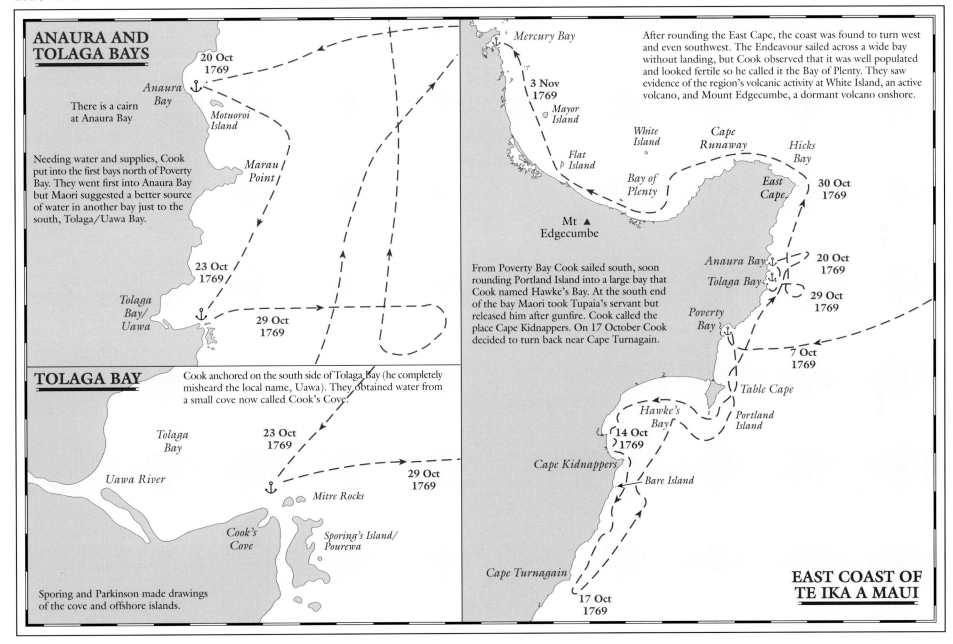

ANAURA AND TOLAGA BAYS

There is a cairn at Anaura Bay

Needing water and supplies, Cook put into the first bays north of Poverty Bay. They went first into Anaura Bay but Maori suggested a better source of water in another bay just to the south, Tolaga/Uawa Bay.

20 Oct 1769

Anaura Bay

Motuoroi Island

Marau Point

23 Oct 1769

Tolaga Bay/ Uawa

29 Oct 1769

TOLAGA BAY

Cook anchored on the south side of Tolaga Bay (he completely misheard the local name, Uawa). They obtained water from a small cove now called Cook's Cove.

Tolaga Bay

23 Oct 1769

Uawa River

29 Oct 1769

Mitre Rocks

Cook's Cove

Sporing's Island/ Pourewa

Sporing and Parkinson made drawings of the cove and offshore islands.

After rounding the East Cape, the coast was found to turn west and even southwest. The Endeavour sailed across a wide bay without landing, but Cook observed that it was well populated and looked fertile so he called it the Bay of Plenty. They saw evidence of the region's volcanic activity at White Island, an active volcano, and Mount Edgecumbe, a dormant volcano onshore.

Mercury Bay

3 Nov 1769

Mayor Island

White Island

Flat Island

Bay of Plenty

Cape Runaway

Hicks Bay

East Cape

30 Oct 1769

Mt ▲ Edgecumbe

From Poverty Bay Cook sailed south, soon rounding Portland Island into a large bay that Cook named Hawke's Bay. At the south end of the bay Maori took Tupaia's servant but released him after gunfire. Cook called the place Cape Kidnappers. On 17 October Cook decided to turn back near Cape Turnagain.

Anaura Bay

Tolaga Bay

20 Oct 1769

29 Oct 1769

Poverty Bay

7 Oct 1769

Table Cape

Hawke's Bay

Portland Island

14 Oct 1769

Cape Kidnappers

Bare Island

Cape Turnagain

17 Oct 1769

EAST COAST OF TE IKA A MAUI

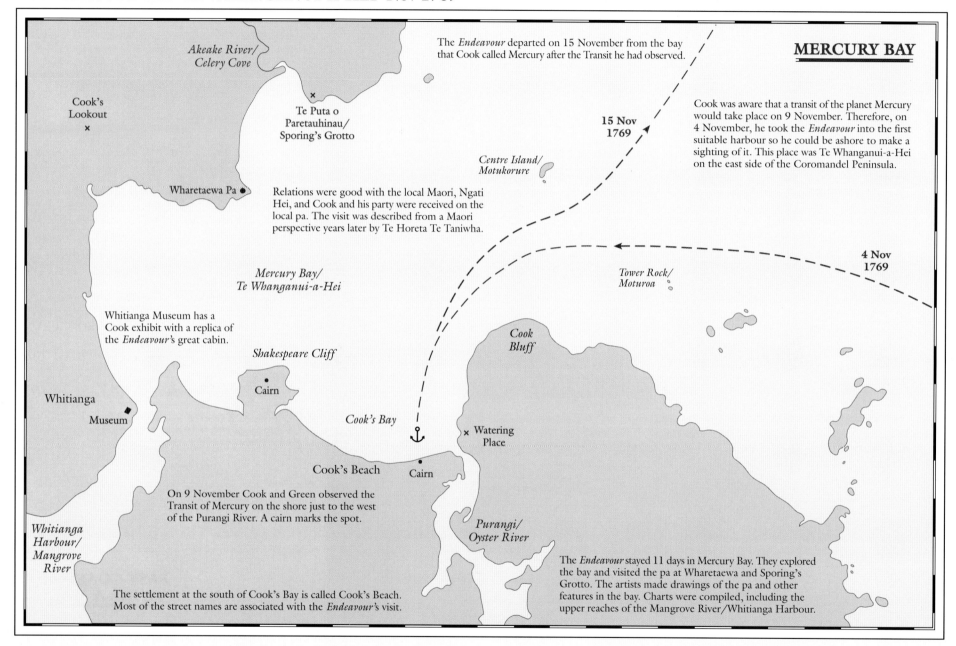

MERCURY BAY

Akeake River/ Celery Cove

Cook's Lookout ×

Te Puta o Paretauhinau/ Sporing's Grotto ×

Wharetaewa Pa ●

Centre Island/ Motukorure

The *Endeavour* departed on 15 November from the bay that Cook called Mercury after the Transit he had observed.

15 Nov 1769

Cook was aware that a transit of the planet Mercury would take place on 9 November. Therefore, on 4 November, he took the *Endeavour* into the first suitable harbour so he could be ashore to make a sighting of it. This place was Te Whanganui-a-Hei on the east side of the Coromandel Peninsula.

Relations were good with the local Maori, Ngati Hei, and Cook and his party were received on the local pa. The visit was described from a Maori perspective years later by Te Horeta Te Taniwha.

Mercury Bay/ Te Whanganui-a-Hei

Tower Rock/ Moturoa

4 Nov 1769

Whitianga Museum has a Cook exhibit with a replica of the *Endeavour*'s great cabin.

Shakespeare Cliff

Cook Bluff

Whitianga
Museum ■

● Cairn

Cook's Bay

⚓

× Watering Place

Cook's Beach   Cairn ●

On 9 November Cook and Green observed the Transit of Mercury on the shore just to the west of the Purangi River. A cairn marks the spot.

Whitianga Harbour/ Mangrove River

Purangi/ Oyster River

The settlement at the south of Cook's Bay is called Cook's Beach. Most of the street names are associated with the *Endeavour*'s visit.

The *Endeavour* stayed 11 days in Mercury Bay. They explored the bay and visited the pa at Wharetaewa and Sporing's Grotto. The artists made drawings of the pa and other features in the bay. Charts were compiled, including the upper reaches of the Mangrove River/Whitianga Harbour.

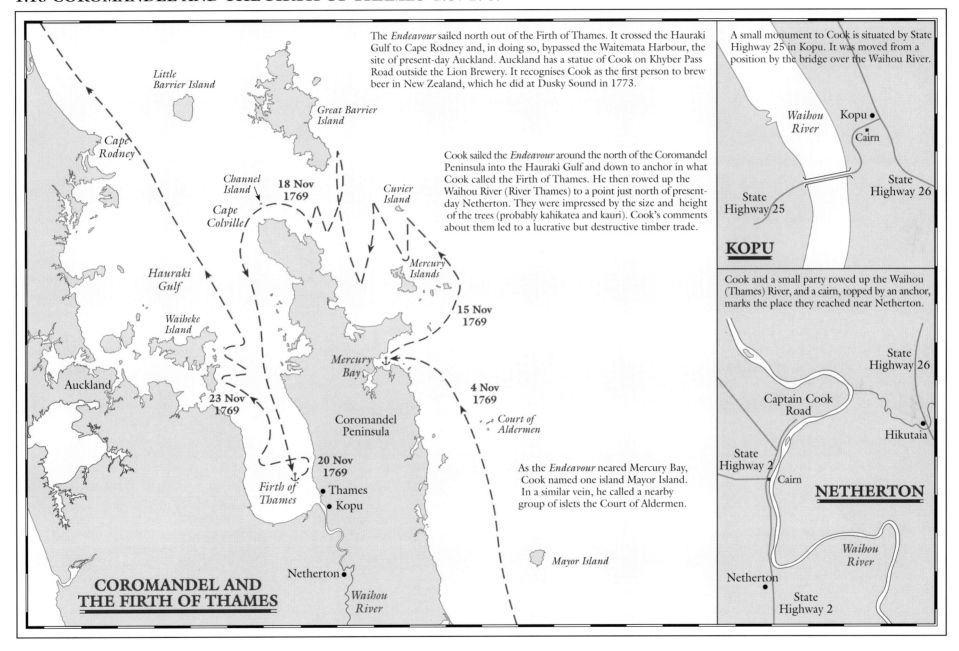

The *Endeavour* sailed north out of the Firth of Thames. It crossed the Hauraki Gulf to Cape Rodney and, in doing so, bypassed the Waitemata Harbour, the site of present-day Auckland. Auckland has a statue of Cook on Khyber Pass Road outside the Lion Brewery. It recognises Cook as the first person to brew beer in New Zealand, which he did at Dusky Sound in 1773.

Cook sailed the *Endeavour* around the north of the Coromandel Peninsula into the Hauraki Gulf and down to anchor in what Cook called the Firth of Thames. He then rowed up the Waihou River (River Thames) to a point just north of present-day Netherton. They were impressed by the size and height of the trees (probably kahikatea and kauri). Cook's comments about them led to a lucrative but destructive timber trade.

As the *Endeavour* neared Mercury Bay, Cook named one island Mayor Island. In a similar vein, he called a nearby group of islets the Court of Aldermen.

A small monument to Cook is situated by State Highway 25 in Kopu. It was moved from a position by the bridge over the Waihou River.

KOPU

Cook and a small party rowed up the Waihou (Thames) River, and a cairn, topped by an anchor, marks the place they reached near Netherton.

NETHERTON

Little Barrier Island

Great Barrier Island

Cape Rodney

Channel Island

18 Nov 1769

Cape Colville

Cuvier Island

Hauraki Gulf

Mercury Islands

15 Nov 1769

Waiheke Island

Mercury Bay

4 Nov 1769

Auckland

23 Nov 1769

Court of Aldermen

Coromandel Peninsula

20 Nov 1769

• Thames
• Kopu

Firth of Thames

Netherton •

Waihou River

Mayor Island

COROMANDEL AND THE FIRTH OF THAMES

Waihou River

Kopu •
Cairn

State Highway 26

State Highway 25

State Highway 26

Captain Cook Road

Hikutaia •

State Highway 2

Cairn

Netherton •

Waihou River

State Highway 2

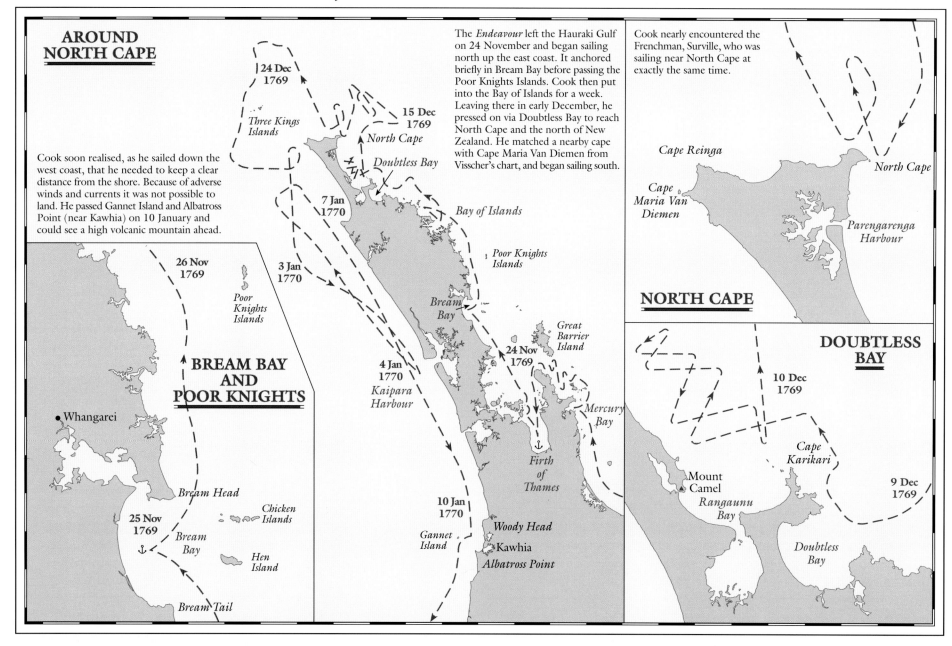

AROUND NORTH CAPE

Cook soon realised, as he sailed down the west coast, that he needed to keep a clear distance from the shore. Because of adverse winds and currents it was not possible to land. He passed Gannet Island and Albatross Point (near Kawhia) on 10 January and could see a high volcanic mountain ahead.

The *Endeavour* left the Hauraki Gulf on 24 November and began sailing north up the east coast. It anchored briefly in Bream Bay before passing the Poor Knights Islands. Cook then put into the Bay of Islands for a week. Leaving there in early December, he pressed on via Doubtless Bay to reach North Cape and the north of New Zealand. He matched a nearby cape with Cape Maria Van Diemen from Visscher's chart, and began sailing south.

Cook nearly encountered the Frenchman, Surville, who was sailing near North Cape at exactly the same time.

BREAM BAY AND POOR KNIGHTS

24 Dec 1769

15 Dec 1769

North Cape

Doubtless Bay

7 Jan 1770

Bay of Islands

Three Kings Islands

3 Jan 1770

26 Nov 1769

Poor Knights Islands

Poor Knights Islands

Bream Bay

Great Barrier Island

24 Nov 1769

• Whangarei

Bream Head

Chicken Islands

4 Jan 1770
Kaipara Harbour

25 Nov 1769

Bream Bay

Hen Island

Mercury Bay

Firth of Thames

Bream Tail

10 Jan 1770

Gannet Island

Woody Head

Kawhia
Albatross Point

NORTH CAPE

Cape Reinga

Cape Maria Van Diemen

North Cape

Parengarenga Harbour

DOUBTLESS BAY

10 Dec 1769

Cape Karikari

9 Dec 1769

Mount Camel

Rangaunu Bay

Doubtless Bay

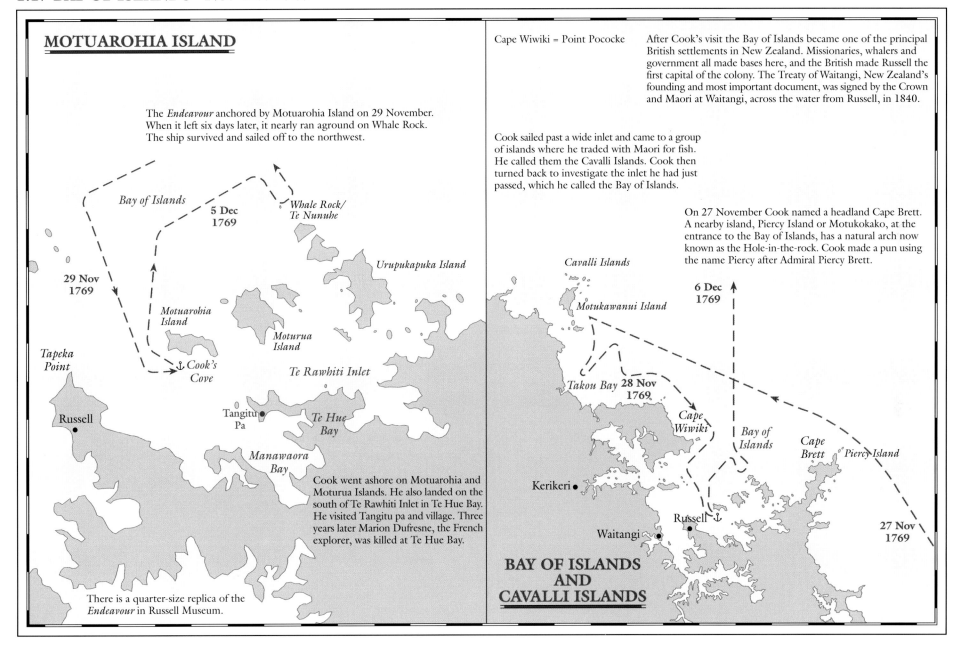

MOTUAROHIA ISLAND

The *Endeavour* anchored by Motuarohia Island on 29 November. When it left six days later, it nearly ran aground on Whale Rock. The ship survived and sailed off to the northwest.

Bay of Islands

5 Dec 1769

Whale Rock/ Te Nunuhe

Urupukapuka Island

29 Nov 1769

Motuarohia Island

Moturua Island

⚓ *Cook's Cove*

Te Rawhiti Inlet

Tapeka Point

Russell

Tangitu Pa •

Te Hue Bay

Manawaora Bay

Cook went ashore on Motuarohia and Moturua Islands. He also landed on the south of Te Rawhiti Inlet in Te Hue Bay. He visited Tangitu pa and village. Three years later Marion Dufresne, the French explorer, was killed at Te Hue Bay.

There is a quarter-size replica of the *Endeavour* in Russell Museum.

Cape Wiwiki = Point Pococke

After Cook's visit the Bay of Islands became one of the principal British settlements in New Zealand. Missionaries, whalers and government all made bases here, and the British made Russell the first capital of the colony. The Treaty of Waitangi, New Zealand's founding and most important document, was signed by the Crown and Maori at Waitangi, across the water from Russell, in 1840.

Cook sailed past a wide inlet and came to a group of islands where he traded with Maori for fish. He called them the Cavalli Islands. Cook then turned back to investigate the inlet he had just passed, which he called the Bay of Islands.

On 27 November Cook named a headland Cape Brett. A nearby island, Piercy Island or Motukokako, at the entrance to the Bay of Islands, has a natural arch now known as the Hole-in-the-rock. Cook made a pun using the name Piercy after Admiral Piercy Brett.

Cavalli Islands

Motukawanui Island

6 Dec 1769

Takou Bay **28 Nov 1769**

Cape Wiwiki

Bay of Islands

Cape Brett *Piercy Island*

Kerikeri •

Russell ⚓

Waitangi

27 Nov 1769

BAY OF ISLANDS AND CAVALLI ISLANDS

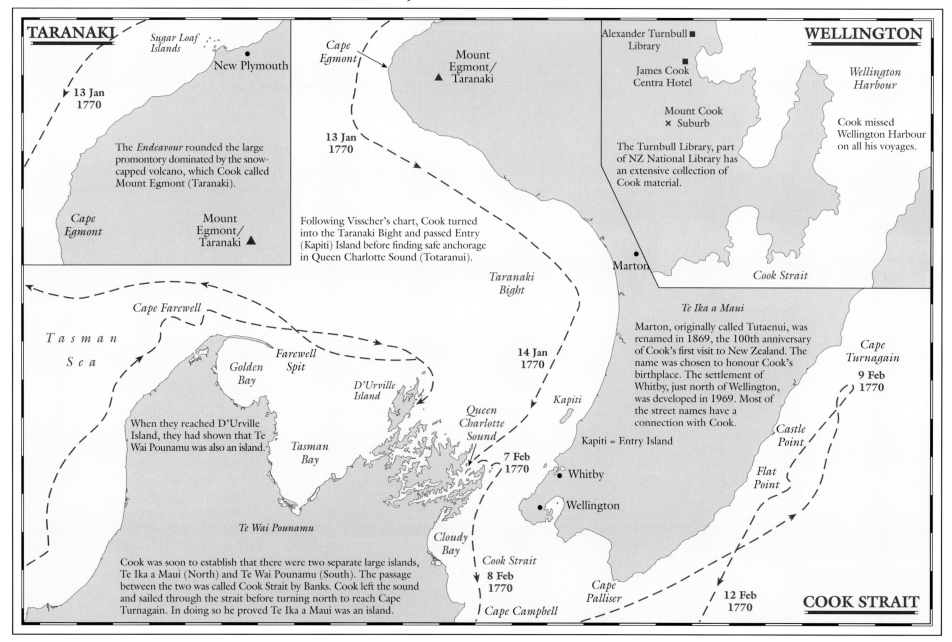

TARANAKI

Sugar Loaf Islands

New Plymouth

13 Jan 1770

The *Endeavour* rounded the large promontory dominated by the snow-capped volcano, which Cook called Mount Egmont (Taranaki).

Cape Egmont

Mount Egmont / Taranaki ▲

Cape Egmont

Mount Egmont / Taranaki ▲

13 Jan 1770

Following Visscher's chart, Cook turned into the Taranaki Bight and passed Entry (Kapiti) Island before finding safe anchorage in Queen Charlotte Sound (Totaranui).

WELLINGTON

Alexander Turnbull ■ Library

James Cook ■ Centra Hotel

Mount Cook ✕ Suburb

Wellington Harbour

Cook missed Wellington Harbour on all his voyages.

The Turnbull Library, part of NZ National Library has an extensive collection of Cook material.

Marton

Cook Strait

Te Ika a Maui

Marton, originally called Tutaenui, was renamed in 1869, the 100th anniversary of Cook's first visit to New Zealand. The name was chosen to honour Cook's birthplace. The settlement of Whitby, just north of Wellington, was developed in 1969. Most of the street names have a connection with Cook.

Taranaki Bight

14 Jan 1770

Kapiti

Kapiti = Entry Island

Cape Turnagain

9 Feb 1770

Castle Point

Flat Point

Cape Farewell

Tasman Sea

Golden Bay

Farewell Spit

D'Urville Island

When they reached D'Urville Island, they had shown that Te Wai Pounamu was also an island.

Tasman Bay

Queen Charlotte Sound

7 Feb 1770

● Whitby

● Wellington

Te Wai Pounamu

Cook was soon to establish that there were two separate large islands, Te Ika a Maui (North) and Te Wai Pounamu (South). The passage between the two was called Cook Strait by Banks. Cook left the sound and sailed through the strait before turning north to reach Cape Turnagain. In doing so he proved Te Ika a Maui was an island.

Cloudy Bay

Cook Strait

8 Feb 1770

Cape Campbell

Cape Palliser

12 Feb 1770

COOK STRAIT

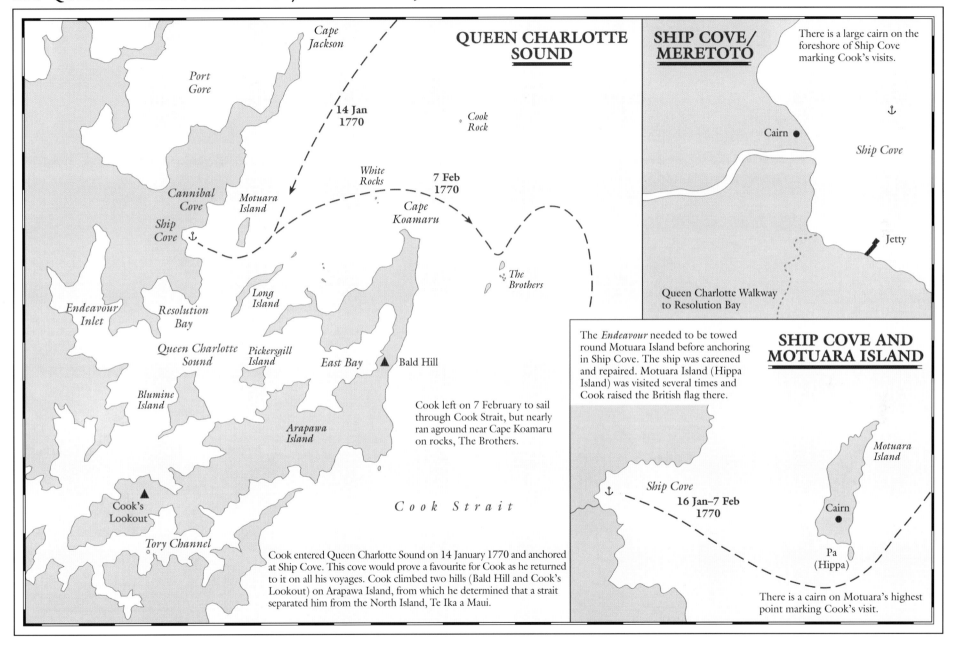

QUEEN CHARLOTTE SOUND

Cape Jackson

Port Gore

14 Jan 1770

Cook Rock

White Rocks

7 Feb 1770

Cannibal Cove

Motuara Island

Ship Cove

Cape Koamaru

The Brothers

Long Island

Endeavour Inlet

Resolution Bay

Queen Charlotte Sound

Pickersgill Island

East Bay

▲ Bald Hill

Blumine Island

Arapawa Island

Cook's Lookout ▲

Tory Channel

C o o k   S t r a i t

Cook left on 7 February to sail through Cook Strait, but nearly ran aground near Cape Koamaru on rocks, The Brothers.

Cook entered Queen Charlotte Sound on 14 January 1770 and anchored at Ship Cove. This cove would prove a favourite for Cook as he returned to it on all his voyages. Cook climbed two hills (Bald Hill and Cook's Lookout) on Arapawa Island, from which he determined that a strait separated him from the North Island, Te Ika a Maui.

SHIP COVE/MERETOTO

There is a large cairn on the foreshore of Ship Cove marking Cook's visits.

Cairn ●

Ship Cove

Jetty

Queen Charlotte Walkway to Resolution Bay

SHIP COVE AND MOTUARA ISLAND

The *Endeavour* needed to be towed round Motuara Island before anchoring in Ship Cove. The ship was careened and repaired. Motuara Island (Hippa Island) was visited several times and Cook raised the British flag there.

Ship Cove

16 Jan–7 Feb 1770

Motuara Island

Cairn ●

Pa (Hippa)

There is a cairn on Motuara's highest point marking Cook's visit.

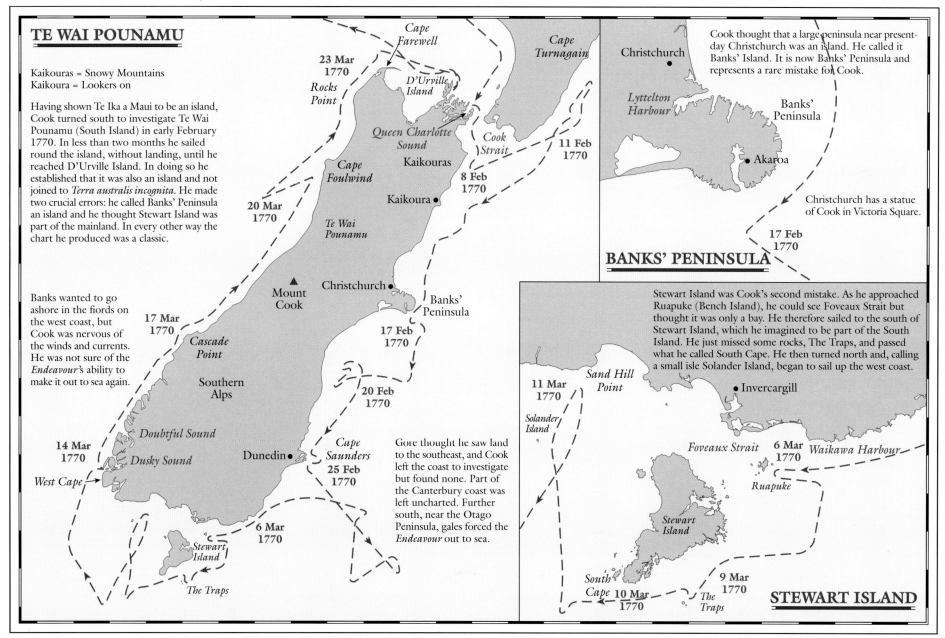

TE WAI POUNAMU

Kaikouras = Snowy Mountains
Kaikoura = Lookers on

Having shown Te Ika a Maui to be an island, Cook turned south to investigate Te Wai Pounamu (South Island) in early February 1770. In less than two months he sailed round the island, without landing, until he reached D'Urville Island. In doing so he established that it was also an island and not joined to *Terra australis incognita*. He made two crucial errors: he called Banks' Peninsula an island and he thought Stewart Island was part of the mainland. In every other way the chart he produced was a classic.

Banks wanted to go ashore in the fiords on the west coast, but Cook was nervous of the winds and currents. He was not sure of the *Endeavour*'s ability to make it out to sea again.

Gore thought he saw land to the southeast, and Cook left the coast to investigate but found none. Part of the Canterbury coast was left uncharted. Further south, near the Otago Peninsula, gales forced the *Endeavour* out to sea.

BANKS' PENINSULA

Cook thought that a large peninsula near present-day Christchurch was an island. He called it Banks' Island. It is now Banks' Peninsula and represents a rare mistake for Cook.

Christchurch has a statue of Cook in Victoria Square.

STEWART ISLAND

Stewart Island was Cook's second mistake. As he approached Ruapuke (Bench Island), he could see Foveaux Strait but thought it was only a bay. He therefore sailed to the south of Stewart Island, which he imagined to be part of the South Island. He just missed some rocks, The Traps, and passed what he called South Cape. He then turned north and, calling a small isle Solander Island, began to sail up the west coast.

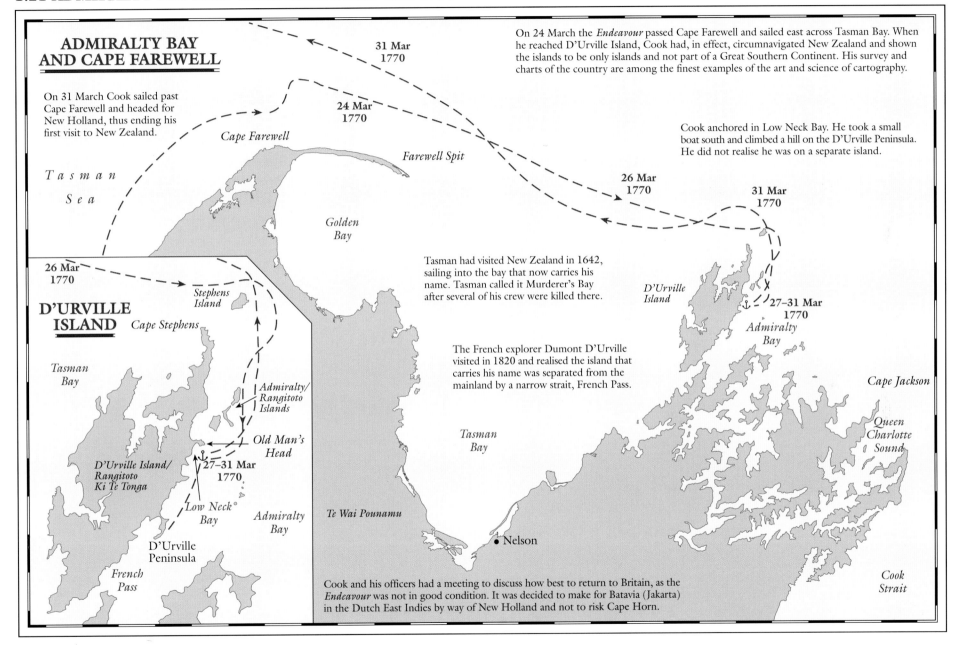

ADMIRALTY BAY AND CAPE FAREWELL

On 31 March Cook sailed past Cape Farewell and headed for New Holland, thus ending his first visit to New Zealand.

On 24 March the *Endeavour* passed Cape Farewell and sailed east across Tasman Bay. When he reached D'Urville Island, Cook had, in effect, circumnavigated New Zealand and shown the islands to be only islands and not part of a Great Southern Continent. His survey and charts of the country are among the finest examples of the art and science of cartography.

Cook anchored in Low Neck Bay. He took a small boat south and climbed a hill on the D'Urville Peninsula. He did not realise he was on a separate island.

31 Mar 1770

24 Mar 1770

26 Mar 1770

31 Mar 1770

Cape Farewell

Farewell Spit

Tasman Sea

Golden Bay

Tasman had visited New Zealand in 1642, sailing into the bay that now carries his name. Tasman called it Murderer's Bay after several of his crew were killed there.

D'Urville Island

27–31 Mar 1770

Admiralty Bay

26 Mar 1770

D'URVILLE ISLAND

Cape Stephens

Stephens Island

Tasman Bay

Admiralty/ Rangitoto Islands

Old Man's Head

The French explorer Dumont D'Urville visited in 1820 and realised the island that carries his name was separated from the mainland by a narrow strait, French Pass.

Cape Jackson

D'Urville Island/ Rangitoto Ki Te Tonga

27–31 Mar 1770

Low Neck Bay

Admiralty Bay

Te Wai Pounamu

Tasman Bay

Queen Charlotte Sound

D'Urville Peninsula

French Pass

● Nelson

Cook and his officers had a meeting to discuss how best to return to Britain, as the *Endeavour* was not in good condition. It was decided to make for Batavia (Jakarta) in the Dutch East Indies by way of New Holland and not to risk Cape Horn.

Cook Strait

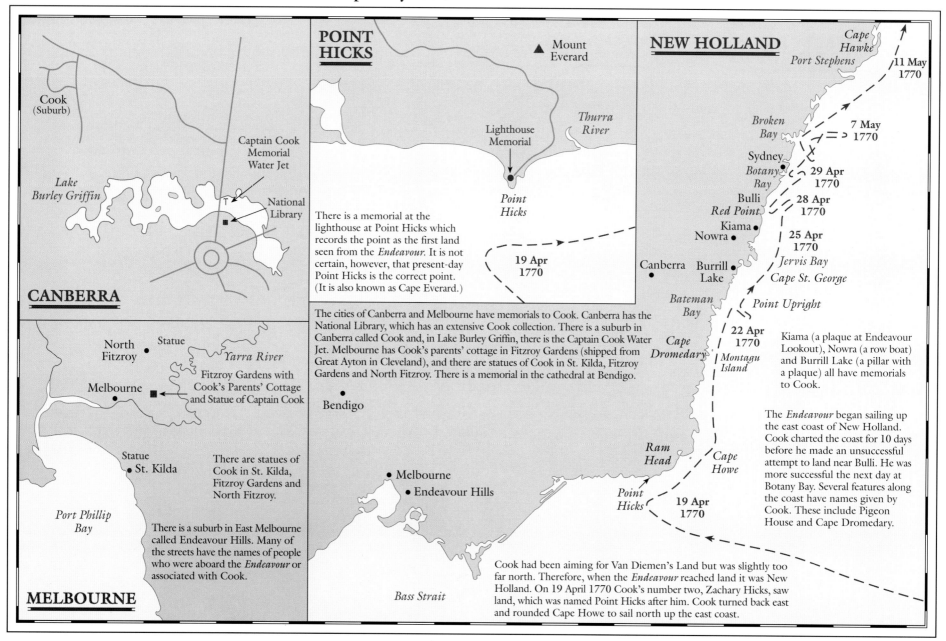

CANBERRA

Cook (Suburb)

Lake Burley Griffin

Captain Cook Memorial Water Jet

National Library

MELBOURNE

North Fitzroy — Statue

Yarra River

Melbourne

Fitzroy Gardens with Cook's Parents' Cottage and Statue of Captain Cook

Statue St. Kilda

Port Phillip Bay

There are statues of Cook in St. Kilda, Fitzroy Gardens and North Fitzroy.

There is a suburb in East Melbourne called Endeavour Hills. Many of the streets have the names of people who were aboard the *Endeavour* or associated with Cook.

POINT HICKS

Mount Everard

Thurra River

Lighthouse Memorial

Point Hicks

There is a memorial at the lighthouse at Point Hicks which records the point as the first land seen from the *Endeavour*. It is not certain, however, that present-day Point Hicks is the correct point. (It is also known as Cape Everard.)

19 Apr 1770

The cities of Canberra and Melbourne have memorials to Cook. Canberra has the National Library, which has an extensive Cook collection. There is a suburb in Canberra called Cook and, in Lake Burley Griffin, there is the Captain Cook Water Jet. Melbourne has Cook's parents' cottage in Fitzroy Gardens (shipped from Great Ayton in Cleveland), and there are statues of Cook in St. Kilda, Fitzroy Gardens and North Fitzroy. There is a memorial in the cathedral at Bendigo.

Canberra

Bendigo

Melbourne
Endeavour Hills

Ram Head

Point Hicks

Bass Strait

19 Apr 1770

NEW HOLLAND

Cape Hawke
Port Stephens

11 May 1770

Broken Bay

7 May 1770

Sydney
Botany Bay

29 Apr 1770

Bulli
Red Point

28 Apr 1770

Kiama
Nowra

25 Apr 1770

Jervis Bay
Cape St. George

Burrill Lake

Point Upright

Bateman Bay

22 Apr 1770

Cape Dromedary
Montagu Island

Cape Howe

Kiama (a plaque at Endeavour Lookout), Nowra (a row boat) and Burrill Lake (a pillar with a plaque) all have memorials to Cook.

The *Endeavour* began sailing up the east coast of New Holland. Cook charted the coast for 10 days before he made an unsuccessful attempt to land near Bulli. He was more successful the next day at Botany Bay. Several features along the coast have names given by Cook. These include Pigeon House and Cape Dromedary.

Cook had been aiming for Van Diemen's Land but was slightly too far north. Therefore, when the *Endeavour* reached land it was New Holland. On 19 April 1770 Cook's number two, Zachary Hicks, saw land, which was named Point Hicks after him. Cook turned back east and rounded Cape Howe to sail north up the east coast.

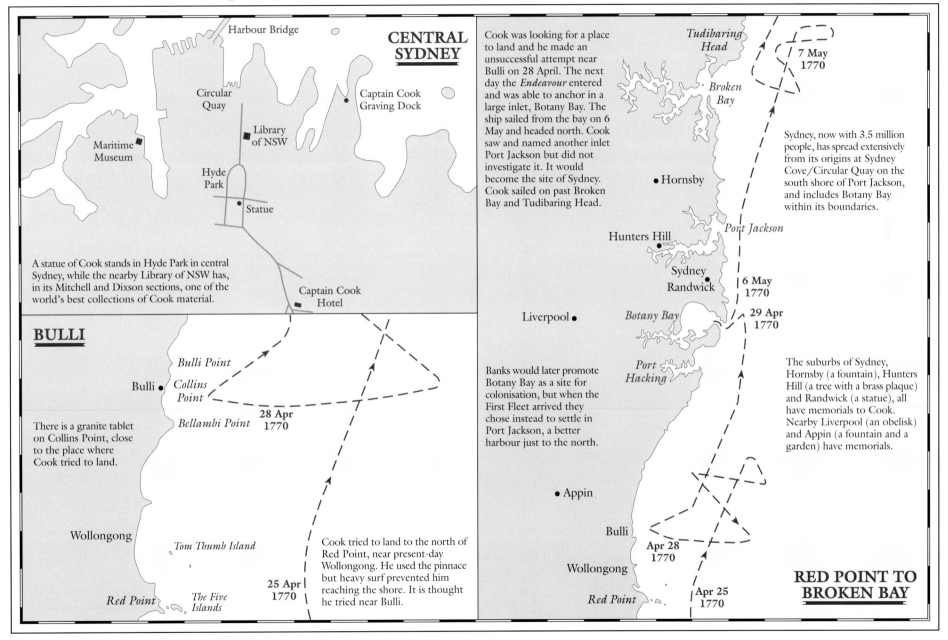

CENTRAL SYDNEY

Harbour Bridge

Circular Quay

Captain Cook Graving Dock

Library of NSW

Maritime Museum

Hyde Park

Statue

A statue of Cook stands in Hyde Park in central Sydney, while the nearby Library of NSW has, in its Mitchell and Dixson sections, one of the world's best collections of Cook material.

Captain Cook Hotel

BULLI

Bulli Point

Bulli

Collins Point

There is a granite tablet on Collins Point, close to the place where Cook tried to land.

Bellambi Point

28 Apr 1770

Wollongong

Tom Thumb Island

Red Point

The Five Islands

25 Apr 1770

Cook tried to land to the north of Red Point, near present-day Wollongong. He used the pinnace but heavy surf prevented him reaching the shore. It is thought he tried near Bulli.

Cook was looking for a place to land and he made an unsuccessful attempt near Bulli on 28 April. The next day the *Endeavour* entered and was able to anchor in a large inlet, Botany Bay. The ship sailed from the bay on 6 May and headed north. Cook saw and named another inlet Port Jackson but did not investigate it. It would become the site of Sydney. Cook sailed on past Broken Bay and Tudibaring Head.

Banks would later promote Botany Bay as a site for colonisation, but when the First Fleet arrived they chose instead to settle in Port Jackson, a better harbour just to the north.

Tudibaring Head

Broken Bay

7 May 1770

Hornsby

Hunters Hill

Port Jackson

Sydney

Randwick

6 May 1770

Liverpool

Botany Bay

29 Apr 1770

Port Hacking

Appin

Bulli

Apr 28 1770

Wollongong

Red Point

Apr 25 1770

Sydney, now with 3.5 million people, has spread extensively from its origins at Sydney Cove/Circular Quay on the south shore of Port Jackson, and includes Botany Bay within its boundaries.

The suburbs of Sydney, Hornsby (a fountain), Hunters Hill (a tree with a brass plaque) and Randwick (a statue), all have memorials to Cook. Nearby Liverpool (an obelisk) and Appin (a fountain and a garden) have memorials.

RED POINT TO BROKEN BAY

1.24 BOTANY BAY Apr–May 1770

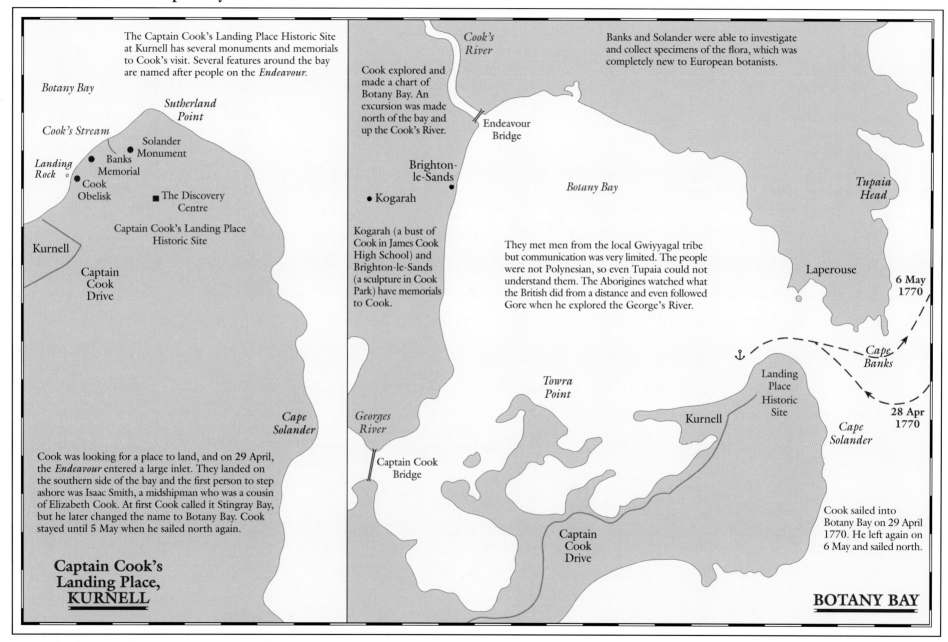

The Captain Cook's Landing Place Historic Site at Kurnell has several monuments and memorials to Cook's visit. Several features around the bay are named after people on the *Endeavour*.

Botany Bay

Cook's Stream

Sutherland Point

Landing Rock

Solander Monument

Banks Memorial

Cook Obelisk

The Discovery Centre

Captain Cook's Landing Place Historic Site

Kurnell

Captain Cook Drive

Cape Solander

Cook was looking for a place to land, and on 29 April, the *Endeavour* entered a large inlet. They landed on the southern side of the bay and the first person to step ashore was Isaac Smith, a midshipman who was a cousin of Elizabeth Cook. At first Cook called it Stingray Bay, but he later changed the name to Botany Bay. Cook stayed until 5 May when he sailed north again.

Captain Cook's Landing Place, KURNELL

Cook explored and made a chart of Botany Bay. An excursion was made north of the bay and up the Cook's River.

Cook's River

Endeavour Bridge

Brighton-le-Sands

Kogarah

Kogarah (a bust of Cook in James Cook High School) and Brighton-le-Sands (a sculpture in Cook Park) have memorials to Cook.

Banks and Solander were able to investigate and collect specimens of the flora, which was completely new to European botanists.

Botany Bay

Tupaia Head

They met men from the local Gwiyyagal tribe but communication was very limited. The people were not Polynesian, so even Tupaia could not understand them. The Aborigines watched what the British did from a distance and even followed Gore when he explored the George's River.

Laperouse

6 May 1770

Cape Banks

28 Apr 1770

Towra Point

Georges River

Landing Place Historic Site

Kurnell

Cape Solander

Captain Cook Bridge

Captain Cook Drive

Cook sailed into Botany Bay on 29 April 1770. He left again on 6 May and sailed north.

BOTANY BAY

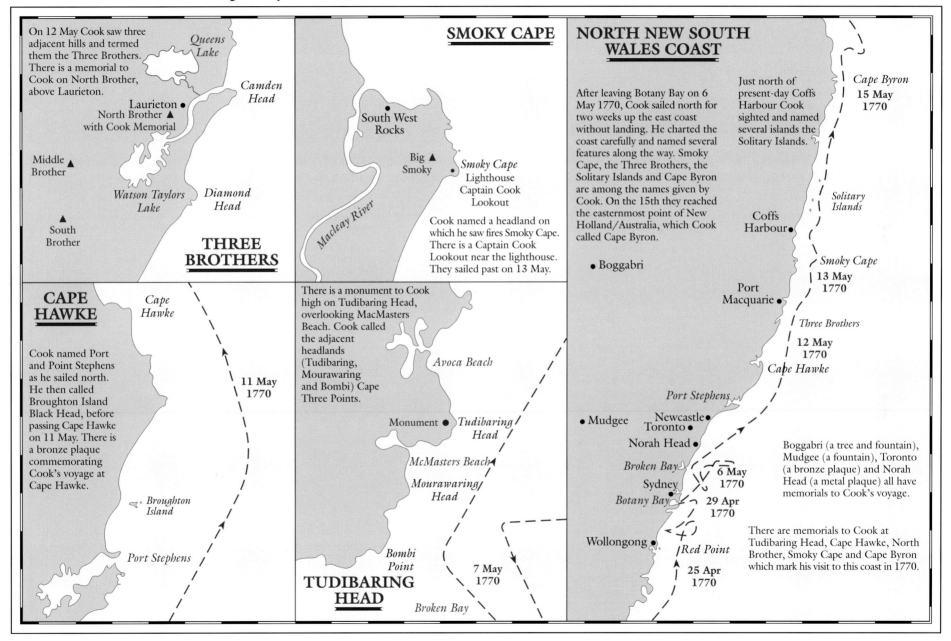

On 12 May Cook saw three adjacent hills and termed them the Three Brothers. There is a memorial to Cook on North Brother, above Laurieton.

Queens Lake

Camden Head

Laurieton •
North Brother ▲
with Cook Memorial

Middle ▲
Brother

Watson Taylors Lake

Diamond Head

South ▲
Brother

THREE BROTHERS

CAPE HAWKE

Cook named Port and Point Stephens as he sailed north. He then called Broughton Island Black Head, before passing Cape Hawke on 11 May. There is a bronze plaque commemorating Cook's voyage at Cape Hawke.

Cape Hawke

11 May 1770

⌒ Broughton Island

Port Stephens

SMOKY CAPE

South West Rocks

Big ▲
Smoky

• Smoky Cape
Lighthouse
Captain Cook
Lookout

Macleay River

Cook named a headland on which he saw fires Smoky Cape. There is a Captain Cook Lookout near the lighthouse. They sailed past on 13 May.

There is a monument to Cook high on Tudibaring Head, overlooking MacMasters Beach. Cook called the adjacent headlands (Tudibaring, Mourawaring and Bombi) Cape Three Points.

Avoca Beach

Monument • Tudibaring Head

McMasters Beach

Mourawaring Head

Bombi Point

7 May 1770

TUDIBARING HEAD

Broken Bay

NORTH NEW SOUTH WALES COAST

After leaving Botany Bay on 6 May 1770, Cook sailed north for two weeks up the east coast without landing. He charted the coast carefully and named several features along the way. Smoky Cape, the Three Brothers, the Solitary Islands and Cape Byron are among the names given by Cook. On the 15th they reached the easternmost point of New Holland/Australia, which Cook called Cape Byron.

Just north of present-day Coffs Harbour Cook sighted and named several islands the Solitary Islands.

Cape Byron
15 May 1770

Solitary Islands

Coffs Harbour •

Smoky Cape
13 May 1770

Port Macquarie •

Three Brothers
12 May 1770

Cape Hawke

Port Stephens

• Boggabri

• Mudgee   Newcastle •
Toronto •

Norah Head •

Broken Bay

Sydney •
Botany Bay •

6 May 1770

29 Apr 1770

Wollongong •

Red Point

25 Apr 1770

Boggabri (a tree and fountain), Mudgee (a fountain), Toronto (a bronze plaque) and Norah Head (a metal plaque) all have memorials to Cook's voyage.

There are memorials to Cook at Tudibaring Head, Cape Hawke, North Brother, Smoky Cape and Cape Byron which mark his visit to this coast in 1770.

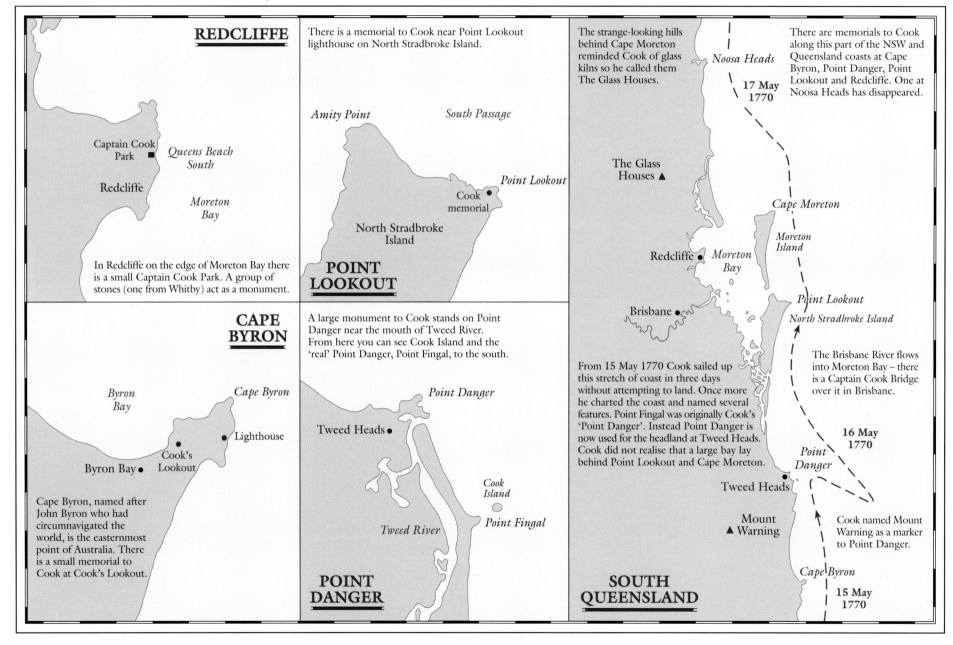

REDCLIFFE

Captain Cook
Park ■

*Queens Beach
South*

Redcliffe

*Moreton
Bay*

In Redcliffe on the edge of Moreton Bay there is a small Captain Cook Park. A group of stones (one from Whitby) act as a monument.

There is a memorial to Cook near Point Lookout lighthouse on North Stradbroke Island.

Amity Point   *South Passage*

Point Lookout

Cook
memorial •

North Stradbroke
Island

POINT LOOKOUT

CAPE BYRON

*Byron
Bay*

Cape Byron

• Lighthouse

Cook's
Lookout •

Byron Bay •

Cape Byron, named after John Byron who had circumnavigated the world, is the easternmost point of Australia. There is a small memorial to Cook at Cook's Lookout.

A large monument to Cook stands on Point Danger near the mouth of Tweed River. From here you can see Cook Island and the 'real' Point Danger, Point Fingal, to the south.

Point Danger

Tweed Heads •

*Cook
Island*

Tweed River   *Point Fingal*

POINT DANGER

The strange-looking hills behind Cape Moreton reminded Cook of glass kilns so he called them The Glass Houses.

~ *Noosa Heads*

**17 May
1770**

The Glass
Houses ▲

Cape Moreton

*Moreton
Island*

Redcliffe • *Moreton
Bay*

Brisbane •

Point Lookout

North Stradbroke Island

From 15 May 1770 Cook sailed up this stretch of coast in three days without attempting to land. Once more he charted the coast and named several features. Point Fingal was originally Cook's 'Point Danger'. Instead Point Danger is now used for the headland at Tweed Heads. Cook did not realise that a large bay lay behind Point Lookout and Cape Moreton.

*Point
Danger*

Tweed Heads •

Mount
▲ Warning

SOUTH QUEENSLAND

There are memorials to Cook along this part of the NSW and Queensland coasts at Cape Byron, Point Danger, Point Lookout and Redcliffe. One at Noosa Heads has disappeared.

The Brisbane River flows into Moreton Bay – there is a Captain Cook Bridge over it in Brisbane.

**16 May
1770**

Cook named Mount Warning as a marker to Point Danger.

Cape Byron

**15 May
1770**

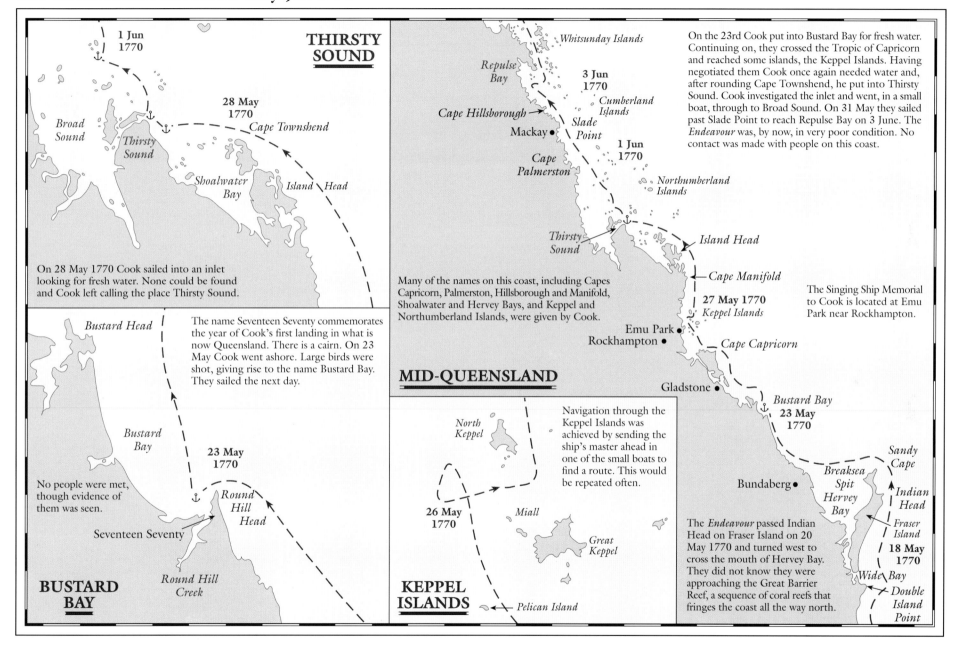

THIRSTY SOUND

1 Jun 1770

28 May 1770

Broad Sound

Thirsty Sound

Cape Townshend

Shoalwater Bay

Island Head

On 28 May 1770 Cook sailed into an inlet looking for fresh water. None could be found and Cook left calling the place Thirsty Sound.

BUSTARD BAY

Bustard Head

Bustard Bay

23 May 1770

Round Hill Head

The name Seventeen Seventy commemorates the year of Cook's first landing in what is now Queensland. There is a cairn. On 23 May Cook went ashore. Large birds were shot, giving rise to the name Bustard Bay. They sailed the next day.

No people were met, though evidence of them was seen.

Seventeen Seventy

Round Hill Creek

MID-QUEENSLAND

Whitsunday Islands

Repulse Bay

3 Jun 1770

Cumberland Islands

Cape Hillsborough

Slade Point

Mackay ●

Cape Palmerston

1 Jun 1770

Northumberland Islands

Thirsty Sound

Island Head

Cape Manifold

27 May 1770
Keppel Islands

Emu Park ●
Rockhampton ●

Cape Capricorn

Gladstone ●

Bustard Bay
23 May 1770

Many of the names on this coast, including Capes Capricorn, Palmerston, Hillsborough and Manifold, Shoalwater and Hervey Bays, and Keppel and Northumberland Islands, were given by Cook.

On the 23rd Cook put into Bustard Bay for fresh water. Continuing on, they crossed the Tropic of Capricorn and reached some islands, the Keppel Islands. Having negotiated them Cook once again needed water and, after rounding Cape Townshend, he put into Thirsty Sound. Cook investigated the inlet and went, in a small boat, through to Broad Sound. On 31 May they sailed past Slade Point to reach Repulse Bay on 3 June. The *Endeavour* was, by now, in very poor condition. No contact was made with people on this coast.

The Singing Ship Memorial to Cook is located at Emu Park near Rockhampton.

KEPPEL ISLANDS

North Keppel

26 May 1770

Miall

Great Keppel

Pelican Island

Navigation through the Keppel Islands was achieved by sending the ship's master ahead in one of the small boats to find a route. This would be repeated often.

Sandy Cape

Breaksea Spit
Hervey Bay

Bundaberg ●

Indian Head

18 May 1770

Fraser Island

Wide Bay

Double Island Point

The *Endeavour* passed Indian Head on Fraser Island on 20 May 1770 and turned west to cross the mouth of Hervey Bay. They did not know they were approaching the Great Barrier Reef, a sequence of coral reefs that fringes the coast all the way north.

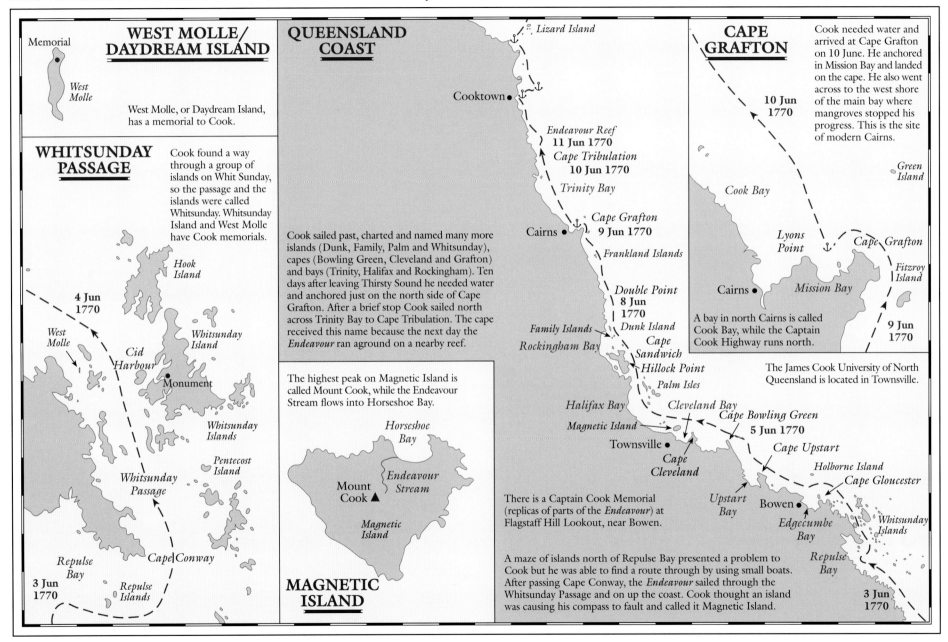

WEST MOLLE/DAYDREAM ISLAND

Memorial

West Molle

West Molle, or Daydream Island, has a memorial to Cook.

WHITSUNDAY PASSAGE

Cook found a way through a group of islands on Whit Sunday, so the passage and the islands were called Whitsunday. Whitsunday Island and West Molle have Cook memorials.

Hook Island

4 Jun 1770

West Molle

Cid Harbour

Monument

Whitsunday Island

Whitsunday Islands

Pentecost Island

Whitsunday Passage

Repulse Bay

Cape Conway

3 Jun 1770

Repulse Islands

QUEENSLAND COAST

Cooktown

Endeavour Reef
11 Jun 1770
Cape Tribulation
10 Jun 1770

Trinity Bay

Cairns

Cape Grafton
9 Jun 1770

Frankland Islands

Double Point
8 Jun 1770

Dunk Island

Family Islands

Rockingham Bay

Cape Sandwich

Hillock Point

Palm Isles

Halifax Bay

Cleveland Bay

Magnetic Island

Townsville

Cape Cleveland

Cook sailed past, charted and named many more islands (Dunk, Family, Palm and Whitsunday), capes (Bowling Green, Cleveland and Grafton) and bays (Trinity, Halifax and Rockingham). Ten days after leaving Thirsty Sound he needed water and anchored just on the north side of Cape Grafton. After a brief stop Cook sailed north across Trinity Bay to Cape Tribulation. The cape received this name because the next day the *Endeavour* ran aground on a nearby reef.

The highest peak on Magnetic Island is called Mount Cook, while the Endeavour Stream flows into Horseshoe Bay.

Horseshoe Bay

Endeavour Stream

Mount Cook ▲

Magnetic Island

MAGNETIC ISLAND

CAPE GRAFTON

Cook needed water and arrived at Cape Grafton on 10 June. He anchored in Mission Bay and landed on the cape. He also went across to the west shore of the main bay where mangroves stopped his progress. This is the site of modern Cairns.

Lizard Island

10 Jun 1770

Green Island

Cook Bay

Lyons Point

Cape Grafton

Cairns

Fitzroy Island

Mission Bay

9 Jun 1770

A bay in north Cairns is called Cook Bay, while the Captain Cook Highway runs north.

The James Cook University of North Queensland is located in Townsville.

Cape Bowling Green
5 Jun 1770

Cape Upstart

Holborne Island

Cape Gloucester

There is a Captain Cook Memorial (replicas of parts of the *Endeavour*) at Flagstaff Hill Lookout, near Bowen.

Upstart Bay

Bowen

Edgecumbe Bay

Whitsunday Islands

Repulse Bay

A maze of islands north of Repulse Bay presented a problem to Cook but he was able to find a route through by using small boats. After passing Cape Conway, the *Endeavour* sailed through the Whitsunday Passage and on up the coast. Cook thought an island was causing his compass to fault and called it Magnetic Island.

3 Jun 1770

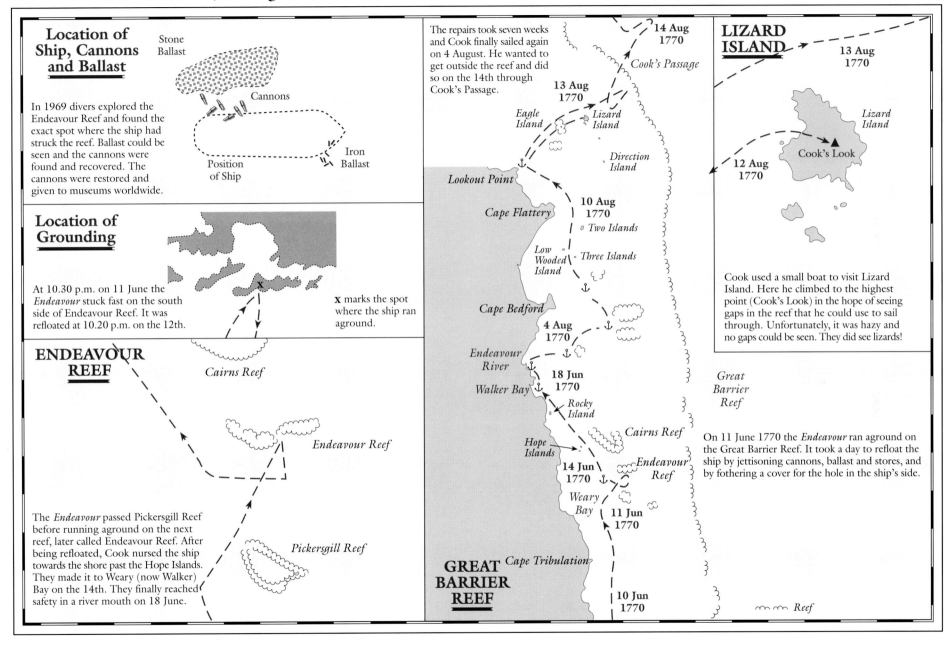

Location of Ship, Cannons and Ballast

Stone Ballast

Cannons

Position of Ship

Iron Ballast

In 1969 divers explored the Endeavour Reef and found the exact spot where the ship had struck the reef. Ballast could be seen and the cannons were found and recovered. The cannons were restored and given to museums worldwide.

Location of Grounding

At 10.30 p.m. on 11 June the *Endeavour* stuck fast on the south side of Endeavour Reef. It was refloated at 10.20 p.m. on the 12th.

x marks the spot where the ship ran aground.

ENDEAVOUR REEF

Cairns Reef

Endeavour Reef

Pickersgill Reef

The *Endeavour* passed Pickersgill Reef before running aground on the next reef, later called Endeavour Reef. After being refloated, Cook nursed the ship towards the shore past the Hope Islands. They made it to Weary (now Walker) Bay on the 14th. They finally reached safety in a river mouth on 18 June.

The repairs took seven weeks and Cook finally sailed again on 4 August. He wanted to get outside the reef and did so on the 14th through Cook's Passage.

14 Aug 1770

Cook's Passage

13 Aug 1770

Eagle Island

Lizard Island

Direction Island

Lookout Point

Cape Flattery

10 Aug 1770

Two Islands

Low Wooded Island

Three Islands

Cape Bedford

4 Aug 1770

Endeavour River

18 Jun 1770

Walker Bay

Rocky Island

Cairns Reef

Hope Islands

Endeavour Reef

14 Jun 1770

Weary Bay

11 Jun 1770

GREAT BARRIER REEF Cape Tribulation

10 Jun 1770

LIZARD ISLAND

13 Aug 1770

Lizard Island

Cook's Look

12 Aug 1770

Cook used a small boat to visit Lizard Island. Here he climbed to the highest point (Cook's Look) in the hope of seeing gaps in the reef that he could use to sail through. Unfortunately, it was hazy and no gaps could be seen. They did see lizards!

Great Barrier Reef

On 11 June 1770 the *Endeavour* ran aground on the Great Barrier Reef. It took a day to refloat the ship by jettisoning cannons, ballast and stores, and by fothering a cover for the hole in the ship's side.

Reef

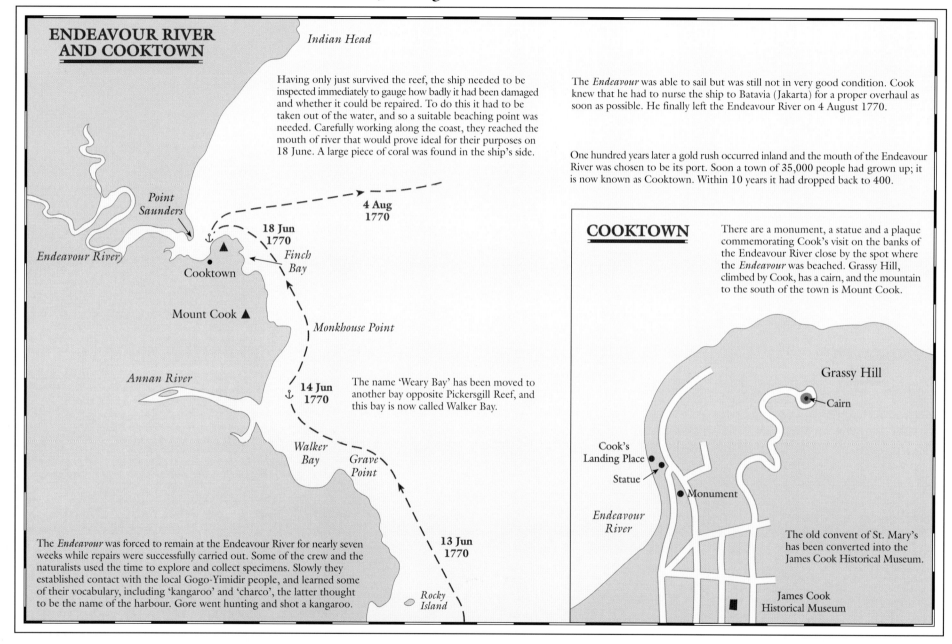

ENDEAVOUR RIVER AND COOKTOWN

Indian Head

Having only just survived the reef, the ship needed to be inspected immediately to gauge how badly it had been damaged and whether it could be repaired. To do this it had to be taken out of the water, and so a suitable beaching point was needed. Carefully working along the coast, they reached the mouth of river that would prove ideal for their purposes on 18 June. A large piece of coral was found in the ship's side.

The *Endeavour* was able to sail but was still not in very good condition. Cook knew that he had to nurse the ship to Batavia (Jakarta) for a proper overhaul as soon as possible. He finally left the Endeavour River on 4 August 1770.

One hundred years later a gold rush occurred inland and the mouth of the Endeavour River was chosen to be its port. Soon a town of 35,000 people had grown up; it is now known as Cooktown. Within 10 years it had dropped back to 400.

Point Saunders

4 Aug 1770

18 Jun 1770

Endeavour River

Cooktown

Finch Bay

Mount Cook ▲

Monkhouse Point

Annan River

14 Jun 1770

The name 'Weary Bay' has been moved to another bay opposite Pickersgill Reef, and this bay is now called Walker Bay.

Walker Bay

Grave Point

13 Jun 1770

Rocky Island

The *Endeavour* was forced to remain at the Endeavour River for nearly seven weeks while repairs were successfully carried out. Some of the crew and the naturalists used the time to explore and collect specimens. Slowly they established contact with the local Gogo-Yimidir people, and learned some of their vocabulary, including 'kangaroo' and 'charco', the latter thought to be the name of the harbour. Gore went hunting and shot a kangaroo.

COOKTOWN

There are a monument, a statue and a plaque commemorating Cook's visit on the banks of the Endeavour River close by the spot where the *Endeavour* was beached. Grassy Hill, climbed by Cook, has a cairn, and the mountain to the south of the town is Mount Cook.

Grassy Hill

Cairn

Cook's Landing Place

Statue

Monument

Endeavour River

The old convent of St. Mary's has been converted into the James Cook Historical Museum.

James Cook Historical Museum

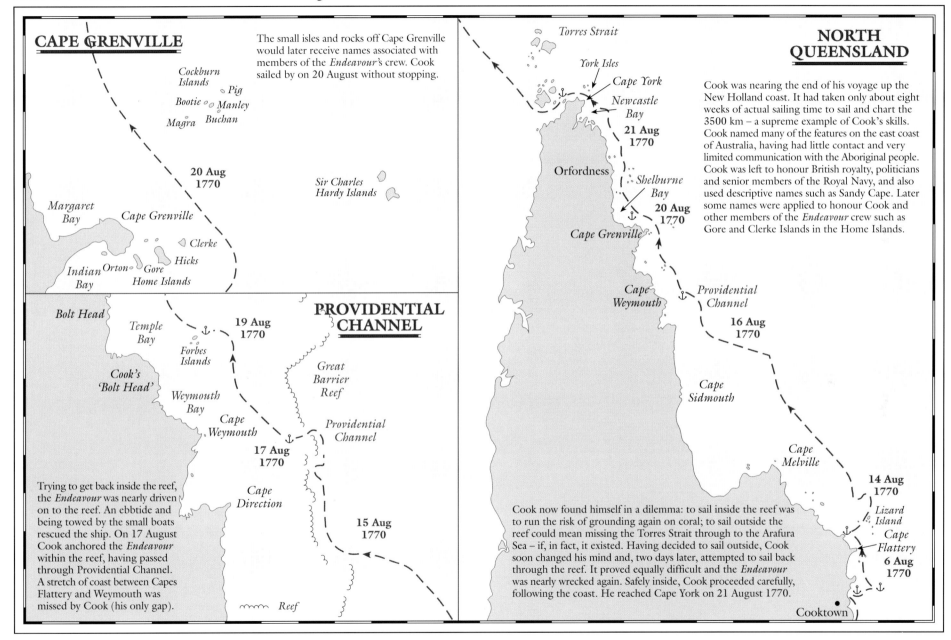

CAPE GRENVILLE

The small isles and rocks off Cape Grenville would later receive names associated with members of the *Endeavour's* crew. Cook sailed by on 20 August without stopping.

Cockburn Islands

Pig

Bootie Manley

Magra Buchan

20 Aug 1770

Sir Charles Hardy Islands

Margaret Bay

Cape Grenville

Clerke

Hicks

Indian Bay Orton Gore

Home Islands

PROVIDENTIAL CHANNEL

Bolt Head

Temple Bay

19 Aug 1770

Forbes Islands

Cook's 'Bolt Head'

Great Barrier Reef

Weymouth Bay

Cape Weymouth

17 Aug 1770

Providential Channel

Cape Direction

15 Aug 1770

Trying to get back inside the reef, the *Endeavour* was nearly driven on to the reef. An ebbtide and being towed by the small boats rescued the ship. On 17 August Cook anchored the *Endeavour* within the reef, having passed through Providential Channel. A stretch of coast between Capes Flattery and Weymouth was missed by Cook (his only gap).

Reef

NORTH QUEENSLAND

Torres Strait

York Isles

Cape York

Newcastle Bay

21 Aug 1770

Orfordness

Shelburne Bay

20 Aug 1770

Cape Grenville

Cape Weymouth

Providential Channel

16 Aug 1770

Cape Sidmouth

Cape Melville

14 Aug 1770

Lizard Island

Cape Flattery

6 Aug 1770

Cook was nearing the end of his voyage up the New Holland coast. It had taken only about eight weeks of actual sailing time to sail and chart the 3500 km – a supreme example of Cook's skills. Cook named many of the features on the east coast of Australia, having had little contact and very limited communication with the Aboriginal people. Cook was left to honour British royalty, politicians and senior members of the Royal Navy, and also used descriptive names such as Sandy Cape. Later some names were applied to honour Cook and other members of the *Endeavour* crew such as Gore and Clerke Islands in the Home Islands.

Cook now found himself in a dilemma: to sail inside the reef was to run the risk of grounding again on coral; to sail outside the reef could mean missing the Torres Strait through to the Arafura Sea – if, in fact, it existed. Having decided to sail outside, Cook soon changed his mind and, two days later, attempted to sail back through the reef. It proved equally difficult and the *Endeavour* was nearly wrecked again. Safely inside, Cook proceeded carefully, following the coast. He reached Cape York on 21 August 1770.

Cooktown

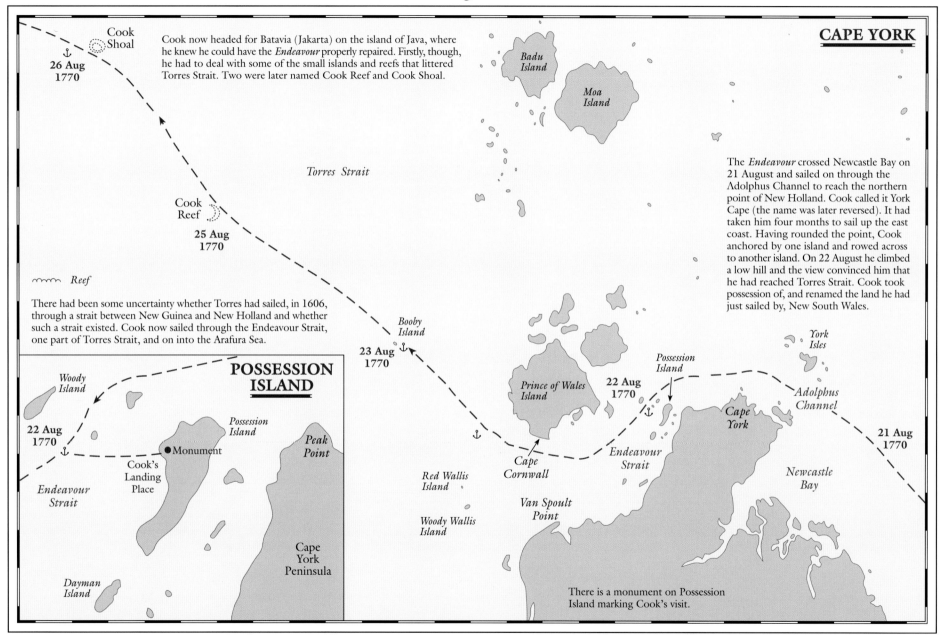

CAPE YORK

Cook now headed for Batavia (Jakarta) on the island of Java, where he knew he could have the *Endeavour* properly repaired. Firstly, though, he had to deal with some of the small islands and reefs that littered Torres Strait. Two were later named Cook Reef and Cook Shoal.

The *Endeavour* crossed Newcastle Bay on 21 August and sailed on through the Adolphus Channel to reach the northern point of New Holland. Cook called it York Cape (the name was later reversed). It had taken him four months to sail up the east coast. Having rounded the point, Cook anchored by one island and rowed across to another island. On 22 August he climbed a low hill and the view convinced him that he had reached Torres Strait. Cook took possession of, and renamed the land he had just sailed by, New South Wales.

There had been some uncertainty whether Torres had sailed, in 1606, through a strait between New Guinea and New Holland and whether such a strait existed. Cook now sailed through the Endeavour Strait, one part of Torres Strait, and on into the Arafura Sea.

POSSESSION ISLAND

There is a monument on Possession Island marking Cook's visit.

Cook Shoal
26 Aug 1770

Cook Reef
25 Aug 1770

Torres Strait

~~~~ Reef

Badu Island

Moa Island

Booby Island
23 Aug 1770

Prince of Wales Island

Cape Cornwall

Red Wallis Island

Woody Wallis Island

Van Spoult Point

Possession Island
22 Aug 1770

Endeavour Strait

Cape York

Newcastle Bay

Adolphus Channel

York Isles

21 Aug 1770

Woody Island

22 Aug 1770

Endeavour Strait

Cook's Landing Place

Monument

Possession Island

Peak Point

Cape York Peninsula

Dayman Island

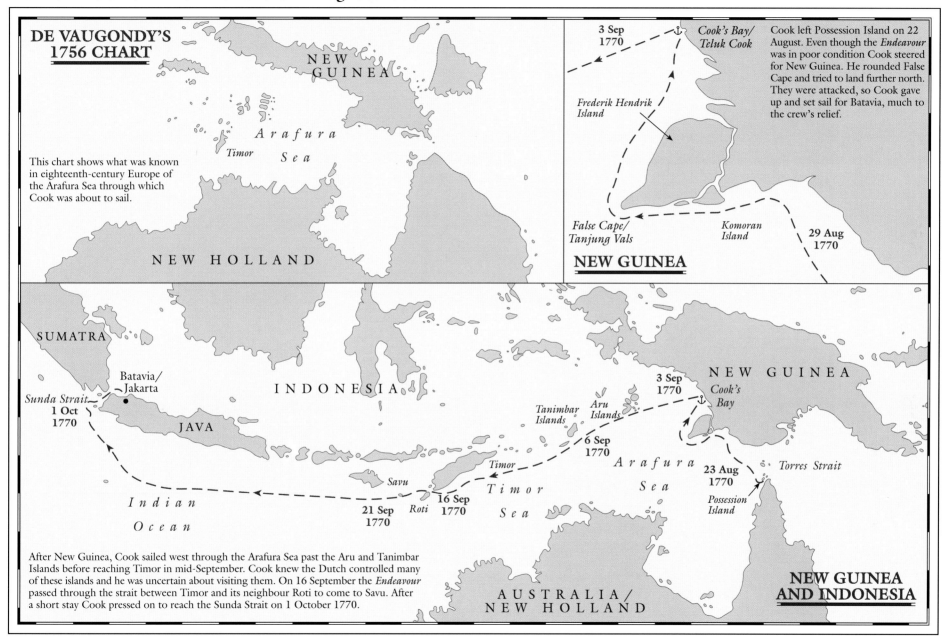

DE VAUGONDY'S 1756 CHART

This chart shows what was known in eighteenth-century Europe of the Arafura Sea through which Cook was about to sail.

NEW GUINEA

Arafura Sea

Timor

NEW HOLLAND

3 Sep 1770

Cook's Bay / Teluk Cook

Frederik Hendrik Island

False Cape / Tanjung Vals

Komoran Island

29 Aug 1770

Cook left Possession Island on 22 August. Even though the *Endeavour* was in poor condition Cook steered for New Guinea. He rounded False Cape and tried to land further north. They were attacked, so Cook gave up and set sail for Batavia, much to the crew's relief.

NEW GUINEA

SUMATRA

Batavia / Jakarta

Sunda Strait **1 Oct 1770**

JAVA

INDONESIA

NEW GUINEA

3 Sep 1770

Cook's Bay

Tanimbar Islands

Aru Islands

6 Sep 1770

Timor

Savu

Roti

16 Sep 1770

21 Sep 1770

Arafura Sea

Torres Strait

23 Aug 1770

Possession Island

Timor Sea

Indian Ocean

AUSTRALIA / NEW HOLLAND

After New Guinea, Cook sailed west through the Arafura Sea past the Aru and Tanimbar Islands before reaching Timor in mid-September. Cook knew the Dutch controlled many of these islands and he was uncertain about visiting them. On 16 September the *Endeavour* passed through the strait between Timor and its neighbour Roti to come to Savu. After a short stay Cook pressed on to reach the Sunda Strait on 1 October 1770.

NEW GUINEA AND INDONESIA

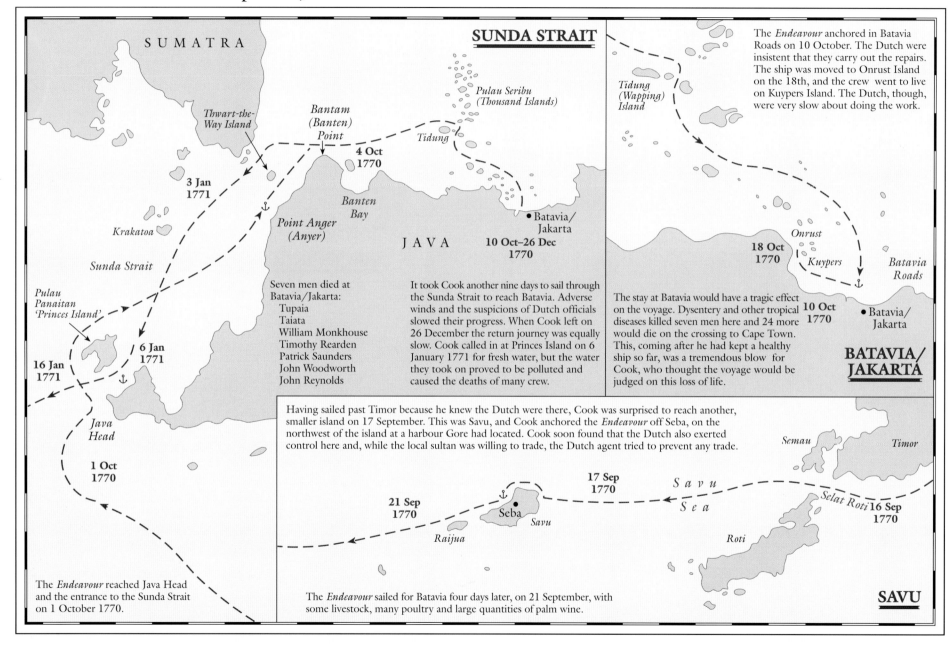

SUNDA STRAIT

SUMATRA

Thwart-the-Way Island

Bantam (Banten) Point

Pulau Seribu (Thousand Islands)

Tidung

4 Oct 1770

3 Jan 1771

Krakatoa

Banten Bay

Point Anger (Anyer)

J A V A

• Batavia/ Jakarta

10 Oct–26 Dec 1770

Sunda Strait

Pulau Panaitan 'Princes Island'

6 Jan 1771

16 Jan 1771

Seven men died at Batavia/Jakarta:
Tupaia
Taiata
William Monkhouse
Timothy Rearden
Patrick Saunders
John Woodworth
John Reynolds

It took Cook another nine days to sail through the Sunda Strait to reach Batavia. Adverse winds and the suspicions of Dutch officials slowed their progress. When Cook left on 26 December the return journey was equally slow. Cook called in at Princes Island on 6 January 1771 for fresh water, but the water they took on proved to be polluted and caused the deaths of many crew.

The *Endeavour* anchored in Batavia Roads on 10 October. The Dutch were insistent that they carry out the repairs. The ship was moved to Onrust Island on the 18th, and the crew went to live on Kuypers Island. The Dutch, though, were very slow about doing the work.

Tidung (Wapping) Island

Onrust

18 Oct 1770

Kuypers

Batavia Roads

The stay at Batavia would have a tragic effect on the voyage. Dysentery and other tropical diseases killed seven men here and 24 more would die on the crossing to Cape Town. This, coming after he had kept a healthy ship so far, was a tremendous blow for Cook, who thought the voyage would be judged on this loss of life.

10 Oct 1770

• Batavia/ Jakarta

BATAVIA/ JAKARTA

Having sailed past Timor because he knew the Dutch were there, Cook was surprised to reach another, smaller island on 17 September. This was Savu, and Cook anchored the *Endeavour* off Seba, on the northwest of the island at a harbour Gore had located. Cook soon found that the Dutch also exerted control here and, while the local sultan was willing to trade, the Dutch agent tried to prevent any trade.

Java Head

1 Oct 1770

Semau

Timor

17 Sep 1770

S a v u

S e a

Selat Roti **16 Sep 1770**

21 Sep 1770

Seba

Savu

Raijua

Roti

The *Endeavour* reached Java Head and the entrance to the Sunda Strait on 1 October 1770.

The *Endeavour* sailed for Batavia four days later, on 21 September, with some livestock, many poultry and large quantities of palm wine.

SAVU

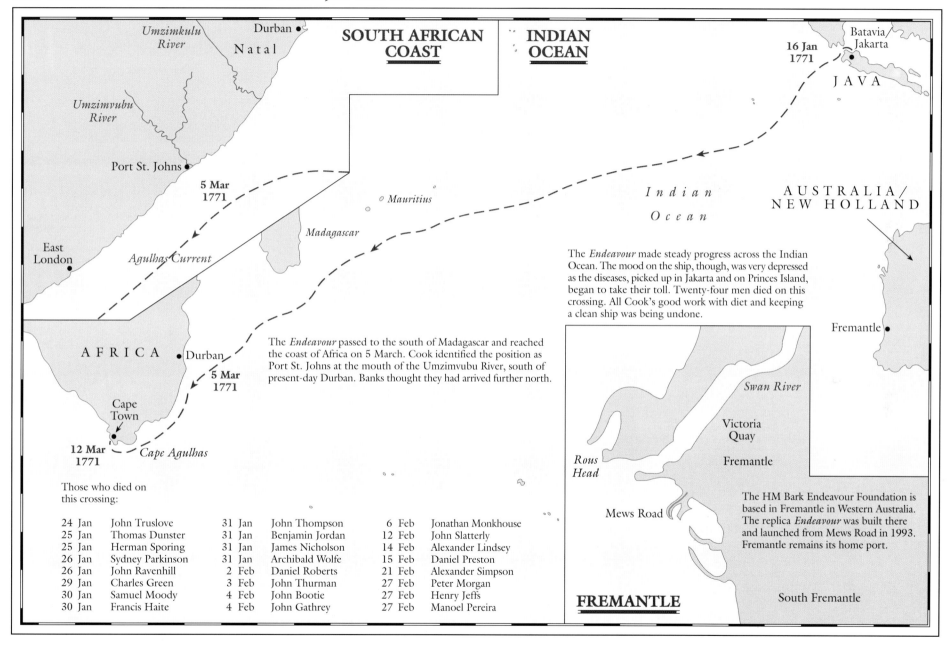

SOUTH AFRICAN COAST **INDIAN OCEAN**

Umzimkulu River

Durban •

Natal

Umzimvubu River

Port St. Johns •

5 Mar 1771

Agulhas Current

East London •

Mauritius

Madagascar

16 Jan 1771

Batavia/ Jakarta •

J A V A

Indian Ocean

AUSTRALIA/ NEW HOLLAND

The *Endeavour* made steady progress across the Indian Ocean. The mood on the ship, though, was very depressed as the diseases, picked up in Jakarta and on Princes Island, began to take their toll. Twenty-four men died on this crossing. All Cook's good work with diet and keeping a clean ship was being undone.

Fremantle •

A F R I C A   • Durban

5 Mar 1771

Cape Town •

12 Mar 1771   Cape Agulhas

The *Endeavour* passed to the south of Madagascar and reached the coast of Africa on 5 March. Cook identified the position as Port St. Johns at the mouth of the Umzimvubu River, south of present-day Durban. Banks thought they had arrived further north.

Swan River

Victoria Quay

Fremantle

Rous Head

Mews Road

The HM Bark Endeavour Foundation is based in Fremantle in Western Australia. The replica *Endeavour* was built there and launched from Mews Road in 1993. Fremantle remains its home port.

South Fremantle

FREMANTLE

Those who died on this crossing:

24 Jan	John Truslove	31 Jan	John Thompson	6 Feb	Jonathan Monkhouse
25 Jan	Thomas Dunster	31 Jan	Benjamin Jordan	12 Feb	John Slatterly
25 Jan	Herman Sporing	31 Jan	James Nicholson	14 Feb	Alexander Lindsey
26 Jan	Sydney Parkinson	31 Jan	Archibald Wolfe	15 Feb	Daniel Preston
26 Jan	John Ravenhill	2 Feb	Daniel Roberts	21 Feb	Alexander Simpson
29 Jan	Charles Green	3 Feb	John Thurman	27 Feb	Peter Morgan
30 Jan	Samuel Moody	4 Feb	John Bootie	27 Feb	Henry Jeffs
30 Jan	Francis Haite	4 Feb	John Gathrey	27 Feb	Manoel Pereira

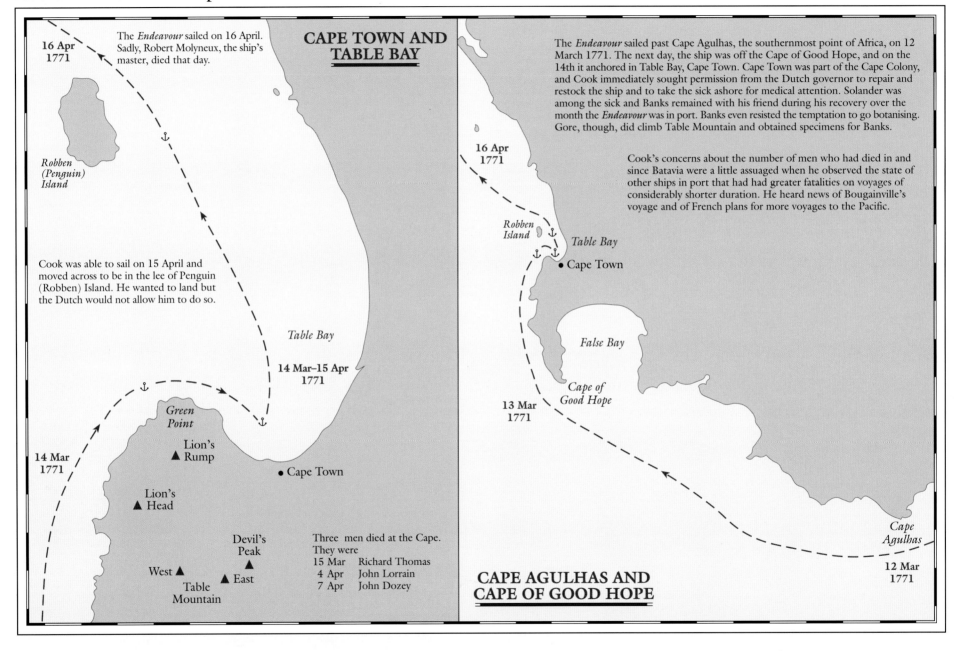

CAPE TOWN AND TABLE BAY

16 Apr 1771

The *Endeavour* sailed on 16 April. Sadly, Robert Molyneux, the ship's master, died that day.

Robben (Penguin) Island

Cook was able to sail on 15 April and moved across to be in the lee of Penguin (Robben) Island. He wanted to land but the Dutch would not allow him to do so.

Table Bay

14 Mar–15 Apr 1771

Green Point

Lion's ▲ Rump

Lion's ▲ Head

14 Mar 1771

• Cape Town

Devil's ▲ Peak

West ▲   ▲ East

Table Mountain

Three men died at the Cape. They were
15 Mar   Richard Thomas
4 Apr   John Lorrain
7 Apr   John Dozey

The *Endeavour* sailed past Cape Agulhas, the southernmost point of Africa, on 12 March 1771. The next day, the ship was off the Cape of Good Hope, and on the 14th it anchored in Table Bay, Cape Town. Cape Town was part of the Cape Colony, and Cook immediately sought permission from the Dutch governor to repair and restock the ship and to take the sick ashore for medical attention. Solander was among the sick and Banks remained with his friend during his recovery over the month the *Endeavour* was in port. Banks even resisted the temptation to go botanising. Gore, though, did climb Table Mountain and obtained specimens for Banks.

Cook's concerns about the number of men who had died in and since Batavia were a little assuaged when he observed the state of other ships in port that had had greater fatalities on voyages of considerably shorter duration. He heard news of Bougainville's voyage and of French plans for more voyages to the Pacific.

16 Apr 1771

Robben Island

Table Bay

• Cape Town

False Bay

Cape of Good Hope

13 Mar 1771

Cape Agulhas

12 Mar 1771

CAPE AGULHAS AND CAPE OF GOOD HOPE

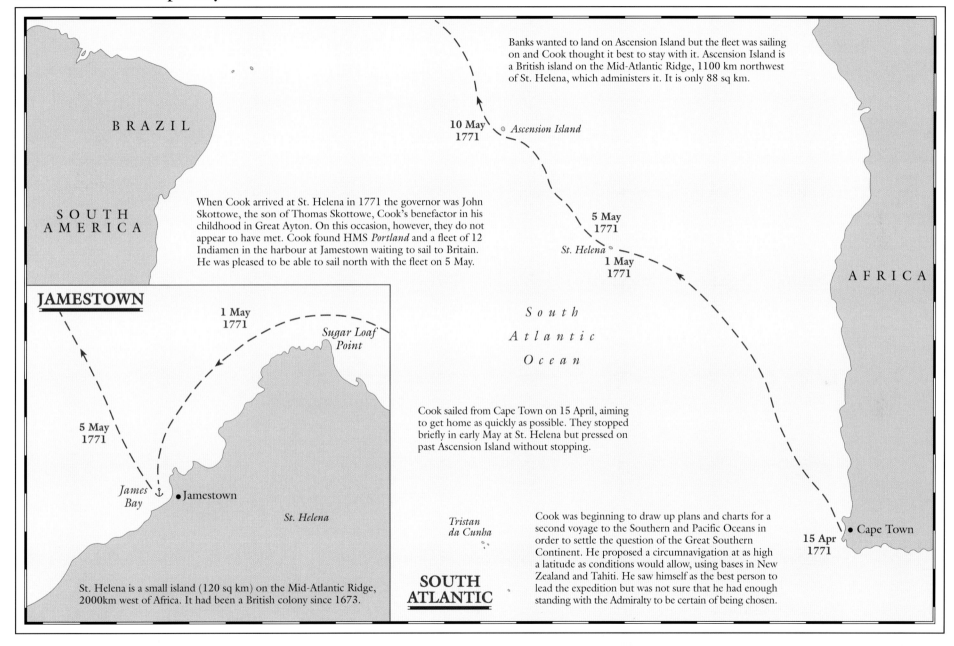

BRAZIL

SOUTH
AMERICA

Banks wanted to land on Ascension Island but the fleet was sailing on and Cook thought it best to stay with it. Ascension Island is a British island on the Mid-Atlantic Ridge, 1100 km northwest of St. Helena, which administers it. It is only 88 sq km.

10 May 1771 ○ *Ascension Island*

When Cook arrived at St. Helena in 1771 the governor was John Skottowe, the son of Thomas Skottowe, Cook's benefactor in his childhood in Great Ayton. On this occasion, however, they do not appear to have met. Cook found HMS *Portland* and a fleet of 12 Indiamen in the harbour at Jamestown waiting to sail to Britain. He was pleased to be able to sail north with the fleet on 5 May.

5 May 1771

St. Helena ○
1 May 1771

AFRICA

South Atlantic Ocean

JAMESTOWN

1 May 1771

Sugar Loaf Point

5 May 1771

James Bay ⚓ ● Jamestown

St. Helena

St. Helena is a small island (120 sq km) on the Mid-Atlantic Ridge, 2000km west of Africa. It had been a British colony since 1673.

Tristan da Cunha

SOUTH ATLANTIC

Cook sailed from Cape Town on 15 April, aiming to get home as quickly as possible. They stopped briefly in early May at St. Helena but pressed on past Ascension Island without stopping.

Cook was beginning to draw up plans and charts for a second voyage to the Southern and Pacific Oceans in order to settle the question of the Great Southern Continent. He proposed a circumnavigation at as high a latitude as conditions would allow, using bases in New Zealand and Tahiti. He saw himself as the best person to lead the expedition but was not sure that he had enough standing with the Admiralty to be certain of being chosen.

● Cape Town
15 Apr 1771

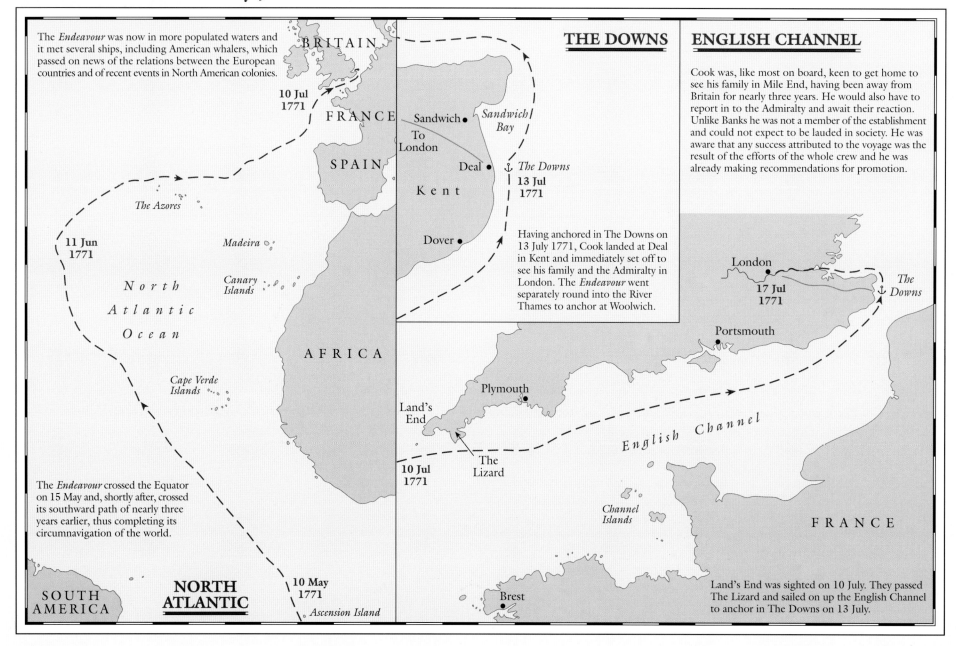

The *Endeavour* was now in more populated waters and it met several ships, including American whalers, which passed on news of the relations between the European countries and of recent events in North American colonies.

BRITAIN

FRANCE

10 Jul 1771

SPAIN

The Azores

11 Jun 1771

Madeira

North Atlantic Ocean

Canary Islands

AFRICA

Cape Verde Islands

The *Endeavour* crossed the Equator on 15 May and, shortly after, crossed its southward path of nearly three years earlier, thus completing its circumnavigation of the world.

SOUTH AMERICA

NORTH ATLANTIC

10 May 1771

Ascension Island

THE DOWNS

Sandwich •   *Sandwich Bay*

To London

Deal •   ⚓ *The Downs*

13 Jul 1771

K e n t

Dover •

Having anchored in The Downs on 13 July 1771, Cook landed at Deal in Kent and immediately set off to see his family and the Admiralty in London. The *Endeavour* went separately round into the River Thames to anchor at Woolwich.

ENGLISH CHANNEL

Cook was, like most on board, keen to get home to see his family in Mile End, having been away from Britain for nearly three years. He would also have to report in to the Admiralty and await their reaction. Unlike Banks he was not a member of the establishment and could not expect to be lauded in society. He was aware that any success attributed to the voyage was the result of the efforts of the whole crew and he was already making recommendations for promotion.

London •

17 Jul 1771   *The Downs* ⚓

Portsmouth •

Plymouth •

Land's End

English Channel

10 Jul 1771

The Lizard

Channel Islands

FRANCE

Brest •

Land's End was sighted on 10 July. They passed The Lizard and sailed on up the English Channel to anchor in The Downs on 13 July.

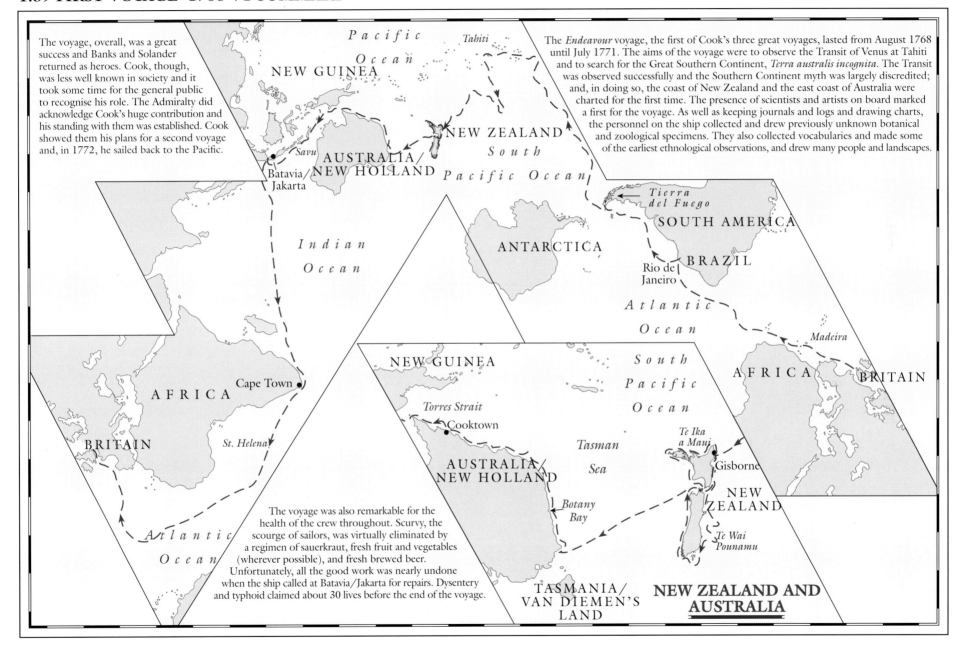

The voyage, overall, was a great success and Banks and Solander returned as heroes. Cook, though, was less well known in society and it took some time for the general public to recognise his role. The Admiralty did acknowledge Cook's huge contribution and his standing with them was established. Cook showed them his plans for a second voyage and, in 1772, he sailed back to the Pacific.

The *Endeavour* voyage, the first of Cook's three great voyages, lasted from August 1768 until July 1771. The aims of the voyage were to observe the Transit of Venus at Tahiti and to search for the Great Southern Continent, *Terra australis incognita*. The Transit was observed successfully and the Southern Continent myth was largely discredited; and, in doing so, the coast of New Zealand and the east coast of Australia were charted for the first time. The presence of scientists and artists on board marked a first for the voyage. As well as keeping journals and logs and drawing charts, the personnel on the ship collected and drew previously unknown botanical and zoological specimens. They also collected vocabularies and made some of the earliest ethnological observations, and drew many people and landscapes.

The voyage was also remarkable for the health of the crew throughout. Scurvy, the scourge of sailors, was virtually eliminated by a regimen of sauerkraut, fresh fruit and vegetables (wherever possible), and fresh brewed beer. Unfortunately, all the good work was nearly undone when the ship called at Batavia/Jakarta for repairs. Dysentery and typhoid claimed about 30 lives before the end of the voyage.

Pacific Ocean · Tahiti

NEW GUINEA

NEW ZEALAND

South Pacific Ocean

AUSTRALIA/NEW HOLLAND

Savu

Batavia/Jakarta

Indian Ocean

AFRICA

Cape Town

BRITAIN

St. Helena

Atlantic Ocean

ANTARCTICA

Tierra del Fuego

SOUTH AMERICA

BRAZIL

Rio de Janeiro

Atlantic Ocean

Madeira

AFRICA

BRITAIN

NEW GUINEA

Torres Strait

Cooktown

AUSTRALIA/NEW HOLLAND

Tasman Sea

South Pacific Ocean

Botany Bay

Te Ika a Maui

Gisborne

NEW ZEALAND

Te Wai Pounamu

TASMANIA/VAN DIEMEN'S LAND

NEW ZEALAND AND AUSTRALIA

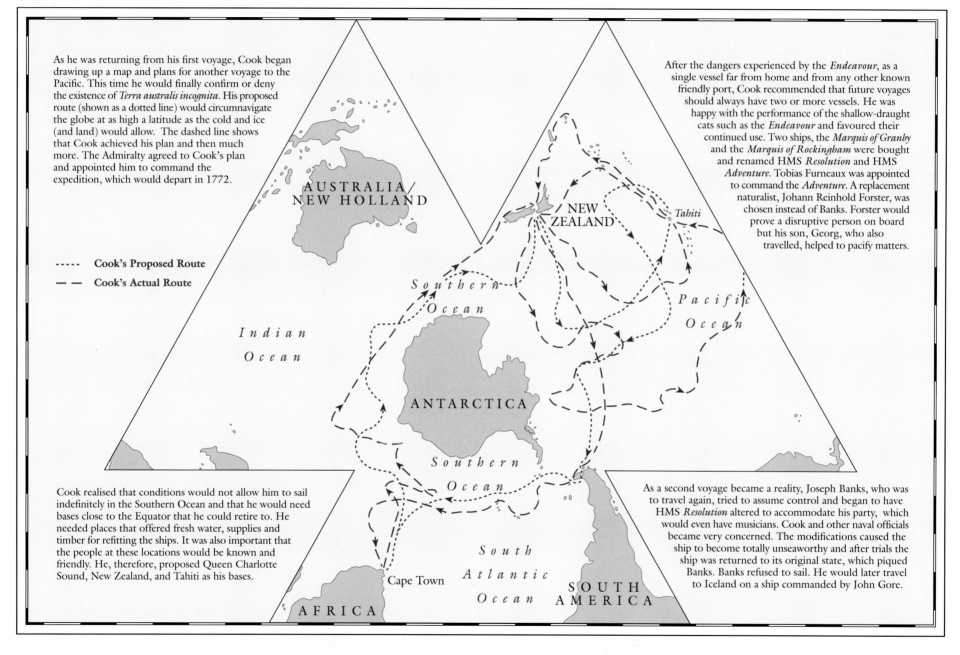

As he was returning from his first voyage, Cook began drawing up a map and plans for another voyage to the Pacific. This time he would finally confirm or deny the existence of *Terra australis incognita*. His proposed route (shown as a dotted line) would circumnavigate the globe at as high a latitude as the cold and ice (and land) would allow. The dashed line shows that Cook achieved his plan and then much more. The Admiralty agreed to Cook's plan and appointed him to command the expedition, which would depart in 1772.

- - - - - Cook's Proposed Route
— — Cook's Actual Route

After the dangers experienced by the *Endeavour*, as a single vessel far from home and from any other known friendly port, Cook recommended that future voyages should always have two or more vessels. He was happy with the performance of the shallow-draught cats such as the *Endeavour* and favoured their continued use. Two ships, the *Marquis of Granby* and the *Marquis of Rockingham* were bought and renamed HMS *Resolution* and HMS *Adventure*. Tobias Furneaux was appointed to command the *Adventure*. A replacement naturalist, Johann Reinhold Forster, was chosen instead of Banks. Forster would prove a disruptive person on board but his son, Georg, who also travelled, helped to pacify matters.

Cook realised that conditions would not allow him to sail indefinitely in the Southern Ocean and that he would need bases close to the Equator that he could retire to. He needed places that offered fresh water, supplies and timber for refitting the ships. It was also important that the people at these locations would be known and friendly. He, therefore, proposed Queen Charlotte Sound, New Zealand, and Tahiti as his bases.

As a second voyage became a reality, Joseph Banks, who was to travel again, tried to assume control and began to have HMS *Resolution* altered to accommodate his party, which would even have musicians. Cook and other naval officials became very concerned. The modifications caused the ship to become totally unseaworthy and after trials the ship was returned to its original state, which piqued Banks. Banks refused to sail. He would later travel to Iceland on a ship commanded by John Gore.

The Second Voyage

Preparations

Even before he arrived back in Britain from his First Voyage, Cook had begun formulating plans for another voyage to the Pacific. The second part of the First Voyage had involved searching for *Terra australis incognita*, and Cook still felt there was much to do in proving or denying its existence. In Britain, Alexander Dalrymple, still smarting at being excluded from the Tahiti expedition, was of the same opinion and criticised Cook for not having searched more extensively.

Cook prepared a plan whereby he would circumnavigate the South Pole at latitudes as high as cold, ice and land would allow. Knowing it would be impossible to stay for long periods in the extreme cold, Cook proposed the use of Queen Charlotte Sound in New Zealand, and Tahiti, as bases for repair and recuperation. He submitted a chart to the Admiralty showing the proposed track close to 60°S. The Admiralty agreed to the plan and nominated Cook to be in charge of the expedition, promoting him to commander. When Cook received his instructions they bore a marked resemblance to his own original suggestions.

On the *Endeavour* voyage, Cook had experienced the problems of using only one ship, so he made strong representations that two vessels should sail this time. The Admiralty agreed, and two more colliers, the *Marquis of Granby* and the *Marquis of Rockingham*, were purchased from Captain Hammond in Hull. They were renamed the *Drake* and the *Raleigh*, but it was felt such names might antagonise the Spanish, so these were abandoned for HMS *Resolution* and HMS *Adventure*. The *Resolution* was 462 tons while the *Adventure* was 340 tons (the *Endeavour* had been 369 tons), and both had been built at the Fishburn yard in Whitby.

Distractions

Joseph Banks, who had sailed with Cook on the *Endeavour*, began to formulate plans of his own for the new voyage. He would travel again himself and take a party of 15, including an artist, draughtsmen, secretaries, servants and even musicians. To accommodate all these people and their associated belongings, Banks determined that the *Resolution* be modified, and he managed to persuade the Navy to carry out changes. Cook's friend, Hugh Palliser, was now the comptroller of the Navy and he was one of the voices arguing against Banks' proposals. Banks, however, was a close friend of Lord Sandwich who had taken over as First Lord of the Admiralty, and through him Banks had his way.

The modifications took time and Cook started to worry that they would not sail on time. On 10 April the *Resolution* was sailed down the Thames to check its seaworthiness, but by the 14th, near the Nore, the pilot in charge gave up [2.01]. The ship was totally unsuitable to be taken to sea. Lieutenant Cooper, who had been acting for Cook, reported the news to Cook. The Navy Board and the Admiralty quickly decided that the *Resolution* should be returned to its original state, and sent the ship to Sheerness for this to be done. The passengers would fit the ship, not the ship the passengers.

Banks visited Sheerness and was livid at developments. He swore that he and his party would not sail if his proposals were not carried out, and he made strong representations to Lord Sandwich. Sandwich now sided with the Navy so that Banks had, in effect, excluded himself from the voyage.

Meanwhile, personnel had been assembled to crew the ships. The *Resolution*'s lieutenants were Cooper, Clerke (who had sailed on *Endeavour*) and Pickersgill. The master was Gilbert, who had worked in Newfoundland. The captain of the *Adventure* was Tobias Furneaux, who had previously sailed to the Pacific with Wallis on the *Dolphin*; his lieutenants were Shank (who lasted only as far as Cape Town), Kempe and Burney.

The last-minute loss of Banks and Solander occasioned the need to replace them quickly with naturalists, and Johann Reinhold Forster and his son, Georg, were chosen. Johann Forster, while most capable as a scientist, was not the easiest person to deal with, especially in the confines of a ship for three years, and he proved a source of friction throughout the voyage and after. Georg worked hard to smooth over many of those frictions and proved an excellent scientist. One person who did not like Forster was William Wales, the astronomer on the *Resolution*. Another astronomer, William Bayley, sailed on the *Adventure*. Another late appointment was William Hodges as artist, and he was to make some memorable records of the voyage in his paintings.

Longitude and marine chronometers

It had always been a problem for sailors to fix their exact position at sea, away from the sight of land. The development of sextants and octants had enabled latitude, the distance north or south of the Equator, to be determined reasonably correctly but longitude, the distance east or west of a prime meridian, remained a problem. At the beginning of the eighteenth century, the scale of this problem had been demonstrated when the British flagship, the *Association*, and three other warships were wrecked on the Scilly Isles in 1707 with the loss of over 2000 men. They had completely miscalculated their longitude. The disaster prompted the British Government to offer a prize to the person who solved the longitude problem and they created the Board of Longitude to oversee the matter.

John Harrison was a carpenter living in the village of Barrow in north Lincolnshire. A self-taught man, Harrison learned mechanics and astronomy and became interested in making clocks. In the 1710s he made several wooden clocks with adaptations of his own design. Aware of the Longitude prize, Harrison believed that a clock, or marine chronometer, would be the answer. He maintained that if a clock on a ship could keep the exact time relative to the time at the port of origin, whose co-ordinates were known, then the co-ordinates of the point of observation could be calculated. In 1730 he took his plans to London to show Edmond Halley, the Astronomer Royal, who referred him to George Graham, the foremost clockmaker of the time. Graham was impressed and funded Harrison's work.

Over the next 40 years Harrison produced a series of marine chronometers but had to fight the Board of Longitude for them to recognise that his instruments satisfied the requirements to win the prize. The Board usually comprised astronomers, such as Nevil Maskelyne, who believed that calculating with lunar tables was the only solution and would accept no alternative. Finally in 1773 after intervention by people such as King George III, Harrison was given proper recognition and given the final instalments of prize money.

In the late 1760s Harrison had produced his fourth in his series of timekeepers, H4. Larcum Kendal, a watchmaker, then made a copy (K1) of this instrument and Cook was asked to test it on his voyage. John Arnold, another watchmaker, made three other watches based on Harrison's originals and these were to be tested also. This work would be entrusted to the astronomers on board.

The chronometers would prove their worth and Cook, who had begun the voyage as an observer of 'a watch on trial', was a committed champion of the instrument by the voyage's end.

To Cape Town

The preparations were ready by the end of June 1772 and Cook joined the *Resolution* at Sheerness [2.01]. The ship sailed from the Thames the next day, and on 3 July it reached Plymouth, where the *Adventure* had been waiting since May. Cook received his instructions and, more interestingly, he took marine chronometers on board from Drake's Island in Plymouth Sound. They were ready to sail at last.

The *Resolution* and the *Adventure* sailed from Plymouth Sound on 13 July 1772 and followed a similar route to the one taken by the *Endeavour* four years earlier through the Bay of Biscay and past Cape Ortegal in northwest Spain [2.01]. On 13 July Cook brought the ships into Funchal harbour in Madeira where they took on board wine, beef, water and onions.

On 2 August they sailed south, passing Ferro in the Canary Islands before coming to the Cape Verde Islands. Rounding Boa Vista, the ships anchored in Praia on the south side of Sao Tiago Island. The scientists took the opportunity to go ashore and while charts were made of the harbour; they sailed again on the 15th. Henry Smock, a ship's carpenter on the *Resolution*, fell overboard on the 20th, and John Lambrecht, a midshipman, died on the *Adventure* on the 27th. The two ships managed to keep together as they crossed the Equator on 7 September. In this part of the voyage the ships were put through their paces to assess their speed and handling abilities, and the scientists trialled new instruments including a submergible thermometer for seawater temperatures and a still for converting salt water into fresh drinking water [2.02].

The ships arrived at Cape Town on 31 October. The Dutch gave them a friendly reception but were slow at producing provisions that had been requested. Cook was already behind schedule owing to Banks' modifications to the *Resolution* and these further delays frustrated him considerably. He knew how important it was to reach high latitudes around Antarctica while it was still summer; later, ice and cold conditions would hinder exploration. Every day in port was a day lost.

Others were not idle: Gilbert, the master, charted Table Bay; Hodges painted; and the Forsters collected. They even collected an assistant called Anders Sparrman, a Swede, who proved a useful addition to the party. Cook gave Furneaux further instruction in health matters, as the *Adventure* had arrived at the Cape with too many men sick (the *Resolution* had none). While in port Cook heard about other explorers, especially the French Kerguelen and Dufresne. Kerguelen was reported as having located land at 48°S, south of Mauritius, while Dufresne had been returning Aotourou, a Tahitian, to his island.

Antarctic waters

Cook was a month behind schedule when the two ships sailed from Cape Town on 23 November 1772, heading for the Antarctic [2.03]. He was keen to settle the question of the existence of a Southern Continent and needed as much sailing time as conditions would allow; summer months were therefore at a premium. By early December they were buffeted by gales, and soon after they saw their first icebergs. These prompted Cook to arrange rendezvous points with Furneaux, should the ships be separated. When dense fog followed, poor visibility and icebergs were a potentially deadly mix.

In 1739 Jacques Bouvet, a French explorer, had located a cape, Cape Circumcision, in these latitudes and Cook, wanting to confirm its location, set a course west when he reached 58°S. Christmas was celebrated in boisterous style, to Forster senior's disapproval. Cook sailed as far as 10°E without any sign of land and then turned back. He was sceptical of the cape's existence, speculating that it had been an iceberg; in fact the co-ordinates were wrong, and the cape was finally fixed in 1898 as part of Bouvet Island.

The crew experimented by loading blocks of ice from icebergs and melting them to produce drinking water. By 12 January 1773 conditions were calm and clear so Cook, at 39°E, turned south, and on 17 January they were the first known ships to cross the Antarctic Circle. The next day, having reached 67°15'S, their passage was blocked by thick ice and they were forced to retreat north. At the end of the month they were finally free of icebergs and Cook began searching for the land described by Kerguelen. They were unsuccessful and then, on 8 February in thick fog, the two vessels were separated. The *Resolution* circled for several days, firing cannons, but could not find the *Adventure*, which was deemed to have sailed off for the rendezvous.

The *Resolution* headed back to higher latitudes, narrowly missing Heard Island, and by late February had reached 60°S, 95°E. On the 24th they sailed to 61°52'S before pack ice stopped them once more and forced them back. Cook was intent on resolving the Southern Continent but he was not to know that he had virtually been at the Antarctic mainland at this point. They were able to see the *Aurora australis*, the first recorded sighting of this phenomenon. Cook sailed east, keeping the *Resolution* close to latitude 60°S for three weeks before deciding to make for warmer waters on 17 March [2.04]. He considered aiming for Van Diemen's Land (Tasmania) but at 146°E he was already too far east and steered instead for New Zealand.

Meanwhile Furneaux had sailed for the rendezvous point after separation, keeping around latitude 40–45°S, so that in early March he had arrived at Van Diemen's Land [2.04]. Tasman had visited the island 130 years earlier and the French explorer Marion Dufresne had been there the year before Furneaux. He called in briefly at Bruny Island off the south coast. He anchored in a bay now known as Adventure Bay off the east coast of the island. Furneaux restocked the ship and, while there were signs of human habitation, no contact was made. The *Adventure* left and sailed up the west coast of the island intending to check whether this land was connected to New Holland (Australia). However, having reached the eastern entrance to Bass Strait on 19 March, Furneaux struck east for New Zealand, where he arrived at Queen Charlotte Sound on 7 April.

On 25 March the southwest corner of Te Wai Pounamu, the South Island of New Zealand, was sighted and the next day Cook brought the *Resolution* into Dusky Sound, one of the inlets he had refused to enter three years earlier. The ship had been at sea for 117 days in inhospitable conditions but only had one case of scurvy and three other people sick. While the *Resolution* waited by Anchor Island, boats were dispatched to find a suitable anchorage. Pickersgill found one on the south side of the inlet; it was later called Pickersgill Harbour [2.05]. A clearing was made ashore for the astronomers to work — it earned the name Astronomer's Point — while a brewery was set up using rimu and manuka. Officers began to explore the sound and, at Cascade Point in Cascade Cove, they saw in the distance Maori who then followed them back to the ship, but no contact resulted. Cook found the Maori's camp but it was deserted. Sparrman climbed a mountain above Cascade Cove, which is now named after him. Hodges, meanwhile, painted the waterfall in Cascade Cove and several other features.

More exploration took place in order to shoot wildfowl and seals for food. Many local features were named for the animals shot there, and the detailed charts compiled show Woodhen Cove, Duck Cove and Seal Rocks. Luncheon Cove and Supper Cove denote the meals enjoyed. Gradually contact was established with local Maori. Gifts were exchanged with a small family on Indian Island, and others visited the ship.

Cook explored the Acheron Passage and realised it gave egress to the sea so that, when they sailed on 30 April, he decided to leave via that route. Progress was very slow and it took until 5 May to reach Passage Point. Pickersgill and the Forsters spent two days up Wet Jacket Arm, while Cook investigated Breaksea Sound and Gilbert charted the passage to the sea. On 11 May they sailed back out into the open sea and north up the coast [2.04]. Cape Farewell was rounded on 17 May but before making Queen Charlotte Sound six large waterspouts were seen and drawn. There was great relief when they arrived at Ship Cove to find the *Adventure* safely anchored there. The *Adventure* had been there for five weeks and Furneaux had the ship stripped for overhaul. Cook, though, gave instructions to prepare to sail immediately.

The First Island Sweep

Cook was not about to sit idly in Queen Charlotte Sound over the winter months and gave instructions to prepare for a sweep of the Central Pacific in order to disprove the existence of the Southern Continent. On 7 June 1773, when the reunited *Resolution* and *Adventure* set sail, Cook's intention was to sail east in latitudes 41–46°S as far as longitude 135–140°W and then make for Tahiti. Leaving through Cook Strait, the ships sailed as far as 133°W without seeing any sign of land, then turned north [2.06].

Furneaux reported that there were cases of scurvy aboard the *Adventure* and their cook had died, so Cook sent over a replacement. On 6 August at latitude 25°S, and when no land had been seen, the ships turned west to sail through the Tuamotus to Tahiti, which was reached on the 15th. As they came to Tahiti, Cook was not on deck and their approach was too far south, at the island's southeastern corner, so that the ships nearly ran onto the fringing reef [2.07]. When he had walked around the island four years earlier, Cook had identified Tautira as a potential safe harbour and it was to here that he was now heading. They managed to sail through a gap in the reef but not without difficulties, and several anchors were lost.

On 17 August the ships anchored at Cook's Anchorage near Tautira in Vaitepiha Bay, where they were received warmly [2.07]. The local chief was now Vehiatua, who as a boy in 1769 had accompanied Cook on part of his walk, and the two men met on the 23rd. Gilbert managed to recover some of the anchors, while Hodges painted scenes of the Vaitepiha River and valley. Another anchor was retrieved years later and is an exhibit in the Museum of the Pacific and the Islands at Punaauia [1.08].

Cook decided to leave Tautira on 24 August, and two days later arrived at Matavai Bay [2.07]. Things had changed since Cook's last visit, with two wars apparently having taken place, and new people were in power. Tu, based in Pare, was now chief, and he visited Cook on 27 August. Entertainments were organised for the visitors when Cook returned Tu's visit the following day. In both Tautira and Matavai provisions were in short supply, probably as a result of the wars, and Cook, realising the situation would not improve, decided to leave. The ships sailed on 1 September for Huahine and the other Leeward Islands of the Society Islands.

They reached Huahine the next day, and Cook sailed the *Resolution* through Passe Avapeihi to anchor near Fare [2.08]. He had to send his boats though to assist the *Adventure*, which nearly hit the reef. Ori, who was still chief on Huahine, greeted Cook warmly, and gifts and compliments were exchanged. Unlike Tahiti, provisions were in good supply and trade was brisk. But Sparrman went inland, where he was robbed and stripped, and this led to a tense situation. Ori offered himself as hostage, but the matter was quickly sorted out and, since the ships were ready, Cook determined to leave. On 7 September they sailed with an extra passenger on the *Adventure*. This was Mai (later known as Omai) who would gain fame in London.

They sailed across to Raiatea and rounded the south end of the island [2.08]. Cook modified his charts as he sailed past, fixing the islands of Haaio and Nao Nao and Vaihuti Bay, before reaching the anchorage at Passe Rautoanui. Orio, the chief, welcomed Cook lavishly with entertainments, dancing, theatre and music every day of the visit. Pickersgill was charged with obtaining fresh supplies and even went north to Tahaa for fresh pigs. The ships left Raiatea on 17 September and Cook, having changed his mind about returning straight to New Zealand, headed instead for some islands, the Tonga group, that Tasman had visited in 1643.

A few days later, on 23 September, an atoll with two small uninhabited islands that Cook called the Hervey Islands were seen [2.06]. They were Manuae and Te Au O Tu; later, they were included in the Cook Islands. Sailing on without stopping, the ships arrived at the Tongan Group on 2 October [2.09].

Tasman and Visscher had visited two islands that they called Amsterdam and Middelburg, and Cook was keen to fix the islands' position. The *Resolution* and *Adventure* approached Middelburg from the east and rounded the south of the island where, passing between it and a smaller island, Kalau, they sailed up to anchor off its northwest shore. The anchorage was called English Roads while the island's traditional name is 'Eua. Cook went ashore at Ohonua to meet Chief Taione (Tionee), and relations were most friendly. Everyone was impressed by the island and its agriculture and well-tended gardens but the Tongans showed no desire to trade, so Cook decided to move on to another island visible to the northwest.

They sailed across to Tongatapu (Tasman's Amsterdam) on 3 October [2.09]. After passing the island's southern point, Houma Toloa or Cook Point, many canoes accompanied the ships to an anchorage, Van Dieman's Roads, at the northwest of the island. Cook was soon introduced to a chief, Ataongo (Otago), who would look after him during his stay, but the social structure of Tonga was complex and Cook never met the King. However, the reception was so cordial that Cook would later give the name 'The Friendly Islands' to the whole island group. For their four days there trade was brisk in coconuts, bananas, pigs, and Cook, despite the short stay, gave a detailed and favourable description of Tongatapu and 'Eua. He also learned about more islands to the north.

Cook could not afford to stay longer as he needed to be ready to return to Antarctic waters at the beginning of summer [2.06]. They departed, therefore, on 8 October, heading for New Zealand. The tiny island of 'Ata was passed the next day. The crossing was uneventful until Table Cape on the Mahia Peninsula was sighted on the 21st. Sailing down the east coast of Te Ika a Maui, Cook gave livestock to Maori who came out to the ships in canoes. When they were near Cape Palliser, gales started that lasted over a week, causing the ships to ply back and forward until, on the 30th, they were separated. The *Resolution* made it into Cook Strait on 2 November and only the tides prevented it entering what would later be called Wellington Harbour; it arrived at Queen Charlotte Sound on the 3rd. The *Adventure* was not there and did not appear.

The Second Island Sweep: to the Antarctic

Cook remained at Queen Charlotte Sound for three weeks repairing the *Resolution* and waiting for the *Adventure* to arrive. By 25 November 1773 the *Resolution* was ready and Cook, who needed to be in the Southern Ocean and could not wait any longer, sailed out into Cook Strait. He spent two days looking in the strait for signs of the *Adventure* before giving up and sailing south. Cook did not expect to find any land north of 60°S and so he plunged south to cross

that latitude on 11 December [2.10]. The next day the first iceberg was seen and three days later the ship was surrounded by loose pack ice. The *Resolution* crossed the Antarctic Circle again on 20 December but the pack ice was always close by and conditions on board were very cold, with ice covering everything.

Many of the crew were sick, so Cook decided to head north for warmth and to check a space on his chart of the Pacific. He continued north to latitude 47°S in longitude 122°W without meeting any land; then, to everyone else's surprise and disappointment, Cook turned once more and struck southwards. By 26 January 1774 they had crossed the Antarctic Circle at longitude 109°W in mild but foggy conditions. They were surrounded by very large icebergs until, on 30 January, having reached 71°0'S, they came to the edge of an impenetrable pack ice that forced them to turn and retreat. It was, by a long way, the furthest south and closest to the South Pole that anyone had been. Both Vancouver and Sparrman claimed to be the individual who was furthest south.

William Wales, the astronomer on the *Resolution*, would later teach at Christ's Hospital School where one of his pupils was Samuel Taylor Coleridge. It is most probable that Wales told stories about his voyage with Cook, and that Coleridge's poem, 'The Ryme of the Ancient Mariner', was partly inspired by the voyage. Many verses show close similarities to descriptions in Cook's journal for this voyage.

Even Cook was now ready to give up searching for *Terra australis incognita* and he wrote, 'I, who had ambition not only to go farther than anyone had done before, but as far as it was possible for man to go, was not sorry at meeting with this interruption.' Cook reckoned that if a Southern Continent did exist it did so at such high latitudes as to be too cold and inhospitable.

Easter Island and the Marquesas

The *Resolution* now worked its way north to warmer waters close to longitude 100°W, with Cook looking for islands designated on Dalrymple's chart of the Pacific [2.10]. Land had been recorded by Juan Fernandez in 1563 and by Edward Davis in 1687, but their locations were vague and Cook saw it as his duty to check them out. By 22 February he had reached 36°S and turned west to sail through the area where the land sighted by Fernandez was supposed to be.

In late February Cook fell seriously ill with stomach complaints and handed over command to Lieutenant Cooper. His condition became critical and only constant nursing by Surgeon Patten, together with some help from the elder Forster, saved him. Forster had his dog killed and made a broth from it, and this was carefully fed to Cook. It is now believed that Cook had a problem with his gall bladder and a paralysed bowel. Given that he was now 46 and had been at sea for a long time, often in terrible conditions, it is not surprising that he should succumb to illness.

The ship meanwhile continued north without sighting any land. The weather was changing and the crew now complained about the heat and a lack of drinking water (parallels again with 'The Ancient Mariner'). In early March the *Resolution* turned west looking for Easter Island, and on the 13th the island — one of the most remote inhabited islands in the world —was sighted [2.11]. It is probable that Davis Island and Easter Island are one and the same. After meeting the people on the island, Cook realised that the Polynesians had reached this distant spot, and called it Te Pito o Te Henua (it later acquired the name Rapa Nui). The Dutch explorer Jacob Roggeveen, who had visited in 1722, gave it its more common name.

The *Resolution* approached the island from the southeast but no harbours or landing places could be seen on the south coast. Cook skirted along the coast and around South Cape before sailing up the west coast, but there was no safe harbour there either. He returned south to stand off and anchor off a small settlement called Hanga Roa. Going ashore on 14 March, Cook found he could communicate with the local people albeit with difficulty. Some trading took place, but fresh drinking water was in short supply.

Cook sent a party ashore to explore the island; he was still too weak to accompany them. The Forsters, Wales and Pickersgill all gave Cook accounts of what they had seen and where they had gone. Local people had accompanied them, with one man carrying a white flag in the lead across what proved to be a treeless and barren terrain that had no surface water and little cultivation. The party crossed to the south coast at Vaihu and then walked to the eastern end of the island, which is 18 kilometres long. They climbed a hill (Puakatiki?) that gave them views of the south and north coasts before returning. The party was fascinated by the many large statues (moai) standing or lying on platforms (ahu), mainly around the coast. Hodges painted one group of statues near Orito.

The ship was under sail on 16 March and they departed the next day [2.10]. Cook was ill again as they sailed north, looking for islands known from Mendana's voyage from Peru in 1595. The Spanish had called these islands Las Marquesas de Mendoca and the name had contracted to the Marquesas, though the Polynesian name was Te Fenua Enata. The islands were thought to be in latitude 10°S, so the *Resolution* started sailing west on 29 March and sighted Fatu Huku on 6 April [2.12].

They sailed through the strait between the islands of Hiva Oa and Tahuata, searching for a harbour described by Mendana on the west coast of Tahuata. They came to the safe harbour or Vaitahu Bay on 8 April. Water and provisions were available and trade began, but misunderstandings arose and a Tahuatan was shot dead. Trade continued but with suspicions on both sides. Someone from the *Resolution* started using red feathers from Tonga as currency and this undermined all other tender, so Cook decided it was time to leave. The *Resolution* sailed from Vaitahu on 12 April and made for the west coast of Hiva Oa, but no landing place could be seen. The ship then headed for Tahiti without seeing the other islands of the Marquesas further to the north. Despite the short stay and the limited contact, the Marquesan people and islands left a very favourable impression on Cook. Few women had been seen, but the men were held to be the most handsome in the Pacific.

To Tahiti and Tonga again

After four days the *Resolution* came to the Northern Tuamotu Islands, which presented another challenge for Cook [2.13]. The atolls and reefs required careful navigation, so Gilbert, the master, was dispatched in a small boat to guide the ship through the maze. On 17 April they arrived at Takaroa, where Cook and Forster went ashore, but the local people did not make them welcome and they moved on to neighbouring Takapoto. After a quick inspection there Cook continued to a cluster of small atolls to which he gave the name Palliser's Isles; they include Apataki, Arutua and Toau.

On 22 April 1774 Cook sailed once more into Matavai Bay on Tahiti [2.14]. Remembering the lack of supplies the previous August, he did not intend to stay long, but was surprised to find pigs and other supplies in profusion. Cook was also amazed by the spectacle he saw a few days later at Pare, where over 300 double canoes were assembled. Cook counted 160 war canoes and 170 smaller support canoes with about 7000 men on board. The purpose of the fleet was uncertain but an attack on the neighbouring island of Moorea seemed most likely. To'ofa was in control of the fleet and seemed to have assumed equal status to Chief Tu. A tense situation arose on 8 May when a musket was stolen, but it was retrieved and, to diffuse matters, Cook gave a fireworks display.

They left Tahiti on 14 May and sailed across to Huahine where they had a lukewarm reception and their stay was marked by several incidents, including Captain Forster's servant Scholient being attacked and robbed. Cook moved on to Raiatea to anchor inside Passe Rautoanui on the west coast, and Chief Orio put on elaborate entertainments featuring his daughter Poetua. They were able to trade, as provisions were plentiful, and they left the island on 4 June. The next day they passed the outlying island of Maupihaa and began following a more northerly course than they had on the first island sweep [2.13].

Two weeks later they came to an atoll where Cook took the ship in close while Gilbert went ashore to examine the string of uninhabited, small islets dotting the fringe of the atoll [2.13]. There was no passage for the *Resolution* into the lagoon so it sailed on. One islet is now called Cook's, while another cluster of small islets has the name Small Cooks. The whole atoll is called Palmerston Atoll and is part of the Cook Islands. On 22 June Cook approached another island, which he skirted to the north while small boats tried to land. As the crew tried to climb a cliff near Tuapa, local people threw coral at them and they retreated to the ship. A second attempt to land was made near Alofi, with the same result. Cook called this island (Niue) Savage Island because of their hostile reception.

Pressing on, Cook reached the Tongan Islands again on 25 June, but this time he was further north in the Ha'apai Group [2.16]. Cook was aiming for Nomuka, or Rotterdam as it was called on Visscher's chart of Tasman's voyage of 1643. He sailed south of Telekitonga and between Tonumea and Mango to arrive from the southwest at Nomuka, where he anchored in the middle of the north coast. The island was able to supply provisions and fresh water in plenty, so trade was brisk. Surgeon Patten and Lieutenant Clerke had their muskets taken, and when they were recovered Cook thought it best to leave.

On 29 June Cook sailed north to the west of Tungua, heading for two interesting islands. On the 30th Cook sailed through the channel between Kao and Tofua, an active volcano. Low cloud prevented those on board from seeing whether the volcano was active and Cook was not prepared to go ashore to investigate. On the stretch from Nomuka to Tofua, Cook had been able to watch Tongan canoes and admire how they were sailed, and their capabilities for speed and manoeuvrability.

Fifteen years later the mutiny on the *Bounty* took place off Tofua. Captain Bligh, who would be the master on the *Resolution* on Cook's Third Voyage, landed his longboat on Tofua but was attacked, losing his quartermaster.

New Hebrides/Vanuatu

In 1606 Quiros, the Spanish explorer, had visited islands that he called Tierra del Espiritu Santo, but their exact location had remained unknown. As he left Tonga, Cook was hoping to find those islands. He kept a course westward in latitude 20°S, and on 3 July he arrived at Vatoa, an outlier of the Fiji Group of islands [2.13]. Some crew went ashore searching for water and turtles but returned with neither. This was the only occasion Cook visited Fiji. The *Resolution* continued westward before turning northwest on 11 July.

The island of Maewo, one of those visited by Quiros, was sighted on 16 July. Cook rounded the north of the island before sailing south between Maewo and Aoba and then down the west coast of Pentecost [2.18]. Though Cook never landed on Pentecost, some rocks near Ateu Point are called Captain Cook's Rocks. He was now surrounded by islands and headed southwest for Malekula, where he found an inlet and anchored the *Resolution* on the 22nd [2.20]. Cook went ashore only to find that the people were Melanesian not Polynesian so communication was extremely difficult. He exchanged green branches with one of the 400–500 people who had assembled on the beach. The British were not encouraged to trade but were allowed to cut wood. Cook and Forster were able to visit a local village. An incident then occurred between the two parties and Cook thought it wise to leave. Cook was not to know that the Malekulans regarded their visitors as ghosts and believed there was no need to supply food or water, as ghosts do not eat or drink.

They sailed from the inlet, Port Sandwich, and turned south. William Wales called a nearby group of small islands Maskelyne's Isles (after the Astronomer Royal). The bay between these islands and Malekula is Cook Bay. *Resolution* continued past the islands of Epi and Emae (a reef to the west of Emae is called Cook Reef) to arrive at a group of small islands that Cook called the Shepherd Islands [2.18]. Turning southwest they passed between Mataso and Wot Rock to arrive at Efate. They passed to the east of this island and could see further islands to the south, but the *Resolution* became becalmed in light winds. Gradually it worked its way to the first island, Erromango.

At the beginning of August, Cook took the *Resolution* down the west coast of Erromango in search of a harbour, but the winds reversed and the ship was forced back north [2.19]. Gilbert was sent off to investigate Elizabeth Bay but Cook had to recall him when they were driven north. Rounding the north of the island, Cook came to a large bay and began looking for an anchorage. Clerke landed on a small island, Goat Island, to search for water but was unsuccessful. Cook in the meantime had anchored in Polenia Bay on 4 August and attempted to land, but his reception was cool if courteous. As he was invited to step ashore, Cook became suspicious and gave orders to return to the ship. A fight broke out and marines fired their muskets, killing four locals. Back on board, winds shifted, and Cook issued instructions to leave. He took the ship around a headland that he named Traitor's Head (Pointe Uvwore), and sailed for another island visible in the distance. The bay south of Pointe Uvwore is named Cook Bay even though Cook never called there.

The next island was Tanna, and Cook anchored the *Resolution* in an inlet near the southeastern corner of the island. The headland to the east of this inlet,

Port Resolution, is called Cape Cook. They were met by a large crowd of local people but the reception was lukewarm and, although the ship stayed for two weeks, relations remained distant. The crew was able to fish and get fresh water, wood and some supplies, but Cook always set a guard of marines when anyone went ashore. The volcano of Yasur overlooks the inlet, but the British were discouraged from exploring it or going anywhere far from the beach. One Tanna man, Paowang, did become friendly and he and a chief were entertained on the ship.

Before they sailed on 20 August a sentry overreacted and shot dead a Tanna man. Cook was shocked and ordered the marine to be flogged but the ship's officers argued his case and he was let off. The *Resolution* sailed east to view two islands, Aniwa and Futuna, but did not land and returned around the south of Tanna to head north past the west of Erromango. One further island, Anatom, lay to the south, unvisited, but Cook felt he had reached the end of the island chain. By the 23rd the ship was off the west coast of Malekula [2.20].

On 24 August, Cook sailed east through the Bougainville Strait between Malekula and Malo, and changed course north along the coast of a larger island. Cook correctly identified this island with Quiros' Tierra del Espiritu Santo, and honoured the Spanish explorer by naming a headland Cape Quiros. Rounding this cape he entered St. Phillip and St. James Bay where he located Quiros' Jordan River flowing into the bay. The island's name has been shortened to Espiritu Santo. The *Resolution* sailed around the northwest cape of the island, Cape Cumberland, and sailed down the west coast before leaving these islands on 1 September 1774.

Bougainville had visited the northern members of the island group and had named them the Great Cyclades. Cook, though, called them the New Hebrides and this name remained until the country gained independence and became known as Vanuatu. Cook's chart of the New Hebrides is one of the early wonders of hydrographic charting, being completed largely by running survey in only four weeks of actual sailing time.

New Caledonia

Sailing south from the New Hebrides, the *Resolution* came to more land three days later on 4 September [2.21]. A reef could be seen fronting land that stretched northwest to southeast. The first bit of land sighted was called Cape Colnett after the midshipman who saw it. Cook stood off until a passage through the reef was located the next day, and he then sailed the ship into a safe anchorage, accompanied by local canoes. Going ashore at Koulnoue M'Balan beach, Cook was received courteously by people who were Melanesian but different from the people he had met in the New Hebrides. A chief, Tibooma, met them and took them to the village of Baio for water. The district was called Balade. Meanwhile an observatory was set up on Poudiou Island, close by the anchorage, to see an eclipse of the sun. A white monument on the island records the visit.

Cook went off to climb Mount Vengaya, south of Balade, and from its summit he could see the wide valley of the River Diahot and, in the distance, the island's parallel south coast. The dryness, the vegetation and the nature of the countryside reminded Cook strongly of New Holland, not so far away to the west in the same latitude. Cook sent parties off along the coast to explore and locate a passage via the north to the other coast recently seen from Mount Vengaya.

On 13 September they sailed north on Gilbert's recommendation, passing Balabio and Belap Islands and keeping a safe distance from the reef (later known as Recif de Cook or Cook Reef). However, the reef persisted to the north and no route west was found, so Cook turned near a sandy isle, Ongombua, and sailed back past Balade. He sailed on, wary of the reef after his time on the Great Barrier Reef, but keeping the coast in sight. They were sufficiently close to be puzzled by the sight of tower-like structures that were increasing in numbers. Cook thought they were trees and was keen to get ashore to investigate. By 24 September they had arrived at the southern end of the island, and Cook named two headlands Cape Coronation and Queen Charlotte's Foreland [2.22].

Reefs and gales prevented the *Resolution* rounding Queen Charlotte's Foreland, and they were forced further southeast near to another smaller island that appeared to be covered in the 'towers'. Cook worked the ship back towards the larger island but found the reefs closing in, forcing him to anchor off a tiny islet. This was Amere Island, Cook's Botany Island. The botanists were able at last to inspect the 'towers' and confirm they were trees, New Caledonia pines, which have a Latin name honouring Cook — *Araucaria columnaris cooki*. The carpenters felled some trees, which were deemed most suitable as ships' timber.

From the little he could learn from the local people, they had no name for the whole of the large island, so Cook now gave it the name of New Caledonia. Sailing down its coast, it had reminded him of Scotland. The smaller island he called the Isle of Pines, though it was called Kounie locally. A headland to the west Cook called Prince of Wales Foreland (it is actually on Ouen Island and not on Grand Terre, as the large island is also known). The reefs prevented the *Resolution* from leaving in any direction but the way it had approached Amere Island. Cook looked for a route near Totea Island but soon gave up and headed southeast for New Zealand on 1 October 1774.

Norfolk Island and back to New Zealand

The *Resolution* sailed southeast and south for several days, and then turned west before sighting another small island on 10 October [2.23]. Cook brought the ship to anchor off the north coast and, taking two of the small boats, went ashore. The flora and fauna reminded him of New Zealand: there was a similar flax, and many of the birds were clearly related. In one respect, though, it was like New Caledonia, having its own version of the tall pine tree (*Araucaria excelsia*, the Norfolk Island pine). He saw no signs of human habitation during his short visit. He quickly reboarded the *Resolution* and sailed off, noting as he left several smaller islands off the south coast of the island he called Norfolk Island.

They neared Cape Egmont on the west coast of Te Ika a Maui, New Zealand, on 17 October, and anchored in Ship Cove in Queen Charlotte Sound the next day. The *Adventure* was not in the cove but there was evidence it had been there since the *Resolution*'s last visit. The bottle left for Furneaux had gone, and trees had been felled recently with axes, but there was no message from the other ship. Repairs and restocking of the ship's provisions began straight away as

Cook was keen to be on his way and to round Cape Horn.

Cook visited Motuara Island but found it to be uninhabited and its vegetable plots untended. He met Maori from whom he received various stories, some contradictory, about killings and ships sinking. The Maori themselves were not at ease. In early November Cook took the pinnace to investigate an inlet further up Queen Charlotte Sound. He had suspected when he climbed Cook's Lookout four years earlier that this inlet connected the sound to Cook Strait and he now found he was correct. Interestingly, a chart of this passage (later called Tory Channel) by Peter Fannin, the master of the *Adventure*, shows he had independently explored the passage.

The *Adventure*'s tale

After the *Adventure* and the *Resolution* became separated in November 1773 off Cape Palliser, the *Resolution* was able to make it into Queen Charlotte Sound four days later, but the *Adventure* was not so fortunate and spent several days being buffeted by gales off Cape Palliser. Furneaux traded with Maori near the cape but was then blown well to the north and, in great need of water and wood, put into Tolaga Bay on 9 November [2.06]. The *Adventure* stayed here until the 12th but, having left the bay, fresh gales forced the ship back. The rigging needed repairs and the ship sailed on the 16th into yet more gales, which it endured out at sea. Finally, on 30 November Furneaux anchored the *Adventure* in Queen Charlotte Sound, only to find the *Resolution* had been and gone five days earlier.

They found a message from Cook in Ship Cove describing what had happened to the *Resolution* and Cook's plans [2.23]. No further rendezvous was suggested. Furneaux set about repairing the ship and restocking water and supplies. A chart by the master, Fannin, shows that he explored well up the sound beyond present-day Picton and also confirmed that Tory Channel connected the sound to Cook Strait.

On 17 December the cutter with Rowe, a midshipman, and nine others aboard set off to the east side of the sound to cut fresh greens. It did not return. The next day Furneaux sent Lieutenant Burney in the launch to find out what had happened. They rowed past Long Island and through East Bay to Wharehunga Bay (Grass Cove) where they found remains of the cutter and, more ominously, remains of the cutter's crew. Burney and Fannin saw several hundred Maori and thought it wise to withdraw to the ship. Furneaux, hearing the news, decided to leave straight away and, with little chance of meeting Cook, set off for Britain.

The *Adventure* sailed on 23 December and crossed the Pacific near latitude 60°S without seeing any land [2.24]. They passed well to the south of Cape Horn in late January 1774 but cold forced them further north in the South Atlantic where Furneaux looked once more for Cape Circumcision (Bouvet Island) without success [2.26]. On 19 March the *Adventure* anchored at Cape Town. It stayed there until 16 April, then sailed for Britain, which it reached on 14 July. (Cook at this time was approaching the New Hebrides two-thirds of the way through his second island sweep.)

Across the Pacific to Tierra del Fuego

Cook set off from Queen Charlotte Sound at the north end of Te Wai Pounamu, New Zealand, on 10 November 1774, exactly two and a half years since he had sailed from Plymouth. By now he and his crew were ready to go home but even so Cook was determined to tidy up loose ends. He proposed to cross the Pacific to Cape Horn and then have another look for Cape Circumcision before sailing up the Atlantic to Britain.

The *Resolution* passed through Cook Strait and headed south, holding a course between those taken on his two Pacific sweeps [2.24]. When they reached latitude 55°S, that of Tierra del Fuego, they headed east on a course that would take them through some parts of the ocean as yet unexplored. On 17 December they arrived at Cape Deseado on Desolation Island after an uneventful passage and no signs of land.

A map of the Pacific with the criss-cross of routes taken by Cook on the *Endeavour* and the *Resolution* shows how Cook was now able to declare that no significant large land masses remained to be located in the South Pacific. If anything did remain out there, it was small or lay in cold and inhospitable latitudes. The map also shows how Cook fixed the positions of islands visited by earlier explorers such as Tasman, Quiros and Mendana, whose surveying and cartographic abilities and tools were far short of those of Cook. In fact, the map that Cook nearly single-handedly produced was virtually identical to the one we know today.

Cook followed the coast of Tierra del Fuego, which comprised hundreds of small islands, some of which were charted and named but many of which were not, making for Cape Horn [2.25]. The *Resolution* was kept at a safe distance from the shore and soon passed the Grafton Islands, Noir Island, Tower Rocks and the Gilbert Islands (named after the master). A large inlet passed on the 19th is now called Cook Bay. Cook needed provisions and to check the state of the *Resolution*. He found an inlet suitable for his purpose on the 20th, and took the ship into it. He stayed here for eight days over Christmas, earning the inlet the name Christmas Sound. Fresh water and vegetables were obtained while Cook, the Forsters, Pickersgill and Clerke made sorties exploring the sound. Local Fuegan people visited the ship and gifts were exchanged. Various birds were shot for food, and features around the sound were named for the birds shot there. A towering rock on Waterman Island was called York Minster.

The *Resolution* sailed on 28 December and rounded Cape Horn safely the next day before making for the Bay of Good Success to check for signs of the *Adventure*. Pickersgill went ashore but found no trace of the other ship having been there. Sailing on, Cook went through the Strait of Le Maire and turned east along the north coast of Staten Island. He came to a group of small islands, the New Year's Isles, on 31 December 1774. Cook anchored the ship in the lee of the largest island, Observatory Island, and sent Gilbert to explore an inlet on Staten Island. Gilbert charted what proved to be a good harbour, which he named New Year's Harbour, and some isles at its mouth, Gull Isles. Two days later they sailed east, passing a bay, later called Cook Bay, and rounding Cape St. John before heading off to explore the South Atlantic.

The South Atlantic, Dalrymple's chart and Bouvet again

Cook had in his possession a chart prepared by Alexander Dalrymple that showed various features seen or thought to have been seen by earlier explorers in the South Atlantic Ocean [2.26]. On 2 January 1775 Cook left Staten Island intending to confirm or deny these features. A large gulf, the Golfo de St. Sebastiano, was supposed to exist and Antoine de La Roche reported seeing land southeast of Tierra del Fuego when he was blown off course after rounding Cape Horn in 1675.

The *Resolution* sailed through the reported location for Golfo de St. Sebastiano without detecting any sign of land, but they did sight land on 14 January, well to the east of Dalrymple's supposed location [2.26]. Gregorio Jerez, in the *Leon* in 1756, had seen an island that he called San Pedro, and it was possibly this that Cook now began to investigate. On the 17th Cook worked the ship through a strait between Willis and Bird Islands and began sailing along the north coast of what appeared to be a mountainous, snow-covered and barren land [2.27]. He named Capes North and Buller and the Bay of Isles before anchoring at the mouth of an inlet.

Cook and Forster took a small boat and landed in the inlet that Cook called Possession Bay. Only three species of plant were found in the cold and bleak environment. Fur seals and various birds, including king penguins, were seen but the large glaciers flowing into the bay had the most effect when one 'calved an iceberg' with a huge bang while Cook's party was there. A small inlet close to where the *Resolution* anchored is now called Cook Bay. The *Resolution* continued along the coast, and by 19 January Cook could see more land to the southeast. On the 20th they rounded Cape Disappointment and could see the coast heading northwest, confirming the land to be an island that Cook called South Georgia. Smaller islands were named after crew members including Pickersgill and Cooper's Islands.

Cook was puzzled that land in 55°S should have such a cold and inhospitable climate with no flowing water and scarcely any vegetation. He could not account for the huge amount of pack ice he had encountered, and wondered whether glaciers were the source of it. They then sailed east to locate the land sighted earlier, but a gale and then dense fog made sailing difficult. On the 23rd they found the land to be only rocks, covered in seabirds, and Cook called them Clerke's Rocks after his officer. The *Resolution* headed off southeast and then south to reach 60°S where it was enveloped in very thick fog.

Cook did not want to meet pack ice in the fog so he turned east on 27 January. Progress was slow, but on the 31st a towering rock was discerned through the fog. Freezland Rock was named after the seaman who first sighted it, while more land seen behind the rock was called Cape Bristol [2.28]. Cook turned and, retracing his path, found more land. The Forsters suggested the name Southern Thule, equating the place with the furthest point south. With visibility continuing to be very poor, Cook could not be sure whether the pieces of land seen were joined or separate islands. He decided on the former and called all his sightings capes; the stretch of water between Thule and Bristol he called Forster Bay (now Forster Passage).

The *Resolution* next sailed north on 1 February, passing two more 'capes', Montagu and Saunders. Cook changed course northeast, while to the northwest he saw a cluster of small islands, the Candlemas Islands (a large rock in Nelson Strait between the two larger islands is called Cook Rock). On 5 February he struck south again and, since he could see no further trace of land, decided the capes of the previous days had been small islands that he grouped and named as the South Sandwich Islands. Russian explorers later located three more islands to the north that belonged to the group; they also showed that Southern Thule was in fact three islands, the middle of which they called Cook Island. Cook made no attempt to land on any of the South Sandwich Islands.

Cook turned east and for eight days sailed close to 58°S through many icebergs [2.26]. He then altered course northeast, aiming for where Bouvet's Cape Circumcision was meant to be, but the longitude was wrong and he was already too far east. By the 25th Cook had despaired of ever finding Bouvet's cape and decided to head north for Cape Town. They had circumnavigated the world in high latitudes as set out in their instructions, and had finally laid to rest the idea of a Great Southern Continent. Two more small islands were shown on Dalrymple's chart, Denia and Marseveen, and Cook made a quick effort to find

them. He soon dismissed their existence (rightly) and headed on to Cape Town, where he anchored in Table Bay on 22 March 1775.

To Britain via the Atlantic

Cook found waiting for him a letter from Furneaux explaining what had happened to the *Adventure* since their separation. It included information about the cutter crew's demise at Wharehunga Bay.

Cook was detained at Cape Town for five weeks while repairs were carried out, especially to the rudder. While the repairs were being carried out, Cook met Julien Marie Crozet, a French explorer, and from him learned about French voyages and discoveries in the Indian and Pacific Oceans. The meeting fired Cook with new ideas for future voyages. Sparrman, who had joined the Forsters as a naturalist two years earlier, left the ship here to resume his studies of the Cape district. Cook sent ahead copies of his journals on board an Indiaman, the *Ceres*.

The *Resolution* departed Cape Town on 27 April in company with another Indiaman, the *Dutton* [2.29]. Using Kendal's chronometer, Cook was able to sail a direct course to St. Helena and tell the *Dutton* exactly when they would reach the island. True to the prediction, the ships anchored at Jamestown, St. Helena, on 15 May, but Cook's own reception was less than warm. At Cape Town he had seen a copy of John Hawkesworth's edition of the journal of Cook's first voyage, which contained unflattering descriptions of St. Helena, and now he found the book had reached the island as well. Cook had to do some quick diplomacy, but as a joke he still received many wheelbarrows: Hawkesworth had said, incorrectly, that there was no wheeled transport on St. Helena. More pleasantly for Cook, the governor of the island was John Skottowe, who was the son of Thomas Skottowe, Cook's employer and benefactor in Great Ayton in his youth. They renewed their friendship and rode about the island by day. Balls and dinners were held for the crew at night.

The *Resolution* sailed north with the *Dutton* on 21 May but the two ships parted company three days later. Cook steered his ship to Acension Island where he hoped to obtain turtles for food. They arrived on 28 May, anchoring at Cross Bay near Georgetown, but turtles were in short supply and the island itself was not fertile, so Cook left on 31 May.

Cook was keen to be home but even now there were the positions of some islands to be fixed, and his conscience and pride caused him to search further. The island of St. Matthew was given only brief attention (it does not exist), but on 9 June the ship came to Fernando de Noronha off Brazil [2.29]. Kendal's chronometer was used to fix the island's position but Cook did not attempt to land. Instead he fired a salute to a fort that could be seen on shore and sailed on.

Leaving Fernando de Noronha, Cook sailed north, crossing the Equator on 11 June. A northerly and then northwesterly course was held until 9 July, when they turned east for the Azores [2.30]. On this passage Cook trialled a still for distilling fresh water, but he felt it required too much fuel even though it produced good quantities of water. On the 11th the *Resolution* anchored at Horta on the island of Fayal in the Central Azores. Cook spent five days at Horta, making a detailed description of the place and its inhabitants. Mr Dent, the acting British consul, helped them restock with beef and water.

Cook sailed again on 19 July, passing to the north of Pico, Sao Jorge and Terceira islands and finally headed for Britain and home. The *Resolution* sighted Plymouth on 29 July and the next day Cook brought the ship to anchor at Spithead, off Portsmouth [2.30]. They had been away for just over three years and only four men had died, one from sickness. Cook went straight to London to report to the Admiralty and to see his family. The *Resolution* meanwhile was directed to Deptford on the Thames via Gallions Reach.

Assessment of Second Voyage

If the *Endeavour* Voyage was a success, Cook's Second Voyage must be regarded as a huge success, and it remains one of the greatest single expeditions of all time [2.31]. To nitpick, the *Resolution* and *Adventure* lost touch with each other twice (the second time permanently); Cook did not reach the Antarctic mainland to confirm its existence; and he failed to locate Bouvet Island in the South Atlantic.

However, these are very minor matters when compared to the positive achievements of the voyage.

Cook had set out a detailed plan for the voyage, especially circumnavigating the world near 60°S to look for the Great Southern Continent, and he was able to carry out the plan virtually in its entirety. The continent was shown to exist only near the pole, and would be too cold and inhospitable for people to live there. He became the first person to cross the Antarctic Circle and came very close to reaching the Antarctic mainland.

The sweeps Cook made of the South Pacific criss-crossed that ocean and left very little for future explorers to locate. Groups of such islands as the Marquesas, New Hebrides (Vanuatu) and Easter Island, previously known although their positions were vague, were charted and fixed. New Caledonia, Niue, Norfolk Island and members of the Cook Islands were located and made known for the first time. Vast tracts of the ocean were shown to have no land at all.

On the First Voyage, Cook had met Polynesian people on widely scattered islands, and had been struck by their dispersal and the sailing and navigational skills required to achieve it. On the Second Voyage, Cook was amazed to find the dispersal was greater than previously realised. Cook and his crew had acquired some ability in Polynesian language, so communication, of sorts, had been possible and relations had generally been good. He also encountered Melanesian people on New Caledonia and the New Hebrides. On the Melanesian islands the languages were quite different and communication was very limited, so the presence of the British was usually just tolerated and not encouraged.

Cook also visited the barren islands of South Georgia and South Sandwich in the South Atlantic, and spoilt Dalrymple's ideas about there being habitable land in the area. Returning up the Atlantic, Cook once more brought home a healthy crew after three years away. The Forsters, despite some friction with others on board, brought home much of interest to scientists, while the marine chronometers had shown their worth as navigational tools. Cook's charts were superb and the paintings of William Hodges provide a wonderful pictoral record of this magnificent voyage.

Cook in Britain, 1775–76

Immediately upon arrival on 31 July 1775, Cook travelled up from Portsmouth to London. Unlike his reception four years earlier, Cook was welcomed as a hero by the general population, as well as by the Admiralty and by his family in Mile End. A notable absentee, though, was Joseph Banks, who stayed away for a month, probably embarrassed at his behaviour prior to the voyage in 1772. When the two men eventually met, all was forgotten and their good friendship resumed.

At Mile End, Elizabeth Cook was relieved to have Cook home. Unfortunately, another of their children, George, had died in October 1772, aged only three months. Only the two boys, James and Nathaniel, survived. James who was now 12 had begun attending the Naval Academy at Portsmouth, while Nathaniel would soon follow his brother. A sixth child, Hugh, would be born in May 1776.

Cook was soon presented at Court and promoted to post-captain of HMS *Kent*. However, before Cook could take up this post, he was appointed to the Greenwich Hospital as fourth captain [0.08]. This was something of a sinecure for Cook, as he received a pension and was entitled to live at the hospital (he chose to remain at Mile End though). It was intended that Cook use the opportunity to write up the records of the Second Voyage for publication, thereby avoiding the problems that had resulted from allowing a non-naval person to write the *Endeavour* voyage. To assist Cook, Canon Douglas was brought in to help with style, grammar, etc. The work was eventually published to great acclaim in May 1777, after Cook's departure on his Third Voyage.

Cook was also moving in more exalted circles. He was elected a Fellow of the Royal Society (the same body that had initiated the *Endeavour* voyage) and admitted to the society in March 1776 [0.08]. A paper that he presented on the prevention of scurvy won him the society's Copley Medal. Cook often dined out and met people such as James Boswell, the diarist. He even had his portrait painted by Nathaniel Dance.

Soon, however, Cook was becoming bored with this life and he required little pressure from the Earl of Sandwich and other members of the Admiralty to accept charge of another expedition, this time to search for the Northwest Passage from the Pacific Ocean.

Plans for Third Voyage

Cook had been a tired man when he returned to Britain at the end of his Second Voyage in 1775. He had been away at sea for three years and had fallen seriously ill halfway through that voyage. He was ready for some rest and the opportunity to recover.

But the sedentary life sat uneasily with him. He wrote to his friend John Walker in Whitby: 'A few months ago the whole southern hemisphere was hardly big enough for me, and now I am to be confined within the limits of Greenwich Hospital.' Fortunately for Cook, at about the same time, the Admiralty was thinking about restarting the search for the Northwest Passage, north of North America, to the Pacific and China (Cathay), and the First Sea Lord, the Earl of Sandwich, was looking for a leader of a possible expedition. He acknowledged that Cook had already done sufficient to warrant his retirement, but he also felt Cook to be the most suitable choice. He manoeuvered his colleagues into offering Cook the position, and Cook needed little persuasion to accept the offer. Cook would take two ships to the Pacific and search for the Northwest Passage from there, while Richard Pickersgill, who had sailed previously with Cook, would take HMS *Lyon* north past Baffin Island to look from the Atlantic in the east.

North European countries had been looking for northern routes to the Pacific for over 200 years [2.32]. There were potentially lucrative markets for trade in Cathay (China) and the Spice Islands (Indonesia), but Spain and Portugal controlled the traditional southern routes for reaching the region, so an alternative was required. Pack ice and extreme cold had always prevented earlier success either by a Northwest Passage or by a Northeast Passage to the north of Russia and Siberia. Nobody was even sure that a navigable sea passage existed, but many had been prepared to find out. In 1728 Vitus Bering, a Dane working for Russia, proved that America and Asia were separated by a strait, but how it was linked to the Atlantic remained unknown.

It would not be until 1878 that Nils Nordenskjold, a Swede, eventually navigated the Northeast Passage, and another 27 years again until Roald Amundsen, a Norwegian, made it through the Northwest Passage in 1905.

Furneaux had returned to Britain in 1774 with a Polynesian on board the *Adventure*. Mai (or Omai as he has generally been known; Mai is a better transcription of his name) was introduced into British society and became a celebrity. In 1776, though, it was felt that Mai should return to the Society Islands, and Cook was given the task of transporting him there.

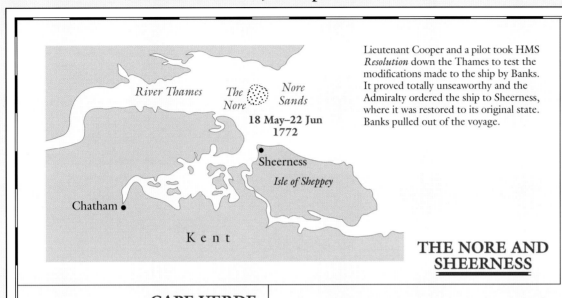

Lieutenant Cooper and a pilot took HMS *Resolution* down the Thames to test the modifications made to the ship by Banks. It proved totally unseaworthy and the Admiralty ordered the ship to Sheerness, where it was restored to its original state. Banks pulled out of the voyage.

18 May–22 Jun 1772

THE NORE AND SHEERNESS

NORTH ATLANTIC

On 25 June the restored *Resolution* sailed from The Nore via The Downs to join the *Adventure* in Plymouth.

CAPE VERDE ISLANDS

The Cape Verde Islands were a Portuguese colony off the west coast of Africa. Cook was able to obtain only limited supplies and little fresh water.

It was agreed that Joseph Banks would sail back to the Pacific with Cook on the new voyage. However, Banks started to take over and saw it as his expedition. He had plans to take a large party with him and arranged to have HMS *Resolution*, the ship chosen to sail, rebuilt to accommodate them. Cook was not happy, but the changes made the ship totally unseaworthy and, when the Navy returned the ship to its original state, Banks withdrew completely from the voyage. The incident soured the relationship between Cook and Banks.

Cook set off on his Second Pacific Voyage in command of HMS *Resolution*. He had successfully convinced the Admiralty that two ships were necessary and so he was accompanied by HMS *Adventure*, commanded by Captain Tobias Furneaux. They sailed from Plymouth on 13 July 1772 with the intention of finally settling the question as to whether a Great Southern Continent existed by circumnavigating the Southern Ocean around Antarctica. Their first stop was for three days at Madeira while the ships were provisioned with wine, fruit and vegetables. Sailing on 2 August, they passed the Canary Islands and reached Port Praia on Sao Tiago in the Cape Verde Islands on 13 August. Again they stayed only a few days and left on the 15th, having made charts of the harbour. The Equator was crossed on 7 September and they were near Ascension Island on 16 September.

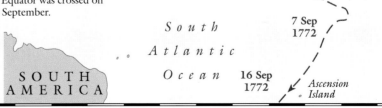

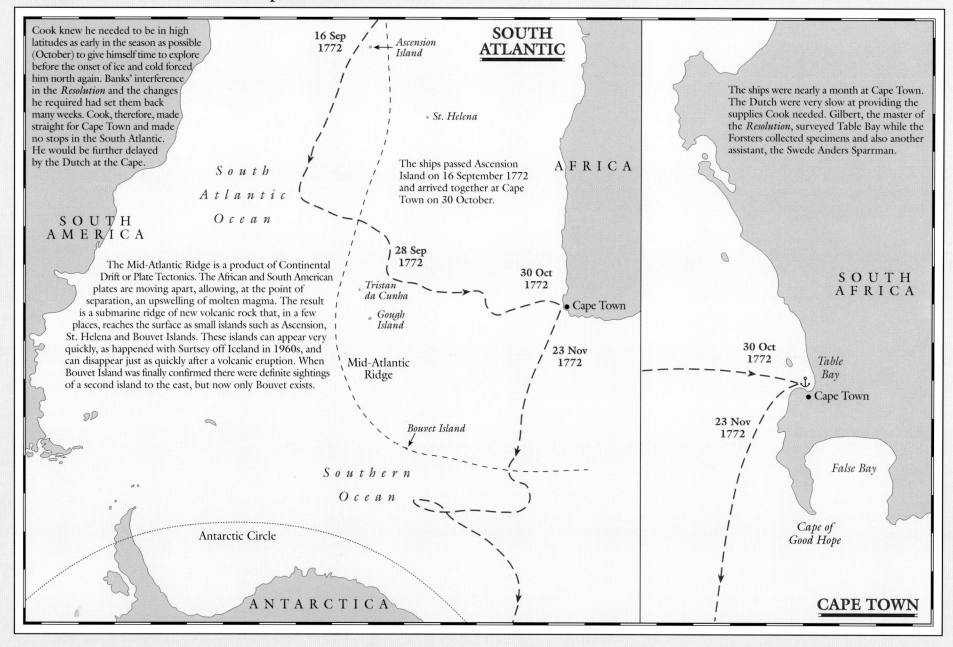

Cook knew he needed to be in high latitudes as early in the season as possible (October) to give himself time to explore before the onset of ice and cold forced him north again. Banks' interference in the *Resolution* and the changes he required had set them back many weeks. Cook, therefore, made straight for Cape Town and made no stops in the South Atlantic. He would be further delayed by the Dutch at the Cape.

The Mid-Atlantic Ridge is a product of Continental Drift or Plate Tectonics. The African and South American plates are moving apart, allowing, at the point of separation, an upswelling of molten magma. The result is a submarine ridge of new volcanic rock that, in a few places, reaches the surface as small islands such as Ascension, St. Helena and Bouvet Islands. These islands can appear very quickly, as happened with Surtsey off Iceland in 1960s, and can disappear just as quickly after a volcanic eruption. When Bouvet Island was finally confirmed there were definite sightings of a second island to the east, but now only Bouvet exists.

The ships passed Ascension Island on 16 September 1772 and arrived together at Cape Town on 30 October.

The ships were nearly a month at Cape Town. The Dutch were very slow at providing the supplies Cook needed. Gilbert, the master of the *Resolution*, surveyed Table Bay while the Forsters collected specimens and also another assistant, the Swede Anders Sparrman.

SOUTH ATLANTIC

South Atlantic Ocean

SOUTH AMERICA

16 Sep 1772

Ascension Island

St. Helena

AFRICA

28 Sep 1772

30 Oct 1772

Cape Town

Tristan da Cunha

Gough Island

Mid-Atlantic Ridge

23 Nov 1772

Bouvet Island

Southern Ocean

Antarctic Circle

ANTARCTICA

SOUTH AFRICA

30 Oct 1772

Table Bay

Cape Town

23 Nov 1772

False Bay

Cape of Good Hope

CAPE TOWN

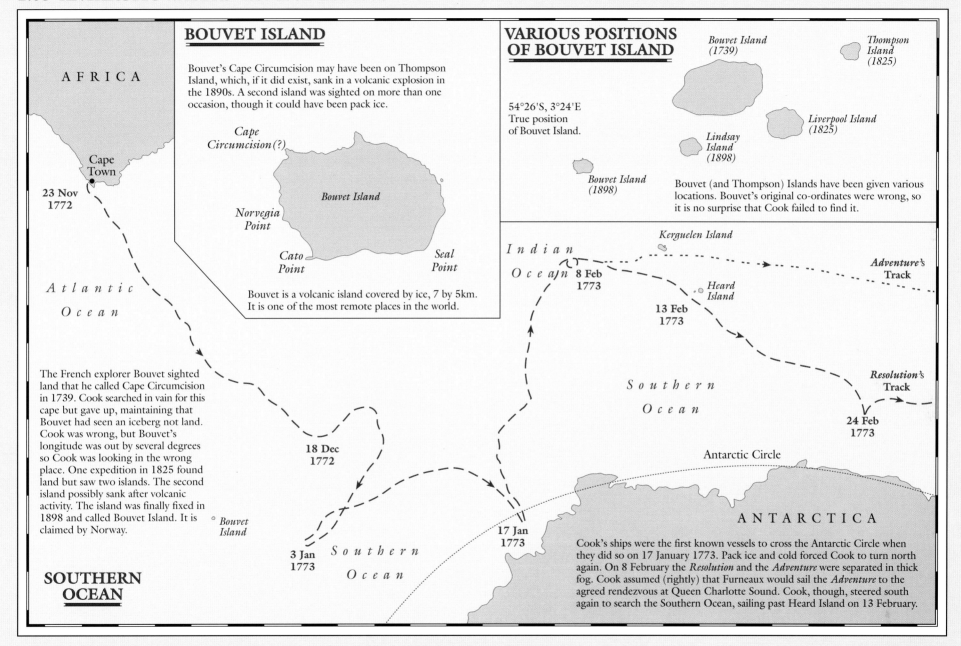

AFRICA

Cape
Town

**23 Nov
1772**

*Atlantic
Ocean*

BOUVET ISLAND

Bouvet's Cape Circumcision may have been on Thompson
Island, which, if it did exist, sank in a volcanic explosion in
the 1890s. A second island was sighted on more than one
occasion, though it could have been pack ice.

*Cape
Circumcision (?)*

Bouvet Island

*Norvegia
Point*

*Cato
Point*

*Seal
Point*

Bouvet is a volcanic island covered by ice, 7 by 5km.
It is one of the most remote places in the world.

VARIOUS POSITIONS
OF BOUVET ISLAND

*Bouvet Island
(1739)*

*Thompson
Island
(1825)*

54°26'S, 3°24'E
True position
of Bouvet Island.

*Liverpool Island
(1825)*

*Lindsay
Island
(1898)*

*Bouvet Island
(1898)*

Bouvet (and Thompson) Islands have been given various
locations. Bouvet's original co-ordinates were wrong, so
it is no surprise that Cook failed to find it.

Kerguelen Island

Indian

Ocean **8 Feb
1773**

*Adventure's
Track*

*Heard
Island*

**13 Feb
1773**

Southern

Ocean

*Resolution's
Track*

**24 Feb
1773**

The French explorer Bouvet sighted
land that he called Cape Circumcision
in 1739. Cook searched in vain for this
cape but gave up, maintaining that
Bouvet had seen an iceberg not land.
Cook was wrong, but Bouvet's
longitude was out by several degrees
so Cook was looking in the wrong
place. One expedition in 1825 found
land but saw two islands. The second
island possibly sank after volcanic
activity. The island was finally fixed in
1898 and called Bouvet Island. It is
claimed by Norway.

° *Bouvet
Island*

**18 Dec
1772**

**3 Jan
1773**

Southern

Ocean

Antarctic Circle

**17 Jan
1773**

A N T A R C T I C A

Cook's ships were the first known vessels to cross the Antarctic Circle when
they did so on 17 January 1773. Pack ice and cold forced Cook to turn north
again. On 8 February the *Resolution* and the *Adventure* were separated in thick
fog. Cook assumed (rightly) that Furneaux would sail the *Adventure* to the
agreed rendezvous at Queen Charlotte Sound. Cook, though, steered south
again to search the Southern Ocean, sailing past Heard Island on 13 February.

**SOUTHERN
OCEAN**

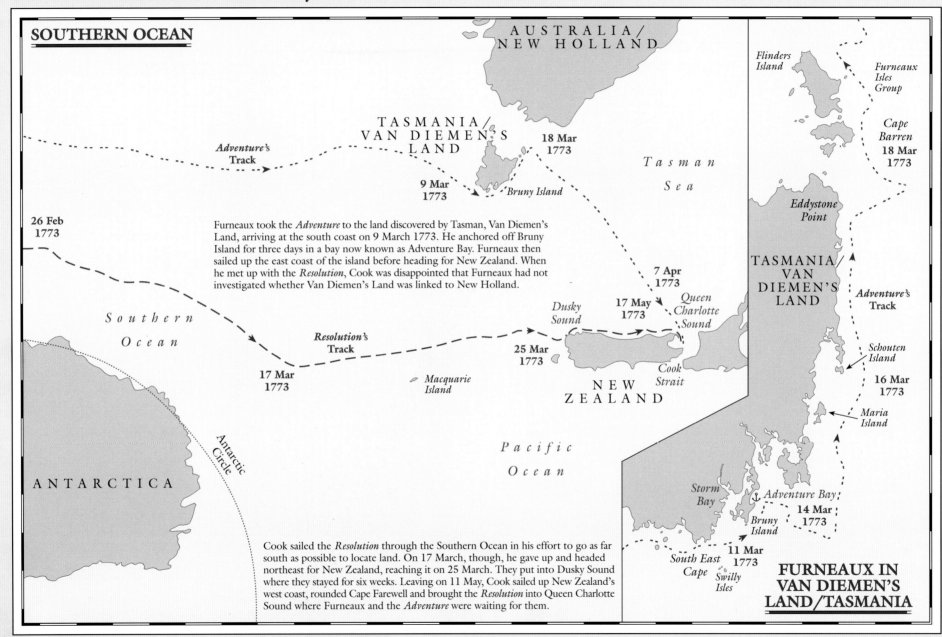

SOUTHERN OCEAN

AUSTRALIA/
NEW HOLLAND

TASMANIA/
VAN DIEMEN'S
LAND

*Tasman
Sea*

**18 Mar
1773**

**9 Mar
1773**

Bruny Island

*Flinders
Island*

*Furneaux
Isles
Group*

*Cape
Barren*

**18 Mar
1773**

*Eddystone
Point*

TASMANIA/
VAN
DIEMEN'S
LAND

*Adventure's
Track*

*Schouten
Island*

**16 Mar
1773**

*Maria
Island*

*Adventure's
Track*

**26 Feb
1773**

Furneaux took the *Adventure* to the land discovered by Tasman, Van Diemen's Land, arriving at the south coast on 9 March 1773. He anchored off Bruny Island for three days in a bay now known as Adventure Bay. Furneaux then sailed up the east coast of the island before heading for New Zealand. When he met up with the *Resolution*, Cook was disappointed that Furneaux had not investigated whether Van Diemen's Land was linked to New Holland.

**7 Apr
1773**

*Dusky
Sound*

**17 May
1773**

*Queen
Charlotte
Sound*

*Southern
Ocean*

*Resolution's
Track*

**25 Mar
1773**

*Cook
Strait*

**17 Mar
1773**

*Macquarie
Island*

NEW
ZEALAND

*Antarctic
Circle*

ANTARCTICA

*Pacific
Ocean*

*Storm
Bay*

⚓ *Adventure Bay*

*Bruny
Island*

**14 Mar
1773**

Cook sailed the *Resolution* through the Southern Ocean in his effort to go as far south as possible to locate land. On 17 March, though, he gave up and headed northeast for New Zealand, reaching it on 25 March. They put into Dusky Sound where they stayed for six weeks. Leaving on 11 May, Cook sailed up New Zealand's west coast, rounded Cape Farewell and brought the *Resolution* into Queen Charlotte Sound where Furneaux and the *Adventure* were waiting for them.

*South East
Cape*

**11 Mar
1773**

*Swilly
Isles*

**FURNEAUX IN
VAN DIEMEN'S
LAND/TASMANIA**

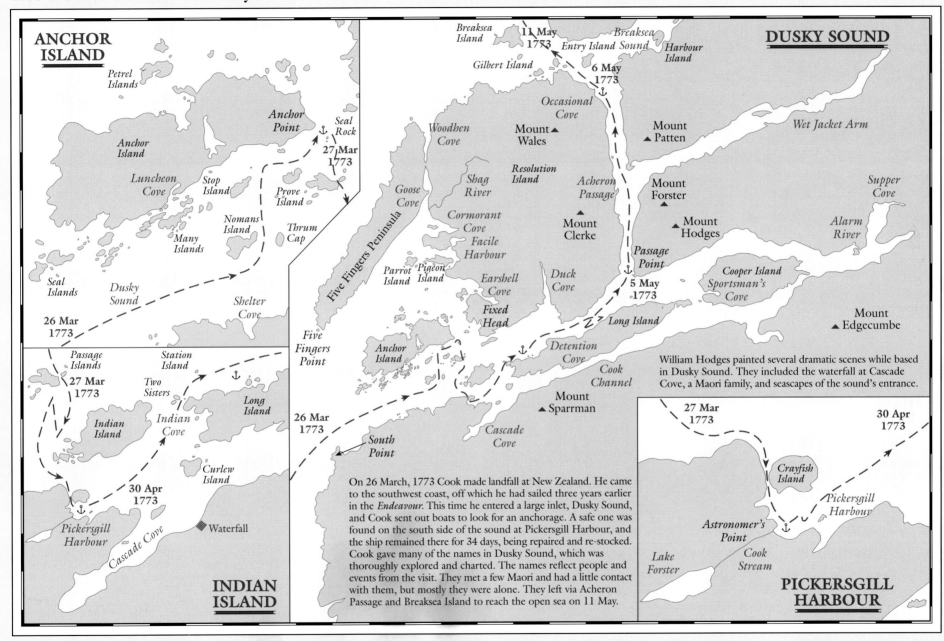

ANCHOR ISLAND

Petrel Islands

Anchor Point

Seal Rock

Anchor Island

Luncheon Cove

Stop Island

Prove Island

27 Mar 1773

Nomans Island

Many Islands

Thrum Cap

Seal Islands

Dusky Sound

Shelter Cove

26 Mar 1773

Passage Islands

27 Mar 1773

Station Island

Two Sisters

Long Island

INDIAN ISLAND

Indian Island

Indian Cove

Curlew Island

30 Apr 1773

Pickersgill Harbour

Cascade Cove

Waterfall

Breaksea Island

11 May 1773

Entry Island Sound

Breaksea Harbour Island

Gilbert Island

6 May 1773

Occasional Cove

Woodhen Cove

Mount Wales

Mount Patten

Wet Jacket Arm

Shag River

Resolution Island

Acheron Passage

Mount Forster

Five Fingers Peninsula

Goose Cove

Cormorant Cove

Facile Harbour

Mount Clerke

Mount Hodges

Supper Cove

Alarm River

Parrot Island

Pigeon Island

Earshell Cove

Duck Cove

Passage Point

Cooper Island

Sportsman's Cove

Fixed Head

5 May 1773

Long Island

Mount Edgecumbe

Five Fingers Point

Anchor Island

Detention Cove

Cook Channel

William Hodges painted several dramatic scenes while based in Dusky Sound. They included the waterfall at Cascade Cove, a Maori family, and seascapes of the sound's entrance.

26 Mar 1773

South Point

Mount Sparrman

Cascade Cove

On 26 March, 1773 Cook made landfall at New Zealand. He came to the southwest coast, off which he had sailed three years earlier in the *Endeavour*. This time he entered a large inlet, Dusky Sound, and Cook sent out boats to look for an anchorage. A safe one was found on the south side of the sound at Pickersgill Harbour, and the ship remained there for 34 days, being repaired and re-stocked. Cook gave many of the names in Dusky Sound, which was thoroughly explored and charted. The names reflect people and events from the visit. They met a few Maori and had a little contact with them, but mostly they were alone. They left via Acheron Passage and Breaksea Island to reach the open sea on 11 May.

DUSKY SOUND

PICKERSGILL HARBOUR

27 Mar 1773

30 Apr 1773

Crayfish Island

Astronomer's Point

Pickersgill Harbour

Lake Forster

Cook Stream

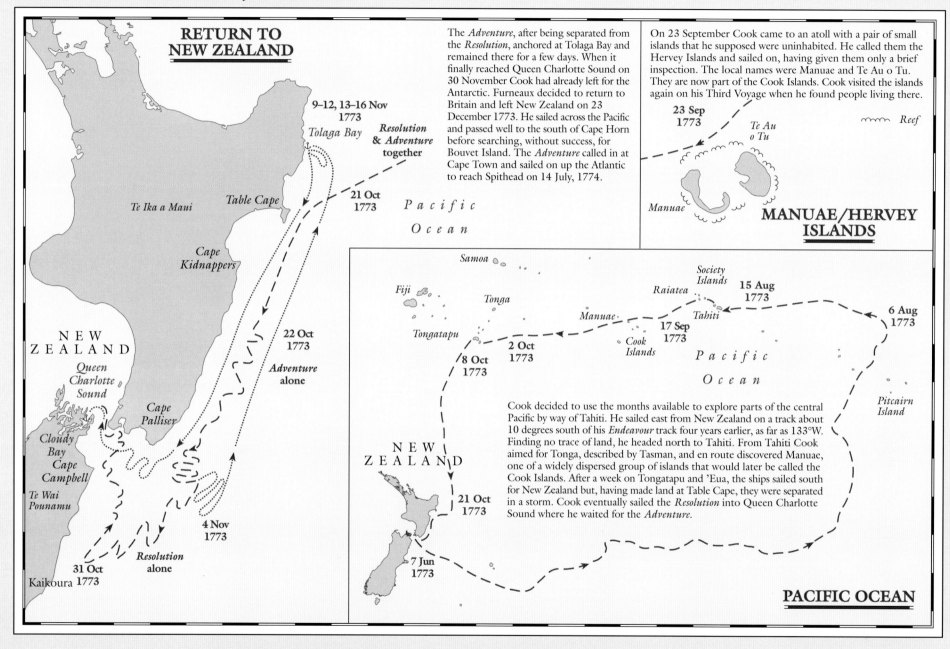

RETURN TO NEW ZEALAND

The *Adventure*, after being separated from the *Resolution*, anchored at Tolaga Bay and remained there for a few days. When it finally reached Queen Charlotte Sound on 30 November Cook had already left for the Antarctic. Furneaux decided to return to Britain and left New Zealand on 23 December 1773. He sailed across the Pacific and passed well to the south of Cape Horn before searching, without success, for Bouvet Island. The *Adventure* called in at Cape Town and sailed on up the Atlantic to reach Spithead on 14 July, 1774.

On 23 September Cook came to an atoll with a pair of small islands that he supposed were uninhabited. He called them the Hervey Islands and sailed on, having given them only a brief inspection. The local names were Manuae and Te Au o Tu. They are now part of the Cook Islands. Cook visited the islands again on his Third Voyage when he found people living there.

23 Sep 1773

Te Au o Tu

~~~~~ *Reef*

Manuae

MANUAE/HERVEY ISLANDS

9–12, 13–16 Nov 1773
Tolaga Bay

Resolution & Adventure **together**

21 Oct 1773

Pacific Ocean

Te Ika a Maui

Table Cape

Cape Kidnappers

22 Oct 1773

Adventure **alone**

N E W Z E A L A N D

Queen Charlotte Sound

Cape Palliser

Cloudy Bay
Cape Campbell

Te Wai Pounamu

4 Nov 1773

31 Oct 1773
Kaikoura

Resolution **alone**

Pacific Ocean map

Samoa

Fiji

Tonga

Society Islands

Raiatea

15 Aug 1773

Manuae

Tahiti

17 Sep 1773

Tongatapu

2 Oct 1773

Cook Islands

8 Oct 1773

6 Aug 1773

Pacific Ocean

Pitcairn Island

Cook decided to use the months available to explore parts of the central Pacific by way of Tahiti. He sailed east from New Zealand on a track about 10 degrees south of his *Endeavour* track four years earlier, as far as 133°W. Finding no trace of land, he headed north to Tahiti. From Tahiti Cook aimed for Tonga, described by Tasman, and en route discovered Manuae, one of a widely dispersed group of islands that would later be called the Cook Islands. After a week on Tongatapu and 'Eua, the ships sailed south for New Zealand but, having made land at Table Cape, they were separated in a storm. Cook eventually sailed the *Resolution* into Queen Charlotte Sound where he waited for the *Adventure*.

N E W Z E A L A N D

21 Oct 1773

7 Jun 1773

PACIFIC OCEAN

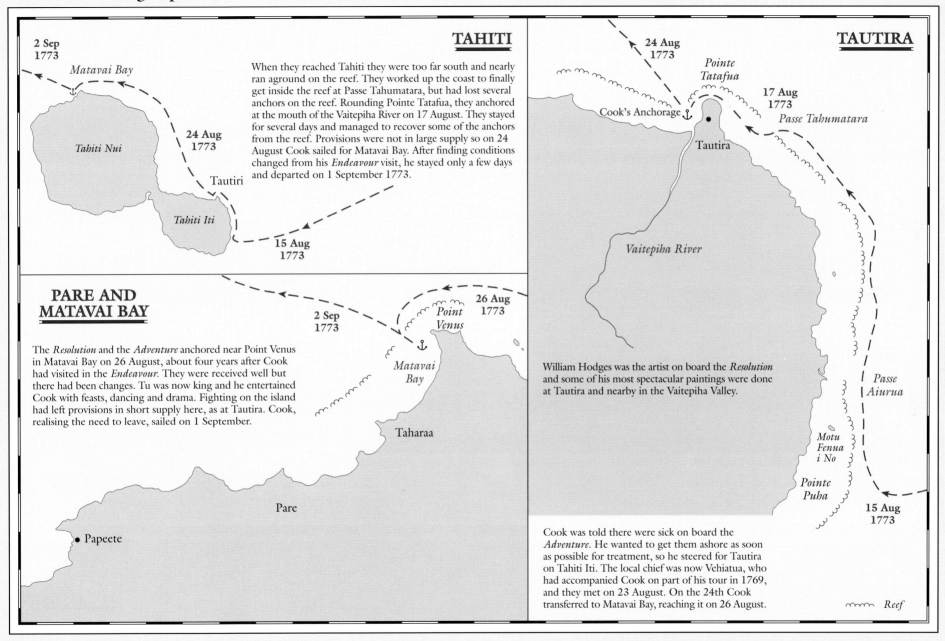

TAHITI

When they reached Tahiti they were too far south and nearly ran aground on the reef. They worked up the coast to finally get inside the reef at Passe Tahumatara, but had lost several anchors on the reef. Rounding Pointe Tatafua, they anchored at the mouth of the Vaitepiha River on 17 August. They stayed for several days and managed to recover some of the anchors from the reef. Provisions were not in large supply so on 24 August Cook sailed for Matavai Bay. After finding conditions changed from his *Endeavour* visit, he stayed only a few days and departed on 1 September 1773.

2 Sep 1773
Matavai Bay
24 Aug 1773
Tautiri
Tahiti Nui
Tahiti Iti
15 Aug 1773

TAUTIRA

24 Aug 1773
Pointe Tatafua
17 Aug 1773
Cook's Anchorage
Passe Tahumatara
Tautira
Vaitepiha River
Passe Aiurua
Motu Fenua i No
Pointe Puha
15 Aug 1773

William Hodges was the artist on board the *Resolution* and some of his most spectacular paintings were done at Tautira and nearby in the Vaitepiha Valley.

PARE AND MATAVAI BAY

The *Resolution* and the *Adventure* anchored near Point Venus in Matavai Bay on 26 August, about four years after Cook had visited in the *Endeavour*. They were received well but there had been changes. Tu was now king and he entertained Cook with feasts, dancing and drama. Fighting on the island had left provisions in short supply here, as at Tautira. Cook, realising the need to leave, sailed on 1 September.

2 Sep 1773
Point Venus
26 Aug 1773
Matavai Bay
Taharaa
Pare
• Papeete

Cook was told there were sick on board the *Adventure*. He wanted to get them ashore as soon as possible for treatment, so he steered for Tautira on Tahiti Iti. The local chief was now Vehiatua, who had accompanied Cook on part of his tour in 1769, and they met on 23 August. On the 24th Cook transferred to Matavai Bay, reaching it on 26 August.

〰〰〰 *Reef*

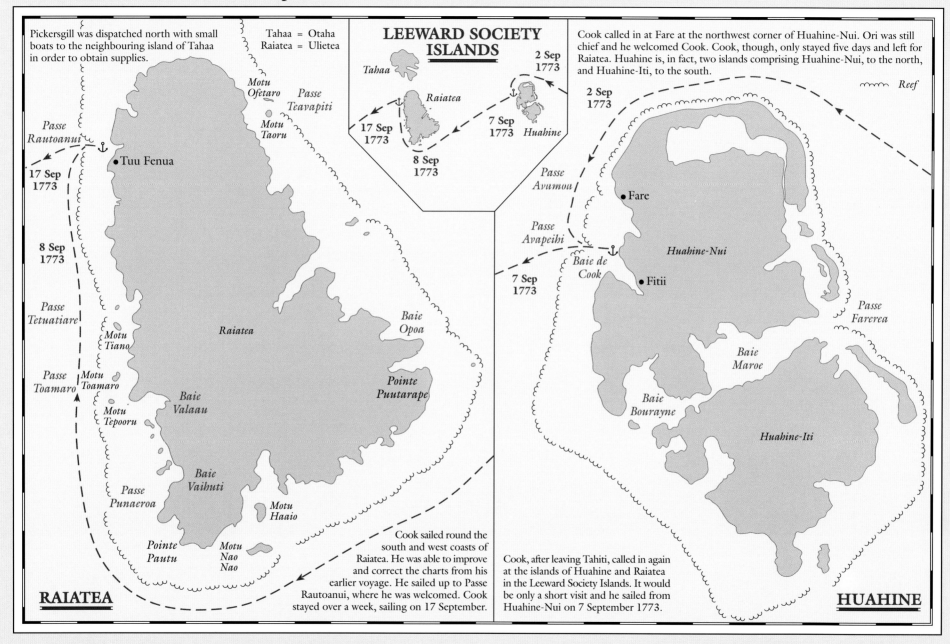

Pickersgill was dispatched north with small boats to the neighbouring island of Tahaa in order to obtain supplies.

Tahaa = Otaha
Raiatea = Ulietea

LEEWARD SOCIETY ISLANDS

Cook called in at Fare at the northwest corner of Huahine-Nui. Ori was still chief and he welcomed Cook. Cook, though, only stayed five days and left for Raiatea. Huahine is, in fact, two islands comprising Huahine-Nui, to the north, and Huahine-Iti, to the south.

Reef

Tahaa

Raiatea

2 Sep 1773

2 Sep 1773

17 Sep 1773

7 Sep 1773

Huahine

8 Sep 1773

Passe Avamoa

Passe Avapeihi

Baie de Cook

Fare

Huahine-Nui

Fitii

7 Sep 1773

Passe Rautoanui

Tuu Fenua

17 Sep 1773

8 Sep 1773

Passe Tetuatiare

Passe Toamaro

Motu Tiano

Motu Toamaro

Motu Tepooru

Motu Ofetaro

Passe Teavapiti

Motu Taoru

Raiatea

Baie Opoa

Baie Valaau

Pointe Puutarape

Passe Farerea

Baie Maroe

Baie Vaihuti

Passe Punaeroa

Motu Haaio

Baie Bourayne

Huahine-Iti

Pointe Pautu

Motu Nao Nao

Cook sailed round the south and west coasts of Raiatea. He was able to improve and correct the charts from his earlier voyage. He sailed up to Passe Rautoanui, where he was welcomed. Cook stayed over a week, sailing on 17 September.

Cook, after leaving Tahiti, called in again at the islands of Huahine and Raiatea in the Leeward Society Islands. It would be only a short visit and he sailed from Huahine-Nui on 7 September 1773.

RAIATEA

HUAHINE

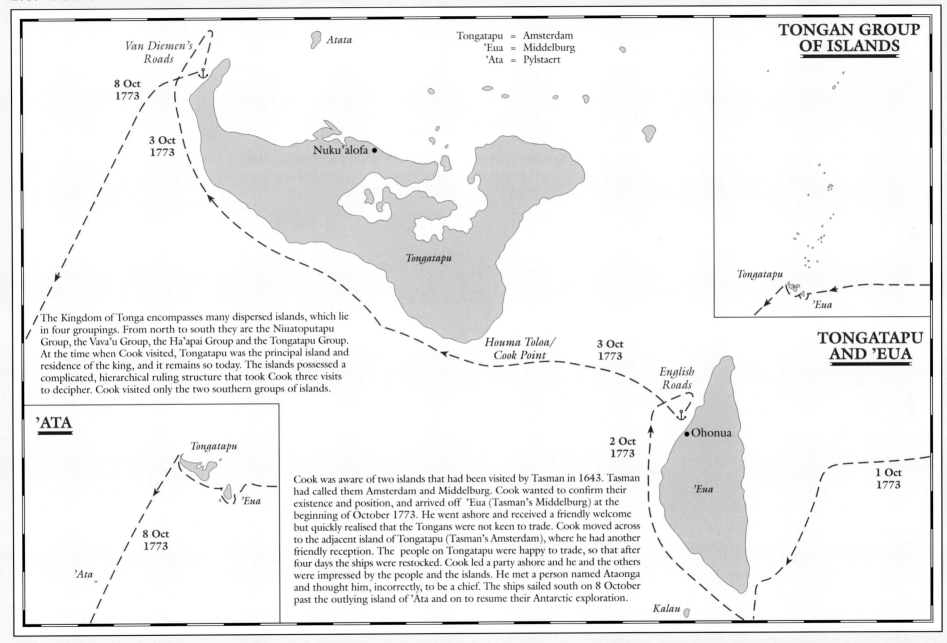

TONGAN GROUP OF ISLANDS

TONGATAPU AND 'EUA

'ATA

Van Diemen's Roads

8 Oct 1773

3 Oct 1773

Atata

Tongatapu = Amsterdam
'Eua = Middelburg
'Ata = Pylstaert

Nuku'alofa •

Tongatapu

The Kingdom of Tonga encompasses many dispersed islands, which lie in four groupings. From north to south they are the Niuatoputapu Group, the Vava'u Group, the Ha'apai Group and the Tongatapu Group. At the time when Cook visited, Tongatapu was the principal island and residence of the king, and it remains so today. The islands possessed a complicated, hierarchical ruling structure that took Cook three visits to decipher. Cook visited only the two southern groups of islands.

Houma Toloa/ Cook Point

3 Oct 1773

English Roads

2 Oct 1773

• Ohonua

'Eua

1 Oct 1773

Tongatapu

'Eua

8 Oct 1773

'Ata

Cook was aware of two islands that had been visited by Tasman in 1643. Tasman had called them Amsterdam and Middelburg. Cook wanted to confirm their existence and position, and arrived off 'Eua (Tasman's Middelburg) at the beginning of October 1773. He went ashore and received a friendly welcome but quickly realised that the Tongans were not keen to trade. Cook moved across to the adjacent island of Tongatapu (Tasman's Amsterdam), where he had another friendly reception. The people on Tongatapu were happy to trade, so that after four days the ships were restocked. Cook led a party ashore and he and the others were impressed by the people and the islands. He met a person named Ataonga and thought him, incorrectly, to be a chief. The ships sailed south on 8 October past the outlying island of 'Ata and on to resume their Antarctic exploration.

Kalau

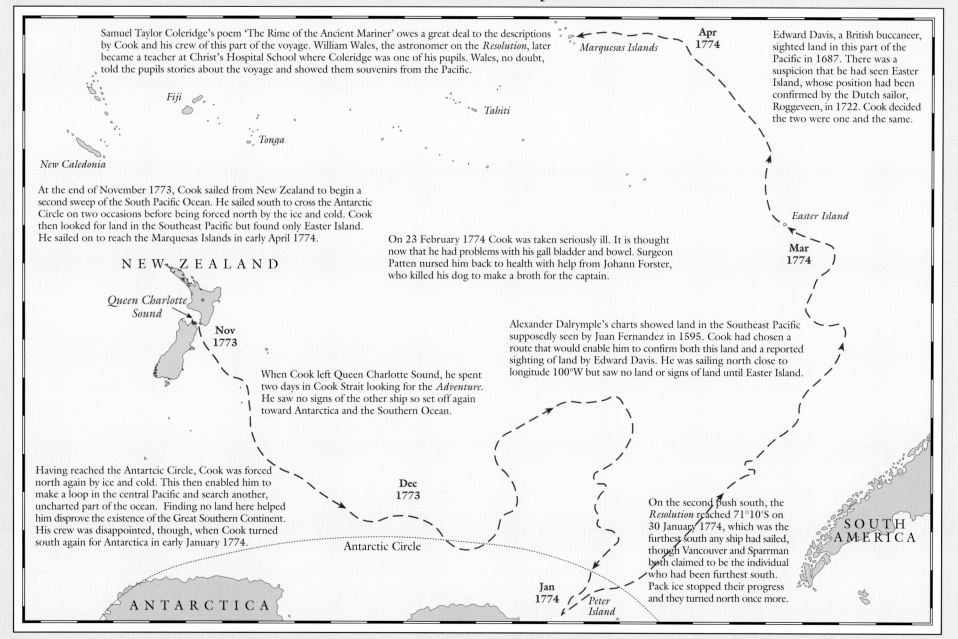

Samuel Taylor Coleridge's poem 'The Rime of the Ancient Mariner' owes a great deal to the descriptions by Cook and his crew of this part of the voyage. William Wales, the astronomer on the *Resolution*, later became a teacher at Christ's Hospital School where Coleridge was one of his pupils. Wales, no doubt, told the pupils stories about the voyage and showed them souvenirs from the Pacific.

Edward Davis, a British buccaneer, sighted land in this part of the Pacific in 1687. There was a suspicion that he had seen Easter Island, whose position had been confirmed by the Dutch sailor, Roggeveen, in 1722. Cook decided the two were one and the same.

At the end of November 1773, Cook sailed from New Zealand to begin a second sweep of the South Pacific Ocean. He sailed south to cross the Antarctic Circle on two occasions before being forced north by the ice and cold. Cook then looked for land in the Southeast Pacific but found only Easter Island. He sailed on to reach the Marquesas Islands in early April 1774.

On 23 February 1774 Cook was taken seriously ill. It is thought now that he had problems with his gall bladder and bowel. Surgeon Patten nursed him back to health with help from Johann Forster, who killed his dog to make a broth for the captain.

When Cook left Queen Charlotte Sound, he spent two days in Cook Strait looking for the *Adventure*. He saw no signs of the other ship so set off again toward Antarctica and the Southern Ocean.

Alexander Dalrymple's charts showed land in the Southeast Pacific supposedly seen by Juan Fernandez in 1595. Cook had chosen a route that would enable him to confirm both this land and a reported sighting of land by Edward Davis. He was sailing north close to longitude 100°W but saw no land or signs of land until Easter Island.

Having reached the Antartcic Circle, Cook was forced north again by ice and cold. This then enabled him to make a loop in the central Pacific and search another, uncharted part of the ocean. Finding no land here helped him disprove the existence of the Great Southern Continent. His crew was disappointed, though, when Cook turned south again for Antarctica in early January 1774.

On the second push south, the *Resolution* reached 71°10'S on 30 January 1774, which was the furthest south any ship had sailed, though Vancouver and Sparrman both claimed to be the individual who had been furthest south. Pack ice stopped their progress and they turned north once more.

Apr 1774

Marquesas Islands

Fiji

Tahiti

Tonga

New Caledonia

Easter Island

Mar 1774

N E W   Z E A L A N D

Queen Charlotte Sound

Nov 1773

Dec 1773

Antarctic Circle

Jan 1774

Peter Island

A N T A R C T I C A

S O U T H   A M E R I C A

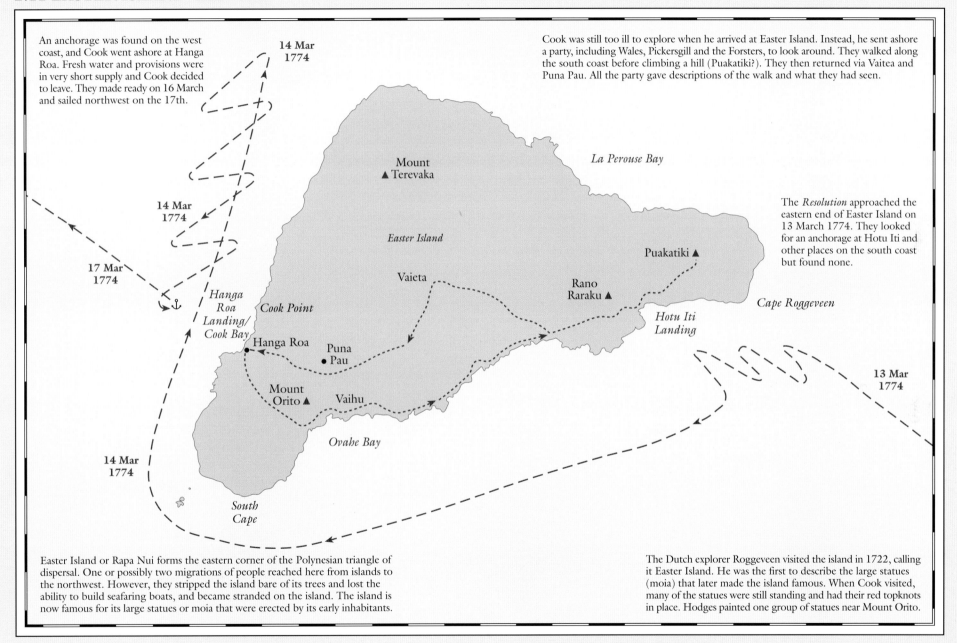

An anchorage was found on the west coast, and Cook went ashore at Hanga Roa. Fresh water and provisions were in very short supply and Cook decided to leave. They made ready on 16 March and sailed northwest on the 17th.

Cook was still too ill to explore when he arrived at Easter Island. Instead, he sent ashore a party, including Wales, Pickersgill and the Forsters, to look around. They walked along the south coast before climbing a hill (Puakatiki?). They then returned via Vaitea and Puna Pau. All the party gave descriptions of the walk and what they had seen.

The *Resolution* approached the eastern end of Easter Island on 13 March 1774. They looked for an anchorage at Hotu Iti and other places on the south coast but found none.

14 Mar 1774

14 Mar 1774

17 Mar 1774

14 Mar 1774

13 Mar 1774

La Perouse Bay

Mount ▲ Terevaka

Easter Island

Puakatiki ▲

Vaieta

Rano Raraku ▲

Cape Roggeveen

Hotu Iti Landing

Hanga Roa Landing / Cook Bay

Cook Point

Hanga Roa

Puna Pau

Mount Orito ▲

Vaihu

Ovahe Bay

South Cape

Easter Island or Rapa Nui forms the eastern corner of the Polynesian triangle of dispersal. One or possibly two migrations of people reached here from islands to the northwest. However, they stripped the island bare of its trees and lost the ability to build seafaring boats, and became stranded on the island. The island is now famous for its large statues or moia that were erected by its early inhabitants.

The Dutch explorer Roggeveen visited the island in 1722, calling it Easter Island. He was the first to describe the large statues (moia) that later made the island famous. When Cook visited, many of the statues were still standing and had their red topknots in place. Hodges painted one group of statues near Mount Orito.

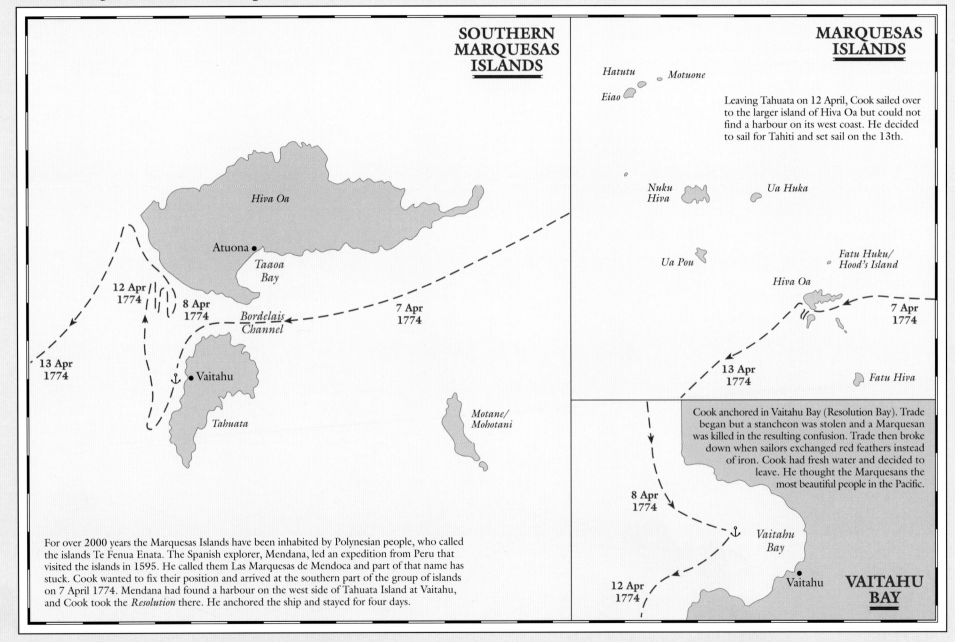

SOUTHERN MARQUESAS ISLANDS

MARQUESAS ISLANDS

Hatutu

Motuone

Eiao

Leaving Tahuata on 12 April, Cook sailed over to the larger island of Hiva Oa but could not find a harbour on its west coast. He decided to sail for Tahiti and set sail on the 13th.

Hiva Oa

Nuku Hiva

Ua Huka

Atuona

Taaoa Bay

Ua Pou

Fatu Huku/ Hood's Island

12 Apr 1774

8 Apr 1774

Bordelais Channel

7 Apr 1774

Hiva Oa

7 Apr 1774

13 Apr 1774

13 Apr 1774

Fatu Hiva

Vaitahu

Cook anchored in Vaitahu Bay (Resolution Bay). Trade began but a stancheon was stolen and a Marquesan was killed in the resulting confusion. Trade then broke down when sailors exchanged red feathers instead of iron. Cook had fresh water and decided to leave. He thought the Marquesans the most beautiful people in the Pacific.

Motane/ Mohotani

Tahuata

8 Apr 1774

Vaitahu Bay

For over 2000 years the Marquesas Islands have been inhabited by Polynesian people, who called the islands Te Fenua Enata. The Spanish explorer, Mendana, led an expedition from Peru that visited the islands in 1595. He called them Las Marquesas de Mendoca and part of that name has stuck. Cook wanted to fix their position and arrived at the southern part of the group of islands on 7 April 1774. Mendana had found a harbour on the west side of Tahuata Island at Vaitahu, and Cook took the *Resolution* there. He anchored the ship and stayed for four days.

12 Apr 1774

Vaitahu

VAITAHU BAY

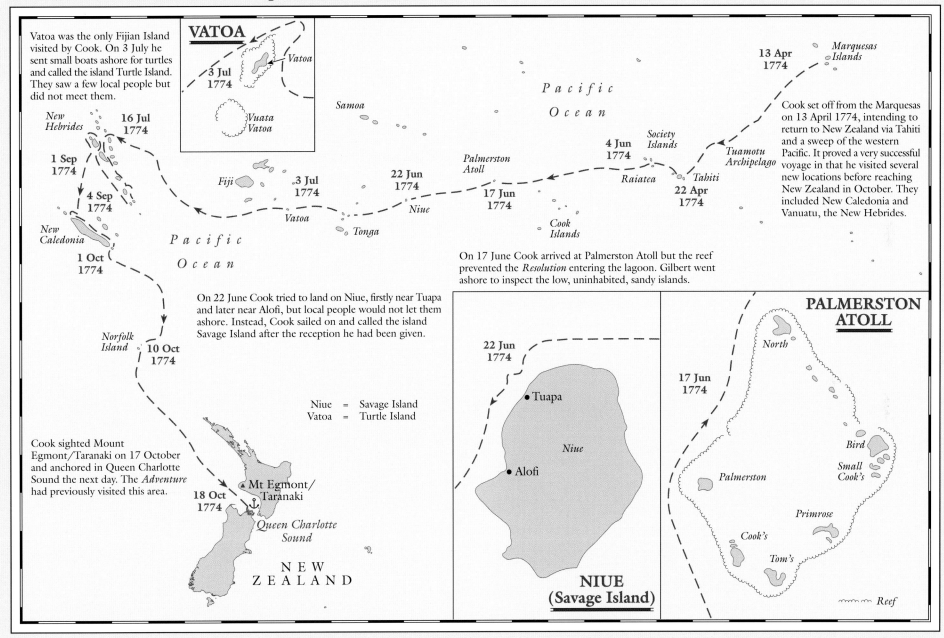

Vatoa was the only Fijian Island visited by Cook. On 3 July he sent small boats ashore for turtles and called the island Turtle Island. They saw a few local people but did not meet them.

VATOA

Vatoa

3 Jul 1774

Vuata Vatoa

Samoa

Pacific Ocean

New Hebrides

16 Jul 1774

1 Sep 1774

4 Sep 1774

New Caledonia

1 Oct 1774

Fiji

3 Jul 1774

22 Jun 1774

Palmerston Atoll

17 Jun 1774

Niue

Cook Islands

Vatoa

Tonga

Pacific Ocean

13 Apr 1774

Marquesas Islands

4 Jun 1774

Society Islands

Tuamotu Archipelago

Raiatea

Tahiti

22 Apr 1774

Cook set off from the Marquesas on 13 April 1774, intending to return to New Zealand via Tahiti and a sweep of the western Pacific. It proved a very successful voyage in that he visited several new locations before reaching New Zealand in October. They included New Caledonia and Vanuatu, the New Hebrides.

On 17 June Cook arrived at Palmerston Atoll but the reef prevented the *Resolution* entering the lagoon. Gilbert went ashore to inspect the low, uninhabited, sandy islands.

On 22 June Cook tried to land on Niue, firstly near Tuapa and later near Alofi, but local people would not let them ashore. Instead, Cook sailed on and called the island Savage Island after the reception he had been given.

Norfolk Island

10 Oct 1774

Niue = Savage Island
Vatoa = Turtle Island

Cook sighted Mount Egmont/Taranaki on 17 October and anchored in Queen Charlotte Sound the next day. The *Adventure* had previously visited this area.

18 Oct 1774

Mt Egmont/ Taranaki

Queen Charlotte Sound

NEW ZEALAND

22 Jun 1774

Tuapa

Alofi

Niue

NIUE (Savage Island)

PALMERSTON ATOLL

North

17 Jun 1774

Bird

Palmerston

Small Cook's

Primrose

Cook's

Tom's

Reef

2.14 TUAMOTU AND SOCIETY ISLANDS Apr–Jun 1774

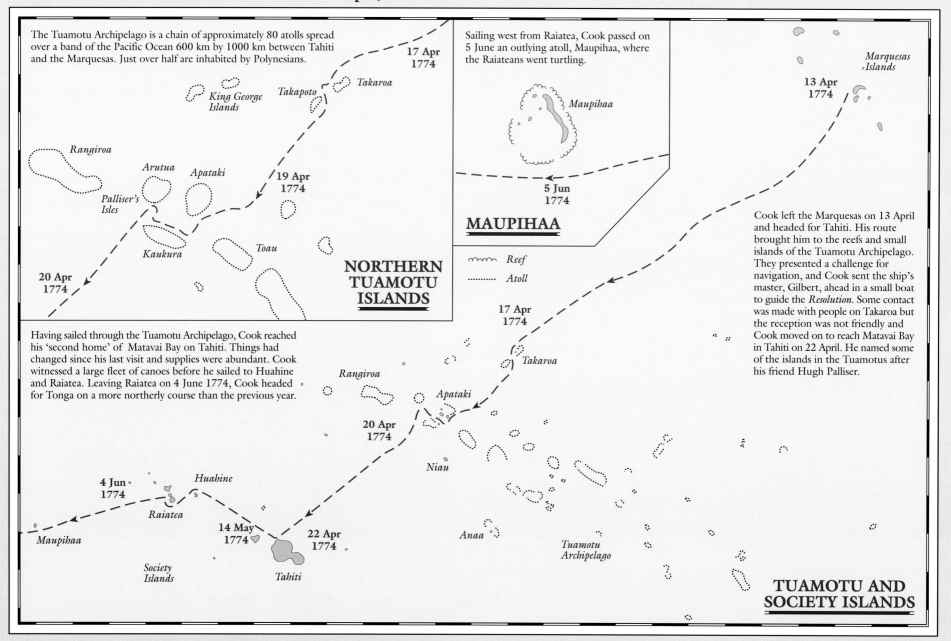

The Tuamotu Archipelago is a chain of approximately 80 atolls spread over a band of the Pacific Ocean 600 km by 1000 km between Tahiti and the Marquesas. Just over half are inhabited by Polynesians.

17 Apr 1774

King George Islands

Takapoto

Takaroa

Rangiroa

Arutua

Apataki

19 Apr 1774

Palliser's Isles

Kaukura

Toau

20 Apr 1774

NORTHERN TUAMOTU ISLANDS

Sailing west from Raiatea, Cook passed on 5 June an outlying atoll, Maupihaa, where the Raiateans went turtling.

Maupihaa

5 Jun 1774

MAUPIHAA

~~~ Reef

········· Atoll

Marquesas Islands

13 Apr 1774

Cook left the Marquesas on 13 April and headed for Tahiti. His route brought him to the reefs and small islands of the Tuamotu Archipelago. They presented a challenge for navigation, and Cook sent the ship's master, Gilbert, ahead in a small boat to guide the *Resolution*. Some contact was made with people on Takaroa but the reception was not friendly and Cook moved on to reach Matavai Bay in Tahiti on 22 April. He named some of the islands in the Tuamotus after his friend Hugh Palliser.

17 Apr 1774

Takaroa

Rangiroa

Apataki

20 Apr 1774

Niau

Having sailed through the Tuamotu Archipelago, Cook reached his 'second home' of Matavai Bay on Tahiti. Things had changed since his last visit and supplies were abundant. Cook witnessed a large fleet of canoes before he sailed to Huahine and Raiatea. Leaving Raiatea on 4 June 1774, Cook headed for Tonga on a more northerly course than the previous year.

4 Jun 1774

Huahine

Raiatea

Maupihaa

14 May 1774

22 Apr 1774

Society Islands

Tahiti

Anaa

Tuamotu Archipelago

TUAMOTU AND SOCIETY ISLANDS

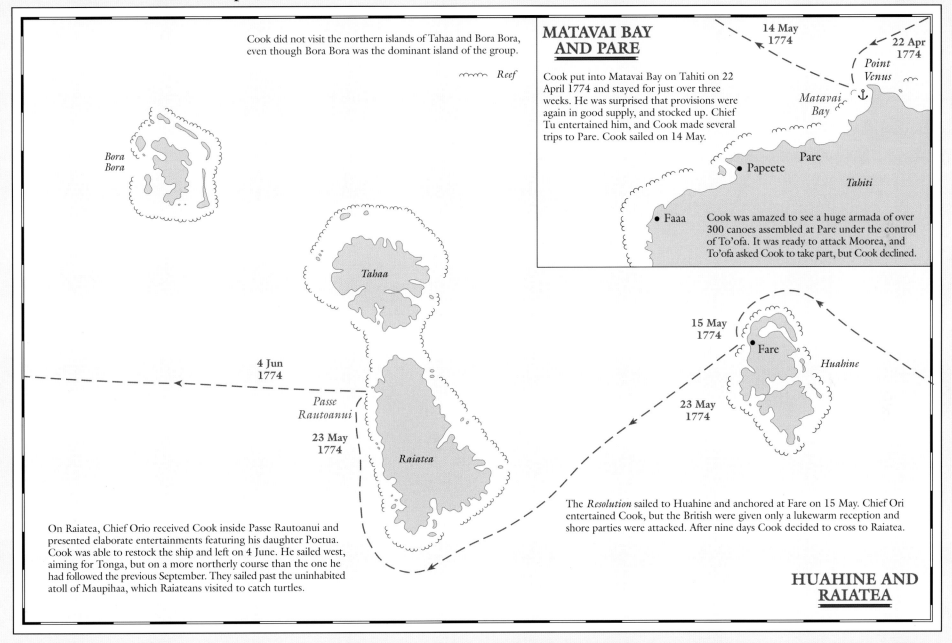

Cook did not visit the northern islands of Tahaa and Bora Bora, even though Bora Bora was the dominant island of the group.

〰〰〰 *Reef*

MATAVAI BAY AND PARE

Cook put into Matavai Bay on Tahiti on 22 April 1774 and stayed for just over three weeks. He was surprised that provisions were again in good supply, and stocked up. Chief Tu entertained him, and Cook made several trips to Pare. Cook sailed on 14 May.

14 May 1774

22 Apr 1774

Point Venus

⚓

Matavai Bay

Pare

● Papeete

Tahiti

● Faaa

Cook was amazed to see a huge armada of over 300 canoes assembled at Pare under the control of To'ofa. It was ready to attack Moorea, and To'ofa asked Cook to take part, but Cook declined.

Bora Bora

Tahaa

15 May 1774

● Fare

Huahine

4 Jun 1774

23 May 1774

Passe Rautoanui

23 May 1774

Raiatea

The *Resolution* sailed to Huahine and anchored at Fare on 15 May. Chief Ori entertained Cook, but the British were given only a lukewarm reception and shore parties were attacked. After nine days Cook decided to cross to Raiatea.

On Raiatea, Chief Orio received Cook inside Passe Rautoanui and presented elaborate entertainments featuring his daughter Poetua. Cook was able to restock the ship and left on 4 June. He sailed west, aiming for Tonga, but on a more northerly course than the one he had followed the previous September. They sailed past the uninhabited atoll of Maupihaa, which Raiateans visited to catch turtles.

HUAHINE AND RAIATEA

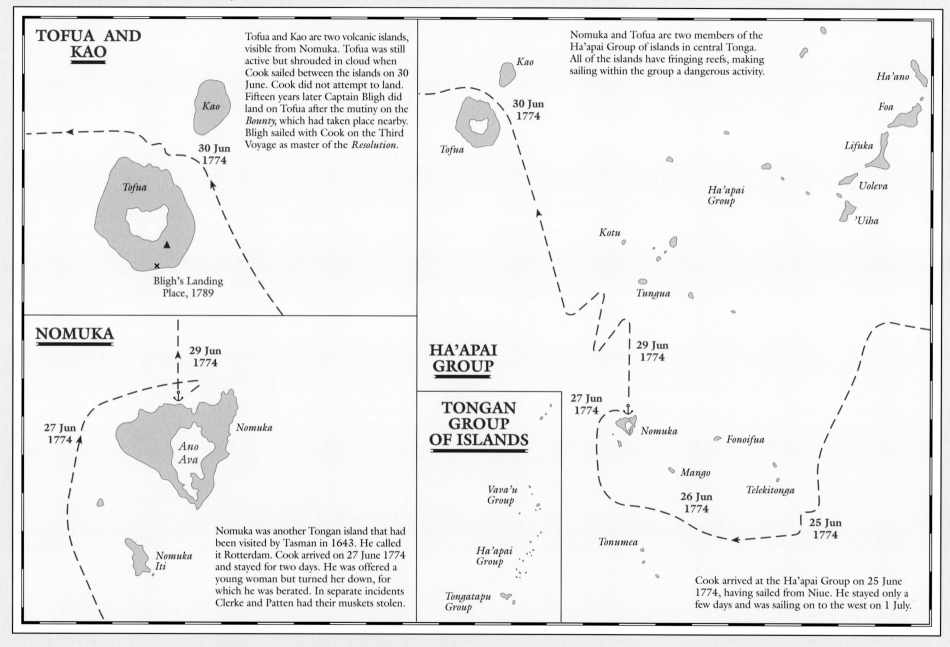

TOFUA AND KAO

Tofua and Kao are two volcanic islands, visible from Nomuka. Tofua was still active but shrouded in cloud when Cook sailed between the islands on 30 June. Cook did not attempt to land. Fifteen years later Captain Bligh did land on Tofua after the mutiny on the *Bounty*, which had taken place nearby. Bligh sailed with Cook on the Third Voyage as master of the *Resolution*.

Kao

30 Jun 1774

Tofua

Bligh's Landing Place, 1789

NOMUKA

29 Jun 1774

27 Jun 1774

Nomuka

Ano Ava

Nomuka Iti

Nomuka was another Tongan island that had been visited by Tasman in 1643. He called it Rotterdam. Cook arrived on 27 June 1774 and stayed for two days. He was offered a young woman but turned her down, for which he was berated. In separate incidents Clerke and Patten had their muskets stolen.

Nomuka and Tofua are two members of the Ha'apai Group of islands in central Tonga. All of the islands have fringing reefs, making sailing within the group a dangerous activity.

Kao

30 Jun 1774

Tofua

Ha'ano

Foa

Lifuka

Uoleva

'Uiha

Ha'apai Group

Kotu

Tungua

HA'APAI GROUP

29 Jun 1774

27 Jun 1774

Nomuka

Fonoifua

Mango

Telekitonga

26 Jun 1774

25 Jun 1774

Tonumea

TONGAN GROUP OF ISLANDS

Vava'u Group

Ha'apai Group

Tongatapu Group

Cook arrived at the Ha'apai Group on 25 June 1774, having sailed from Niue. He stayed only a few days and was sailing on to the west on 1 July.

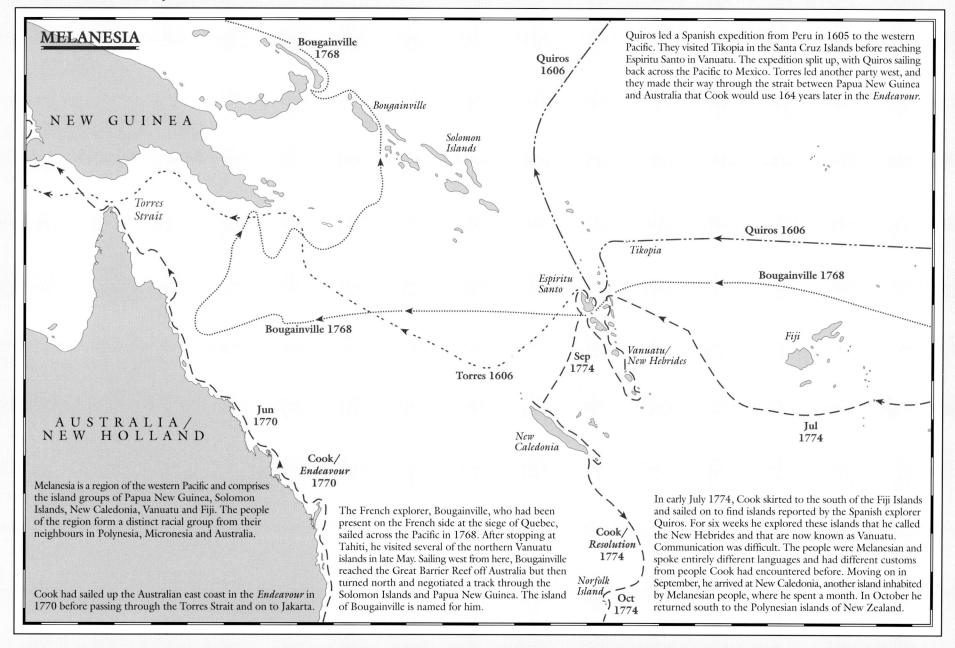

MELANESIA

NEW GUINEA

Torres Strait

AUSTRALIA/ NEW HOLLAND

Bougainville 1768

Bougainville

Solomon Islands

Quiros 1606

Quiros 1606

Tikopia

Bougainville 1768

Espiritu Santo

Bougainville 1768

Torres 1606

Sep 1774

Vanuatu/ New Hebrides

Fiji

Jun 1770

New Caledonia

Jul 1774

Cook/ Endeavour 1770

Cook/ Resolution 1774

Norfolk Island

Oct 1774

Quiros led a Spanish expedition from Peru in 1605 to the western Pacific. They visited Tikopia in the Santa Cruz Islands before reaching Espiritu Santo in Vanuatu. The expedition split up, with Quiros sailing back across the Pacific to Mexico. Torres led another party west, and they made their way through the strait between Papua New Guinea and Australia that Cook would use 164 years later in the *Endeavour*.

Melanesia is a region of the western Pacific and comprises the island groups of Papua New Guinea, Solomon Islands, New Caledonia, Vanuatu and Fiji. The people of the region form a distinct racial group from their neighbours in Polynesia, Micronesia and Australia.

Cook had sailed up the Australian east coast in the *Endeavour* in 1770 before passing through the Torres Strait and on to Jakarta.

The French explorer, Bougainville, who had been present on the French side at the siege of Quebec, sailed across the Pacific in 1768. After stopping at Tahiti, he visited several of the northern Vanuatu islands in late May. Sailing west from here, Bougainville reached the Great Barrier Reef off Australia but then turned north and negotiated a track through the Solomon Islands and Papua New Guinea. The island of Bougainville is named for him.

In early July 1774, Cook skirted to the south of the Fiji Islands and sailed on to find islands reported by the Spanish explorer Quiros. For six weeks he explored these islands that he called the New Hebrides and that are now known as Vanuatu. Communication was difficult. The people were Melanesian and spoke entirely different languages and had different customs from people Cook had encountered before. Moving on in September, he arrived at New Caledonia, another island inhabited by Melanesian people, where he spent a month. In October he returned south to the Polynesian islands of New Zealand.

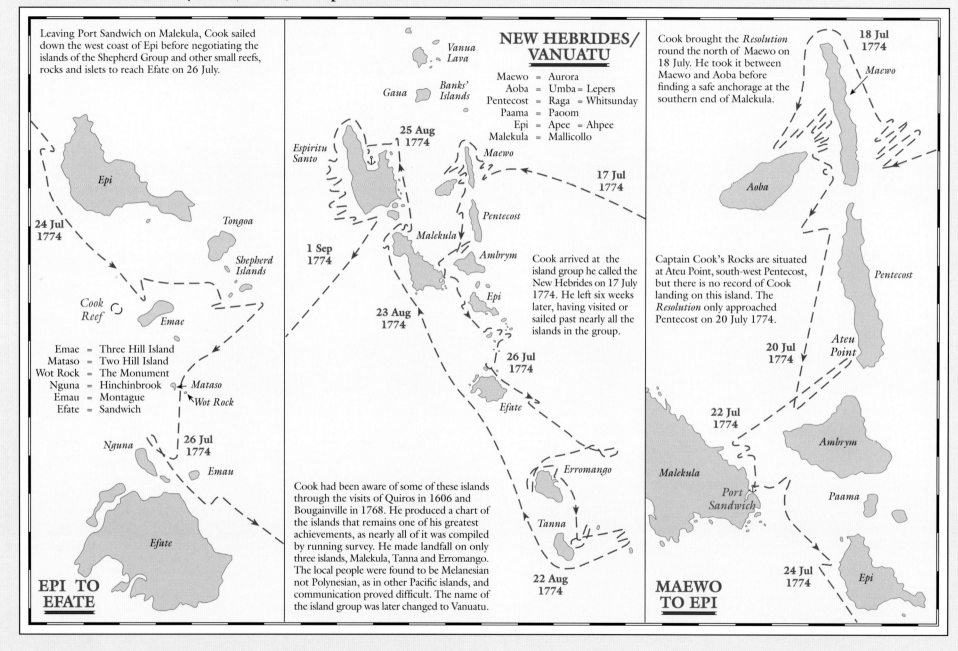

Leaving Port Sandwich on Malekula, Cook sailed down the west coast of Epi before negotiating the islands of the Shepherd Group and other small reefs, rocks and islets to reach Efate on 26 July.

NEW HEBRIDES/ VANUATU

Maewo	= Aurora	
Aoba	= Umba	= Lepers
Pentecost	= Raga	= Whitsunday
Paama	= Paoom	
Epi	= Apee	= Ahpee
Malekula	= Mallicollo	

Cook brought the *Resolution* round the north of Maewo on 18 July. He took it between Maewo and Aoba before finding a safe anchorage at the southern end of Malekula.

Cook arrived at the island group he called the New Hebrides on 17 July 1774. He left six weeks later, having visited or sailed past nearly all the islands in the group.

Captain Cook's Rocks are situated at Ateu Point, south-west Pentecost, but there is no record of Cook landing on this island. The *Resolution* only approached Pentecost on 20 July 1774.

Emae = Three Hill Island
Mataso = Two Hill Island
Wot Rock = The Monument
Nguna = Hinchinbrook
Emau = Montague
Efate = Sandwich

Cook had been aware of some of these islands through the visits of Quiros in 1606 and Bougainville in 1768. He produced a chart of the islands that remains one of his greatest achievements, as nearly all of it was compiled by running survey. He made landfall on only three islands, Malekula, Tanna and Erromango. The local people were found to be Melanesian not Polynesian, as in other Pacific islands, and communication proved difficult. The name of the island group was later changed to Vanuatu.

EPI TO EFATE

MAEWO TO EPI

Map labels: Vanua Lava, Gaua, Banks' Islands, Espiritu Santo, Maewo, Pentecost, Malekula, Ambrym, Epi, Efate, Erromango, Tanna, Aoba, Pentecost, Ateu Point, Malekula, Port Sandwich, Ambrym, Paama, Epi, Epi, Tongoa, Shepherd Islands, Cook Reef, Emae, Mataso, Wot Rock, Nguna, Emau, Efate

Dates: 18 Jul 1774, 17 Jul 1774, 20 Jul 1774, 22 Jul 1774, 24 Jul 1774, 25 Aug 1774, 1 Sep 1774, 23 Aug 1774, 26 Jul 1774, 22 Aug 1774, 24 Jul 1774, 26 Jul 1774

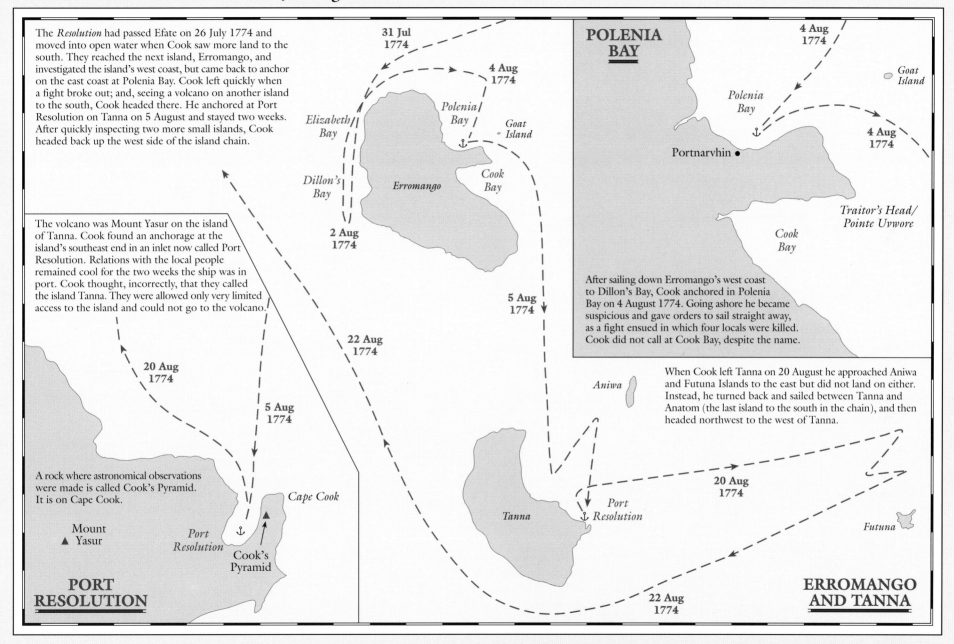

The *Resolution* had passed Efate on 26 July 1774 and moved into open water when Cook saw more land to the south. They reached the next island, Erromango, and investigated the island's west coast, but came back to anchor on the east coast at Polenia Bay. Cook left quickly when a fight broke out; and, seeing a volcano on another island to the south, Cook headed there. He anchored at Port Resolution on Tanna on 5 August and stayed two weeks. After quickly inspecting two more small islands, Cook headed back up the west side of the island chain.

The volcano was Mount Yasur on the island of Tanna. Cook found an anchorage at the island's southeast end in an inlet now called Port Resolution. Relations with the local people remained cool for the two weeks the ship was in port. Cook thought, incorrectly, that they called the island Tanna. They were allowed only very limited access to the island and could not go to the volcano.

A rock where astronomical observations were made is called Cook's Pyramid. It is on Cape Cook.

POLENIA BAY

After sailing down Erromango's west coast to Dillon's Bay, Cook anchored in Polenia Bay on 4 August 1774. Going ashore he became suspicious and gave orders to sail straight away, as a fight ensued in which four locals were killed. Cook did not call at Cook Bay, despite the name.

When Cook left Tanna on 20 August he approached Aniwa and Futuna Islands to the east but did not land on either. Instead, he turned back and sailed between Tanna and Anatom (the last island to the south in the chain), and then headed northwest to the west of Tanna.

PORT RESOLUTION

ERROMANGO AND TANNA

31 Jul 1774

4 Aug 1774

Polenia Bay

Goat Island

Elizabeth Bay

Dillon's Bay

Erromango

Cook Bay

2 Aug 1774

5 Aug 1774

22 Aug 1774

4 Aug 1774

Polenia Bay

Portnarvhin •

Goat Island

Traitor's Head/ Pointe Uvwore

Cook Bay

Aniwa

20 Aug 1774

22 Aug 1774

Futuna

Tanna

Port Resolution

20 Aug 1774

5 Aug 1774

Mount ▲ Yasur

Port Resolution

Cook's Pyramid

Cape Cook

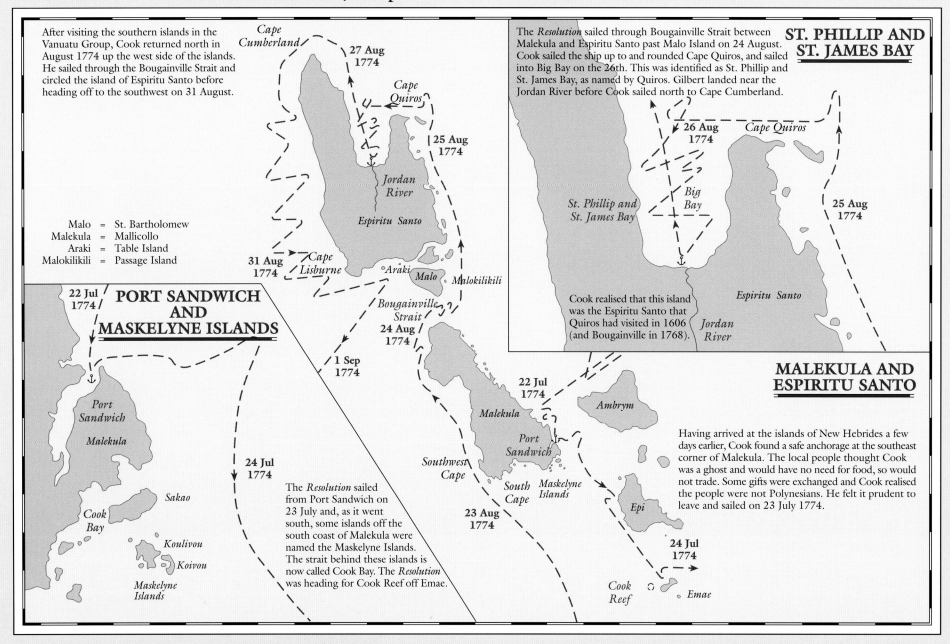

After visiting the southern islands in the Vanuatu Group, Cook returned north in August 1774 up the west side of the islands. He sailed through the Bougainville Strait and circled the island of Espiritu Santo before heading off to the southwest on 31 August.

Malo = St. Bartholomew
Malekula = Mallicollo
Araki = Table Island
Malokilikili = Passage Island

Cape Cumberland

27 Aug 1774

Cape Quiros

25 Aug 1774

Jordan River

Espiritu Santo

31 Aug 1774

Cape Lisburne

Araki

Malo

Malokilikili

Bougainville Strait

24 Aug 1774

1 Sep 1774

ST. PHILLIP AND ST. JAMES BAY

The *Resolution* sailed through Bougainville Strait between Malekula and Espiritu Santo past Malo Island on 24 August. Cook sailed the ship up to and rounded Cape Quiros, and sailed into Big Bay on the 26th. This was identified as St. Phillip and St. James Bay, as named by Quiros. Gilbert landed near the Jordan River before Cook sailed north to Cape Cumberland.

26 Aug 1774

Cape Quiros

St. Phillip and St. James Bay

Big Bay

25 Aug 1774

Espiritu Santo

Cook realised that this island was the Espiritu Santo that Quiros had visited in 1606 (and Bougainville in 1768).

Jordan River

PORT SANDWICH AND MASKELYNE ISLANDS

22 Jul 1774

Port Sandwich

Malekula

24 Jul 1774

Sakao

Cook Bay

Koulivou

Koivou

Maskelyne Islands

The *Resolution* sailed from Port Sandwich on 23 July and, as it went south, some islands off the south coast of Malekula were named the Maskelyne Islands. The strait behind these islands is now called Cook Bay. The *Resolution* was heading for Cook Reef off Emae.

MALEKULA AND ESPIRITU SANTO

22 Jul 1774

Ambrym

Malekula

Port Sandwich

Southwest Cape

South Cape

Maskelyne Islands

23 Aug 1774

Epi

24 Jul 1774

Cook Reef

Emae

Having arrived at the islands of New Hebrides a few days earlier, Cook found a safe anchorage at the southeast corner of Malekula. The local people thought Cook was a ghost and would have no need for food, so would not trade. Some gifts were exchanged and Cook realised the people were not Polynesians. He felt it prudent to leave and sailed on 23 July 1774.

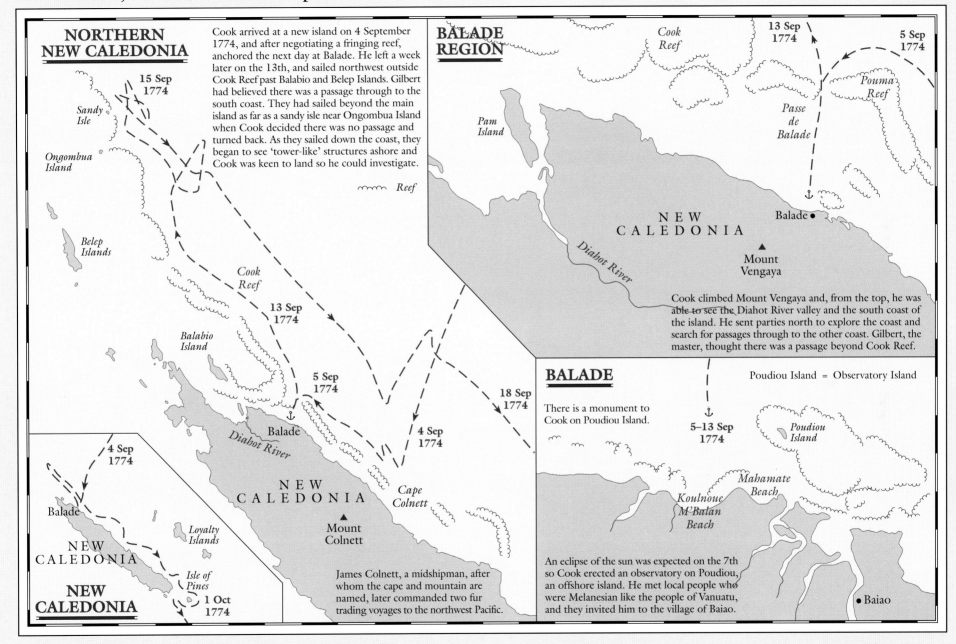

NORTHERN NEW CALEDONIA

15 Sep 1774

Sandy Isle

Ongombua Island

Belep Islands

Cook Reef

13 Sep 1774

Balabio Island

5 Sep 1774

Balade

Diahot River

NEW CALEDONIA

Mount Colnett

Cape Colnett

James Colnett, a midshipman, after whom the cape and mountain are named, later commanded two fur trading voyages to the northwest Pacific.

Cook arrived at a new island on 4 September 1774, and after negotiating a fringing reef, anchored the next day at Balade. He left a week later on the 13th, and sailed northwest outside Cook Reef past Balabio and Belep Islands. Gilbert had believed there was a passage through to the south coast. They had sailed beyond the main island as far as a sandy isle near Ongombua Island when Cook decided there was no passage and turned back. As they sailed down the coast, they began to see 'tower-like' structures ashore and Cook was keen to land so he could investigate.

Reef

4 Sep 1774

Balade

NEW CALEDONIA

Loyalty Islands

Isle of Pines

1 Oct 1774

NEW CALEDONIA

18 Sep 1774

4 Sep 1774

BALADE REGION

Cook Reef

13 Sep 1774

5 Sep 1774

Pouma Reef

Pam Island

Passe de Balade

NEW CALEDONIA

Balade

Diahot River

Mount Vengaya

Cook climbed Mount Vengaya and, from the top, he was able to see the Diahot River valley and the south coast of the island. He sent parties north to explore the coast and search for passages through to the other coast. Gilbert, the master, thought there was a passage beyond Cook Reef.

BALADE

Poudiou Island = Observatory Island

There is a monument to Cook on Poudiou Island.

5–13 Sep 1774

Poudiou Island

Mahamate Beach

Koulnoue M'Balan Beach

Baiao

An eclipse of the sun was expected on the 7th so Cook erected an observatory on Poudiou, an offshore island. He met local people who were Melanesian like the people of Vanuatu, and they invited him to the village of Baiao.

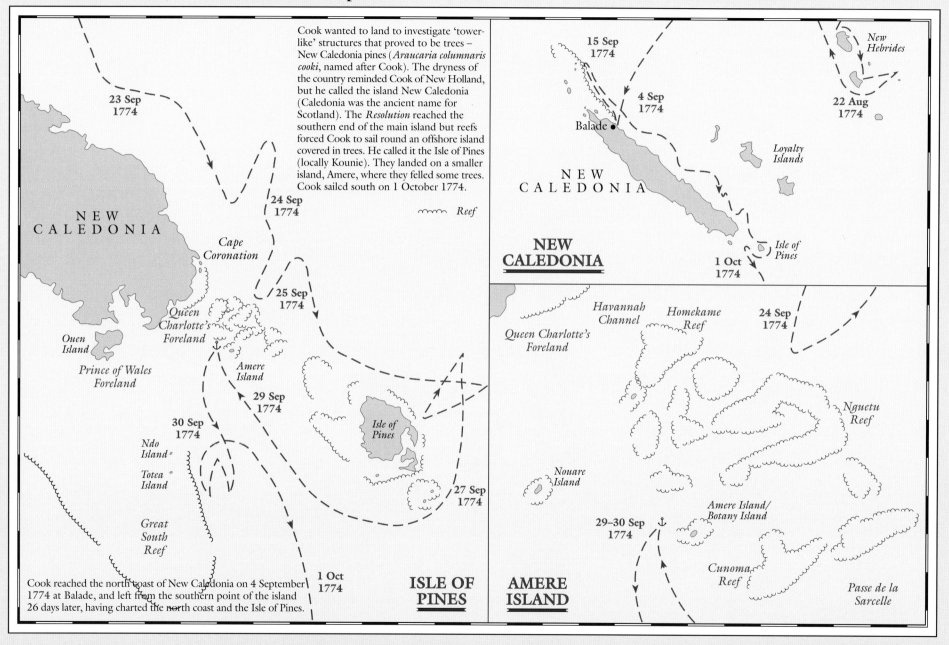

Cook wanted to land to investigate 'tower-like' structures that proved to be trees – New Caledonia pines (*Araucaria columnaris cooki*, named after Cook). The dryness of the country reminded Cook of New Holland, but he called the island New Caledonia (Caledonia was the ancient name for Scotland). The *Resolution* reached the southern end of the main island but reefs forced Cook to sail round an offshore island covered in trees. He called it the Isle of Pines (locally Kounie). They landed on a smaller island, Amere, where they felled some trees. Cook sailed south on 1 October 1774.

～～～ *Reef*

NEW CALEDONIA

15 Sep 1774

4 Sep 1774

Balade

New Hebrides

22 Aug 1774

Loyalty Islands

N E W C A L E D O N I A

Isle of Pines

1 Oct 1774

23 Sep 1774

N E W C A L E D O N I A

Cape Coronation

24 Sep 1774

25 Sep 1774

Queen Charlotte's Foreland

Ouen Island

Prince of Wales Foreland

Amere Island

29 Sep 1774

30 Sep 1774

Ndo Island

Totea Island

Isle of Pines

27 Sep 1774

Great South Reef

1 Oct 1774

ISLE OF PINES

Cook reached the north coast of New Caledonia on 4 September 1774 at Balade, and left from the southern point of the island 26 days later, having charted the north coast and the Isle of Pines.

Queen Charlotte's Foreland

Havannah Channel

Homekame Reef

24 Sep 1774

Nguetu Reef

Nouare Island

Amere Island/ Botany Island

29–30 Sep 1774

Cunoma Reef

Passe de la Sarcelle

AMERE ISLAND

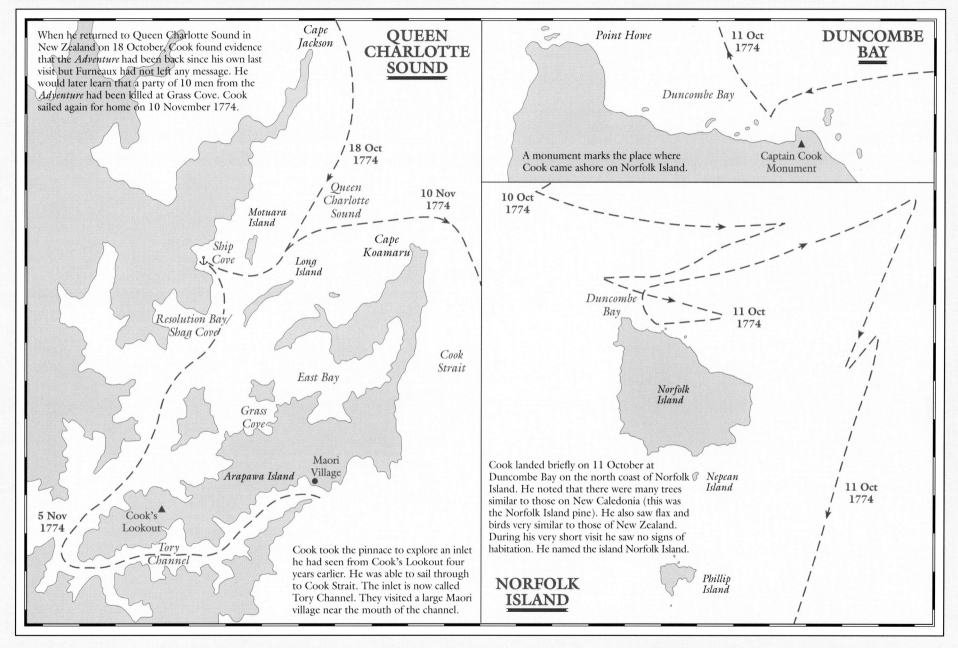

When he returned to Queen Charlotte Sound in New Zealand on 18 October, Cook found evidence that the *Adventure* had been back since his own last visit but Furneaux had not left any message. He would later learn that a party of 10 men from the *Adventure* had been killed at Grass Cove. Cook sailed again for home on 10 November 1774.

Cape Jackson

QUEEN CHARLOTTE SOUND

18 Oct 1774

Queen Charlotte Sound

10 Nov 1774

Motuara Island

Ship Cove

Long Island

Cape Koamaru

Resolution Bay/ Shag Cove

Cook Strait

East Bay

Grass Cove

5 Nov 1774

Cook's Lookout

Arapawa Island

Maori Village

Tory Channel

Cook took the pinnace to explore an inlet he had seen from Cook's Lookout four years earlier. He was able to sail through to Cook Strait. The inlet is now called Tory Channel. They visited a large Maori village near the mouth of the channel.

Point Howe

11 Oct 1774

DUNCOMBE BAY

Duncombe Bay

A monument marks the place where Cook came ashore on Norfolk Island.

Captain Cook Monument

10 Oct 1774

11 Oct 1774

Duncombe Bay

11 Oct 1774

Norfolk Island

11 Oct 1774

Cook landed briefly on 11 October at Duncombe Bay on the north coast of Norfolk Island. He noted that there were many trees similar to those on New Caledonia (this was the Norfolk Island pine). He also saw flax and birds very similar to those of New Zealand. During his very short visit he saw no signs of habitation. He named the island Norfolk Island.

Nepean Island

NORFOLK ISLAND

Phillip Island

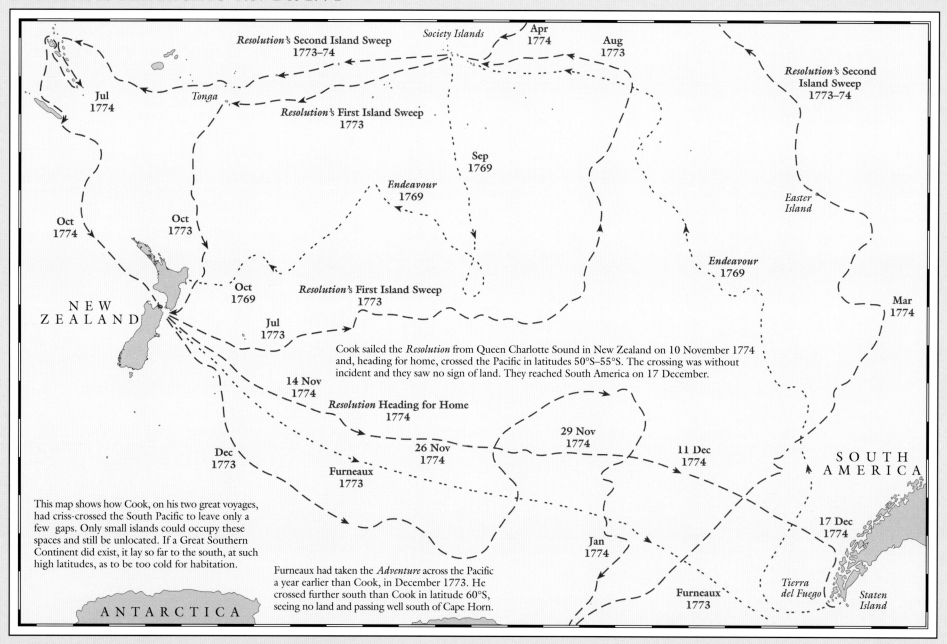

Resolution's Second Island Sweep
1773–74

Society Islands

Apr
1774

Aug
1773

Resolution's Second
Island Sweep
1773–74

Jul
1774

Tonga

Resolution's First Island Sweep
1773

Sep
1769

Endeavour
1769

*Easter
Island*

Oct
1774

Oct
1773

Oct
1769

Endeavour
1769

Oct
1769

Resolution's First Island Sweep
1773

Mar
1774

NEW
ZEALAND

Jul
1773

Cook sailed the *Resolution* from Queen Charlotte Sound in New Zealand on 10 November 1774 and, heading for home, crossed the Pacific in latitudes 50°S–55°S. The crossing was without incident and they saw no sign of land. They reached South America on 17 December.

14 Nov
1774

Resolution Heading for Home
1774

29 Nov
1774

11 Dec
1774

SOUTH
AMERICA

26 Nov
1774

Dec
1773

Furneaux
1773

17 Dec
1774

This map shows how Cook, on his two great voyages, had criss-crossed the South Pacific to leave only a few gaps. Only small islands could occupy these spaces and still be unlocated. If a Great Southern Continent did exist, it lay so far to the south, at such high latitudes, as to be too cold for habitation.

Jan
1774

Furneaux had taken the *Adventure* across the Pacific a year earlier than Cook, in December 1773. He crossed further south than Cook in latitude 60°S, seeing no land and passing well south of Cape Horn.

Furneaux
1773

*Tierra
del Fuego*

*Staten
Island*

ANTARCTICA

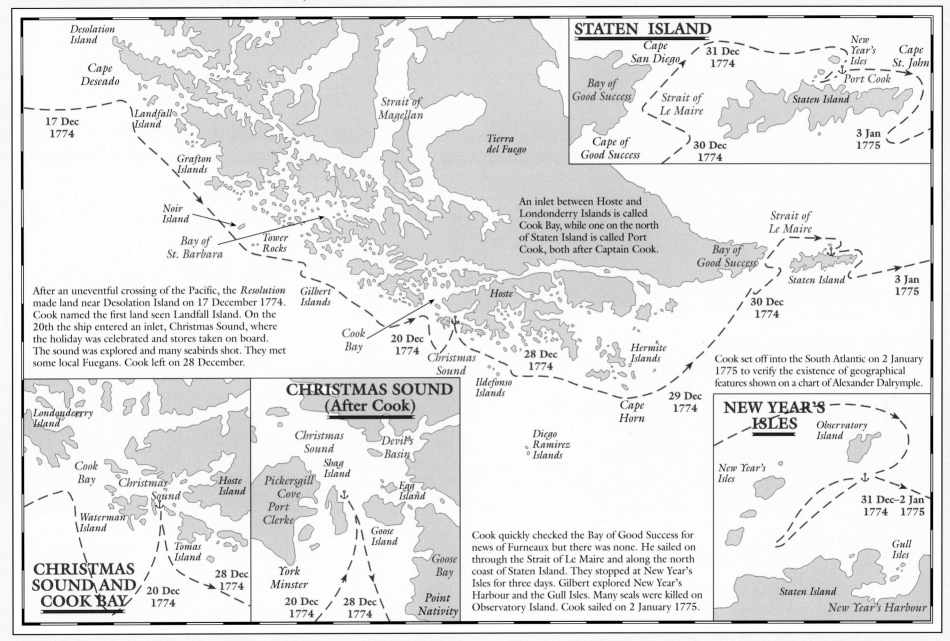

STATEN ISLAND

Cape San Diego
31 Dec 1774
New Year's Isles
Cape St. John
Port Cook
Bay of Good Success
Strait of Le Maire
Staten Island
Cape of Good Success
30 Dec 1774
3 Jan 1775

Desolation Island
Cape Deseado
Landfall Island
17 Dec 1774
Grafton Islands
Noir Island
Bay of St. Barbara
Tower Rocks
Strait of Magellan
Tierra del Fuego

An inlet between Hoste and Londonderry Islands is called Cook Bay, while one on the north of Staten Island is called Port Cook, both after Captain Cook.

Strait of Le Maire
Bay of Good Success
Staten Island
3 Jan 1775
30 Dec 1774

After an uneventful crossing of the Pacific, the *Resolution* made land near Desolation Island on 17 December 1774. Cook named the first land seen Landfall Island. On the 20th the ship entered an inlet, Christmas Sound, where the holiday was celebrated and stores taken on board. The sound was explored and many seabirds shot. They met some local Fuegans. Cook left on 28 December.

Gilbert Islands
Cook Bay
20 Dec 1774
Christmas Sound
Hoste
28 Dec 1774
Ildefonso Islands
Hermite Islands
Cape Horn
29 Dec 1774
Diego Ramirez Islands

Cook set off into the South Atlantic on 2 January 1775 to verify the existence of geographical features shown on a chart of Alexander Dalrymple.

CHRISTMAS SOUND (After Cook)

Londonderry Island
Cook Bay
Christmas Sound
Hoste Island
Waterman Island
Tomas Island
28 Dec 1774
20 Dec 1774

CHRISTMAS SOUND AND COOK BAY

Christmas Sound
Devil's Basin
Shag Island
Pickersgill Cove Port Clerke
Egg Island
Goose Island
Goose Bay
York Minster
20 Dec 1774
28 Dec 1774
Point Nativity

NEW YEAR'S ISLES

Observatory Island
New Year's Isles
31 Dec–2 Jan 1774 1775
Gull Isles
Staten Island
New Year's Harbour

Cook quickly checked the Bay of Good Success for news of Furneaux but there was none. He sailed on through the Strait of Le Maire and along the north coast of Staten Island. They stopped at New Year's Isles for three days. Gilbert explored New Year's Harbour and the Gull Isles. Many seals were killed on Observatory Island. Cook sailed on 2 January 1775.

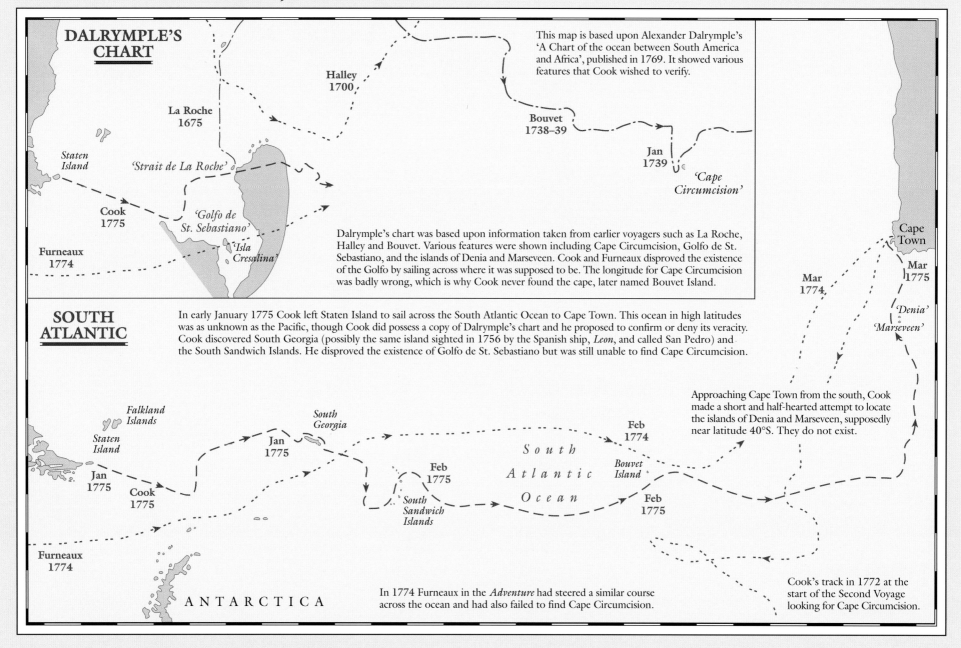

DALRYMPLE'S CHART

This map is based upon Alexander Dalrymple's 'A Chart of the ocean between South America and Africa', published in 1769. It showed various features that Cook wished to verify.

Halley 1700

La Roche 1675

Bouvet 1738–39

Staten Island

'Strait de La Roche'

Jan 1739

'Cape Circumcision'

Cook 1775

'Golfo de St. Sebastiano'

'Isla Cresalina'

Furneaux 1774

Dalrymple's chart was based upon information taken from earlier voyagers such as La Roche, Halley and Bouvet. Various features were shown including Cape Circumcision, Golfo de St. Sebastiano, and the islands of Denia and Marseveen. Cook and Furneaux disproved the existence of the Golfo by sailing across where it was supposed to be. The longitude for Cape Circumcision was badly wrong, which is why Cook never found the cape, later named Bouvet Island.

Cape Town

Mar 1775

Mar 1774

'Denia'
'Marseveen'

SOUTH ATLANTIC

In early January 1775 Cook left Staten Island to sail across the South Atlantic Ocean to Cape Town. This ocean in high latitudes was as unknown as the Pacific, though Cook did possess a copy of Dalrymple's chart and he proposed to confirm or deny its veracity. Cook discovered South Georgia (possibly the same island sighted in 1756 by the Spanish ship, *Leon*, and called San Pedro) and the South Sandwich Islands. He disproved the existence of Golfo de St. Sebastiano but was still unable to find Cape Circumcision.

Falkland Islands

South Georgia

Feb 1774

Staten Island

Jan 1775

Approaching Cape Town from the south, Cook made a short and half-hearted attempt to locate the islands of Denia and Marseveen, supposedly near latitude 40°S. They do not exist.

Jan 1775

Cook 1775

Feb 1775

South Atlantic Ocean

Bouvet Island

South Sandwich Islands

Feb 1775

Feb 1775

Furneaux 1774

ANTARCTICA

In 1774 Furneaux in the *Adventure* had steered a similar course across the ocean and had also failed to find Cape Circumcision.

Cook's track in 1772 at the start of the Second Voyage looking for Cape Circumcision.

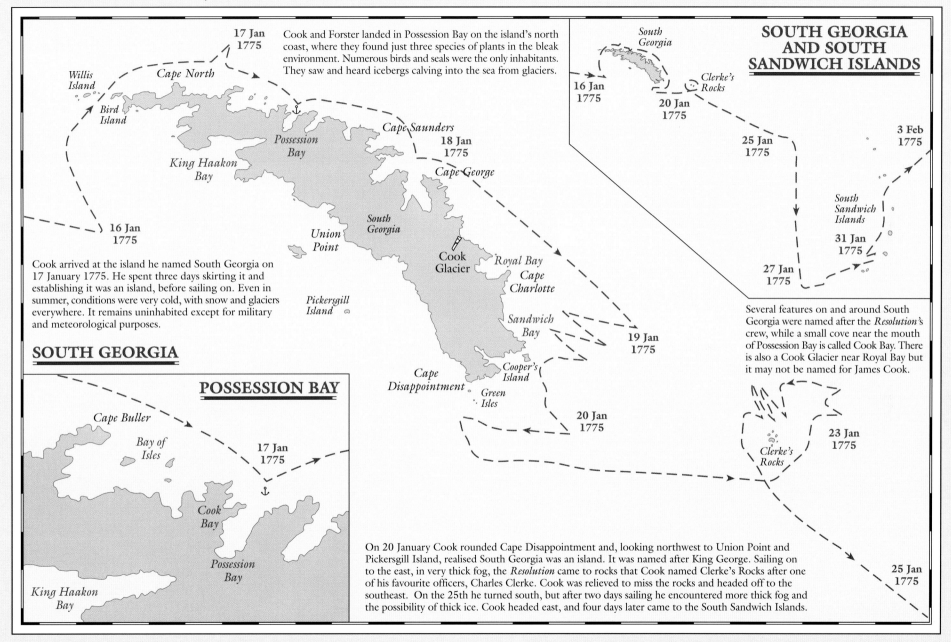

Cook and Forster landed in Possession Bay on the island's north coast, where they found just three species of plants in the bleak environment. Numerous birds and seals were the only inhabitants. They saw and heard icebergs calving into the sea from glaciers.

SOUTH GEORGIA AND SOUTH SANDWICH ISLANDS

Cook arrived at the island he named South Georgia on 17 January 1775. He spent three days skirting it and establishing it was an island, before sailing on. Even in summer, conditions were very cold, with snow and glaciers everywhere. It remains uninhabited except for military and meteorological purposes.

SOUTH GEORGIA

POSSESSION BAY

Several features on and around South Georgia were named after the *Resolution*'s crew, while a small cove near the mouth of Possession Bay is called Cook Bay. There is also a Cook Glacier near Royal Bay but it may not be named for James Cook.

On 20 January Cook rounded Cape Disappointment and, looking northwest to Union Point and Pickersgill Island, realised South Georgia was an island. It was named after King George. Sailing on to the east, in very thick fog, the *Resolution* came to rocks that Cook named Clerke's Rocks after one of his favourite officers, Charles Clerke. Cook was relieved to miss the rocks and headed off to the southeast. On the 25th he turned south, but after two days sailing he encountered more thick fog and the possibility of thick ice. Cook headed east, and four days later came to the South Sandwich Islands.

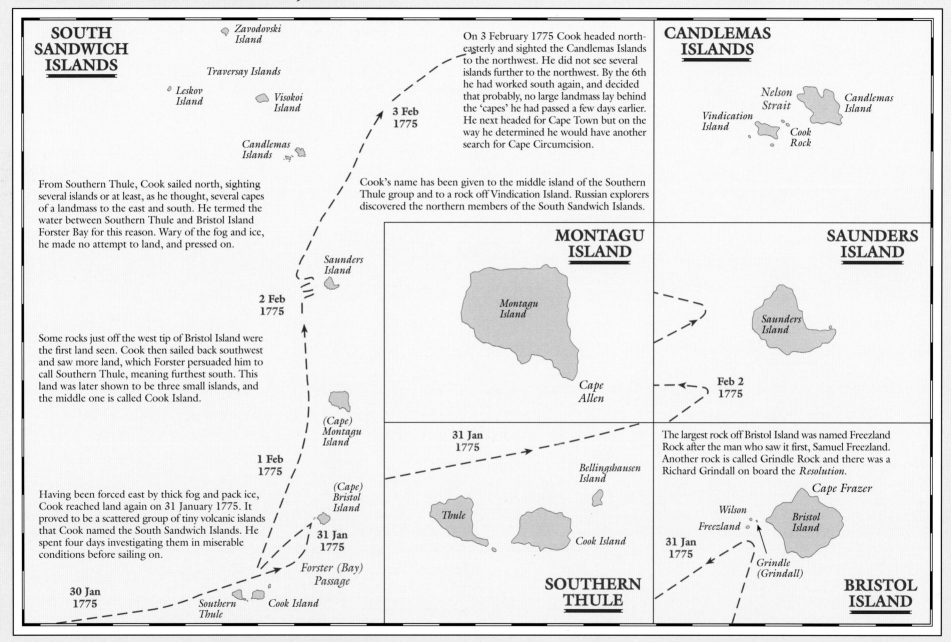

SOUTH SANDWICH ISLANDS

Zavodovski Island

Traversay Islands

Leskov Island *Visokoi Island*

Candlemas Islands

From Southern Thule, Cook sailed north, sighting several islands or at least, as he thought, several capes of a landmass to the east and south. He termed the water between Southern Thule and Bristol Island Forster Bay for this reason. Wary of the fog and ice, he made no attempt to land, and pressed on.

Some rocks just off the west tip of Bristol Island were the first land seen. Cook then sailed back southwest and saw more land, which Forster persuaded him to call Southern Thule, meaning furthest south. This land was later shown to be three small islands, and the middle one is called Cook Island.

Having been forced east by thick fog and pack ice, Cook reached land again on 31 January 1775. It proved to be a scattered group of tiny volcanic islands that Cook named the South Sandwich Islands. He spent four days investigating them in miserable conditions before sailing on.

Saunders Island

2 Feb 1775

1 Feb 1775

(Cape) Montagu Island

(Cape) Bristol Island

31 Jan 1775

30 Jan 1775

Southern Thule *Cook Island*

Forster (Bay) Passage

3 Feb 1775

On 3 February 1775 Cook headed north-easterly and sighted the Candlemas Islands to the northwest. He did not see several islands further to the northwest. By the 6th he had worked south again, and decided that probably, no large landmass lay behind the 'capes' he had passed a few days earlier. He next headed for Cape Town but on the way he determined he would have another search for Cape Circumcision.

Cook's name has been given to the middle island of the Southern Thule group and to a rock off Vindication Island. Russian explorers discovered the northern members of the South Sandwich Islands.

CANDLEMAS ISLANDS

Nelson Strait *Candlemas Island*

Vindication Island *Cook Rock*

MONTAGU ISLAND

Montagu Island

Cape Allen

SAUNDERS ISLAND

Saunders Island

Feb 2 1775

SOUTHERN THULE

31 Jan 1775

Bellingshausen Island

Thule

Cook Island

BRISTOL ISLAND

The largest rock off Bristol Island was named Freezland Rock after the man who saw it first, Samuel Freezland. Another rock is called Grindle Rock and there was a Richard Grindall on board the *Resolution*.

Cape Frazer

Wilson Freezland *Bristol Island*

31 Jan 1775

Grindle (Grindall)

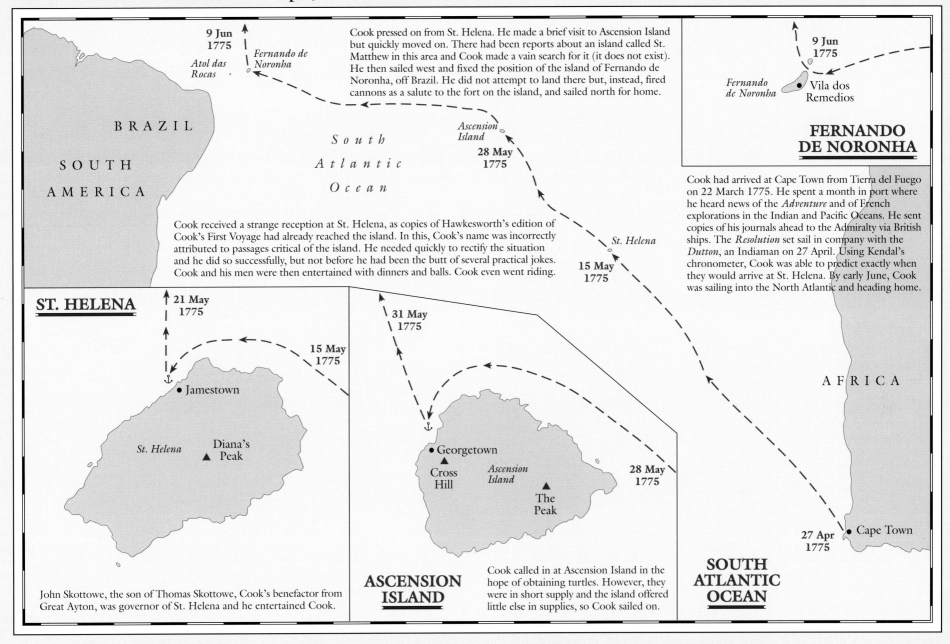

Cook pressed on from St. Helena. He made a brief visit to Ascension Island but quickly moved on. There had been reports about an island called St. Matthew in this area and Cook made a vain search for it (it does not exist). He then sailed west and fixed the position of the island of Fernando de Noronha, off Brazil. He did not attempt to land there but, instead, fired cannons as a salute to the fort on the island, and sailed north for home.

BRAZIL

SOUTH AMERICA

South Atlantic Ocean

Cook received a strange reception at St. Helena, as copies of Hawkesworth's edition of Cook's First Voyage had already reached the island. In this, Cook's name was incorrectly attributed to passages critical of the island. He needed quickly to rectify the situation and he did so successfully, but not before he had been the butt of several practical jokes. Cook and his men were then entertained with dinners and balls. Cook even went riding.

9 Jun 1775
Atol das Rocas
Fernando de Noronha

Ascension Island
28 May 1775

St. Helena
15 May 1775

FERNANDO DE NORONHA

9 Jun 1775
Fernando de Noronha
Vila dos Remedios

Cook had arrived at Cape Town from Tierra del Fuego on 22 March 1775. He spent a month in port where he heard news of the *Adventure* and of French explorations in the Indian and Pacific Oceans. He sent copies of his journals ahead to the Admiralty via British ships. The *Resolution* set sail in company with the *Dutton*, an Indiaman on 27 April. Using Kendal's chronometer, Cook was able to predict exactly when they would arrive at St. Helena. By early June, Cook was sailing into the North Atlantic and heading home.

ST. HELENA

21 May 1775

15 May 1775

• Jamestown

St. Helena
Diana's
▲ Peak

31 May 1775

• Georgetown
▲
Cross Hill
Ascension Island
▲ The Peak

28 May 1775

AFRICA

27 Apr 1775
• Cape Town

SOUTH ATLANTIC OCEAN

John Skottowe, the son of Thomas Skottowe, Cook's benefactor from Great Ayton, was governor of St. Helena and he entertained Cook.

ASCENSION ISLAND

Cook called in at Ascension Island in the hope of obtaining turtles. However, they were in short supply and the island offered little else in supplies, so Cook sailed on.

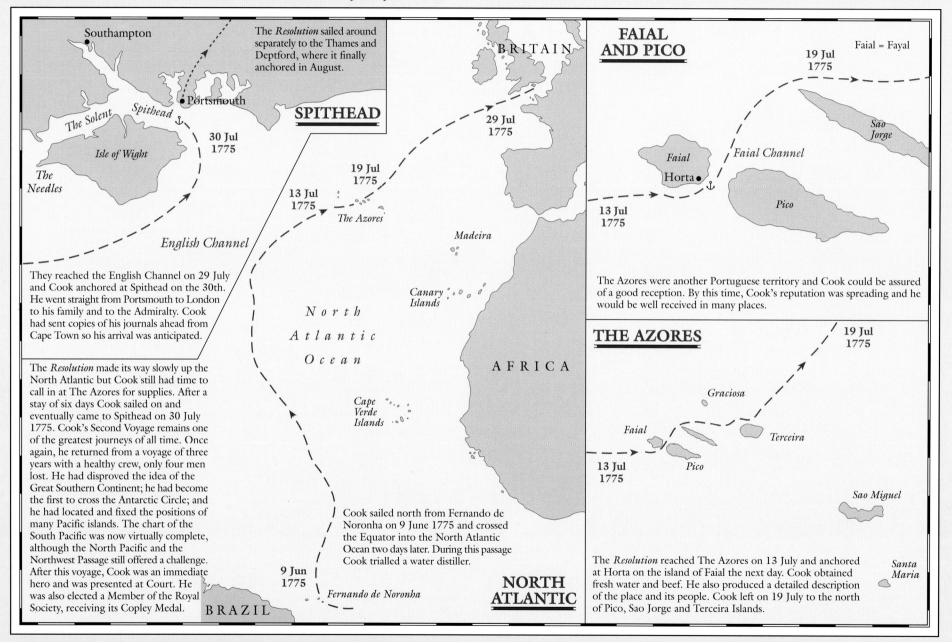

Southampton

The *Resolution* sailed around separately to the Thames and Deptford, where it finally anchored in August.

SPITHEAD

The Solent

Spithead

Portsmouth

30 Jul 1775

The Needles

Isle of Wight

English Channel

29 Jul 1775

BRITAIN

19 Jul 1775

13 Jul 1775

The Azores

Madeira

Canary Islands

North Atlantic Ocean

AFRICA

They reached the English Channel on 29 July and Cook anchored at Spithead on the 30th. He went straight from Portsmouth to London to his family and to the Admiralty. Cook had sent copies of his journals ahead from Cape Town so his arrival was anticipated.

The *Resolution* made its way slowly up the North Atlantic but Cook still had time to call in at The Azores for supplies. After a stay of six days Cook sailed on and eventually came to Spithead on 30 July 1775. Cook's Second Voyage remains one of the greatest journeys of all time. Once again, he returned from a voyage of three years with a healthy crew, only four men lost. He had disproved the idea of the Great Southern Continent; he had become the first to cross the Antarctic Circle; and he had located and fixed the positions of many Pacific islands. The chart of the South Pacific was now virtually complete, although the North Pacific and the Northwest Passage still offered a challenge. After this voyage, Cook was an immediate hero and was presented at Court. He was also elected a Member of the Royal Society, receiving its Copley Medal.

BRAZIL

9 Jun 1775

Cape Verde Islands

Fernando de Noronha

Cook sailed north from Fernando de Noronha on 9 June 1775 and crossed the Equator into the North Atlantic Ocean two days later. During this passage Cook trialled a water distiller.

NORTH ATLANTIC

FAIAL AND PICO

Faial = Fayal

19 Jul 1775

Faial Channel

Sao Jorge

Faial

Horta

Pico

13 Jul 1775

The Azores were another Portuguese territory and Cook could be assured of a good reception. By this time, Cook's reputation was spreading and he would be well received in many places.

THE AZORES

19 Jul 1775

Graciosa

Faial

Terceira

Pico

13 Jul 1775

Sao Miguel

Santa Maria

The *Resolution* reached The Azores on 13 July and anchored at Horta on the island of Faial the next day. Cook obtained fresh water and beef. He also produced a detailed description of the place and its people. Cook left on 19 July to the north of Pico, Sao Jorge and Terceira Islands.

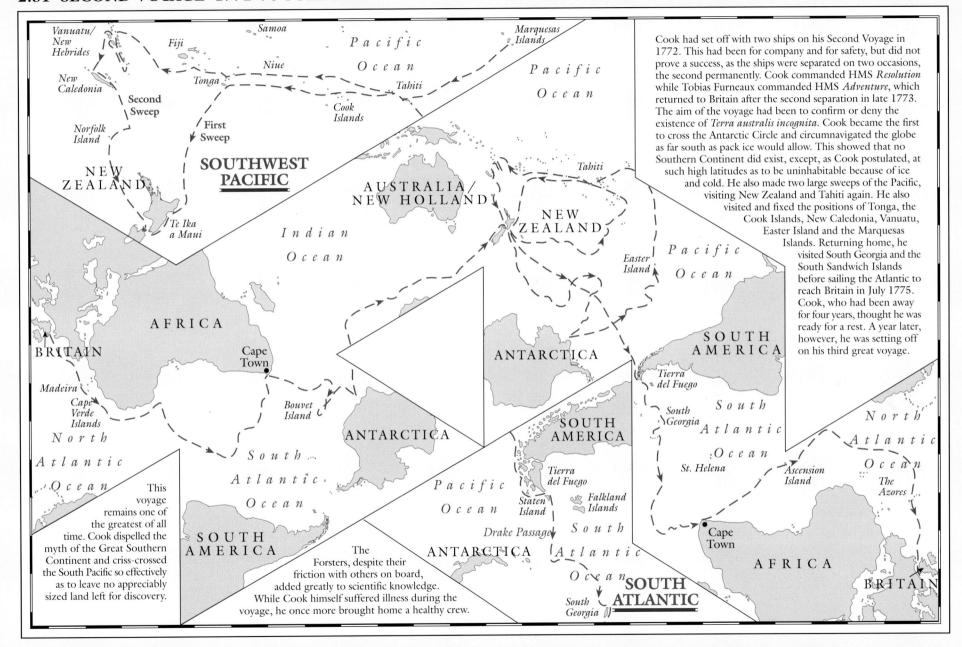

Cook had set off with two ships on his Second Voyage in 1772. This had been for company and for safety, but did not prove a success, as the ships were separated on two occasions, the second permanently. Cook commanded HMS *Resolution* while Tobias Furneaux commanded HMS *Adventure*, which returned to Britain after the second separation in late 1773. The aim of the voyage had been to confirm or deny the existence of *Terra australis incognita*. Cook became the first to cross the Antarctic Circle and circumnavigated the globe as far south as pack ice would allow. This showed that no Southern Continent did exist, except, as Cook postulated, at such high latitudes as to be uninhabitable because of ice and cold. He also made two large sweeps of the Pacific, visiting New Zealand and Tahiti again. He also visited and fixed the positions of Tonga, the Cook Islands, New Caledonia, Vanuatu, Easter Island and the Marquesas Islands. Returning home, he visited South Georgia and the South Sandwich Islands before sailing the Atlantic to reach Britain in July 1775. Cook, who had been away for four years, thought he was ready for a rest. A year later, however, he was setting off on his third great voyage.

This voyage remains one of the greatest of all time. Cook dispelled the myth of the Great Southern Continent and criss-crossed the South Pacific so effectively as to leave no appreciably sized land left for discovery.

The Forsters, despite their friction with others on board, added greatly to scientific knowledge. While Cook himself suffered illness during the voyage, he once more brought home a healthy crew.

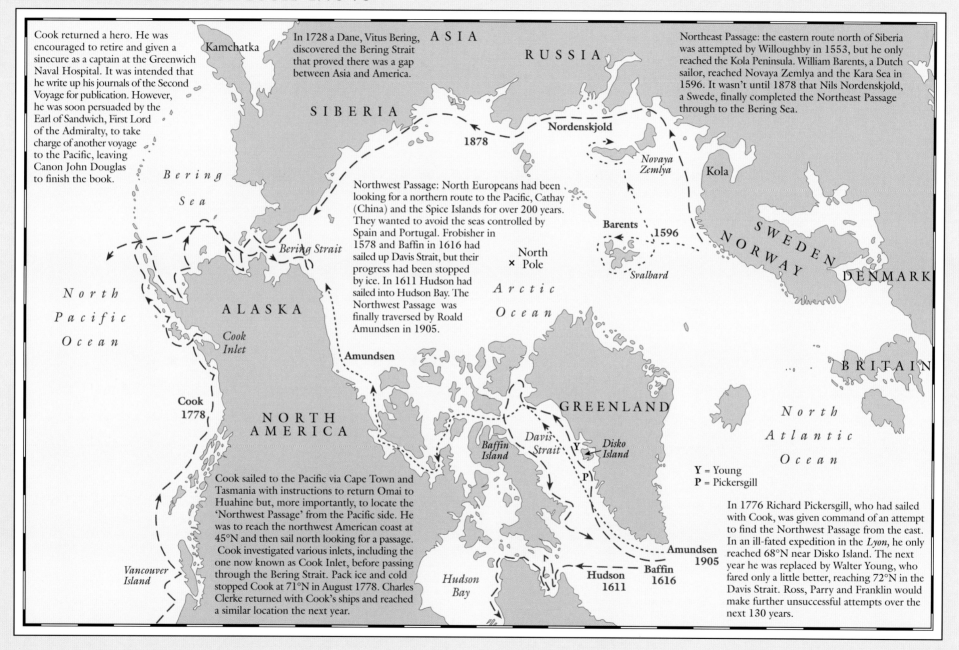

Cook returned a hero. He was encouraged to retire and given a sinecure as a captain at the Greenwich Naval Hospital. It was intended that he write up his journals of the Second Voyage for publication. However, he was soon persuaded by the Earl of Sandwich, First Lord of the Admiralty, to take charge of another voyage to the Pacific, leaving Canon John Douglas to finish the book.

In 1728 a Dane, Vitus Bering, discovered the Bering Strait that proved there was a gap between Asia and America.

Northeast Passage: the eastern route north of Siberia was attempted by Willoughby in 1553, but he only reached the Kola Peninsula. William Barents, a Dutch sailor, reached Novaya Zemlya and the Kara Sea in 1596. It wasn't until 1878 that Nils Nordenskjold, a Swede, finally completed the Northeast Passage through to the Bering Sea.

Northwest Passage: North Europeans had been looking for a northern route to the Pacific, Cathay (China) and the Spice Islands for over 200 years. They wanted to avoid the seas controlled by Spain and Portugal. Frobisher in 1578 and Baffin in 1616 had sailed up Davis Strait, but their progress had been stopped by ice. In 1611 Hudson had sailed into Hudson Bay. The Northwest Passage was finally traversed by Roald Amundsen in 1905.

Cook sailed to the Pacific via Cape Town and Tasmania with instructions to return Omai to Huahine but, more importantly, to locate the 'Northwest Passage' from the Pacific side. He was to reach the northwest American coast at 45°N and then sail north looking for a passage. Cook investigated various inlets, including the one now known as Cook Inlet, before passing through the Bering Strait. Pack ice and cold stopped Cook at 71°N in August 1778. Charles Clerke returned with Cook's ships and reached a similar location the next year.

Y = Young
P = Pickersgill

In 1776 Richard Pickersgill, who had sailed with Cook, was given command of an attempt to find the Northwest Passage from the east. In an ill-fated expedition in the *Lyon*, he only reached 68°N near Disko Island. The next year he was replaced by Walter Young, who fared only a little better, reaching 72°N in the Davis Strait. Ross, Parry and Franklin would make further unsuccessful attempts over the next 130 years.

Map labels: Kamchatka · ASIA · RUSSIA · SIBERIA · Nordenskjold · 1878 · Novaya Zemlya · Kola · Bering Sea · Barents · 1596 · SWEDEN · NORWAY · DENMARK · Bering Strait · North Pole · Svalbard · Arctic Ocean · North Pacific Ocean · ALASKA · Cook Inlet · Amundsen · GREENLAND · North Atlantic Ocean · BRITAIN · Cook 1778 · NORTH AMERICA · Baffin Island · Davis Strait · Y · Disko Island · P · Vancouver Island · Hudson Bay · Hudson 1611 · Baffin 1616 · Amundsen 1905

The Third Voyage

Preparations

In 1776 Cook was ready to sail, and it was decided again to use HMS *Resolution*, which had served him well on the Second Voyage. HMS *Adventure* would not be used again and would be replaced by HMS *Discovery*, under the captaincy of Charles Clerke, who had already completed three Pacific voyages, two of them with Cook. Before the voyage, however, Clerke was involved in some events that probably had fatal repercussions for him. His brother had left the country with large debts and Clerke, who had stood as guarantor, was arrested and placed in debtors' prison. Not only did this delay Clerke's participation in the voyage, but it is also thought that at this time he contracted the tuberculosis that would kill him four years later off Kamchatka.

As for Cook, he was now 47 years old and, though much recovered, he was no longer the fit man who had sailed in the *Endeavour*. He was sailing against the wishes of his wife Elizabeth, who had just given birth to their sixth child, Hugh, in May 1776. Two other boys were still alive, James now 12 and Nathaniel now 11, while Elizabeth, Joseph and George had already died.

The crew chosen to sail on the *Resolution* included as first lieutenant John Gore, who had sailed with Cook on the *Endeavour*. Not included on the Second Voyage, Gore had taken Banks and Solander on their scientific expedition to Iceland. The other lieutenants were James King, who would later edit the journals of this voyage, and James Williamson. No scientists were taken (possibly Cook refused to have any on board after his experiences with the Forsters on the previous voyage), and Surgeon William Anderson doubled as naturalist and ethnologist. John Webber sailed as artist, while Midshipman Henry Roberts proved skilled at drafting charts. The most famous person on board, other than Cook, was William Bligh, the master, who would later gain notoriety as captain of HMS *Bounty* and governor of New South Wales.

With Clerke on the *Discovery* were Lieutenants James Burney and John Rickman. The ship's master was Thomas Edgar and its surgeon was David Samwell. The surgeon's assistant, William Ellis, contributed many drawings. William Bayly was the astronomer and David Nelson was aboard to collect botanical specimens for Joseph Banks. George Vancouver, who would later lead his own expeditions to the Pacific, was a midshipman.

Plymouth to Cape Town

The *Resolution* sailed by itself from Plymouth on 12 July 1776 [3.01]. Captain Clerke had not yet sorted out his problems, so Cook left instructions for the *Discovery* to sail as soon as possible and for the two ships to meet at Cape Town. For once Cook did not choose to stop at Madeira but made instead for Tenerife in the Canary Islands, which he reached on 1 August.

While wine, water and supplies were taken on board the ship, Cook met Captain Borda, a Frenchman who was using chronometers to fix the longitude of the island's Pico de Teide. This mountain had long been used by sailors as the base marker for determining longitude when setting out on their voyages, so it was important that its co-ordinates were as accurate as possible.

Sailing again on 4 August the *Resolution* made for the Cape Verde Islands, but Cook and his crew were taken by surprise when, on the 10th, they nearly ran aground on Boa Vista Island. Either Cook or the ship's master, William Bligh, was guilty of an unusually slack piece of sailing, but disaster was avoided and the ship sailed on. Cook paused outside Port Praia on Sao Tiago Island but decided not to call in and pressed on to the south. They crossed the Equator in early September, and the ship then steered for the Brazilian coast.

Cook kept a course down this coast before making a large sweep across the South Atlantic to Cape Town [3.02]. This leg was uneventful except for sightings of birds on 8 October, suggesting to the crew that they were near Gough Island (discovered 45 years earlier but whose exact location was uncertain). They were in fact closer to Tristan da Cunha. On 17 October Africa was sighted and the *Resolution* arrived at Cape Town the following day. The ship had been leaking and needed repairing. Cook was entertained by the governor and wrote letters to Britain, which were taken north by French ships then in port.

The *Discovery*, meanwhile, had finally sailed from Plymouth on 1 August, three weeks after Cook. The ship was delayed further by gales close to Cape Town after an otherwise straightforward voyage, and reached port on 10 November. It also needed repairs.

The stock animals on the *Resolution* were taken ashore, but when sheep and cattle were stolen Cook was forced to buy replacements. Anderson and Nelson went on a botanical and scientific expedition to Stellenbosch and Paarl in the hinterland. An observatory was set up ashore but the same gale that delayed Clerke wrecked it; fortunately, the instruments were rescued.

After the experiences on the previous voyage when the ships were separated, Cook gave Clerke instructions that they should rendezvous at Queen Charlotte Sound in New Zealand should they be parted on the next stage of the voyage. At Cape Town in 1775 Cook had met Crozet, a French captain, who had shown him charts and told him about French exploration and discoveries in the Southern Ocean. Cook sailed on 1 December to investigate those discoveries [3.03].

Kerguelen Island

On 12 December, at 47°S, the ships sailed between two small islands marked on the French charts but not named. Cook did not attempt to land. He named the smaller, northern island Prince Edward Island and honoured Crozet's sailing companion Marion Dufresne by calling the larger island Marion Island. Another French explorer, Kerguelen-Tremarec, had discovered an island further to the southeast, and Cook began searching for it.

A high small isle, Kerguelen's Ile de Croy, emerged from fog on 24 December. The ships worked around this and several other small isles and rocks, including Ilot du Rendezvous (Bligh's Cap), before anchoring in the first harbour encountered on the main island. This was Baie de L'Oiseau, but in light of the date Cook called it Christmas Harbour. They stayed for four days, finding water, seals and many birds, especially penguins, but no trees or shrubs. Surgeon Anderson, in his capacity as naturalist, produced the first of many excellent reports on natural history. A bottle was found, left by Kerguelen, and Cook added his own message. Cook climbed Table Mount but the views were only of snow-covered mountains, glaciers and rocks.

On 29 December they sailed along the north coast past many inlets and islands to anchor in an inlet that Cook called Port Palliser. Cook went ashore while Bligh surveyed the harbour. Sailing again, they rounded a large peninsula and went a little way down the island's east coast before striking off to the east on 30 December 1776. Cook called this inhospitable island Isle of Desolation, but the name Kerguelen Island has become the accepted norm. The largest glacier on the island is called Cook Glacier.

Tasmania and New Zealand

Leaving Kerguelen Island, Cook sailed east in the same latitudes, 45–50°S, as far as 110°E before heading north towards Van Diemen's Land (Tasmania), which Cook still thought was part of the mainland of New South Wales [3.04]. In 1773, Furneaux, in the *Adventure*, had visited a bay on the south coast and Cook now made for it. On 24 January 1777 they were off Southwest Cape [3.05]. They then sailed along the south coast past South and Southeast Capes, and rocks offshore that were given names, Mew Stone and Eddystone, from Devon and Cornwall, as they reminded Cook of features on that coast.

They crossed a large bay, now known as D'Entrecasteaux Channel but called Storm Bay by Cook, before rounding Penguin Island to anchor in Adventure Bay on 26 January. Cook and the crew went ashore, and obtained plenty of wood and water from around the bay and Penguin Island. After three days, local Aboriginal people visited the parties ashore but communication was nearly impossible. Cook realised that these people were similar to those he had met further north seven years earlier but he described various differences. More locals visited the next day, including women and children. On the 30th Cook sailed, crossing (modern) Storm Bay and passing Tasman Peninsula before making for New Zealand. He had not realised that his landing spot had been on a small island, later to be called Bruny Island.

When Cook had sailed in the *Endeavour* across the Tasman Sea from New Zealand to New Holland (as it then was) in 1770, he had intended to make land at Van Diemen's Land but conditions had forced him north instead. In 1773 Furneaux had only sailed along the south and east coasts, and Cook had reproached him for not investigating the possibility of Van Diemen's Land being an island. Now when he himself had the chance to explore, he sailed off to New Zealand. This was, perhaps, the first indication that, on this voyage,

Cook had lost some of his drive and curiosity.

It would be left to Bass and Flinders in the late 1790s to show that Tasmania, as the land was later named, was indeed an island. Various points around Adventure Bay mark Cook's visit: Cook Creek, Cookville and Mount Cook. Bligh, the *Resolution*'s master, would return later in his own ship, and a museum records that and visits by other European explorers, including Cook.

Crossing the Tasman Sea the *Discovery* lost a marine, George Moody, overboard. Rocks Point on the west coast of Te Wai Pounamu, New Zealand, was sighted on 10 February. The ships sailed round Cape Farewell to anchor in Ship Cove, Queen Charlotte Sound, on the 12th. The Maori were from the same tribe or iwi that had been in the sound during the previous visit in 1774, and while they came to the ships they were very wary. Cook realised that the Maori expected retaliation or utu for the attack carried out at Grass Cove on that last voyage when men in Furneaux's crew had been killed. Members of Cook's crew and Omai, the Tahitian aboard, also expected Cook to take some action, but he surprised them all by not doing so. Instead he even entertained Kahura, the local chief suspected of leading the attack. However Cook did set a guard of marines every time a party went ashore.

An observatory was set up and spruce beer was brewed at Ship Cove. Gradually a small village grew up as the Maori became friendlier and many moved to live at the cove. The ships were carrying many farm animals destined to be gifts to people of the Pacific, and a great deal of grass and hay needed to be taken on board as feed. Cook was keen to know the progress of gardens he had planted on Motuara Island, but when he visited he found the island deserted and the gardens untended.

Cook also visited Grass Cove (Wharehunga) to inspect the site where Rowe and other members of the *Adventure*'s crew had been killed. He wondered about a longer trip to find the source of the greenstone or pounamu (that gave the South Island its local name, Te Wai Pounamu) but did not go. Cook was ready to depart, and on 24 February he stood off Motuara Island before sailing out of the sound the next day for the last time.

On into the Pacific

Cook had needed to time his earlier voyages so that he could take advantage of Southern Hemisphere summers, but on this voyage he would be attempting to sail north of the Arctic Circle and therefore needed to arrive in the Northern Pacific in the northern spring. He left New Zealand in late February 1777, but showed little inclination to sail into the North Pacific. Instead, he began another (for Cook) leisurely sweep of the South Pacific, revisiting several of the islands in that ocean.

Cook Islands

The ships sailed east from New Zealand to about 160°W, then, in mid-March, they turned north [3.06]. On 29 March 1777 they arrived at the island of Mangaia, a member of a scattered group of islands that, 50 years later, Von Krusenstern, a Russian explorer, named the Cook Islands in memory of Cook [3.07]. The ships approached from the south, but heavy surf and a reef prevented them getting ashore. From the ship they could see people walking about. Cook sailed up the island's west coast while Gore led a party of men in small boats to find a way of landing. He was unsuccessful but he did make contact with islanders in canoes who told him the island's name, Mangaia. One local, Mourua, came out and boarded the *Resolution*.

Sailing the *Resolution* northwards, they saw another island, Atiu, two days later, but lack of wind delayed their arrival there. Cook again sent Gore off to attempt to land on Atiu but the reef stopped them getting ashore. A double canoe brought a chief out to the ships. He presented Cook with a pig and made a speech asking for a dog. Omai gave the chief one of his dogs. On 3 April canoes took Gore, Anderson, Omai and Burney ashore, where the sailors were presented to three chiefs. They stayed all day on the beach while an umukai (feast) was prepared for them. Omai feared they were about to be eaten but eventually they were returned unharmed to the ships.

Cook left on 4 April for a smaller sandy isle that could be seen to the northwest. The animals needed feed and Gore obtained scurvy grass and coconuts. This isle, Takutea, was uninhabited. Cook then sailed north for Manuae (his Hervey Island, which he had visited four years earlier), which he reached on 6 April. It was now inhabited, and this surprised Cook as he had seen no signs of life in 1773.

The ships set sail west towards Tonga via Palmerston Atoll, off which they anchored on 14 April [3.07]. More grass and young coconut palms were collected from Tom's and Cook's Islands as feed for the animals before the ships continued on their way on the 17th. Cook never visited Rarotonga, the largest of the Cook Islands, nor any of the Northern Cooks.

Tonga

They reached the Tonga Group of islands on 28 April, when Cook briefly anchored off Mango. King was sent ashore for supplies [3.08]. They soon moved on to Nomuka but were forced west and had to anchor off the southwest of the island. On 1 May Cook was able to transfer to his preferred mooring on the north coast and, on going ashore, was welcomed by the island's chief, Tupoulangi. Five days later a high chief, Finau, arrived from Tongatapu to see Cook. With fresh provisions on board, Cook sailed north on 14 May to explore the other islands in the Ha'apai Group that made up the central part of the Tongan Archipelago.

Finau, who would prove a regular companion for Cook over the next few weeks, accompanied him on the *Resolution*. Reefs and shoals forced Cook round Kotu and then, with care, he sailed east between Fotuha'a and Lofanga. On 17 May the *Resolution* anchored off the northern end on Lifuka, and Cook went ashore near Kuolo. Over the next few days there were feasts and entertainments, such as dancing, boxing and wrestling, and the British let off fireworks. Afterwards it emerged that the entertainments had been part of a plot to kill Cook, but the Tongans could not agree about the time or the method and Cook escaped. Finau left to go north to the Vava'u Group of islands but lied to Cook about suitable anchorages there for Cook's ships when Cook wanted to accompany him. Cook instead decided to sail south and made a stop at the southern end of Lifuka.

Fatafehi Paulaho, the Tu'i Tonga (a king), suddenly arrived and, after gift exchanges and ceremonies, they all sailed south. Bligh recommended that they should return the way they had come, to avoid more reefs, so they made for Niniva and Fotuha'a before heading to Lofanga. There was supposed to be a safe anchorage there, but none was located. They continued on, and on 30 May were off Kotu, where conditions forced them to ply back and forth. Many of the Tongans on board were alarmed and they were put ashore on Kotu.

Cook arrived back at Nomuka on 5 June. Here he was rejoined the next day by Finau and, on the 7th, by the Tu'i Tonga. Cook was able to observe the hierarchy of Tongan society and the protocols involved. On the 8th they all departed for Tongatapu, passing the two outlying islands of Hunga Ha'apai and Hunga Tonga. They sighted Tongatapu on 9 June. Tongan pilots on board helped Cook bring the ships through the reefs to a safe anchorage off Holeva Point on the north coast of the island [3.09].

The British were welcomed by the Tu'i Tonga. Cook arranged for the animals to be taken ashore and had an observatory erected near the point. He himself visited Pangaimotu for water, and arranged for repairs to be carried out on the ships. However, during the stay on Tongatapu more signs of a differently behaved Cook appeared. He stayed on the island for a month, doing little except taking part in feasts and entertainments. His drive to be always exploring and investigating seemed to dry up, and stories about nearby and yet unvisited island groups, such as Samoa and Fiji, failed to fire his imagination. Nor were Cook's tolerance and good nature in evidence, as he reacted to the prevalent thieving by having offenders flogged and taking hostages until items were returned.

On 12 June, Cook was taken in the king's canoe to visit Maealiuaki (the king's father) at Mu'a on the central lagoon. A banyan tree (Captain Cook's Tree) and a monument mark the visit. Unfortunately, Maealiuaki was not present but he did appear at Holeva the next day. A further round of entertaining followed, with Cook making gifts of cattle, sheep and horses to the Tu'i, Maealiuaki and Finau.

All repairs had been completed by 25 June but Cook decided to wait to observe a solar eclipse on 5 July, which was only partly recorded. The ships were then loaded but could not sail, so Cook was invited by the Tu'i to a ceremony

for one of his sons at Mu'a that lasted two days.

Finally on 10 July the ships sailed, but they made only slow progress via the Piha Passage out to the east. They came to 'Eua on the 12th and were welcomed by Ta'aufa'a. Already they needed fresh water, but they found little on the island. Cook went across to and climbed a hill from which he admired the island. His servant, William Collett, was attacked and robbed, so Cook decided to leave, sailing on 17 July.

Tonga to Tahiti

Cook sailed east from Tonga on 17 July 1777 before turning north to reach Tahiti. Eight years earlier in the *Endeavour* he had seen the island of Rurutu and now, on 9 August, he came to another of the Austral Group of islands [3.06]. This was Tubuai, 300 kilometres to the east of Rurutu. Cook skirted the island but made no attempt to land, even though people could be seen ashore and some, from whom the name was established, came out in canoes.

Three days later, on 12 August, Mehetia and the southernmost end of Tahiti Iti were sighted. The ships anchored near Tautira at the mouth of the Vaitepiha River the next day [3.10]. Cook was welcomed warmly. However, the previous chief or Vehiatua had died and had been replaced by his brother who was not present at that moment. The British learned that Spanish ships from Peru had made two visits since their own last visit and that the Spanish had made attempts to convert islanders to Roman Catholic Christianity.

On 23 August, Cook transferred to Matavai Bay where crews set about general repairs and restocking. Cook soon found himself being entertained by and entertaining local dignitaries, of whom Tu was still the paramount chief. At the time of Cook's previous visit a warfleet had been assembled with the purpose of attacking Moorea, and Cook was now informed that the conflict was still happening. The fleet's commander To'ofa tried to involve Cook but, to To'ofa's disgust, Cook declined. Instead he accepted an invitation to attend a ceremony at Atehuru Marae where a human sacrifice was made to the gods to gain assistance against Moorea.

To'ofa went across to Moorea and engaged in a short battle before a peace was declared, prompting another ceremony that Cook was unable to attend because of illness. Tu's female relatives gave Cook a series of massages and he recovered.

Moorea to Kauai

Cook had never been to Moorea, so on 29 September he farewelled Tu and left Tahiti to investigate the neighbouring island [3.11]. However, when Cook sailed into Oponohu Bay on the island's north coast the next day, he was not received by the chief, Mahine. Mahine probably thought Cook had helped the Tahitians in the recent war against Moorea. The people were more friendly, though, and much fruit and wood were obtained.

Mahine then appeared and, during the welcome, he asked for goats. A short time later two animals were stolen, and this led to a series of incidents. One goat disappeared completely and so did Mahine. Cook was informed they had gone to the south of the island and dispatched two midshipmen to recover the goat. They returned empty-handed so Cook, angry now, marched over the island's central hills to Maatea. He did not find the goat either. He then returned via the west coast, burning some houses and destroying several canoes along the way in an uncharacteristic display of temper. Cook went on to Paopao Bay (now known as Baie de Cook) and destroyed more canoes before, eventually, the goat was recovered. Cook was ready to leave, and did so on 11 October.

The ships arrived at Fare on Huahine to find that Cook's friend Ori was no longer the chief. Their reason for visiting Huahine was to install Omai on the island. They purchased land, and the ships' carpenters set about building him a house. On 2 November Cook sailed, leaving a sad Omai with his retinue.

Chief Orio welcomed the ships to Raiatea. Cook stayed for a month, prolonged by the desertion of crew members and the time taken for search parties to locate them. Cook went to Tahaa in search of two men, only to find they had gone on to Tupai. Another man went round to eastern Raiatea.

Cook had never landed on Bora Bora and, on 7 December, he headed there from Raiatea. Cook had heard that Chief Puni of Bora Bora had acquired an anchor from one of Bougainville's ships, and he wished to purchase it so he would have a source of iron. On 8 December they stood off the west coast of Bora Bora, as winds and tides prevented them entering Teavanui Harbour. Cook went ashore in a small boat but had to wait for the anchor to be retrieved from Tevairoa Island. Various gifts, including sheep, were exchanged before Cook sailed north, leaving the Society Islands for the last time.

As they crossed the Equator on 22 December Captain Clerke and Surgeon Anderson were already very ill with tuberculosis. On the 24th the *Resolution* came to a new island and anchored off its southwest point [3.06]. After the masters had sounded the coast and a large lagoon, the ships were moved north to a new anchorage. An observatory was set up on a small isle, Cook Island, where Cook sighted a solar eclipse on 30 December 1777. Parties went ashore on what was an uninhabited, hot and fairly barren island to collect fish and turtles. Two seamen, delirious because of sunstroke and lack of water, were lost for over 24 hours. Cook left a note in a bottle to record his visit to Christmas Island, as he named the place. The ships sailed north on 2 January 1778 [3.06].

Sandwich/Hawaiian Islands

After another 2000 kilometres the *Resolution* and the *Discovery* sighted land once more on 18 January. It proved to be the island of Oahu, a member of the group which Cook would later call the Sandwich Islands [3.12], although the name of the largest island, Hawaii, soon became used for the whole group. On the 19th Cook approached high cliffs at the southeast corner of Kauai Island, and even though there were no settlements nearby, the ships were soon surrounded by people in canoes. They sailed along the south coast past Poipu, watched by people on shore, until they located an anchorage at the mouth of the Waimea River.

Cook was amazed to find he could communicate with the Hawaiians, another example of the Polynesian diaspora. He speculated about the sailing and navigation ability of the Polynesians that had enabled them to spread all around the Pacific. The crews began obtaining water while Cook was taken a little way up the Waimea Valley and shown a heiau (a stone platform used as a place of worship). Returning to the beach, Cook found everyone trading. Waimea now has a statue of Cook in the middle of town, and a cairn in Lucy Wright Beach Park marks the spot where Cook landed.

Cook raised the *Resolution*'s anchor on 23 January and moved west looking for a better mooring. Strong winds drove them back and, after regaining the *Discovery*, the ships sailed across to the neighbouring island of Nihau [3.12]. Conditions were difficult and it took until the 29th to reach Nihau. Bligh was dispatched near the southeastern point, Kawaihoa Point, to find a landing and water. Cook meantime sailed around the point and anchored between Pahau and Leahi Points near Keelinawi.

Gore went ashore first, but heavy surf prevented his returning to the ship or Cook joining him ashore. Cook did get ashore the next day and went for a walk, climbing Mauuloa, a small hill. On 2 February the ships sailed north, having at first been forced south towards Kaula.

To New Albion/North America

Cook was about to pursue the main reason for this voyage and to search for the Northwest Passage from the Pacific. Many people had tried unsuccessfully to find it from the Atlantic side, but it was still thought to exist and might be more accessible from the Pacific. It was known that the Spanish and Russians had made explorations along the American coast, and charts recording their journeys showed inlets that could easily be entrances to the passage. The English seaman/pirate, Francis Drake, had sailed a little way up this coast and called it New Albion. Cook now directed his ships there [3.13].

Cook's lack of activity in Tonga and the Society Islands was partly attributable to his realisation that he needed to be heading into northern waters in February–March so as to be able to reach Arctic waters in the northern summer months of July and August. He had reached the Pacific too late in 1777, and so had had to find other activities to fill his time. It was the reverse of his previous experience

of high-latitude sailing: before now, he had only been south of the Equator in the South Pacific; he was moving into new waters.

Cook did have to help him a copy of Muller's map of the North Pacific that showed the paths and discoveries of the Russian voyages of 1741, as well as some of the Spanish discoveries further south [3.13]. In 1741 Bering, who had previously shown that the Bering Strait lay between Asia and America, took two ships on an expedition east from Kamchatka. His ship, the *St. Peter*, was soon separated from the *St. Paul*, under Chirikov, but both ships sailed on to make some discoveries on the American mainland. The Spanish had sailed north from their base at Monterey in California to explore the coast and to lay claims to new lands. Among many inlets shown on their charts was a large bay, seen by Juan de Fuca at 49°N.

Oregon and Nootka Sound

Cook had been instructed to reach the New Albion coast at 45°N and, after an uneventful crossing, the *Resolution* and the *Discovery* sighted land on 7 March at 44°50'N [3.14]. Bad weather caused Cook to name the first visible headland Cape Foulweather, and the conditions, together with no apparent harbours, forced him to stand off the coast. The ships began to sail south, passing two capes that Cook named for saints' days: Gregory (now usually called Cape Arago) and Perpetua (there are now a Captain Cook Point and a Cook's Chasm close by Cape Perpetua).

Before gales forced them further out to sea on 13 March Cook identified a larger cape as Cape Blanco, named by Martin de Agualar. Having established his bearings, Cook turned north and regained the coast on the 22nd at 47°N. He sighted some rocks, the Flattery Rocks, near a headland he called Cape Flattery before being driven off the coast again by a series of gales that lasted several days. Cook was mistakenly dismissive of the Spanish charts and records, and was not to know that Cape Flattery was the southern entrance to Strait of Juan de Fuca as depicted on Muller's chart.

Several days later they steered towards snow-covered, mountainous land.

They were in need of a harbour in which to repair the ships. A midshipman on the *Discovery*, George Vancouver, would sail into the Strait of Juan de Fuca 15 years later and show that the land Cook was now approaching was, in fact, an island. It would be named Vancouver Island after him, and in Victoria, the island's largest city, there is a statue of Cook in front of the Empress Hotel near the Inner Harbour. There is also a Captain Cook Room in the British Columbia Maritime Museum.

As Cook approached land on 29 March he described a stretch of coast between Point Estevan and Woody Point as Hope Bay (a name no longer used), and steered into an inlet near Point Estevan. Cook's Woody Point was later renamed Cape Cook. It lies on the Brooks Peninsula where there is also a Cape Clerke and a Solander Island [3.14].

Lack of wind necessitated the ships being towed into the inlet, Nootka Sound [3.15]. The inlet divided into several channels, and Cook and King spent some time looking for an anchorage before Cook settled on a small cove near the entrance of the right-hand channel, the Zuclarte Channel. This was Ship Cove, later called Resolution Cove. Over 30 canoes full of local people paddled around the ships as they arrived, and trading commenced immediately. The local people were selling animal skins, especially those of the sea otter (sea beaver).

For two very wet weeks the crews worked to replace rigging and masts using timber that was felled from coniferous forests growing down to the water's edge. The local people were, for once, not Polynesian but North American Indian (or Native American), and communication was difficult. Gradually, however, communication was established and Surgeon Anderson produced a vocabulary of the local language, though a mistake was made about the name of the place and the people: When Cook had asked them the name of the inlet, it is probable the people had not understood the question. The word Nootka (or Nutka) that Cook thought was their reply does not appear in their language but the name has stuck, as in Nootka People and Nootka Sound (Cook called it King George's Sound but that name soon lapsed). On 20 April Cook set off to explore and went first to the village of Yuquot in Friendly Cove near the mouth of the inlet. The British were made very welcome and shown all around the village and into houses. From Yuquot they rowed up Cook Channel past the Saavedra Islands and across the mouths of the Kendrick and Tahsis Channels. Cook remarked that the trees here (probably Douglas firs) were the tallest he had ever seen. They landed at another village where they received a much cooler reception. Proceeding, they realised that they had rounded an island (Bligh Island) against which they were anchored. More Nootkans visited the ships, entertaining them with music from their canoes. Many features in Nootka Sound now carry names associated with people from the visit.

North to Alaska

On 26 April Cook sailed from Nootka Sound, but storms immediately forced the ships away from the coast and caused the *Resolution* to spring a leak. Cook was aware that he had strayed too far from land to be able to investigate inlets for the Northwest Passage, and Muller's chart showed a possible strait in these latitudes, found by the Spaniard, de Fonte. When he was able, Cook steered back towards the coast [3.16]. Unbeknown to Cook, he was sailing north outside a series of islands and had already passed Queen Charlotte Island. Land was sighted on 2 May on Prince of Wales Island, thought to have been visited by the Russian Chirikov in 1741.

The next day a mountain was observed and called Mount Edgcombe. It is on Kruzof Island, to the east of Baranof Island. Cook could see many small inlets and channels, such as Olga Strait and Salisbury Sound, and speculated about them joining up to form islands of the visible land. Cook had reached Alaska. The islands to the north were Chichagof and Yakobi where Chirikov may have landed and where some of his men may have been stranded 37 years earlier. Cape Cross and Cross Sound, seen on 3 May, mark the northern end of the islands.

The coast had begun trending more to the northwest, and a high mountain, Mount Fairweather, dominated this part of it. They were approaching the area explored by Bering and, as yet, had seen no likely passage. Cook was having difficulty reconciling features on the chart with what he could see, but on 5 May he saw another snow-covered mountain ahead that he equated with Bering's

Mount St. Elias. He was confused, though, about a bay on the chart visited by Bering. Dry, Yakutat and Icy Bays were all possibilities, but Yakutat Bay is most likely. A mountain overlooking Yakutat Bay is called Mount Cook [3.17].

On 10 May the *Resolution* and the *Discovery* approached some islands and a headland (called Cape Suckling by Cook after the Navy controller). Cook was keen to repair leaks and landed briefly on the largest island, but decided to sail on. He left a bottle with some coins on the island, which he called Kayes' Island but which is now known as Kayak Island.

Prince William Sound

Though the coast was now trending east–west Cook was still looking out for the Northwest Passage, and on the 12th he rounded Cape Hinchinbrook to investigate a large inlet. Another map he had on board, by the Russian Stahlin, showed northward-running channels linking to a northern ocean, and he surmised that this inlet could be such a channel. Cook put into a cove just inside the inlet and was surrounded by local people in kayaks keen to trade. The next day Cook transferred to another anchorage, Snug Corner Bay, deeper in the inlet in Port Fidalgo. Repairs were carried out as more people, a different Native American tribe from those met at Nootka, visited the ships to trade furs. Gore and Roberts rowed up the Valdez Arm to check for the passage but returned unsuccessfully, although Roberts thought he had seen a channel.

The ships sailed on 17 May and waited off Bligh Island before heading southwest; they had given up on the inlet being the passage. Cook called the inlet Sandwich Sound but the Earl of Sandwich later changed it to Prince William Sound. Cook sailed through the Montague Strait past Green Island and between Montague Island and the mainland.

Cook Inlet and Kodiak Island

Another large inlet presented itself on 25 May when Cook worked the ships past the Barren Islands and a headland, Cape Douglas, in towards Mount St. Augustine on the western shore (this later proved to be an island) [3.18]. The inlet stretched north, and Cook sailed back to its eastern shore at Cape Bede and crossed Kachemak Bay to an anchorage. The ships proceeded with high hopes up the inlet past Kalgin Island, and anchored off Fire Island on 1 June. Their hopes were not realised, as Cook was already aware that the water of the inlet was fresh and not salty, so it was improbable that this was the passage. The head of the inlet divided into two and Bligh was sent north up Knik Arm to check, while Cook tried the other arm. Believing it was a waste of time and not being prepared to waste any more, Cook called it Turnagain Arm and, with Bligh's return, decided to leave.

King landed at Possession Point, near Fire Island, and buried a bottle. On the return journey south Cook nearly ran aground on shoals, but by 6 June he had left the inlet that the Earl of Sandwich later directed should be called Cook's River. George Vancouver changed it to Cook Inlet. Anchorage, at the head of Cook Inlet, has a statue of Cook in Resolution Park.

As he passed the Barren Islands to be back in the open ocean, Cook was concerned that the trend of the coast was now to the southwest and, instead of being in latitude 65°N, he was now at 58°N and sailing south. Valuable time for exploring higher latitudes appeared to be disappearing quickly. He sailed to the east of land, unaware that it was a cluster of islands separated from the mainland by Shelikof Strait. The two largest islands are Kodiak Island and Afognak Island. Cook identified Bering's St. Hermogenes with Marmot Island, off Afognak Island. Fog slowed their progress as they crossed Marmot Bay between the two larger islands and passed down the coast of Kodiak Island. Sightings of land were confused and infrequent but, on 14 June, Cook was able to sail west, passing Sitkinak and Tugidak Islands. Cook called these the Trinity Islands [3.18].

Alaska Peninsula and Aleutian Islands

Cook was looking out for Bering's Foggy Island, and several islands and capes loomed out of the fog but the most probable, Chirikof Island (sighted and named by Vancouver in 1794), remained unseen [3.19]. Cook regained the mainland in the form of the Alaska Peninsula but there was still no passage and he was forced further south. On 17 June he came to an island where one of Bering's crew, Nikita Shumagin, had died. Bering had named it Nagai, and Cook sailed between it and its neighbour, Unga, both members of the Shumagin Group.

The presence of Russians in the area was demonstrated when local people, Aleuts, approached them in kayaks and passed on notes written in Russian. Rocks and breakers forced the ships south of the Sanak Islands (Cook's Halibut Island). Fog continued to slow progress, but on 21 June a volcano, Shishaldin, on Unimak Island (the first island in the Aleutian Chain) was seen [3.20]. After two more days Cook approached the western end of Unimak but turned back before realising there was a passage through Unimak Pass to the north. Instead he steered south of the Krenitzin Islands and on the 26th was lucky to anchor off Sedanka Island, having narrowly avoided large rocks in thick fog.

The next day they changed their anchorage to one between Egg and Sedanka Islands. They sailed north through Unalga Pass before taking shelter in Samgoonoodha Harbour (English Bay) on Unalaska Island. Here they met more Aleuts, with whom they traded, before Cook sailed north out into the Bering Sea on 2 July.

North across the Arctic Circle

Cook departed from Samgoonoodha Harbour on 2 July 1778 and sailed out into the Bering Sea [3.20]. After several weeks' frustration at not being able to sail north, and so losing valuable summer time for exploring above the Arctic Circle (should he reach there), Cook seemed to be back on track. He saw he could sail northeast and set a course following the coast, so that for a week he traced the north side of the Alaska Peninsula [3.19]. On the 9th the ships arrived at a river mouth and shallows and, as the coast turned west, Cook followed suit. Cook used the name Bristol for the river and the bay into which it flows, but the river is now called the Kvichak.

The ships continued past the Walrus and Round Islands, and sighted Calm Point on Hagemeister Island on 13 July before stopping near a headland, Cape Newenham. Cook sent Williamson ashore to climb it, and from there he could see the coastline stretching to the north. Cook attempted to sail north into Kuskokwim Bay, but shoals prevented him doing so and he turned west past Nunivak Island [3.19].

On 29 July the *Resolution* and the *Discovery* neared the island of St. Matthew in the Bering Sea [3.21]. While Cook did have maps on board he was not happy with their accuracy and mistakenly called the island Bird Island. The ships then headed northeast but there was sadness on 3 August when the surgeon, and one of Cook's favourites, William Anderson, died. Shortly after, another island was sighted that Cook, unsure of his position, called Anderson Island (it was Bering's St. Lawrence Island). Sailing on, they approached the Alaskan shore and anchored near a small island on the 5th. Going ashore, they found a sledge, which gave the island its name, Sledge Island.

Following the coast northwards past Cape Rodney and King Island, the ships came to Bering Strait on 8 August. Cook called the westernmost point of America (unseen by Bering) Cape Prince of Wales, before passing the Diomede Islands to reach the Asian Coast. The ships worked southwest to an inlet, St. Lawrence Bay, where Cook landed for a few hours and met some of the local Chukchi people. Returning to sea, Cook sailed back through the Bering Strait on 11 August past the East Cape (Cape Dezhneva) of Asia into the Chukchi Sea and the Arctic Ocean. He headed northeast to Alaska and came to the coast again near the Mulgrave Hills [3.21].

In increasingly cold conditions they sailed north and round Cape Lisburne, hoping to find the Northwest Passage, but on 18 August near Icy Cape and at 70°44'N ice fields stopped their progress. Cook turned, and for ten days he sailed west across the Arctic Ocean, but the ice prevented any attempts to go any further north. Cook had not found the Northwest Passage but he was probably the first person to have crossed both the 70° lines of latitude.

Back to Unalaska

On 29 August they sighted Cape Shmidta on the Asian mainland, and Cook turned south to return to the Bering Strait, keeping close to the coastline [3.21]. He had decided that the summer was nearly over and that conditions would only worsen and not allow any more exploration. They noted the lagoons and capes along the north side of the Chukotskiy Peninsula before they rounded East Cape on 2 September. Keeping close to the Asia shore, the ships passed St. Lawrence Bay and Cape Chukotskiy before heading southeast. On the 5th they came to St. Lawrence Island but once again Cook did not equate it with Bering's island or even with his own Anderson Island of a month earlier [3.22]. He now called it Clerke's Island.

Sailing on, Cook headed east, possibly to have a final search for the passage in that part of the Alaskan coast he had not already investigated. On 8 September the ships passed to the south of Cape Darby and entered a large bay. This was Norton Bay, the inner part of Norton Sound. Cook anchored in two places, near Capes Darby and Denbigh, and he went ashore. He sent parties to explore possible 'passages' such as Koyuk River. They met local people at Shaktoolik.

By now Cook despaired of the Russian maps he was using and decided to sail south to winter in the Sandwich (Hawaiian) Islands. He sailed south on the 17th round Norton Sound and past Cape Stephens and Stuart Island into waters that shoaled. Cook decided to give them a wide berth and sailed west, thus avoiding the shallows off the Yukon Delta that protrudes out into the Bering Sea. He sighted a point to the south and named it Point Shallow Water (probably Point Romanov).

On 20 September they were off St. Lawrence Island yet again and also sighted the Punuk Islets off its eastern cape [3.22]. They tried unsuccessfully to land. Three days later they were back at St. Matthew Island (Cook now called it Gores Island) where they saw and named the nearby Hall Island and Pinnacle Rocks. They pressed on and after four gruelling months in Arctic waters Cook arrived back at Unalaska on 3 October [3.20]. They entered Unalaska Bay on the north coast where the Russians had a post at Dutch Harbour/Unalaska, but Cook left straight away without attempting contact. He moved back to Samgoonoodha at the eastern end of the island. Work began refitting both ships. Notes in Russian were received and on the 8th Cook sent John Ledyard to Unalaska to make enquiries. Ledyard returned with three Russians with whom communication was possible if difficult. Another Russian, the factor Gerassim Gregoriev Ismailov, came with charts from which Cook made copies, especially of the Aleutian Islands. Cook pointed out the errors in Muller's and Stahlin's maps that he had been using. Ismailov gave Cook letters of introduction to the governor of Kamchatka while Cook wrote a letter to the Admiralty, which he asked Ismailov to forward across Russia (it reached London!).

South to Hawaii

Ismailov left on 21 October and Cook sailed on the 24th. He went west to check his recently acquired information, but terrible weather and high seas stopped him. He could just see Umnak Island when, on the 29th near Bogoslof Islet, he turned, passed Unalaska Island again, and sailed through Unalga Pass out into the Pacific [3.20]. The ships headed south, and on 26 November, after an uneventful passage, they were off the coast of Maui in the Hawaiian Islands [3.22].

The *Resolution* and the *Discovery* sailed along the north coast of Maui to stand off Kahului, from where many canoes came to visit the ships [3.23]. After moving east to be near the northeast point of the island, Cook was visited by Kalani'opu'u, the king of the island of Hawaii, and by Kamehameha, the future king of the whole Hawaiian chain.

Cook decided to visit Hawaii Island, and as he approached Upolu Point on 1 December he could see the snow-covered volcano of Mauna Kea. For unknown reasons Cook now began a slow clockwise circumnavigation of the island without trying to land, even though the ships were leaking. The nature of the coast in any case made it hard to land and strong winds made it difficult for the ships to stay together. They had reached Cape Kumukahi, the easternmost point on the island, by 19 December, only to be forced back north. Working their way south, they rounded the south of the island in early January 1779, passing Ka Lae on the 5th. Reaching the west coast they sailed north before Cook asked Bligh to sound a large bay that might prove an anchorage. Bligh reported favourably, and on 17 January the *Resolution* and the *Discovery* anchored in Kealakekua Bay [3.24]. The ships' crews were all very tired and more than ready to go ashore. They had not understood why Cook had skirted the island for six weeks without landing.

The reception by the Hawaiians remains a topic for speculation and debate by American academics. They continue to argue about whether Cook was regarded as a god by the Hawaiian people. Certainly the ships were greeted by a flotilla of more than 1000 canoes, and Cook was welcomed ashore by Chiefs Palea and Kanina and the priests Koaa and Keli'ikea in a ceremony at Hikiau Heiau. His arrival also coincided with Makahiki, a part of the year associated with the Hawaiian god Lono. The people accorded Cook a special status and treated him with reverence, but it is a matter or debate whether Cook was actually equated with Lono.

Land near the Heiau was acquired for an observatory and as a work area for repairs. Relations were most cordial and trade was brisk. On 25 January King Kalani'opu'u appeared (Cook had met him off Maui) and settled at Kaawaloa across the bay. Gifts were exchanged the next day near the Heiau at Napoopoo. Things began to deteriorate on 1 February. Relations were seriously harmed by members of crew not respecting local religious sensibilities when, collecting firewood, they took fence posts and wooden carvings from the Heiau. Then William Watman, a sailor, died and was buried near the Heiau, showing the mortality of the Europeans.

Cook realised it was time to leave and did so on 4 February. They were escorted by canoes, and the priest Koaa came on board to sail with them [3.23]. Before they had cleared the north of the island, gales began and Bligh took Koaa ashore in Kaiwaihae Bay. The gales continued and broke the *Resolution*'s mast, forcing Cook to return, reluctantly, to Kealakekua Bay where Kamehameha received him on the 11th [3.24].

Their reception this time was less warm. The British had already overstayed their welcome and King Kalani'opu'u made known his displeasure at their return. Relations were now strained and incidents began to occur. Thieving became more frequent and shore parties were harrassed. After one incident Cook went ashore at Kaawaloa early in the morning of 14 February, intending to take the king hostage. Before he could return to his ship, however, a fight broke out on the foreshore and he, four marines and seventeen Hawaiians died.

Charles Clerke assumed command of the *Resolution,* and Gore switched to take charge of the *Discovery.* Everyone was in a state of shock, but Clerke quickly decided to take no reprisals, instead concentrating on recovering the remains of Cook and the marines. Cook had been dismembered and his body parts distributed to various people, so their retrieval took time. The priest Koaa acted as an intermediary, and on 20 February some parts of Cook were handed over. These parts included the hand burned 16 years earlier in Newfoundland, which acted as a proof of identity. Cook was buried in the waters of Kealakekua Bay on 21 February and the ships sailed the next day. Relations between the two sides were largely restored.

To Kamchatka

Clerke sailed from Kealakekua Bay on Hawaii intent on continuing what Captain Cook had started. He would take the ships back to Arctic waters to search for the Northwest Passage but before then he would explore the rest of the Hawaiian Islands. The ships sailed northwest on 21 February 1779 and quickly investigated the smaller islands of Lanai, Molokai and Kahoolawe, west of Maui, before heading on to Oahu [3.25]. On the 26th they sailed through the Kaiwi Channel to be off Mokapu Point on Oahu's east coast. Rounding the northern point of the island, Kahuku Point, they anchored in Waimea Bay on the northwest coast. They quickly decided Kauai would serve them better, and pressed on.

On 2 March the ships anchored again at Waimea on Kauai. Their reception was cool and the British wondered if the news of Cook's death had preceded them. Hundreds gathered on the beach to watch the crew get water. However, a 'civil war' had just occurred and matters had not yet settled down. Contact gradually improved and many pigs were obtained. Queen Tu'mutta'ha'no, recently restored to power, visited the ships and gifts were exchanged.

Clerke wanted more yams for the voyage ahead and felt Nihau would provide a better source, so on 8 March the ships sailed across to anchor near Leahi Point [3.25]. They landed but found that yams were in short supply. The ships were caulked while Bligh located another anchorage further north, near Nonopapa. Clerke, though, was ready to leave, but before he sailed canoes arrived from Queen Tu'mutta'ha'no of Kauai laden with yams and pigs.

The *Resolution* and the *Discovery* set sail for Kamchatka on 15 March, intending to make Petropavlosk in Avacha Bay their base for a renewed search for the Northwest Passage [3.26]. Sailing west from Nihau, they made brief but unsuccessful efforts to locate another islet beyond Kaula from where the Hawaiians obtained turtles. Continuing, the ships held a westerly course until they reached 180°W and there struck northwards. After this sweep of the North Pacific, where no land was seen, the ships approached Kamchatka on 24 April, but fog separated them and delayed their arrival.

Kamchatka

The *Resolution* sailed past Starichkova Island and entered Avacha Bay, which was still covered by pack ice, on 28 April [3.27]. Clerke sent King, with their letters of introduction from Ismailov in Unalaska, over the ice to meet the Russians in their post at Petropavlosk. They found that Behm, the governor of Kamchatka, resided in Bol'sheretsk on the far side of the peninsula and only a sergeant was based in Avacha Bay. The *Discovery* joined them on 2 May and the ships moved to anchor off a sand spit near Petropavlosk.

Emissaries arrived from the governor inviting them to visit, but Clerke's health was failing so it was King, Gore and Webber who left on 7 May for Bol'sheretsk [3.27]. The party used boats to go up the Avacha River as far as Karatchin, from where sledges took them over to Nachiki. Reverting to canoes, they travelled down past Apacha to the Sea of Okhotsk. On 12 May they were met and entertained by Governor Behm. After four days they returned, accompanied by the governor, who met Clerke on board the *Resolution* on 16 May.

In the meantime Clerke had been receiving milk and cheese from a priest at Paratunka. On 31 May, Gore and Samwell led a party to visit the priest, Feodowitz Vereshagin [3.27]. Twenty cows arrived from Verkhene, further north on the peninsula, as fresh beef for the crews [3.26]. Midshipman Riou made a detailed chart of Avacha Bay [3.27].

On to the Arctic

On 16 June 1779 the ships sailed for the Arctic. Their departure was marked by the eruption of Sopka (volcano) Avacha, which showered the ships with volcanic ash. They sailed north up the east coast of the Kamchatka Peninsula, past Capes Shipunskiy, Kronotskiy and Kamchatskiy, and inside the Komandor Islands, before coming to Cape Olyutorskiy on the Koryakskiy coast on 25 June [3.26]. Opuka and Khatyrka Rivers, and Anastasii and Natalii Bays were sighted on this coast before they passed Cape Navarin on 29 June.

The ships sailed across the Gulf of Anadyr to pass between Cape Chaplina, on the Chukotskiy Peninsula, and St. Lawrence Island and head up to the Bering Strait. Sailing through the strait on 6 July they made for the American shore, but pack ice forced them west and even south. On the 12th they went north again and then worked east to look for the passage. However, they admitted defeat on the 18th in latitude 70°33'N, not very far from where Cook had given up a year earlier.

They returned south with Clerke now very ill. The ships crossed the Chukchi Sea to reach Cape Serdtse Kamen on 27 July and pass through the Bering Strait on the 30th. Sailing south across the Bering Sea they kept a more easterly course, meeting no land until they saw Mednyy Island in the Komandor Group on 17 August. On the 21st Sopka Zhupanova on the Kamchatka Peninsula was sighted.

Captain Charles Clerke died of consumption on 22 August, so two sombre ships re-entered Avacha Bay two days later with Gore in command [3.27]. The British wanted to bury Clerke and, after some discussion, Priest Vereshagin finally agreed to Clerke being buried in Petropavlosk at the site of its future church. Meanwhile, the ships were repaired. On 10 September a Russian sloop arrived in the harbour with letters and supplies from Governor Behm. In return, copies of letters and journals were sent to Behm with the request that, as he was returning to St. Petersburg, he take them and forward them to London [3.29]. Behm was as good as his word, and it was through him that the first news of Cook's death reached Europe in January 1780.

Ivashkin, a translator, arrived from Verkhene and he took Gore on a bear shoot while Smyslov, Behm's replacement as governor, came to visit on 22 September. Priest Vereshagin brought his family to visit the ship. Gore had escutcheons for Clerke made and erected at Paratunka and Petropavlosk [3.27]. There is still a memorial to Clerke in Petropavlosk.

South to Macao

The *Resolution*, under Gore, and the *Discovery*, now under King, departed from Avacha Bay on 10 October 1779. Before they sailed, Gore had convened a meeting to discuss the journey home. It was agreed that the ships were no longer in good condition and that as direct a route as possible be taken, with little or no attempt at further exploration. Sailing via Japan, China and Cape Town would be best; and they would avoid Batavia (Jakarta).

After passing the southern tip of Kamchatka, Cape Lopatka, winds forced them away from land and they sailed south without seeing the Kuril Islands [3.28]. On 26 October they sighted Cape Shiriya, the northeast point of the Japanese island of Honshu. Working down Honshu's east coast, often in strong gales, they saw many Japanese ships but none would make contact or respond to signals. The southeast point, Cape Inubo, was seen on 1 November and behind it the volcanic mountain of Fujiyama.

Winds drove the ships from land out to the east before they could resume sailing south. They then passed through sea with a great deal of pumice floating on the surface. They sailed close to Iwo-Jima (Sulphur Island) on 14 November and headed west for Macao in South China. Their route took them through the Bashi Channel between Formosa (Taiwan) and the Philippine island of Luzon. Gore was looking out for the Bashi Islands but missed them.

The ships passed Pratas before rounding the Lema Islands, south of Hong Kong, to arrive at the Portuguese port of Macao on 4 December 1779. Anchoring off Taipa Island, they found supplies difficult to obtain in Macao itself [3.28]. King was dispatched in a sampan up the Pearl River (Zhu Jiang) to merchants at Wampoo (Huangpu) and on to Canton (Guang Zhou). Supplies were obtained but, more significantly, sea otter pelts, obtained in North America, were sold for very high prices. This started a flourishing trade in which several men who had sailed with Cook took part. More importantly, it nearly killed off the sea otter.

Macao to the Cape

The *Resolution* and the *Discovery* sailed out of Macao on 13 January 1780 into the South China Sea, where they experienced gales for seven days. With some relief the ships stopped at the Con Son Islands (Pulau Condore) to the south of the Mekong Delta in Vietnam [3.29]. They were able to buy 10 buffalo for fresh meat, and caught large quantities of fish.

Gore sailed on from Con Son on 28 January and made for Sumatra. The ships negotiated the Bangka Strait on Sumatra's north coast and then sailed through the Sunda Strait between Sumatra and Java. They obtained fresh water from Krakatoa (this is the volcanic island that exploded so violently in 1883) and Princes Island in the Sunda Strait. This was somewhat surprising, as they had avoided Jakarta because of health risks yet Princes Island had proven equally unhealthy on the *Endeavour* voyage in 1770.

The passage across the Indian Ocean was uneventful. Approaching Cape Town, though, the ships could not make it round the Cape of Good Hope and into Table Bay. Instead they sailed into False Bay to anchor at Simon's Bay on 13 April [3.29]. They restocked and fitted a new rudder on the *Resolution*. They heard about the American War of Independence and that Britain was at war with France and Spain. They also heard that France had guaranteed their neutrality and would not attack Captain Cook's ships. Gore, therefore, determined to sail home unaccompanied by any other British ships that might undermine their position.

The Atlantic and Orkney

They sailed north on 9 May 1780 and had a slow passage up the Atlantic, even though they made no landfalls on the journey. On 9 August they neared the English Channel but strong winds forced them north and to the west of Ireland. They briefly considered calling in at Galway in West Ireland but pressed on instead [3.30]. They sighted the Outer Hebrides on 21 August, and the next day the ships anchored at Stromness in Orkney.

Gore amazed everyone by staying in port when conditions would have allowed them to continue. After six days the winds changed, preventing their departure. The midshipmen wrote letters in which they voiced their disapproval and frustration about being so close and yet not home. King was dispatched in early September to Aberdeen and on to the Admiralty with the remaining journals and charts. With his departure Burney took over command of the *Discovery*. Marine Sergeant Gibson, who had sailed on all three of Cook's voyages, was married on Orkney.

Orkney to London

Finally, on 20 September the ships sailed south. Three days later the recently married Sergeant Gibson died, and on the 29th John Davis also died. The ships anchored in Yarmouth Roads off Norfolk on 30 September so that both ships could be fitted with new cables [3.30]. On 2 October they continued south, and reached the mouth of the River Thames on the 4th.

After proceeding slowly up the Thames, the ships tied up in their home port — the *Discovery* at Woolwich and the *Resolution* at Deptford — on 7 October 1780 after more than four and a half years away. Most of the crew were paid off, while Lieutenant King was kept busy helping edit the journals of the voyage, and Midshipman Roberts helped prepare the charts for publication.

Assessment of voyage

Cook had needed little persuasion to take command of the expedition to search for the Northwest Passage. In hindsight, he probably should not have attempted the mission, as he had been ill on his previous voyage and was close to 50 years of age. He had spent most of the previous ten years away at sea, and retirement, or a long period of relaxation, would have served him better. His poor health and tiredness on this voyage led to erratic behaviour and actions not witnessed before. He seemed to lose some of his drive, and his failure to visit Fiji and Samoa would not have occurred on the earlier voyages. He became much harder on his crew, and less amiable and tolerant toward island people he met. He even exhibited signs of anger and violence not seen before. This may have contributed to his death on Hawaii, where he reacted in a way that a younger Cook would not have condoned.

The voyage was unable to find the Northwest Passage, and the ships returned to Britain without their two captains, Cook and Clerke; but even so it was not a failure. The expedition had explored and charted a large section of the North American coast from Oregon to Alaska and a similar stretch of the Asian coastline from Kamchatka northwards. In the Pacific Ocean, the Hawaiian Island Group had been located, together with islands in the Cook, Tonga and Austral Groups, and Kerguelen Island in the Indian Ocean had been described better. As with the Second Voyage, part of its success came from not finding land, thus showing that the Pacific was a very large mass of water with only scatterings of tiny, isolated islands.

Cook's death — the aftermath

The news of Cook's death first reached London in January 1780 via St. Petersburg. Governor Behm, from Kamchatka, had been true to his word and had carried copies of the journals across Russia to be forwarded on to England. When the *Resolution* and *Discovery* finally tied up in the Thames nine months later, people had largely come to terms with the news. Lieutenant King edited the logs and journals for publication in 1784, while Midshipman Roberts prepared the maps. The *Resolution*'s master, William Bligh, claimed to have drawn most of the maps but to have received no acknowledgement of his work.

In death, Cook's status rose. Poems and plays were written about him. The Royal Society had a medal struck, and in 1785 Cook was granted posthumously a coat of arms. However, no official statue or monument was erected and it was left to Cook's friend, Hugh Palliser, to erect a monument on his estate, The Vache, near Chalfont St. Giles [0.23].

No biography of Cook was written until 1788, when Andrew Kippis published his *Life of Captain James Cook*. It seems to have been written with a minimum of research; he appears, for example, not to have travelled north to consult people who knew Cook in Cleveland. Cook's life prior to the First Voyage is dealt with in seven and a half pages, replete with many errors that later writers would perpetuate. Similarly, he met only briefly with Elizabeth Cook, and with friends of Cook such as Banks and Palliser. Unfortunately Elizabeth Cook also destroyed most of Cook's letters and other personal belongings, and this has made the job of Cook biographers even more difficult. Such omissions and errors have made it very difficult for other biographers to write about Cook the person.

Cook's family after his death

When Cook died in Hawaii, Elizabeth, his wife, was only 38 years old, and three of their six children were still alive. Elizabeth lived for another 56 years until she died in Clapham, South London, in 1835 aged 94. She was granted a pension after Cook's death and used it to buy a house in Clapham in 1788 [0.08]. For much of the time she lived there, she shared the house with her cousin, Isaac Smith, after his retirement from the Navy. Smith had been the first of the *Endeavour*'s party to land in Botany Bay and had later risen to be a rear-admiral [1.23].

Of their remaining children, Nathaniel was the first to die when HMS *Thunderer*, the ship on which he was a midshipman, sank in the Caribbean during a hurricane in 1780. He was 16. Hugh, the youngest child, attended Christ's College, Cambridge, but he died from fever in December 1793, aged 17. A month later his older brother and his mother's last surviving child, James, died in strange circumstances in Poole Harbour near the Isle of Wight [0.23]. He was 31 and had been commander of the sloop, the *Spitfire*.

When Elizabeth Cook died in 1835 she was buried with several of her children in St. Andrew the Great Church in Cambridge [0.23].

In the North of England, Cook's father died in April 1779, just two months after Cook died in Hawaii and before the news of Cook's death reached England. He had been living with his daughter, Margaret, in Redcar and was buried in nearby Marske [0.02]. He was 85 years old. Margaret had married a local fisherman named James Fleck and they had eight children. It is through them that anyone claiming a family relationship to Cook must trace a link, as none of the Cooks' children had children of their own. Margaret died in 1804, aged 62, and was buried in Marske. Another sister, Christiana, had married a man called Cocker, but details of their life and whether they had children remain largely unknown. It is believed that Christiana died in 1795, aged 64.

The *Resolution* Trust

The *Resolution* Trust has been set up in Whitby in the North of England to celebrate the maritime history of the seaport and to celebrate its connections to James Cook. As a key part of its plans the Trust has committed itself to building a full replica of HMS *Resolution*, the ship used by Cook on both his Second and Third Voyages. Cook's ship, originally known as the *Marquis of Granby* was a Whitby vessel, built in 1770 by Thomas Fishburn at his yards. A museum and heritage centre will be built on the site of Fishburn's yard next to the River Esk.

After Gore brought the ship home to Britain at the end of the Third Voyage, the *Resolution* had a less than deserved old age. The exact details are uncertain but after it was converted into an armed transport it sailed to the East Indies. It may have sunk in the Sunda Strait in 1783.

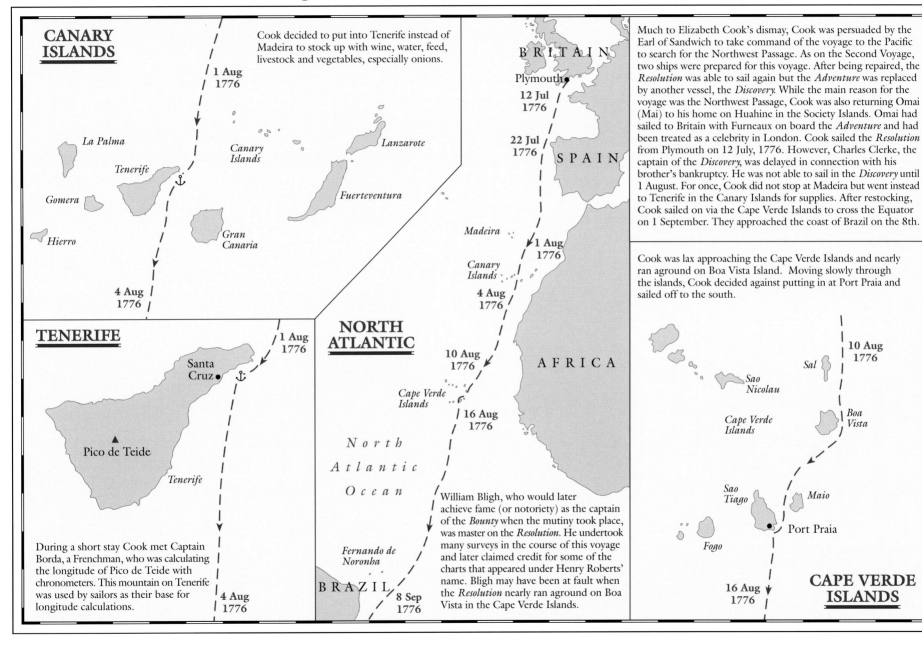

CANARY ISLANDS

1 Aug 1776

La Palma

Tenerife

Gomera

Hierro

Canary Islands

Lanzarote

Fuerteventura

Gran Canaria

4 Aug 1776

Cook decided to put into Tenerife instead of Madeira to stock up with wine, water, feed, livestock and vegetables, especially onions.

TENERIFE

1 Aug 1776

Santa Cruz

▲ Pico de Teide

Tenerife

During a short stay Cook met Captain Borda, a Frenchman, who was calculating the longitude of Pico de Teide with chronometers. This mountain on Tenerife was used by sailors as their base for longitude calculations.

4 Aug 1776

NORTH ATLANTIC

10 Aug 1776

Cape Verde Islands

16 Aug 1776

North Atlantic Ocean

Fernando de Noronha

BRAZIL

8 Sep 1776

William Bligh, who would later achieve fame (or notoriety) as the captain of the *Bounty* when the mutiny took place, was master on the *Resolution*. He undertook many surveys in the course of this voyage and later claimed credit for some of the charts that appeared under Henry Roberts' name. Bligh may have been at fault when the *Resolution* nearly ran aground on Boa Vista in the Cape Verde Islands.

BRITAIN

Plymouth
12 Jul 1776

22 Jul 1776

SPAIN

Madeira

Canary Islands

1 Aug 1776

4 Aug 1776

AFRICA

Much to Elizabeth Cook's dismay, Cook was persuaded by the Earl of Sandwich to take command of the voyage to the Pacific to search for the Northwest Passage. As on the Second Voyage, two ships were prepared for this voyage. After being repaired, the *Resolution* was able to sail again but the *Adventure* was replaced by another vessel, the *Discovery*. While the main reason for the voyage was the Northwest Passage, Cook was also returning Omai (Mai) to his home on Huahine in the Society Islands. Omai had sailed to Britain with Furneaux on board the *Adventure* and had been treated as a celebrity in London. Cook sailed the *Resolution* from Plymouth on 12 July, 1776. However, Charles Clerke, the captain of the *Discovery*, was delayed in connection with his brother's bankruptcy. He was not able to sail in the *Discovery* until 1 August. For once, Cook did not stop at Madeira but went instead to Tenerife in the Canary Islands for supplies. After restocking, Cook sailed on via the Cape Verde Islands to cross the Equator on 1 September. They approached the coast of Brazil on the 8th.

Cook was lax approaching the Cape Verde Islands and nearly ran aground on Boa Vista Island. Moving slowly through the islands, Cook decided against putting in at Port Praia and sailed off to the south.

10 Aug 1776

Sal

Sao Nicolau

Boa Vista

Cape Verde Islands

Sao Tiago

Maio

Port Praia

Fogo

16 Aug 1776

CAPE VERDE ISLANDS

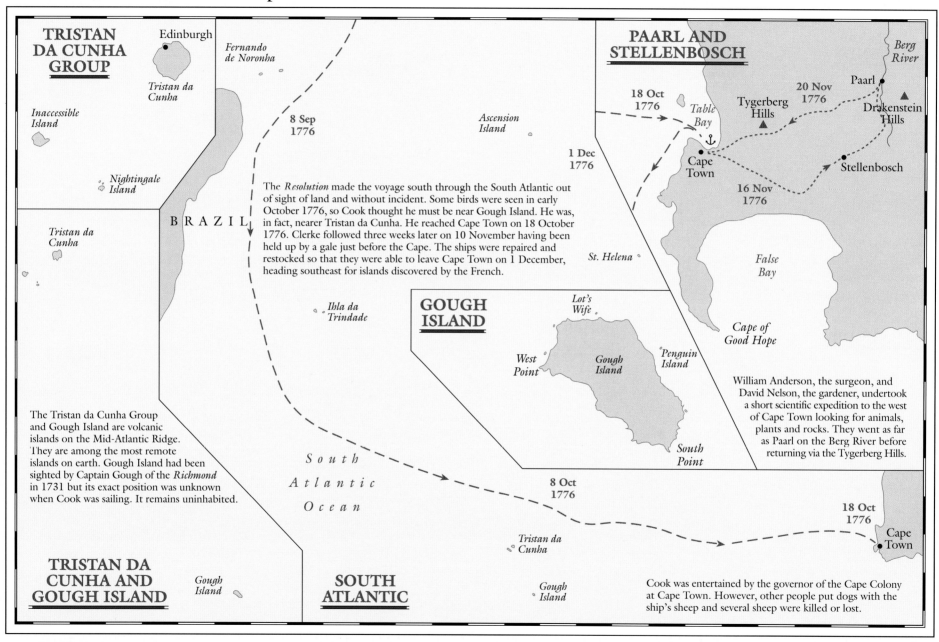

TRISTAN DA CUNHA GROUP

Edinburgh

Fernando de Noronha

Tristan da Cunha

Inaccessible Island

Nightingale Island

Tristan da Cunha

B R A Z I L

8 Sep 1776

The *Resolution* made the voyage south through the South Atlantic out of sight of land and without incident. Some birds were seen in early October 1776, so Cook thought he must be near Gough Island. He was, in fact, nearer Tristan da Cunha. He reached Cape Town on 18 October 1776. Clerke followed three weeks later on 10 November having been held up by a gale just before the Cape. The ships were repaired and restocked so that they were able to leave Cape Town on 1 December, heading southeast for islands discovered by the French.

Ascension Island

1 Dec 1776

St. Helena

Ihla da Trindade

GOUGH ISLAND

Lot's Wife

West Point

Gough Island

Penguin Island

South Point

The Tristan da Cunha Group and Gough Island are volcanic islands on the Mid-Atlantic Ridge. They are among the most remote islands on earth. Gough Island had been sighted by Captain Gough of the *Richmond* in 1731 but its exact position was unknown when Cook was sailing. It remains uninhabited.

S o u t h

A t l a n t i c

O c e a n

8 Oct 1776

TRISTAN DA CUNHA AND GOUGH ISLAND

Gough Island

SOUTH ATLANTIC

Tristan da Cunha

Gough Island

PAARL AND STELLENBOSCH

Berg River

18 Oct 1776

Table Bay

Tygerberg Hills

20 Nov 1776

Paarl

Drakenstein Hills

Cape Town

16 Nov 1776

Stellenbosch

False Bay

Cape of Good Hope

William Anderson, the surgeon, and David Nelson, the gardener, undertook a short scientific expedition to the west of Cape Town looking for animals, plants and rocks. They went as far as Paarl on the Berg River before returning via the Tygerberg Hills.

18 Oct 1776

Cape Town

Cook was entertained by the governor of the Cape Colony at Cape Town. However, other people put dogs with the ship's sheep and several sheep were killed or lost.

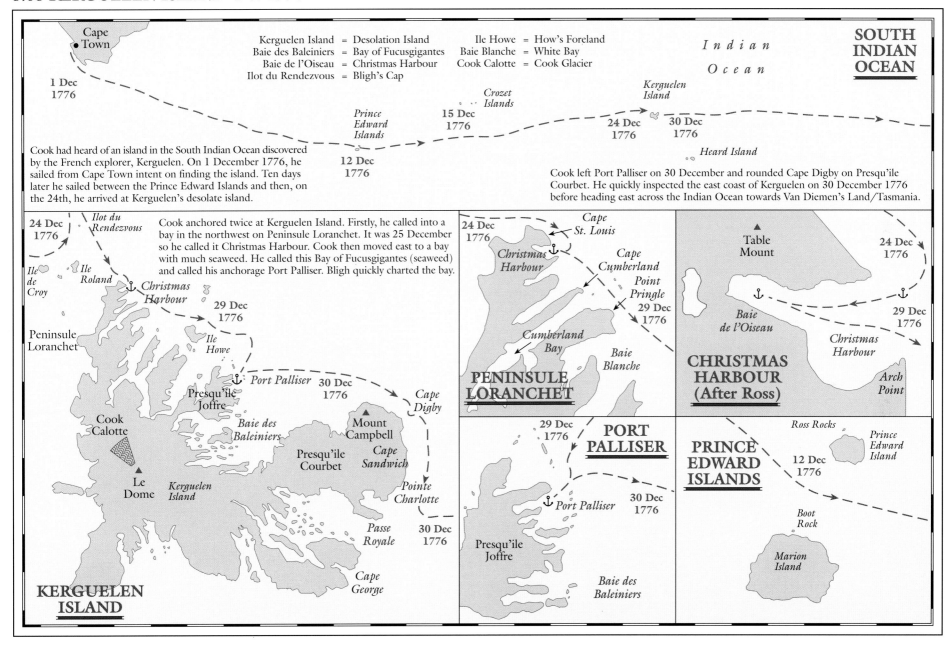

SOUTH INDIAN OCEAN

Indian Ocean

Kerguelen Island = Desolation Island
Baie des Baleiniers = Bay of Fucusgigantes
Baie de l'Oiseau = Christmas Harbour
Ilot du Rendezvous = Bligh's Cap

Ile Howe = How's Foreland
Baie Blanche = White Bay
Cook Calotte = Cook Glacier

Cape Town

1 Dec 1776

Prince Edward Islands

12 Dec 1776

15 Dec 1776

Crozet Islands

24 Dec 1776

Kerguelen Island

30 Dec 1776

Heard Island

Cook had heard of an island in the South Indian Ocean discovered by the French explorer, Kerguelen. On 1 December 1776, he sailed from Cape Town intent on finding the island. Ten days later he sailed between the Prince Edward Islands and then, on the 24th, he arrived at Kerguelen's desolate island.

Cook left Port Palliser on 30 December and rounded Cape Digby on Presqu'ile Courbet. He quickly inspected the east coast of Kerguelen on 30 December 1776 before heading east across the Indian Ocean towards Van Diemen's Land/Tasmania.

Cook anchored twice at Kerguelen Island. Firstly, he called into a bay in the northwest on Peninsule Loranchet. It was 25 December so he called it Christmas Harbour. Cook then moved east to a bay with much seaweed. He called this Bay of Fucusgigantes (seaweed) and called his anchorage Port Palliser. Bligh quickly charted the bay.

24 Dec 1776

Ilot du Rendezvous

Ile de Croy

Ile Roland

Christmas Harbour

29 Dec 1776

Ile Howe

Port Palliser

30 Dec 1776

Peninsule Loranchet

Cook Calotte

Presqu'ile Joffre

Baie des Baleiniers

Mount Campbell

Presqu'ile Courbet

Cape Sandwich

Cape Digby

Le Dome

Kerguelen Island

Pointe Charlotte

Passe Royale

30 Dec 1776

Cape George

KERGUELEN ISLAND

24 Dec 1776

Cape St. Louis

Christmas Harbour

Cape Cumberland

Point Pringle

29 Dec 1776

Cumberland Bay

Baie Blanche

PENINSULE LORANCHET

Table Mount

24 Dec 1776

Baie de l'Oiseau

29 Dec 1776

Christmas Harbour

Arch Point

CHRISTMAS HARBOUR (After Ross)

29 Dec 1776

PORT PALLISER

Port Palliser

30 Dec 1776

Presqu'ile Joffre

Baie des Baleiniers

Ross Rocks

Prince Edward Island

12 Dec 1776

Boot Rock

Marion Island

PRINCE EDWARD ISLANDS

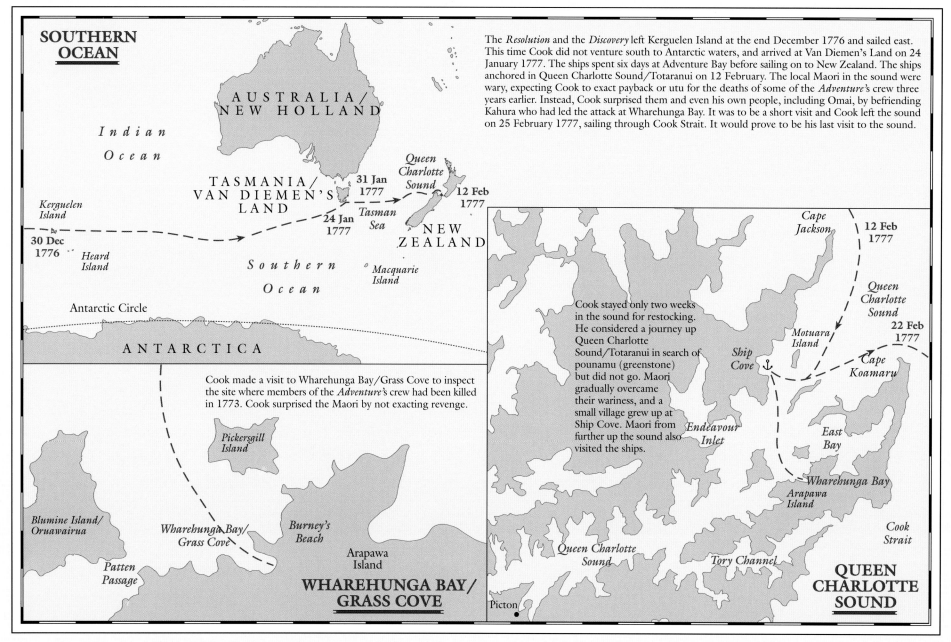

SOUTHERN OCEAN

AUSTRALIA/ NEW HOLLAND

Indian Ocean

TASMANIA/ VAN DIEMEN'S LAND

Kerguelen Island

30 Dec 1776

Heard Island

Southern Ocean

Antarctic Circle

ANTARCTICA

31 Jan 1777

24 Jan 1777

Tasman Sea

Queen Charlotte Sound

12 Feb 1777

NEW ZEALAND

Macquarie Island

The *Resolution* and the *Discovery* left Kerguelen Island at the end December 1776 and sailed east. This time Cook did not venture south to Antarctic waters, and arrived at Van Diemen's Land on 24 January 1777. The ships spent six days at Adventure Bay before sailing on to New Zealand. The ships anchored in Queen Charlotte Sound/Totaranui on 12 February. The local Maori in the sound were wary, expecting Cook to exact payback or utu for the deaths of some of the *Adventure*'s crew three years earlier. Instead, Cook surprised them and even his own people, including Omai, by befriending Kahura who had led the attack at Wharehunga Bay. It was to be a short visit and Cook left the sound on 25 February 1777, sailing through Cook Strait. It would prove to be his last visit to the sound.

Cook made a visit to Wharehunga Bay/Grass Cove to inspect the site where members of the *Adventure*'s crew had been killed in 1773. Cook surprised the Maori by not exacting revenge.

Pickersgill Island

Blumine Island/ Oruawairua

Wharehunga Bay/ Grass Cove

Burney's Beach

Patten Passage

Arapawa Island

WHAREHUNGA BAY/ GRASS COVE

Cape Jackson

12 Feb 1777

Queen Charlotte Sound

22 Feb 1777

Cook stayed only two weeks in the sound for restocking. He considered a journey up Queen Charlotte Sound/Totaranui in search of pounamu (greenstone) but did not go. Maori gradually overcame their wariness, and a small village grew up at Ship Cove. Maori from further up the sound also visited the ships.

Motuara Island

Ship Cove ⚓

Cape Koamaru

Endeavour Inlet

East Bay

Wharehunga Bay

Arapawa Island

Queen Charlotte Sound

Tory Channel

Cook Strait

Picton •

QUEEN CHARLOTTE SOUND

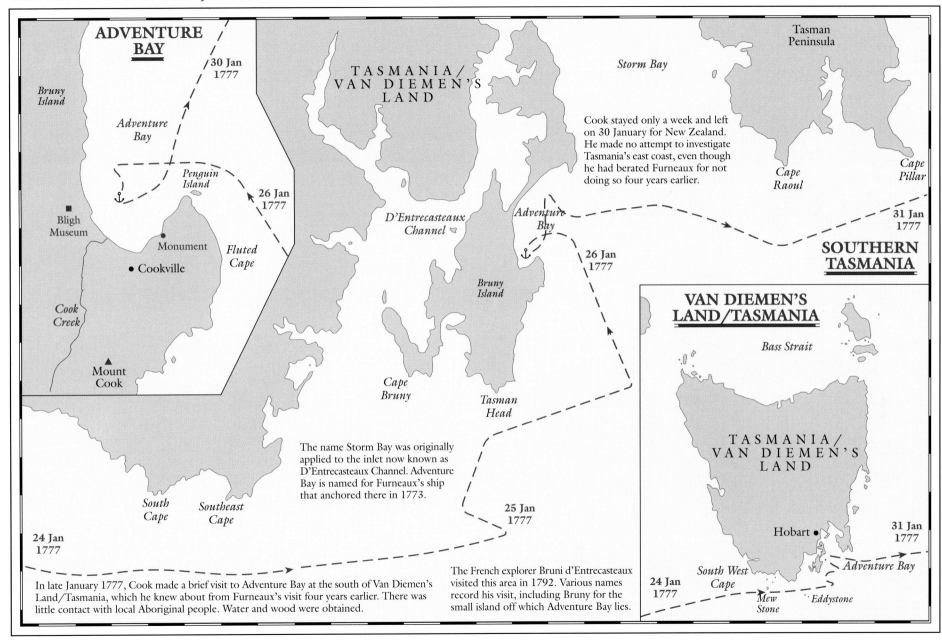

ADVENTURE BAY

Bruny Island

Adventure Bay

30 Jan 1777

Penguin Island

26 Jan 1777

Bligh Museum

Monument

• Cookville

Fluted Cape

Cook Creek

▲ Mount Cook

TASMANIA/ VAN DIEMEN'S LAND

Storm Bay

Tasman Peninsula

Cook stayed only a week and left on 30 January for New Zealand. He made no attempt to investigate Tasmania's east coast, even though he had berated Furneaux for not doing so four years earlier.

Cape Raoul

Cape Pillar

D'Entrecasteaux Channel

Adventure Bay

31 Jan 1777

SOUTHERN TASMANIA

26 Jan 1777

Bruny Island

Cape Bruny

Tasman Head

The name Storm Bay was originally applied to the inlet now known as D'Entrecasteaux Channel. Adventure Bay is named for Furneaux's ship that anchored there in 1773.

South Cape

Southeast Cape

25 Jan 1777

24 Jan 1777

In late January 1777, Cook made a brief visit to Adventure Bay at the south of Van Diemen's Land/Tasmania, which he knew about from Furneaux's visit four years earlier. There was little contact with local Aboriginal people. Water and wood were obtained.

The French explorer Bruni d'Entrecasteaux visited this area in 1792. Various names record his visit, including Bruny for the small island off which Adventure Bay lies.

VAN DIEMEN'S LAND/TASMANIA

Bass Strait

TASMANIA/ VAN DIEMEN'S LAND

Hobart •

31 Jan 1777

24 Jan 1777

South West Cape

Adventure Bay

Mew Stone

Eddystone

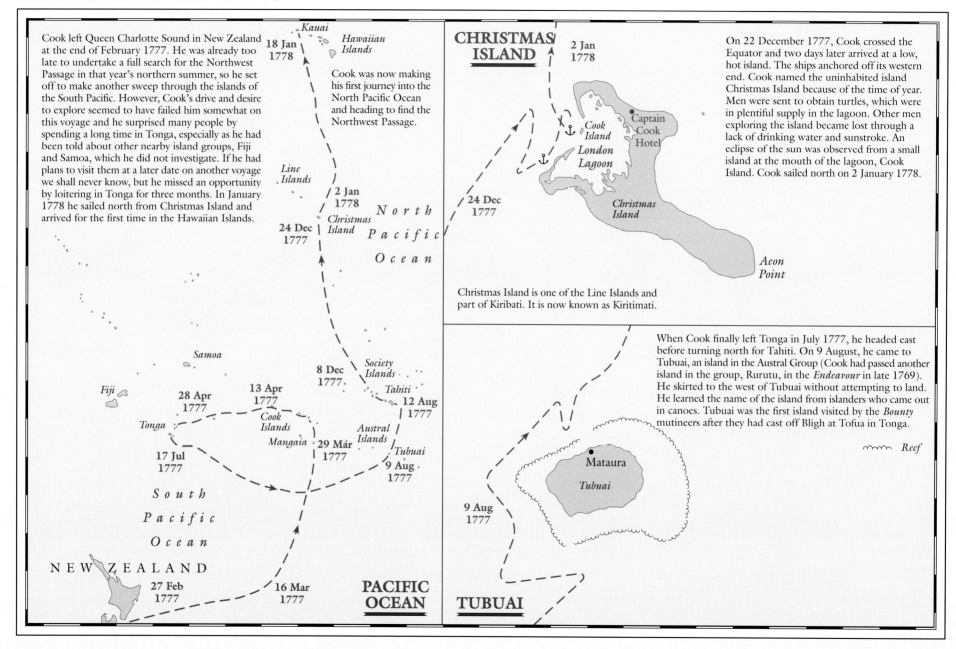

Cook left Queen Charlotte Sound in New Zealand at the end of February 1777. He was already too late to undertake a full search for the Northwest Passage in that year's northern summer, so he set off to make another sweep through the islands of the South Pacific. However, Cook's drive and desire to explore seemed to have failed him somewhat on this voyage and he surprised many people by spending a long time in Tonga, especially as he had been told about other nearby island groups, Fiji and Samoa, which he did not investigate. If he had plans to visit them at a later date on another voyage we shall never know, but he missed an opportunity by loitering in Tonga for three months. In January 1778 he sailed north from Christmas Island and arrived for the first time in the Hawaiian Islands.

Cook was now making his first journey into the North Pacific Ocean and heading to find the Northwest Passage.

CHRISTMAS ISLAND

On 22 December 1777, Cook crossed the Equator and two days later arrived at a low, hot island. The ships anchored off its western end. Cook named the uninhabited island Christmas Island because of the time of year. Men were sent to obtain turtles, which were in plentiful supply in the lagoon. Other men exploring the island became lost through a lack of drinking water and sunstroke. An eclipse of the sun was observed from a small island at the mouth of the lagoon, Cook Island. Cook sailed north on 2 January 1778.

Christmas Island is one of the Line Islands and part of Kiribati. It is now known as Kiritimati.

When Cook finally left Tonga in July 1777, he headed east before turning north for Tahiti. On 9 August, he came to Tubuai, an island in the Austral Group (Cook had passed another island in the group, Rurutu, in the *Endeavour* in late 1769). He skirted to the west of Tubuai without attempting to land. He learned the name of the island from islanders who came out in canoes. Tubuai was the first island visited by the *Bounty* mutineers after they had cast off Bligh at Tofua in Tonga.

~~~~ Reef

TUBUAI

PACIFIC OCEAN

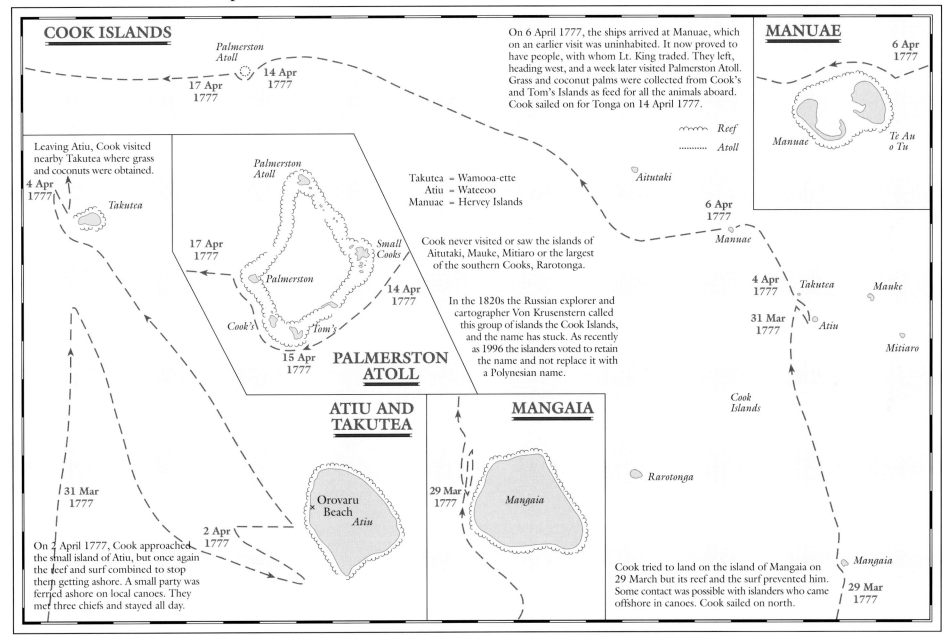

COOK ISLANDS

Palmerston Atoll

14 Apr 1777

17 Apr 1777

On 6 April 1777, the ships arrived at Manuae, which on an earlier visit was uninhabited. It now proved to have people, with whom Lt. King traded. They left, heading west, and a week later visited Palmerston Atoll. Grass and coconut palms were collected from Cook's and Tom's Islands as feed for all the animals aboard. Cook sailed on for Tonga on 14 April 1777.

~~~~~ *Reef*

.... *Atoll*

MANUAE

6 Apr 1777

Manuae   *Te Au o Tu*

Leaving Atiu, Cook visited nearby Takutea where grass and coconuts were obtained.

4 Apr 1777

Takutea

Aitutaki

Takutea = Wamooa-ette
Atiu = Wateeoo
Manuae = Hervey Islands

6 Apr 1777

Palmerston Atoll

17 Apr 1777

Small Cooks

Palmerston

Manuae

Cook never visited or saw the islands of Aitutaki, Mauke, Mitiaro or the largest of the southern Cooks, Rarotonga.

4 Apr 1777   *Takutea*   *Mauke*

31 Mar 1777   *Atiu*

14 Apr 1777

Cook's   *Tom's*

In the 1820s the Russian explorer and cartographer Von Krusenstern called this group of islands the Cook Islands, and the name has stuck. As recently as 1996 the islanders voted to retain the name and not replace it with a Polynesian name.

Mitiaro

15 Apr 1777

PALMERSTON ATOLL

ATIU AND TAKUTEA

MANGAIA

Cook Islands

31 Mar 1777

29 Mar 1777

Rarotonga

2 Apr 1777

Orovaru Beach   *Atiu*

Mangaia

On 2 April 1777, Cook approached the small island of Atiu, but once again the reef and surf combined to stop them getting ashore. A small party was ferried ashore on local canoes. They met three chiefs and stayed all day.

Cook tried to land on the island of Mangaia on 29 March but its reef and the surf prevented him. Some contact was possible with islanders who came offshore in canoes. Cook sailed on north.

Mangaia

29 Mar 1777

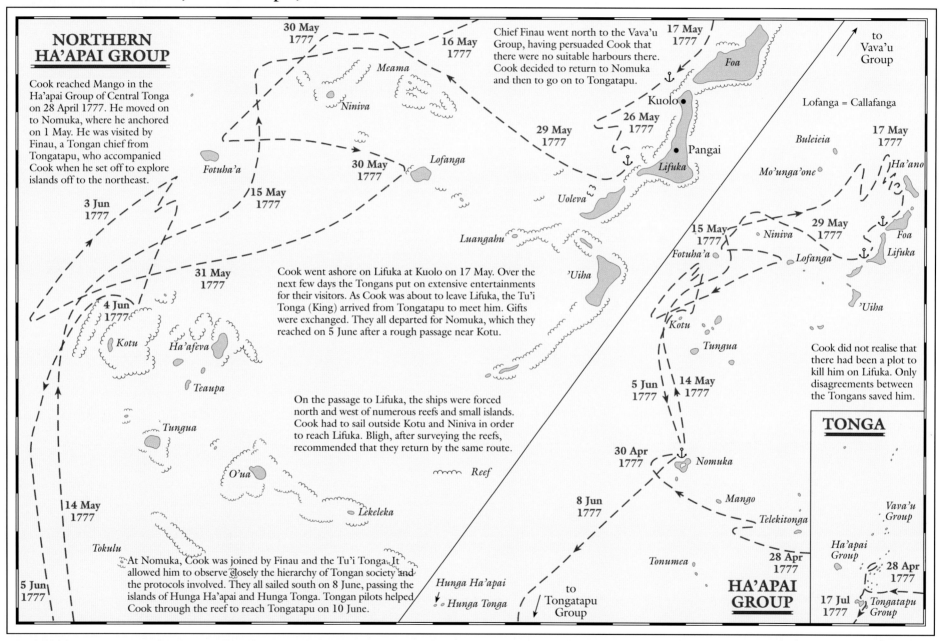

NORTHERN HA'APAI GROUP

Cook reached Mango in the Ha'apai Group of Central Tonga on 28 April 1777. He moved on to Nomuka, where he anchored on 1 May. He was visited by Finau, a Tongan chief from Tongatapu, who accompanied Cook when he set off to explore islands off to the northeast.

Chief Finau went north to the Vava'u Group, having persuaded Cook that there were no suitable harbours there. Cook decided to return to Nomuka and then to go on to Tongatapu.

Cook went ashore on Lifuka at Kuolo on 17 May. Over the next few days the Tongans put on extensive entertainments for their visitors. As Cook was about to leave Lifuka, the Tu'i Tonga (King) arrived from Tongatapu to meet him. Gifts were exchanged. They all departed for Nomuka, which they reached on 5 June after a rough passage near Kotu.

On the passage to Lifuka, the ships were forced north and west of numerous reefs and small islands. Cook had to sail outside Kotu and Niniva in order to reach Lifuka. Bligh, after surveying the reefs, recommended that they return by the same route.

At Nomuka, Cook was joined by Finau and the Tu'i Tonga. It allowed him to observe closely the hierarchy of Tongan society and the protocols involved. They all sailed south on 8 June, passing the islands of Hunga Ha'apai and Hunga Tonga. Tongan pilots helped Cook through the reef to reach Tongatapu on 10 June.

Cook did not realise that there had been a plot to kill him on Lifuka. Only disagreements between the Tongans saved him.

Lofanga = Callafanga

TONGA

HA'APAI GROUP

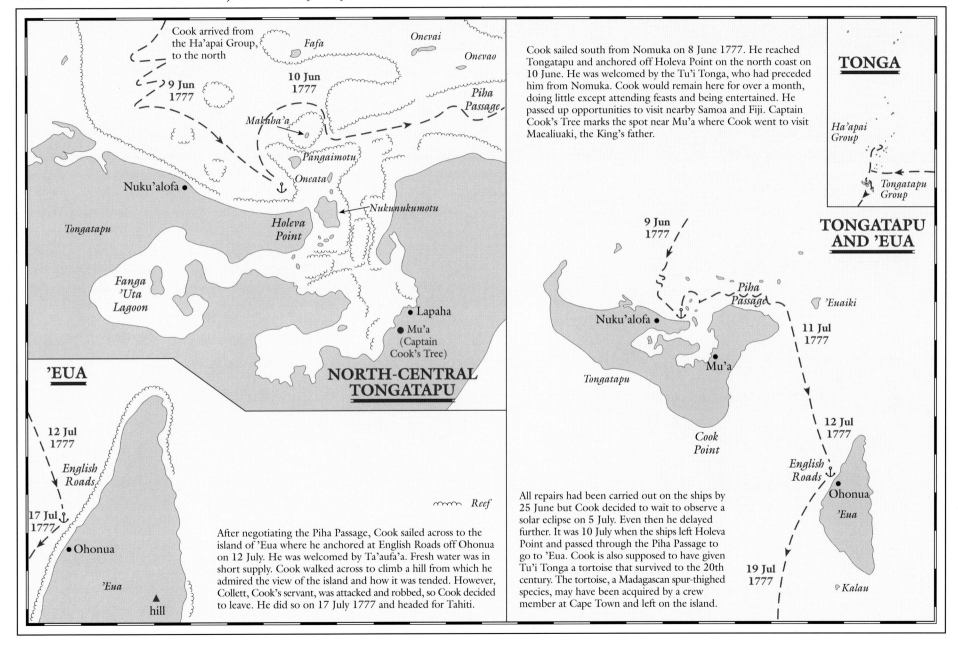

Cook arrived from the Ha'apai Group, to the north

9 Jun 1777

Fafa

Onevai

Onevao

10 Jun 1777

Piha Passage

Makaha'a

Pangaimotu

Oneata

Nukunukumotu

Nuku'alofa •

Holeva Point

Tongatapu

Fanga 'Uta Lagoon

• Lapaha

• Mu'a (Captain Cook's Tree)

NORTH-CENTRAL TONGATAPU

'EUA

12 Jul 1777

English Roads

17 Jul 1777

• Ohonua

'Eua

▲ hill

Cook sailed south from Nomuka on 8 June 1777. He reached Tongatapu and anchored off Holeva Point on the north coast on 10 June. He was welcomed by the Tu'i Tonga, who had preceded him from Nomuka. Cook would remain here for over a month, doing little except attending feasts and being entertained. He passed up opportunities to visit nearby Samoa and Fiji. Captain Cook's Tree marks the spot near Mu'a where Cook went to visit Maealiuaki, the King's father.

TONGA

Ha'apai Group

Tongatapu Group

TONGATAPU AND 'EUA

9 Jun 1777

Piha Passage

'Euaiki

Nuku'alofa •

11 Jul 1777

• Mu'a

Tongatapu

Cook Point

12 Jul 1777

English Roads

• Ohonua

'Eua

19 Jul 1777

Kalau

〰〰〰 *Reef*

After negotiating the Piha Passage, Cook sailed across to the island of 'Eua where he anchored at English Roads off Ohonua on 12 July. He was welcomed by Ta'aufa'a. Fresh water was in short supply. Cook walked across to climb a hill from which he admired the view of the island and how it was tended. However, Collett, Cook's servant, was attacked and robbed, so Cook decided to leave. He did so on 17 July 1777 and headed for Tahiti.

All repairs had been carried out on the ships by 25 June but Cook decided to wait to observe a solar eclipse on 5 July. Even then he delayed further. It was 10 July when the ships left Holeva Point and passed through the Piha Passage to go to 'Eua. Cook is also supposed to have given Tu'i Tonga a tortoise that survived to the 20th century. The tortoise, a Madagascan spur-thighed species, may have been acquired by a crew member at Cape Town and left on the island.

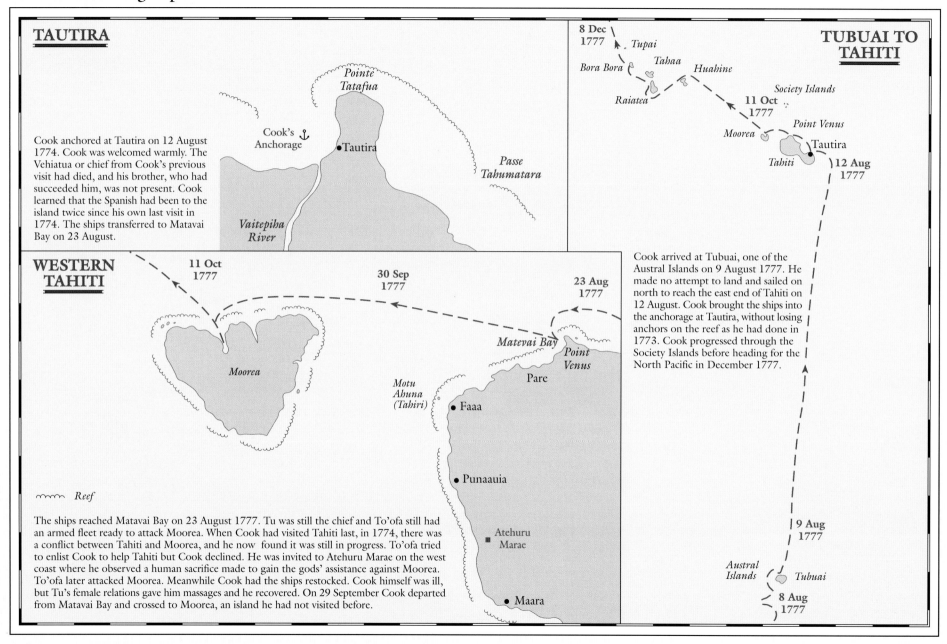

TAUTIRA

Cook anchored at Tautira on 12 August 1774. Cook was welcomed warmly. The Vehiatua or chief from Cook's previous visit had died, and his brother, who had succeeded him, was not present. Cook learned that the Spanish had been to the island twice since his own last visit in 1774. The ships transferred to Matavai Bay on 23 August.

Pointe Tatafua

Cook's Anchorage

•Tautira

Passe Tahumatara

Vaitepiha River

TUBUAI TO TAHITI

8 Dec 1777 — *Tupai*

Bora Bora *Tahaa* *Huahine*

Raiatea **11 Oct 1777** *Society Islands*

Point Venus

Moorea Tautira

Tahiti **12 Aug 1777**

Cook arrived at Tubuai, one of the Austral Islands on 9 August 1777. He made no attempt to land and sailed on north to reach the east end of Tahiti on 12 August. Cook brought the ships into the anchorage at Tautira, without losing anchors on the reef as he had done in 1773. Cook progressed through the Society Islands before heading for the North Pacific in December 1777.

WESTERN TAHITI

11 Oct 1777

30 Sep 1777

23 Aug 1777

Matevai Bay

Point Venus

Pare

Moorea

Motu Ahuna (Tahiri)

•Faaa

•Punaauia

Atehuru Marae ■

•Maara

〰〰〰 *Reef*

The ships reached Matavai Bay on 23 August 1777. Tu was still the chief and To'ofa still had an armed fleet ready to attack Moorea. When Cook had visited Tahiti last, in 1774, there was a conflict between Tahiti and Moorea, and he now found it was still in progress. To'ofa tried to enlist Cook to help Tahiti but Cook declined. He was invited to Atehuru Marae on the west coast where he observed a human sacrifice made to gain the gods' assistance against Moorea. To'ofa later attacked Moorea. Meanwhile Cook had the ships restocked. Cook himself was ill, but Tu's female relations gave him massages and he recovered. On 29 September Cook departed from Matavai Bay and crossed to Moorea, an island he had not visited before.

9 Aug 1777

Austral Islands *Tubuai*

8 Aug 1777

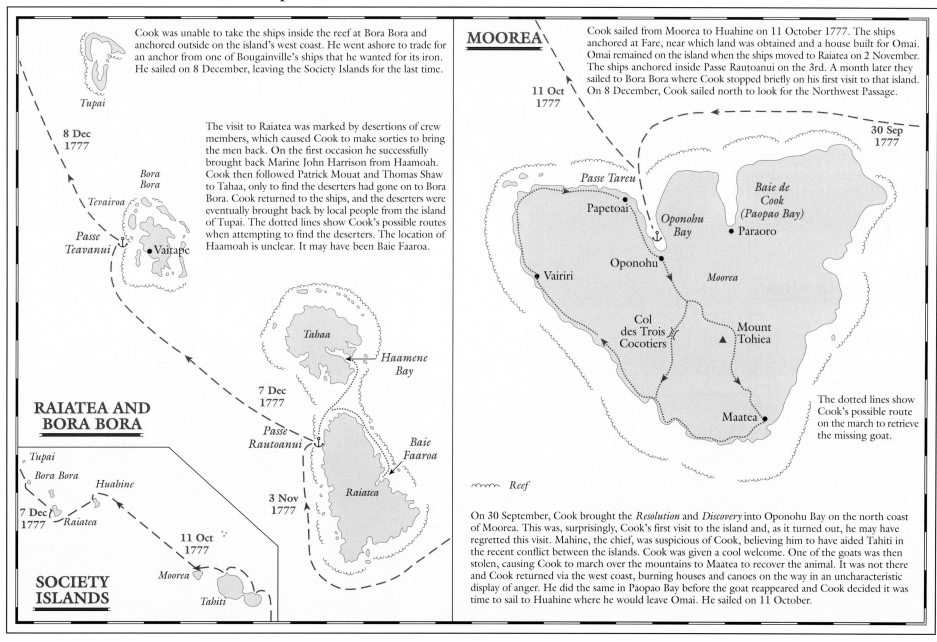

Cook was unable to take the ships inside the reef at Bora Bora and anchored outside on the island's west coast. He went ashore to trade for an anchor from one of Bougainville's ships that he wanted for its iron. He sailed on 8 December, leaving the Society Islands for the last time.

Tupai

8 Dec 1777

The visit to Raiatea was marked by desertions of crew members, which caused Cook to make sorties to bring the men back. On the first occasion he successfully brought back Marine John Harrison from Haamoah. Cook then followed Patrick Mouat and Thomas Shaw to Tahaa, only to find the deserters had gone on to Bora Bora. Cook returned to the ships, and the deserters were eventually brought back by local people from the island of Tupai. The dotted lines show Cook's possible routes when attempting to find the deserters. The location of Haamoah is unclear. It may have been Baie Faaroa.

Bora Bora

Tevairoa

Passe Teavanui ⚓ • *Vaitape*

RAIATEA AND BORA BORA

Tupai

Bora Bora   *Huahine*

7 Dec 1777 *Raiatea*

11 Oct 1777

Moorea

SOCIETY ISLANDS

Tahiti

Tahaa

Haamene Bay

7 Dec 1777

Passe Rautoanui ⚓

3 Nov 1777

Baie Faaroa

Raiatea

MOOREA

Cook sailed from Moorea to Huahine on 11 October 1777. The ships anchored at Fare, near which land was obtained and a house built for Omai. Omai remained on the island when the ships moved to Raiatea on 2 November. The ships anchored inside Passe Rautoanui on the 3rd. A month later they sailed to Bora Bora where Cook stopped briefly on his first visit to that island. On 8 December, Cook sailed north to look for the Northwest Passage.

11 Oct 1777

30 Sep 1777

Passe Tareu

Papetoai

Oponohu Bay ⚓

Baie de Cook (Paopao Bay)

• *Paraoro*

Oponohu

• *Vairiri*

Moorea

Col des Trois Cocotiers

Mount Tohiea ▲

Maatea •

The dotted lines show Cook's possible route on the march to retrieve the missing goat.

〜〜〜 *Reef*

On 30 September, Cook brought the *Resolution* and *Discovery* into Oponohu Bay on the north coast of Moorea. This was, surprisingly, Cook's first visit to the island and, as it turned out, he may have regretted this visit. Mahine, the chief, was suspicious of Cook, believing him to have aided Tahiti in the recent conflict between the islands. Cook was given a cool welcome. One of the goats was then stolen, causing Cook to march over the mountains to Maatea to recover the animal. It was not there and Cook returned via the west coast, burning houses and canoes on the way in an uncharacteristic display of anger. He did the same in Paopao Bay before the goat reappeared and Cook decided it was time to sail to Huahine where he would leave Omai. He sailed on 11 October.

3.12 KAUAI AND NIHAU Jan–Feb 1778

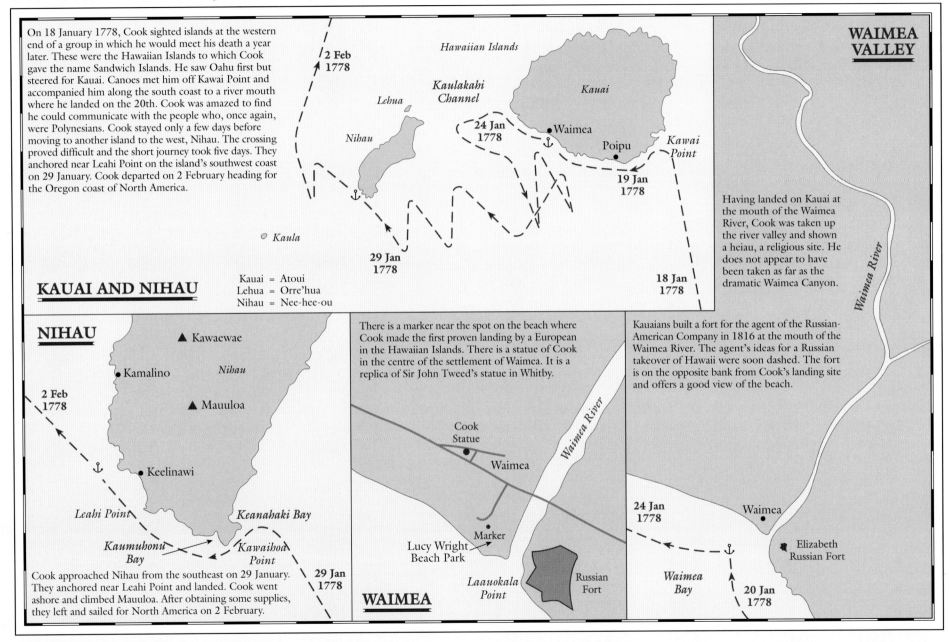

On 18 January 1778, Cook sighted islands at the western end of a group in which he would meet his death a year later. These were the Hawaiian Islands to which Cook gave the name Sandwich Islands. He saw Oahu first but steered for Kauai. Canoes met him off Kawai Point and accompanied him along the south coast to a river mouth where he landed on the 20th. Cook was amazed to find he could communicate with the people who, once again, were Polynesians. Cook stayed only a few days before moving to another island to the west, Nihau. The crossing proved difficult and the short journey took five days. They anchored near Leahi Point on the island's southwest coast on 29 January. Cook departed on 2 February heading for the Oregon coast of North America.

KAUAI AND NIHAU

Kauai = Atoui
Lehua = Orre'hua
Nihau = Nee-hee-ou

Hawaiian Islands

2 Feb 1778

Kaulakahi Channel

Lehua

Nihau

Kauai

Kaula

24 Jan 1778

• Waimea

Poipu •

Kawai Point

19 Jan 1778

29 Jan 1778

18 Jan 1778

WAIMEA VALLEY

Having landed on Kauai at the mouth of the Waimea River, Cook was taken up the river valley and shown a heiau, a religious site. He does not appear to have been taken as far as the dramatic Waimea Canyon.

Waimea River

NIHAU

▲ Kawaewae

• Kamalino

Nihau

▲ Mauuloa

2 Feb 1778

• Keelinawi

Leahi Point

Keanahaki Bay

Kaumuhonu Bay

Kawaihoa Point

29 Jan 1778

Cook approached Nihau from the southeast on 29 January. They anchored near Leahi Point and landed. Cook went ashore and climbed Mauuloa. After obtaining some supplies, they left and sailed for North America on 2 February.

WAIMEA

There is a marker near the spot on the beach where Cook made the first proven landing by a European in the Hawaiian Islands. There is a statue of Cook in the centre of the settlement of Waimea. It is a replica of Sir John Tweed's statue in Whitby.

Cook Statue

Waimea

Waimea River

Lucy Wright Beach Park

• Marker

Laauokala Point

Russian Fort

Kauaians built a fort for the agent of the Russian-American Company in 1816 at the mouth of the Waimea River. The agent's ideas for a Russian takeover of Hawaii were soon dashed. The fort is on the opposite bank from Cook's landing site and offers a good view of the beach.

24 Jan 1778

Waimea •

Elizabeth Russian Fort

Waimea Bay

20 Jan 1778

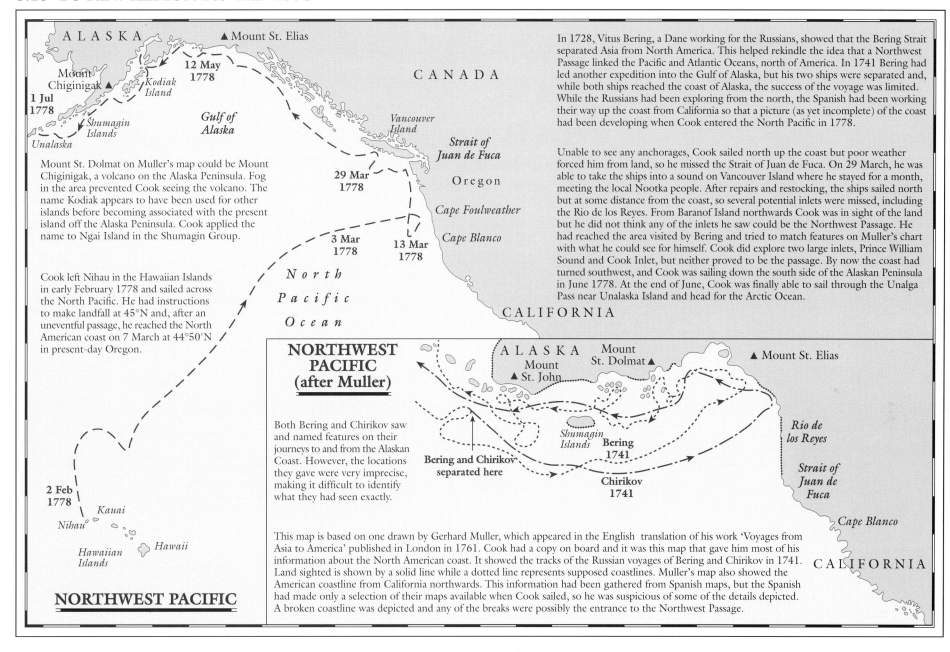

In 1728, Vitus Bering, a Dane working for the Russians, showed that the Bering Strait separated Asia from North America. This helped rekindle the idea that a Northwest Passage linked the Pacific and Atlantic Oceans, north of America. In 1741 Bering had led another expedition into the Gulf of Alaska, but his two ships were separated and, while both ships reached the coast of Alaska, the success of the voyage was limited. While the Russians had been exploring from the north, the Spanish had been working their way up the coast from California so that a picture (as yet incomplete) of the coast had been developing when Cook entered the North Pacific in 1778.

Unable to see any anchorages, Cook sailed north up the coast but poor weather forced him from land, so he missed the Strait of Juan de Fuca. On 29 March, he was able to take the ships into a sound on Vancouver Island where he stayed for a month, meeting the local Nootka people. After repairs and restocking, the ships sailed north but at some distance from the coast, so several potential inlets were missed, including the Rio de los Reyes. From Baranof Island northwards Cook was in sight of the land but he did not think any of the inlets he saw could be the Northwest Passage. He had reached the area visited by Bering and tried to match features on Muller's chart with what he could see for himself. Cook did explore two large inlets, Prince William Sound and Cook Inlet, but neither proved to be the passage. By now the coast had turned southwest, and Cook was sailing down the south side of the Alaskan Peninsula in June 1778. At the end of June, Cook was finally able to sail through the Unalga Pass near Unalaska Island and head for the Arctic Ocean.

Mount St. Dolmat on Muller's map could be Mount Chiginigak, a volcano on the Alaska Peninsula. Fog in the area prevented Cook seeing the volcano. The name Kodiak appears to have been used for other islands before becoming associated with the present island off the Alaska Peninsula. Cook applied the name to Ngai Island in the Shumagin Group.

Cook left Nihau in the Hawaiian Islands in early February 1778 and sailed across the North Pacific. He had instructions to make landfall at 45°N and, after an uneventful passage, he reached the North American coast on 7 March at 44°50'N in present-day Oregon.

NORTHWEST PACIFIC (after Muller)

Both Bering and Chirikov saw and named features on their journeys to and from the Alaskan Coast. However, the locations they gave were very imprecise, making it difficult to identify what they had seen exactly.

This map is based on one drawn by Gerhard Muller, which appeared in the English translation of his work 'Voyages from Asia to America' published in London in 1761. Cook had a copy on board and it was this map that gave him most of his information about the North American coast. It showed the tracks of the Russian voyages of Bering and Chirikov in 1741. Land sighted is shown by a solid line while a dotted line represents supposed coastlines. Muller's map also showed the American coastline from California northwards. This information had been gathered from Spanish maps, but the Spanish had made only a selection of their maps available when Cook sailed, so he was suspicious of some of the details depicted. A broken coastline was depicted and any of the breaks were possibly the entrance to the Northwest Passage.

NORTHWEST PACIFIC

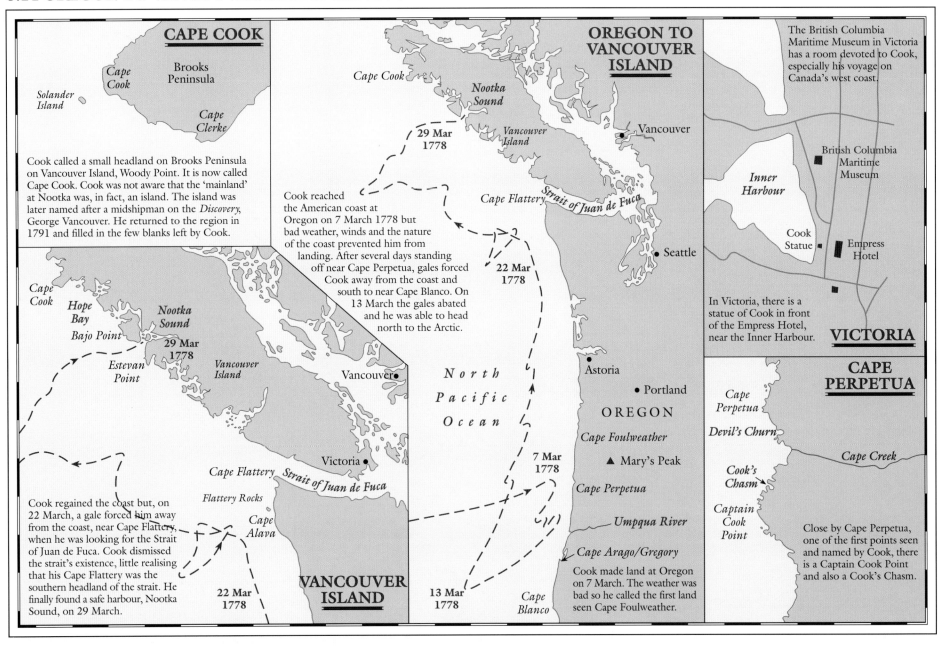

CAPE COOK

Cape Cook

Brooks Peninsula

Solander Island

Cape Clerke

Cook called a small headland on Brooks Peninsula on Vancouver Island, Woody Point. It is now called Cape Cook. Cook was not aware that the 'mainland' at Nootka was, in fact, an island. The island was later named after a midshipman on the *Discovery*, George Vancouver. He returned to the region in 1791 and filled in the few blanks left by Cook.

Cape Cook

Hope Bay

Nootka Sound

Bajo Point

Estevan Point

29 Mar 1778

Vancouver Island

Vancouver•

Victoria •

Cape Flattery

Strait of Juan de Fuca

Flattery Rocks

Cape Alava

Cook regained the coast but, on 22 March, a gale forced him away from the coast, near Cape Flattery, when he was looking for the Strait of Juan de Fuca. Cook dismissed the strait's existence, little realising that his Cape Flattery was the southern headland of the strait. He finally found a safe harbour, Nootka Sound, on 29 March.

22 Mar 1778

VANCOUVER ISLAND

OREGON TO VANCOUVER ISLAND

Cape Cook

Nootka Sound

Vancouver Island

• Vancouver

Cape Flattery

Strait of Juan de Fuca

29 Mar 1778

Cook reached the American coast at Oregon on 7 March 1778 but bad weather, winds and the nature of the coast prevented him from landing. After several days standing off near Cape Perpetua, gales forced Cook away from the coast and south to near Cape Blanco. On 13 March the gales abated and he was able to head north to the Arctic.

22 Mar 1778

• Seattle

North Pacific Ocean

• Astoria

• Portland

OREGON

Cape Foulweather

▲ Mary's Peak

7 Mar 1778

Cape Perpetua

Umpqua River

Cape Arago/Gregory

13 Mar 1778

Cape Blanco

Cook made land at Oregon on 7 March. The weather was bad so he called the first land seen Cape Foulweather.

The British Columbia Maritime Museum in Victoria has a room devoted to Cook, especially his voyage on Canada's west coast.

British Columbia Maritime Museum

Inner Harbour

Cook Statue

Empress Hotel

In Victoria, there is a statue of Cook in front of the Empress Hotel, near the Inner Harbour.

VICTORIA

CAPE PERPETUA

Cape Perpetua

Devil's Churn

Cape Creek

Cook's Chasm

Captain Cook Point

Close by Cape Perpetua, one of the first points seen and named by Cook, there is a Captain Cook Point and also a Cook's Chasm.

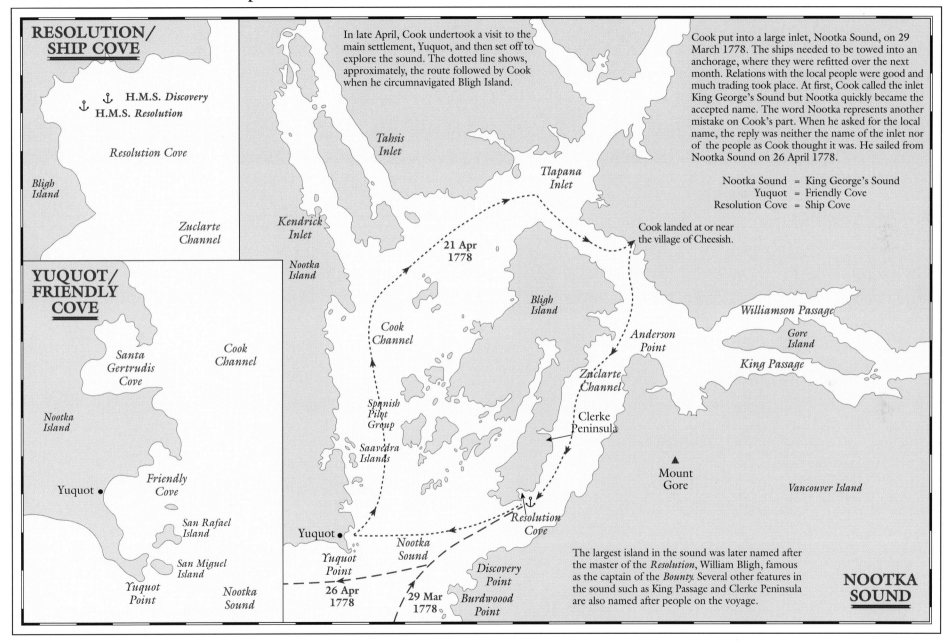

RESOLUTION/ SHIP COVE

⚓ H.M.S. *Discovery*
⚓ H.M.S. *Resolution*

Resolution Cove

Bligh Island

Zuclarte Channel

YUQUOT/ FRIENDLY COVE

Santa Gertrudis Cove

Cook Channel

Nootka Island

Friendly Cove

Yuquot ●

San Rafael Island

San Miguel Island

Yuquot Point

Nootka Sound

Tahsis Inlet

In late April, Cook undertook a visit to the main settlement, Yuquot, and then set off to explore the sound. The dotted line shows, approximately, the route followed by Cook when he circumnavigated Bligh Island.

Cook put into a large inlet, Nootka Sound, on 29 March 1778. The ships needed to be towed into an anchorage, where they were refitted over the next month. Relations with the local people were good and much trading took place. At first, Cook called the inlet King George's Sound but Nootka quickly became the accepted name. The word Nootka represents another mistake on Cook's part. When he asked for the local name, the reply was neither the name of the inlet nor of the people as Cook thought it was. He sailed from Nootka Sound on 26 April 1778.

Nootka Sound = King George's Sound
Yuquot = Friendly Cove
Resolution Cove = Ship Cove

Tlapana Inlet

Cook landed at or near the village of Cheesish.

Kendrick Inlet

Nootka Island

21 Apr 1778

Cook Channel

Bligh Island

Williamson Passage

Gore Island

Anderson Point

King Passage

Zuclarte Channel

Clerke Peninsula

Spanish Pilot Group

Saavedra Islands

▲ *Mount Gore*

Vancouver Island

Yuquot ●

Yuquot Point

26 Apr 1778

Nootka Sound

29 Mar 1778

Discovery Point

Burdwoood Point

Resolution Cove

The largest island in the sound was later named after the master of the *Resolution*, William Bligh, famous as the captain of the *Bounty*. Several other features in the sound such as King Passage and Clerke Peninsula are also named after people on the voyage.

NOOTKA SOUND

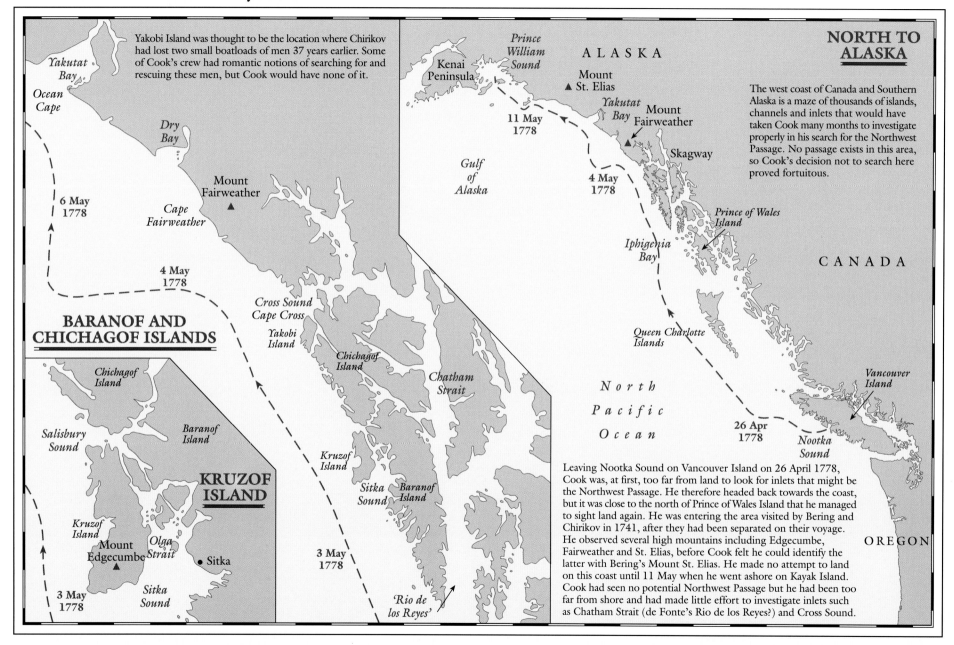

Yakobi Island was thought to be the location where Chirikov had lost two small boatloads of men 37 years earlier. Some of Cook's crew had romantic notions of searching for and rescuing these men, but Cook would have none of it.

Yakutat Bay

Ocean Cape

Dry Bay

6 May 1778

Mount Fairweather ▲

Cape Fairweather

4 May 1778

BARANOF AND CHICHAGOF ISLANDS

Cross Sound
Cape Cross

Yakobi Island

Chichagof Island

KRUZOF ISLAND

Salisbury Sound

Baranof Island

Kruzof Island

Mount Edgecumbe ▲

Olga Strait

• Sitka

3 May 1778

Sitka Sound

Kruzof Island

Sitka Sound

Baranof Island

3 May 1778

Chatham Strait

3 May 1778

'Rio de los Reyes'

Prince William Sound

A L A S K A

Kenai Peninsula

Mount ▲ St. Elias

Yakutat Bay

Mount Fairweather

11 May 1778

▲

Skagway

Gulf of Alaska

4 May 1778

Iphigenia Bay

Prince of Wales Island

C A N A D A

Queen Charlotte Islands

North Pacific Ocean

Vancouver Island

26 Apr 1778

Nootka Sound

NORTH TO ALASKA

The west coast of Canada and Southern Alaska is a maze of thousands of islands, channels and inlets that would have taken Cook many months to investigate properly in his search for the Northwest Passage. No passage exists in this area, so Cook's decision not to search here proved fortuitous.

OREGON

Leaving Nootka Sound on Vancouver Island on 26 April 1778, Cook was, at first, too far from land to look for inlets that might be the Northwest Passage. He therefore headed back towards the coast, but it was close to the north of Prince of Wales Island that he managed to sight land again. He was entering the area visited by Bering and Chirikov in 1741, after they had been separated on their voyage. He observed several high mountains including Edgecumbe, Fairweather and St. Elias, before Cook felt he could identify the latter with Bering's Mount St. Elias. He made no attempt to land on this coast until 11 May when he went ashore on Kayak Island. Cook had seen no potential Northwest Passage but he had been too far from shore and had made little effort to investigate inlets such as Chatham Strait (de Fonte's Rio de los Reyes?) and Cross Sound.

3.17 PRINCE WILLIAM SOUND May 1778

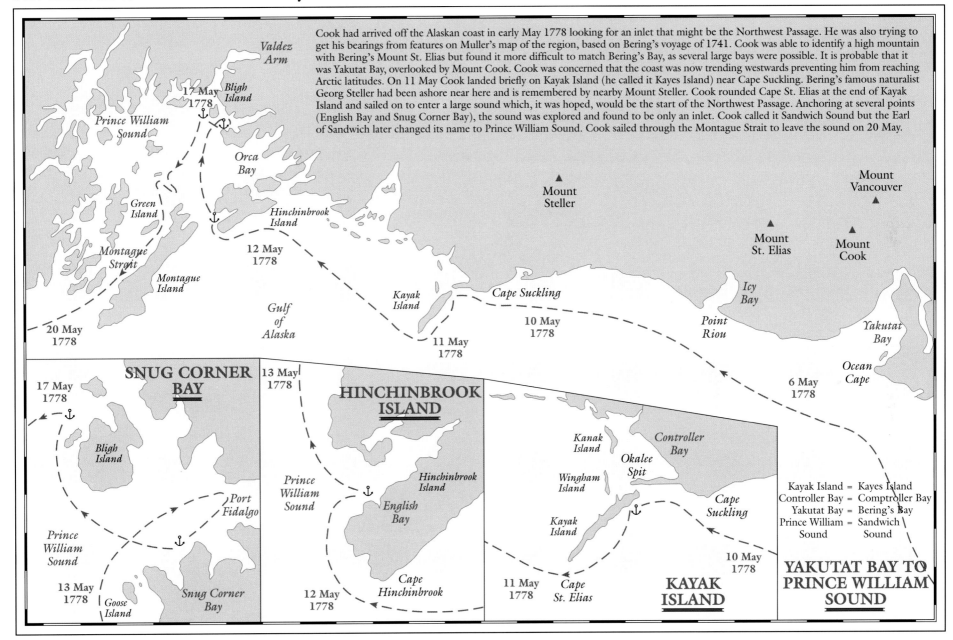

Cook had arrived off the Alaskan coast in early May 1778 looking for an inlet that might be the Northwest Passage. He was also trying to get his bearings from features on Muller's map of the region, based on Bering's voyage of 1741. Cook was able to identify a high mountain with Bering's Mount St. Elias but found it more difficult to match Bering's Bay, as several large bays were possible. It is probable that it was Yakutat Bay, overlooked by Mount Cook. Cook was concerned that the coast was now trending westwards preventing him from reaching Arctic latitudes. On 11 May Cook landed briefly on Kayak Island (he called it Kayes Island) near Cape Suckling. Bering's famous naturalist Georg Steller had been ashore near here and is remembered by nearby Mount Steller. Cook rounded Cape St. Elias at the end of Kayak Island and sailed on to enter a large sound which, it was hoped, would be the start of the Northwest Passage. Anchoring at several points (English Bay and Snug Corner Bay), the sound was explored and found to be only an inlet. Cook called it Sandwich Sound but the Earl of Sandwich later changed its name to Prince William Sound. Cook sailed through the Montague Strait to leave the sound on 20 May.

Valdez Arm

17 May 1778   *Bligh Island*

Prince William Sound

Orca Bay

▲ Mount Steller

Mount Vancouver ▲

Green Island

Hinchinbrook Island

▲ Mount St. Elias

▲ Mount Cook

Montague Strait

12 May 1778

Montague Island

Kayak Island

Cape Suckling

Icy Bay

Gulf of Alaska

11 May 1778

10 May 1778

Point Riou

Yakutat Bay

20 May 1778

Ocean Cape

SNUG CORNER BAY

17 May 1778

Bligh Island

Port Fidalgo

Prince William Sound

13 May 1778   *Goose Island*

Snug Corner Bay

13 May 1778

HINCHINBROOK ISLAND

Prince William Sound

Hinchinbrook Island

English Bay

12 May 1778

Cape Hinchinbrook

KAYAK ISLAND

Kanak Island

Controller Bay

Wingham Island

Okalee Spit

Kayak Island

Cape Suckling

11 May 1778   *Cape St. Elias*

6 May 1778

10 May 1778

Kayak Island = Kayes Island
Controller Bay = Comptroller Bay
Yakutat Bay = Bering's Bay
Prince William Sound = Sandwich Sound

YAKUTAT BAY TO PRINCE WILLIAM SOUND

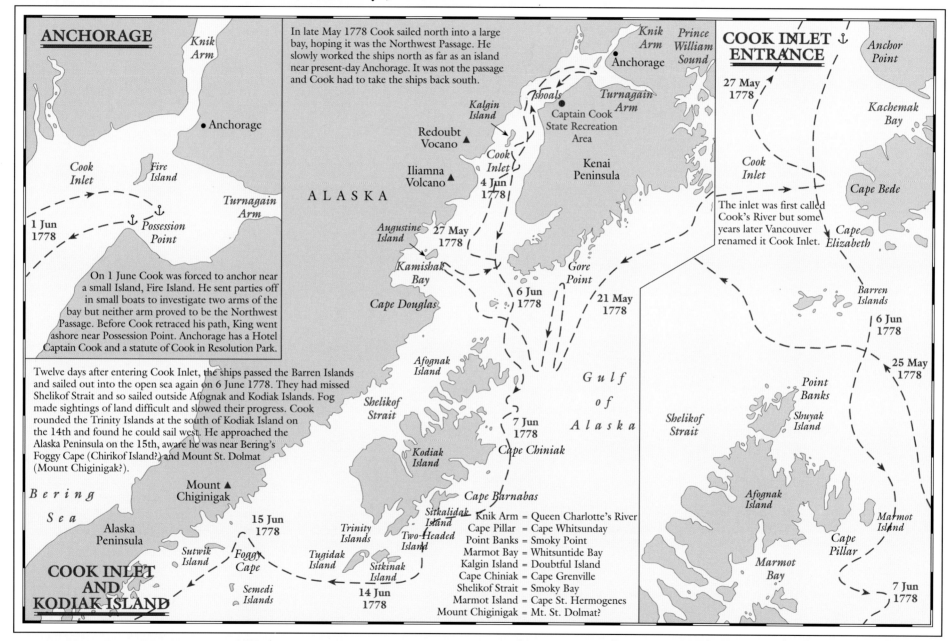

ANCHORAGE

Knik Arm

• Anchorage

Cook Inlet

Fire Island

Turnagain Arm

1 Jun 1778

⚓ *Possession Point*

On 1 June Cook was forced to anchor near a small Island, Fire Island. He sent parties off in small boats to investigate two arms of the bay but neither arm proved to be the Northwest Passage. Before Cook retraced his path, King went ashore near Possession Point. Anchorage has a Hotel Captain Cook and a statute of Cook in Resolution Park.

Twelve days after entering Cook Inlet, the ships passed the Barren Islands and sailed out into the open sea again on 6 June 1778. They had missed Shelikof Strait and so sailed outside Afognak and Kodiak Islands. Fog made sightings of land difficult and slowed their progress. Cook rounded the Trinity Islands at the south of Kodiak Island on the 14th and found he could sail west. He approached the Alaska Peninsula on the 15th, aware he was near Bering's Foggy Cape (Chirikof Island?) and Mount St. Dolmat (Mount Chiginigak?).

In late May 1778 Cook sailed north into a large bay, hoping it was the Northwest Passage. He slowly worked the ships north as far as an island near present-day Anchorage. It was not the passage and Cook had to take the ships back south.

Knik Arm

• Anchorage

Prince William Sound

Shoals

Turnagain Arm

Kalgin Island

Captain Cook State Recreation Area

Redoubt Vocano ▲

Cook Inlet

Kenai Peninsula

4 Jun 1778

Iliamna Volcano ▲

ALASKA

Augustine Island

27 May 1778

Kamishak Bay

Cape Douglas

Gore Point

6 Jun 1778

21 May 1778

Afognak Island

Shelikof Strait

7 Jun 1778

Gulf of Alaska

Cape Chiniak

Kodiak Island

Cape Barnabas

Mount ▲ Chiginigak

Bering Sea

Alaska Peninsula

15 Jun 1778

Sutwik Island

Foggy Cape

Tugidak Island

Trinity Islands

Sitkalidak Island

Two-Headed Island

Sitkinak Island

14 Jun 1778

Semedi Islands

COOK INLET AND KODIAK ISLAND

Knik Arm = Queen Charlotte's River
Cape Pillar = Cape Whitsunday
Point Banks = Smoky Point
Marmot Bay = Whitsuntide Bay
Kalgin Island = Doubtful Island
Cape Chiniak = Cape Grenville
Shelikof Strait = Smoky Bay
Marmot Island = Cape St. Hermogenes
Mount Chiginigak = Mt. St. Dolmat?

COOK INLET ⚓ ENTRANCE

Anchor Point

27 May 1778

Kachemak Bay

Cook Inlet

Cape Bede

The inlet was first called Cook's River but some years later Vancouver renamed it Cook Inlet.

Cape Elizabeth

Barren Islands

6 Jun 1778

25 May 1778

Point Banks

Shuyak Island

Shelikof Strait

Afognak Island

Marmot Island

Cape Pillar

Marmot Bay

7 Jun 1778

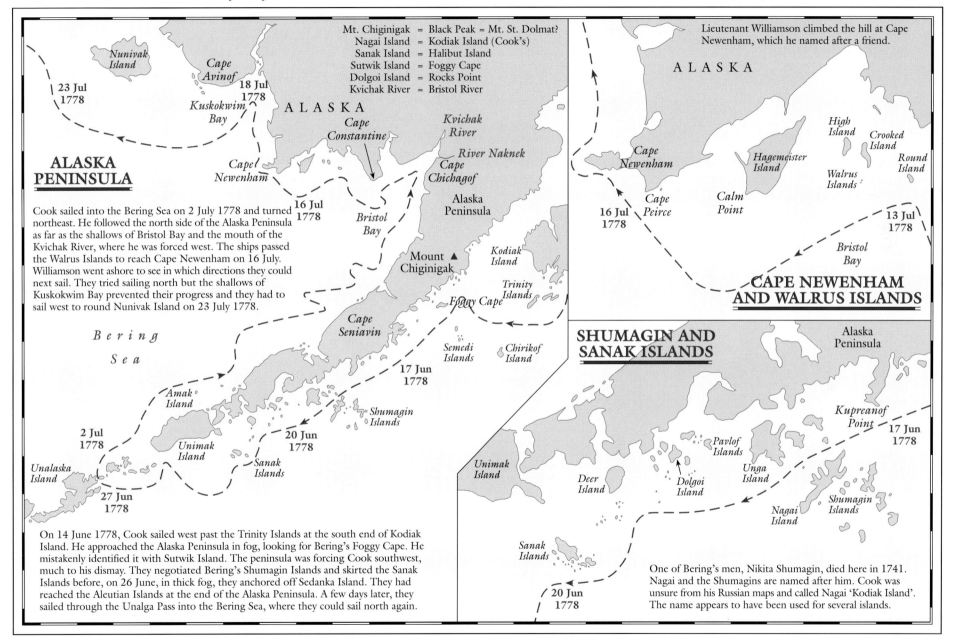

Mt. Chiginigak = Black Peak = Mt. St. Dolmat?
Nagai Island = Kodiak Island (Cook's)
Sanak Island = Halibut Island
Sutwik Island = Foggy Cape
Dolgoi Island = Rocks Point
Kvichak River = Bristol River

Lieutenant Williamson climbed the hill at Cape Newenham, which he named after a friend.

ALASKA PENINSULA

Cook sailed into the Bering Sea on 2 July 1778 and turned northeast. He followed the north side of the Alaska Peninsula as far as the shallows of Bristol Bay and the mouth of the Kvichak River, where he was forced west. The ships passed the Walrus Islands to reach Cape Newenham on 16 July. Williamson went ashore to see in which directions they could next sail. They tried sailing north but the shallows of Kuskokwim Bay prevented their progress and they had to sail west to round Nunivak Island on 23 July 1778.

On 14 June 1778, Cook sailed west past the Trinity Islands at the south end of Kodiak Island. He approached the Alaska Peninsula in fog, looking for Bering's Foggy Cape. He mistakenly identified it with Sutwik Island. The peninsula was forcing Cook southwest, much to his dismay. They negotiated Bering's Shumagin Islands and skirted the Sanak Islands before, on 26 June, in thick fog, they anchored off Sedanka Island. They had reached the Aleutian Islands at the end of the Alaska Peninsula. A few days later, they sailed through the Unalga Pass into the Bering Sea, where they could sail north again.

CAPE NEWENHAM AND WALRUS ISLANDS

SHUMAGIN AND SANAK ISLANDS

One of Bering's men, Nikita Shumagin, died here in 1741. Nagai and the Shumagins are named after him. Cook was unsure from his Russian maps and called Nagai 'Kodiak Island'. The name appears to have been used for several islands.

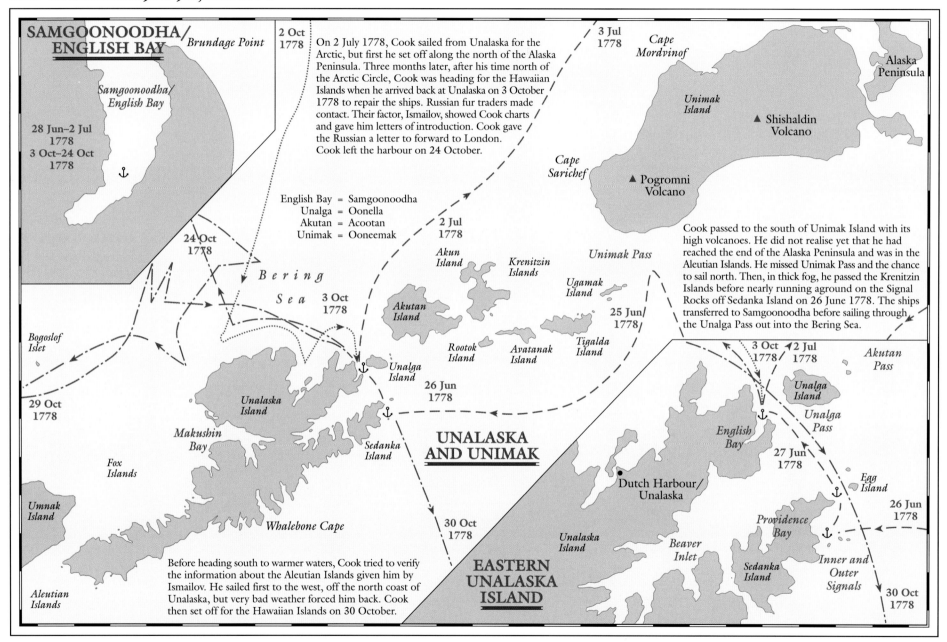

SAMGOONOODHA/ ENGLISH BAY

Brundage Point

Samgoonoodha/ English Bay

28 Jun–2 Jul 1778
3 Oct–24 Oct 1778

2 Oct 1778

On 2 July 1778, Cook sailed from Unalaska for the Arctic, but first he set off along the north of the Alaska Peninsula. Three months later, after his time north of the Arctic Circle, Cook was heading for the Hawaiian Islands when he arrived back at Unalaska on 3 October 1778 to repair the ships. Russian fur traders made contact. Their factor, Ismailov, showed Cook charts and gave him letters of introduction. Cook gave the Russian a letter to forward to London. Cook left the harbour on 24 October.

English Bay = Samgoonoodha
Unalga = Oonella
Akutan = Acootan
Unimak = Ooneemak

3 Jul 1778

Cape Mordvinof

Alaska Peninsula

Unimak Island

▲ Shishaldin Volcano

Cape Sarichef

▲ Pogromni Volcano

Cook passed to the south of Unimak Island with its high volcanoes. He did not realise yet that he had reached the end of the Alaska Peninsula and was in the Aleutian Islands. He missed Unimak Pass and the chance to sail north. Then, in thick fog, he passed the Krenitzin Islands before nearly running aground on the Signal Rocks off Sedanka Island on 26 June 1778. The ships transferred to Samgoonoodha before sailing through the Unalga Pass out into the Bering Sea.

2 Jul 1778

Akun Island

Krenitzin Islands

Unimak Pass

Ugamak Island

24 Oct 1778

B e r i n g

S e a

3 Oct 1778

Akutan Island

25 Jun 1778

Bogoslof Islet

Rootok Island

Avatanak Island

Tigalda Island

29 Oct 1778

Unalaska Island

Unalga Island

26 Jun 1778

UNALASKA AND UNIMAK

3 Oct 1778 **2 Jul 1778**

Akutan Pass

Makushin Bay

Fox Islands

Sedanka Island

English Bay

Unalga Island

Unalga Pass

27 Jun 1778

Egg Island

Umnak Island

● Dutch Harbour/ Unalaska

30 Oct 1778

Unalaska Island

Beaver Inlet

Providence Bay

26 Jun 1778

Whalebone Cape

Sedanka Island

Inner and Outer Signals

Aleutian Islands

EASTERN UNALASKA ISLAND

Before heading south to warmer waters, Cook tried to verify the information about the Aleutian Islands given him by Ismailov. He sailed first to the west, off the north coast of Unalaska, but very bad weather forced him back. Cook then set off for the Hawaiian Islands on 30 October.

30 Oct 1778

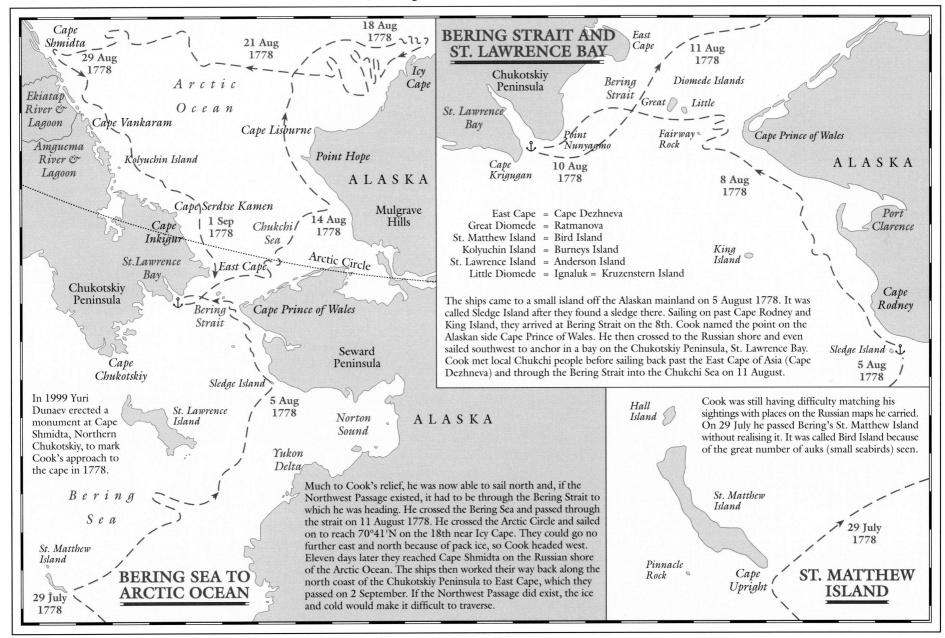

Cape Shmidta

29 Aug 1778

21 Aug 1778

18 Aug 1778

Arctic

Ocean

Icy Cape

Ekiatap River & Lagoon

Cape Vankaram

Amguema River & Lagoon

Cape Lisburne

Point Hope

ALASKA

Kolyuchin Island

Cape Serdtse Kamen

1 Sep 1778

Cape Inkigur

Chukchi Sea

14 Aug 1778

Mulgrave Hills

Arctic Circle

St.Lawrence Bay

East Cape

Chukotskiy Peninsula

Bering Strait

Cape Prince of Wales

Seward Peninsula

Cape Chukotskiy

Sledge Island

5 Aug 1778

Norton Sound

ALASKA

In 1999 Yuri Dunaev erected a monument at Cape Shmidta, Northern Chukotskiy, to mark Cook's approach to the cape in 1778.

St. Lawrence Island

Yukon Delta

Bering

Sea

St. Matthew Island

29 July 1778

BERING SEA TO ARCTIC OCEAN

BERING STRAIT AND ST. LAWRENCE BAY

East Cape

Chukotskiy Peninsula

Bering Strait

Diomede Islands

11 Aug 1778

St. Lawrence Bay

Great   Little

Cape Krigugan

Point Nunyagmo

10 Aug 1778

Fairway Rock

Cape Prince of Wales

ALASKA

8 Aug 1778

King Island

Port Clarence

East Cape	=	Cape Dezhneva
Great Diomede	=	Ratmanova
St. Matthew Island	=	Bird Island
Kolyuchin Island	=	Burneys Island
St. Lawrence Island	=	Anderson Island
Little Diomede	= Ignaluk =	Kruzenstern Island

Cape Rodney

Sledge Island

5 Aug 1778

The ships came to a small island off the Alaskan mainland on 5 August 1778. It was called Sledge Island after they found a sledge there. Sailing on past Cape Rodney and King Island, they arrived at Bering Strait on the 8th. Cook named the point on the Alaskan side Cape Prince of Wales. He then crossed to the Russian shore and even sailed southwest to anchor in a bay on the Chukotskiy Peninsula, St. Lawrence Bay. Cook met local Chukchi people before sailing back past the East Cape of Asia (Cape Dezhneva) and through the Bering Strait into the Chukchi Sea on 11 August.

Much to Cook's relief, he was now able to sail north and, if the Northwest Passage existed, it had to be through the Bering Strait to which he was heading. He crossed the Bering Sea and passed through the strait on 11 August 1778. He crossed the Arctic Circle and sailed on to reach 70°41'N on the 18th near Icy Cape. They could go no further east and north because of pack ice, so Cook headed west. Eleven days later they reached Cape Shmidta on the Russian shore of the Arctic Ocean. The ships then worked their way back along the north coast of the Chukotskiy Peninsula to East Cape, which they passed on 2 September. If the Northwest Passage did exist, the ice and cold would make it difficult to traverse.

Hall Island

Cook was still having difficulty matching his sightings with places on the Russian maps he carried. On 29 July he passed Bering's St. Matthew Island without realising it. It was called Bird Island because of the great number of auks (small seabirds) seen.

St. Matthew Island

29 July 1778

Pinnacle Rock

Cape Upright

ST. MATTHEW ISLAND

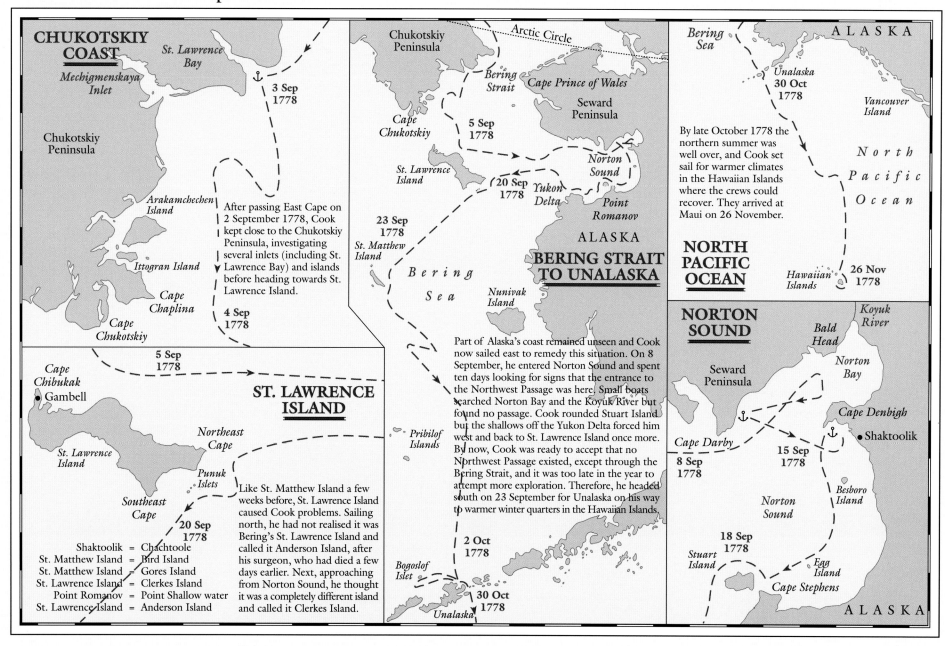

CHUKOTSKIY COAST

Mechigmenskaya Inlet

St. Lawrence Bay

3 Sep 1778

Chukotskiy Peninsula

Arakamchechen Island

Ittogran Island

Cape Chaplina

Cape Chukotskiy

After passing East Cape on 2 September 1778, Cook kept close to the Chukotskiy Peninsula, investigating several inlets (including St. Lawrence Bay) and islands before heading towards St. Lawrence Island.

4 Sep 1778

5 Sep 1778

Cape Chibukak
● Gambell

St. Lawrence Island

Northeast Cape

Punuk Islets

Southeast Cape

20 Sep 1778

ST. LAWRENCE ISLAND

Shaktoolik = Chachtoole
St. Matthew Island = Bird Island
St. Matthew Island = Gores Island
St. Lawrence Island = Clerkes Island
Point Romanov = Point Shallow water
St. Lawrence Island = Anderson Island

Like St. Matthew Island a few weeks before, St. Lawrence Island caused Cook problems. Sailing north, he had not realised it was Bering's St. Lawrence Island and called it Anderson Island, after his surgeon, who had died a few days earlier. Next, approaching from Norton Sound, he thought it was a completely different island and called it Clerkes Island.

Chukotskiy Peninsula

Arctic Circle

Bering Strait

Cape Prince of Wales

Seward Peninsula

Cape Chukotskiy

5 Sep 1778

St. Lawrence Island

Norton Sound

20 Sep 1778

Yukon Delta

Point Romanov

23 Sep 1778

St. Matthew Island

ALASKA

BERING STRAIT TO UNALASKA

Bering Sea

Nunivak Island

Pribilof Islands

Part of Alaska's coast remained unseen and Cook now sailed east to remedy this situation. On 8 September, he entered Norton Sound and spent ten days looking for signs that the entrance to the Northwest Passage was here. Small boats searched Norton Bay and the Koyuk River but found no passage. Cook rounded Stuart Island but the shallows off the Yukon Delta forced him west and back to St. Lawrence Island once more. By now, Cook was ready to accept that no Northwest Passage existed, except through the Bering Strait, and it was too late in the year to attempt more exploration. Therefore, he headed south on 23 September for Unalaska on his way to warmer winter quarters in the Hawaiian Islands.

2 Oct 1778

Bogoslof Islet

30 Oct 1778

Unalaska

Bering Sea

ALASKA

Unalaska
30 Oct 1778

Vancouver Island

By late October 1778 the northern summer was well over, and Cook set sail for warmer climates in the Hawaiian Islands where the crews could recover. They arrived at Maui on 26 November.

North Pacific Ocean

NORTH PACIFIC OCEAN

Hawaiian Islands

26 Nov 1778

NORTON SOUND

Koyuk River

Bald Head

Norton Bay

Seward Peninsula

Cape Denbigh

Shaktoolik ●

Cape Darby

15 Sep 1778

8 Sep 1778

Besboro Island

Norton Sound

18 Sep 1778

Stuart Island

Egg Island

Cape Stephens

ALASKA

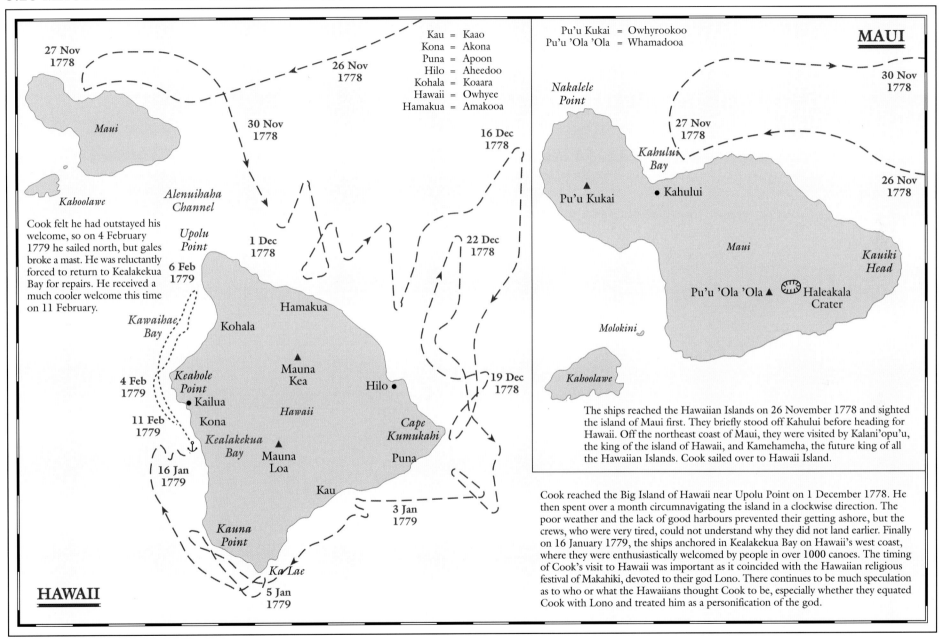

27 Nov 1778

26 Nov 1778

30 Nov 1778

16 Dec 1778

Kau	=	Kaao
Kona	=	Akona
Puna	=	Apoon
Hilo	=	Aheedoo
Kohala	=	Koaara
Hawaii	=	Owhyee
Hamakua	=	Amakooa

Pu'u Kukai = Owhyrookoo
Pu'u 'Ola 'Ola = Whamadooa

MAUI

Maui

Kahoolawe

Alenuihaha Channel

Upolu Point

1 Dec 1778

22 Dec 1778

Cook felt he had outstayed his welcome, so on 4 February 1779 he sailed north, but gales broke a mast. He was reluctantly forced to return to Kealakekua Bay for repairs. He received a much cooler welcome this time on 11 February.

Kawaihae Bay

6 Feb 1779

4 Feb 1779

11 Feb 1779

Keahole Point
• Kailua

Kohala

Hamakua

▲ Mauna Kea

Hawaii

Hilo •

Kona

Kealakekua Bay

▲ Mauna Loa

16 Jan 1779

Cape Kumukahi

Puna

Kau

19 Dec 1778

3 Jan 1779

Kauna Point

HAWAII

Ka Lae

5 Jan 1779

Nakalele Point

30 Nov 1778

27 Nov 1778

Kahului Bay

26 Nov 1778

Pu'u Kukai ▲

• Kahului

Maui

Kauiki Head

Pu'u 'Ola 'Ola ▲ ⊚ Haleakala Crater

Molokini

Kahoolawe

The ships reached the Hawaiian Islands on 26 November 1778 and sighted the island of Maui first. They briefly stood off Kahului before heading for Hawaii. Off the northeast coast of Maui, they were visited by Kalani'opu'u, the king of the island of Hawaii, and Kamehameha, the future king of all the Hawaiian Islands. Cook sailed over to Hawaii Island.

Cook reached the Big Island of Hawaii near Upolu Point on 1 December 1778. He then spent over a month circumnavigating the island in a clockwise direction. The poor weather and the lack of good harbours prevented their getting ashore, but the crews, who were very tired, could not understand why they did not land earlier. Finally on 16 January 1779, the ships anchored in Kealakekua Bay on Hawaii's west coast, where they were enthusiastically welcomed by people in over 1000 canoes. The timing of Cook's visit to Hawaii was important as it coincided with the Hawaiian religious festival of Makahiki, devoted to their god Lono. There continues to be much speculation as to who or what the Hawaiians thought Cook to be, especially whether they equated Cook with Lono and treated him as a personification of the god.

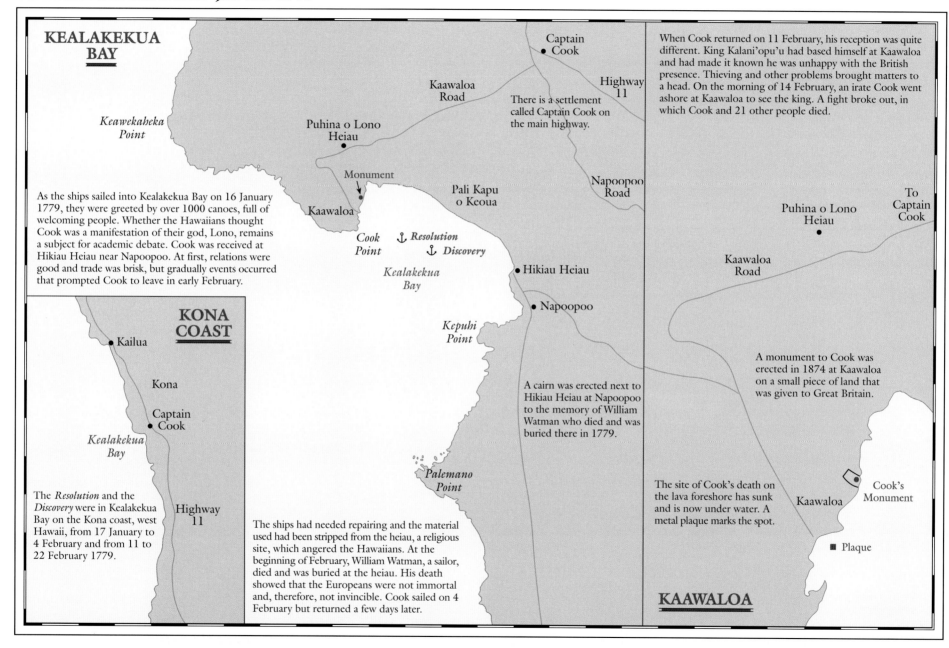

KEALAKEKUA BAY

Keawekaheka Point

As the ships sailed into Kealakekua Bay on 16 January 1779, they were greeted by over 1000 canoes, full of welcoming people. Whether the Hawaiians thought Cook was a manifestation of their god, Lono, remains a subject for academic debate. Cook was received at Hikiau Heiau near Napoopoo. At first, relations were good and trade was brisk, but gradually events occurred that prompted Cook to leave in early February.

Captain Cook

Kaawaloa Road

Puhina o Lono Heiau

Monument

Kaawaloa

Cook Point

⚓ *Resolution*
⚓ *Discovery*

Kealakekua Bay

There is a settlement called Captain Cook on the main highway.

Highway 11

Pali Kapu o Keoua

Napoopoo Road

● Hikiau Heiau

● Napoopoo

Kepuhi Point

When Cook returned on 11 February, his reception was quite different. King Kalani'opu'u had based himself at Kaawaloa and had made it known he was unhappy with the British presence. Thieving and other problems brought matters to a head. On the morning of 14 February, an irate Cook went ashore at Kaawaloa to see the king. A fight broke out, in which Cook and 21 other people died.

To Captain Cook

Puhina o Lono Heiau

Kaawaloa Road

A monument to Cook was erected in 1874 at Kaawaloa on a small piece of land that was given to Great Britain.

KONA COAST

● Kailua

Kona

● Captain Cook

Kealakekua Bay

Highway 11

The *Resolution* and the *Discovery* were in Kealakekua Bay on the Kona coast, west Hawaii, from 17 January to 4 February and from 11 to 22 February 1779.

The ships had needed repairing and the material used had been stripped from the heiau, a religious site, which angered the Hawaiians. At the beginning of February, William Watman, a sailor, died and was buried at the heiau. His death showed that the Europeans were not immortal and, therefore, not invincible. Cook sailed on 4 February but returned a few days later.

Palemano Point

A cairn was erected next to Hikiau Heiau at Napoopoo to the memory of William Watman who died and was buried there in 1779.

The site of Cook's death on the lava foreshore has sunk and is now under water. A metal plaque marks the spot.

Kaawaloa

Cook's Monument

■ Plaque

KAAWALOA

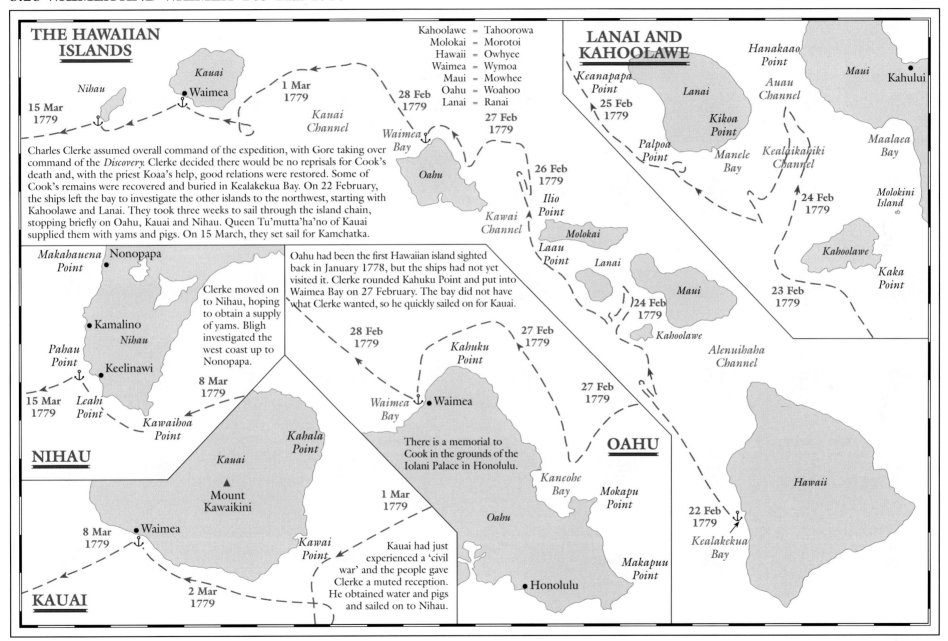

THE HAWAIIAN ISLANDS

Kahoolawe = Tahoorowa
Molokai = Morotoi
Hawaii = Owhyee
Waimea = Wymoa
Maui = Mowhee
Oahu = Woahoo
Lanai = Ranai

Charles Clerke assumed overall command of the expedition, with Gore taking over command of the *Discovery*. Clerke decided there would be no reprisals for Cook's death and, with the priest Koaa's help, good relations were restored. Some of Cook's remains were recovered and buried in Kealakekua Bay. On 22 February, the ships left the bay to investigate the other islands to the northwest, starting with Kahoolawe and Lanai. They took three weeks to sail through the island chain, stopping briefly on Oahu, Kauai and Nihau. Queen Tu'mutta'ha'no of Kauai supplied them with yams and pigs. On 15 March, they set sail for Kamchatka.

Clerke moved on to Nihau, hoping to obtain a supply of yams. Bligh investigated the west coast up to Nonopapa.

Oahu had been the first Hawaiian island sighted back in January 1778, but the ships had not yet visited it. Clerke rounded Kahuku Point and put into Waimea Bay on 27 February. The bay did not have what Clerke wanted, so he quickly sailed on for Kauai.

There is a memorial to Cook in the grounds of the Iolani Palace in Honolulu.

Kauai had just experienced a 'civil war' and the people gave Clerke a muted reception. He obtained water and pigs and sailed on to Nihau.

LANAI AND KAHOOLAWE

NIHAU

KAUAI

OAHU

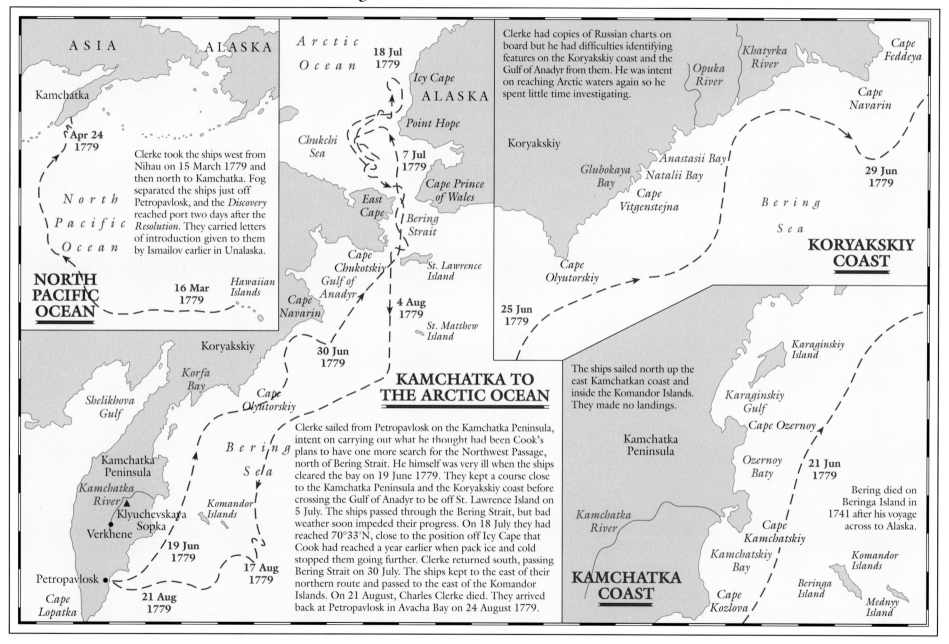

ASIA   ALASKA

Arctic Ocean

18 Jul 1779

Icy Cape
ALASKA

Kamchatka

Point Hope

Apr 24 1779

Clerke took the ships west from Nihau on 15 March 1779 and then north to Kamchatka. Fog separated the ships just off Petropavlosk, and the *Discovery* reached port two days after the *Resolution*. They carried letters of introduction given to them by Ismailov earlier in Unalaska.

Chukchi Sea

7 Jul 1779

Cape Prince of Wales

East Cape

Bering Strait

North Pacific Ocean

NORTH PACIFIC OCEAN

16 Mar 1779

Hawaiian Islands

Clerke had copies of Russian charts on board but he had difficulties identifying features on the Koryakskiy coast and the Gulf of Anadyr from them. He was intent on reaching Arctic waters again so he spent little time investigating.

Khatyrka River

Cape Feddeya

Opuka River

Cape Navarin

Koryakskiy

Anastasii Bay
Natalii Bay
Glubokaya Bay
Cape Vitgenstejna

Cape Olyutorskiy

Bering Sea

29 Jun 1779

KORYAKSKIY COAST

Cape Chukotskiy
Gulf of Anadyr

St. Lawrence Island

Koryakskiy

Cape Navarin

30 Jun 1779

4 Aug 1779

St. Matthew Island

25 Jun 1779

KAMCHATKA TO THE ARCTIC OCEAN

Korfa Bay

Shelikhova Gulf

Cape Olyutorskiy

Bering Sea

The ships sailed north up the east Kamchatkan coast and inside the Komandor Islands. They made no landings.

Clerke sailed from Petropavlosk on the Kamchatka Peninsula, intent on carrying out what he thought had been Cook's plans to have one more search for the Northwest Passage, north of Bering Strait. He himself was very ill when the ships cleared the bay on 19 June 1779. They kept a course close to the Kamchatka Peninsula and the Koryakskiy coast before crossing the Gulf of Anadyr to be off St. Lawrence Island on 5 July. The ships passed through the Bering Strait, but bad weather soon impeded their progress. On 18 July they had reached 70°33'N, close to the position off Icy Cape that Cook had reached a year earlier when pack ice and cold stopped them going further. Clerke returned south, passing Bering Strait on 30 July. The ships kept to the east of their northern route and passed to the east of the Komandor Islands. On 21 August, Charles Clerke died. They arrived back at Petropavlosk in Avacha Bay on 24 August 1779.

Kamchatka Peninsula

Karaginskiy Island

Karaginskiy Gulf

Cape Ozernoy

Kamchatka Peninsula

Ozernoy Baty

21 Jun 1779

Kamchatka River
Klyuchevskaya Sopka
Verkhene

Komandor Islands

19 Jun 1779

17 Aug 1779

Petropavlosk

Kamchatka River

Cape Kamchatskiy

Kamchatskiy Bay

Komandor Islands

Bering died on Beringa Island in 1741 after his voyage across to Alaska.

KAMCHATKA COAST

Cape Kozlova

Beringa Island

Mednyy Island

21 Aug 1779

Cape Lopatka

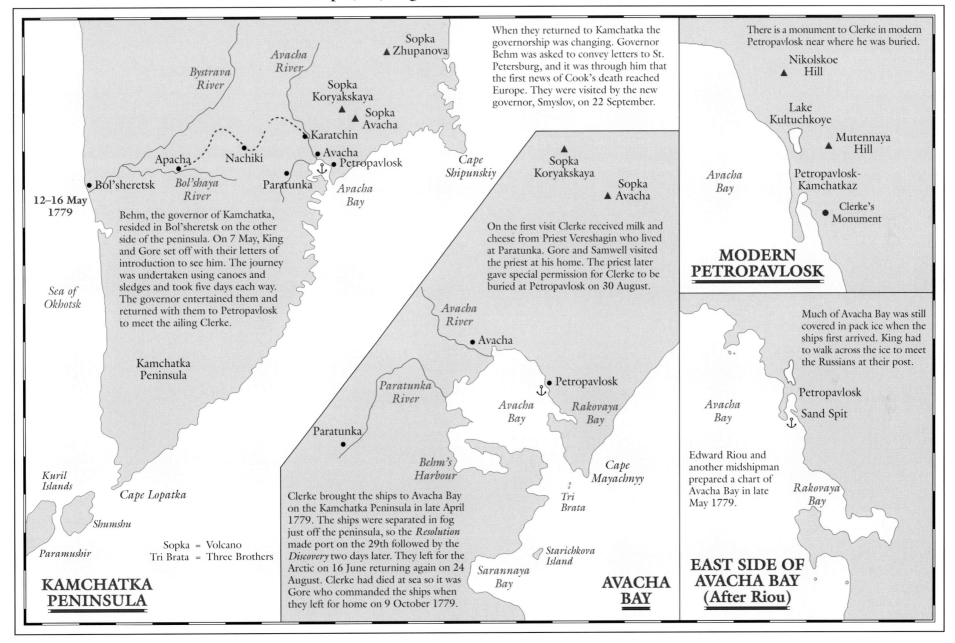

KAMCHATKA PENINSULA

Avacha River

Sopka ▲ Zhupanova

Bystrava River

Sopka Koryakskaya ▲
▲ Sopka Avacha

Karatchin
Avacha
⚓ Petropavlosk

Apacha · Nachiki
· Bol'sheretsk · *Bol'shaya River* · Paratunka

Avacha Bay

Cape Shipunskiy

12–16 May 1779

Behm, the governor of Kamchatka, resided in Bol'sheretsk on the other side of the peninsula. On 7 May, King and Gore set off with their letters of introduction to see him. The journey was undertaken using canoes and sledges and took five days each way. The governor entertained them and returned with them to Petropavlosk to meet the ailing Clerke.

Sea of Okhotsk

Kamchatka Peninsula

Kuril Islands

Cape Lopatka

Shumshu

Paramushir

Sopka = Volcano
Tri Brata = Three Brothers

When they returned to Kamchatka the governorship was changing. Governor Behm was asked to convey letters to St. Petersburg, and it was through him that the first news of Cook's death reached Europe. They were visited by the new governor, Smyslov, on 22 September.

Sopka ▲ Koryakskaya
Sopka ▲ Avacha

On the first visit Clerke received milk and cheese from Priest Vereshagin who lived at Paratunka. Gore and Samwell visited the priest at his home. The priest later gave special permission for Clerke to be buried at Petropavlosk on 30 August.

Avacha River

· Avacha

Paratunka River

· Petropavlosk ⚓
Avacha Bay · *Rakovaya Bay*

· Paratunka

Behm's Harbour

Cape Mayachnyy

Tri Brata

Starichkova Island

Sarannaya Bay

Clerke brought the ships to Avacha Bay on the Kamchatka Peninsula in late April 1779. The ships were separated in fog just off the peninsula, so the *Resolution* made port on the 29th followed by the *Discovery* two days later. They left for the Arctic on 16 June returning again on 24 August. Clerke had died at sea so it was Gore who commanded the ships when they left for home on 9 October 1779.

AVACHA BAY

There is a monument to Clerke in modern Petropavlosk near where he was buried.

Nikolskoe ▲ Hill

Lake Kultuchkoye
▲ Mutennaya Hill

Avacha Bay

Petropavlosk-Kamchatkaz

· Clerke's Monument

MODERN PETROPAVLOSK

Much of Avacha Bay was still covered in pack ice when the ships first arrived. King had to walk across the ice to meet the Russians at their post.

Avacha Bay

Petropavlosk
Sand Spit ⚓

Edward Riou and another midshipman prepared a chart of Avacha Bay in late May 1779.

Rakovaya Bay

EAST SIDE OF AVACHA BAY (After Riou)

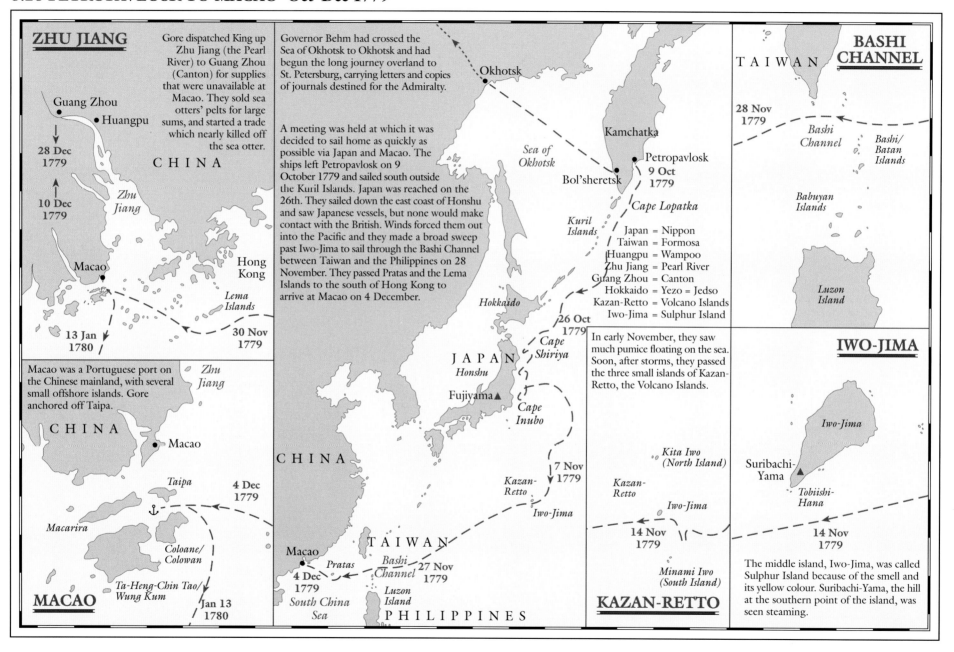

ZHU JIANG

Gore dispatched King up Zhu Jiang (the Pearl River) to Guang Zhou (Canton) for supplies that were unavailable at Macao. They sold sea otters' pelts for large sums, and started a trade which nearly killed off the sea otter.

Guang Zhou
● Huangpu

28 Dec 1779
CHINA

10 Dec 1779

Zhu Jiang

Macao ●

Hong Kong

Lema Islands

13 Jan 1780   30 Nov 1779

Macao was a Portuguese port on the Chinese mainland, with several small offshore islands. Gore anchored off Taipa.

Zhu Jiang

CHINA

● Macao

Taipa   4 Dec 1779

Macarira

Coloane/ Colowan

Ta-Heng-Chin Tao/ Wung Kum   Jan 13 1780

MACAO

Governor Behm had crossed the Sea of Okhotsk to Okhotsk and had begun the long journey overland to St. Petersburg, carrying letters and copies of journals destined for the Admiralty.

A meeting was held at which it was decided to sail home as quickly as possible via Japan and Macao. The ships left Petropavlosk on 9 October 1779 and sailed south outside the Kuril Islands. Japan was reached on the 26th. They sailed down the east coast of Honshu and saw Japanese vessels, but none would make contact with the British. Winds forced them out into the Pacific and they made a broad sweep past Iwo-Jima to sail through the Bashi Channel between Taiwan and the Philippines on 28 November. They passed Pratas and the Lema Islands to the south of Hong Kong to arrive at Macao on 4 December.

Okhotsk

Kamchatka

Sea of Okhotsk

Petropavlosk
9 Oct 1779
Bol'sheretsk

Cape Lopatka

Kuril Islands

Japan = Nippon
Taiwan = Formosa
Huangpu = Wampoo
Zhu Jiang = Pearl River
Guang Zhou = Canton
Hokkaido = Yezo = Jedso
Kazan-Retto = Volcano Islands
Iwo-Jima = Sulphur Island

Hokkaido

26 Oct 1779

Cape Shiriya

JAPAN
Honshu

Fujiyama ▲

Cape Inubo

CHINA

Kazan-Retto   7 Nov 1779

Iwo-Jima

Macao
4 Dec 1779
South China Sea   *Pratas*   *Bashi Channel*   27 Nov 1779
Luzon Island
TAIWAN
PHILIPPINES

In early November, they saw much pumice floating on the sea. Soon, after storms, they passed the three small islands of Kazan-Retto, the Volcano Islands.

Kita Iwo (North Island)

Kazan-Retto

Iwo-Jima

14 Nov 1779

Minami Iwo (South Island)

KAZAN-RETTO

BASHI CHANNEL

TAIWAN

28 Nov 1779
Bashi Channel   *Bashi/ Batan Islands*

Babuyan Islands

Luzon Island

IWO-JIMA

Iwo-Jima

Suribachi-Yama ▲

Tobiishi-Hana

14 Nov 1779

The middle island, Iwo-Jima, was called Sulphur Island because of the smell and its yellow colour. Suribachi-Yama, the hill at the southern point of the island, was seen steaming.

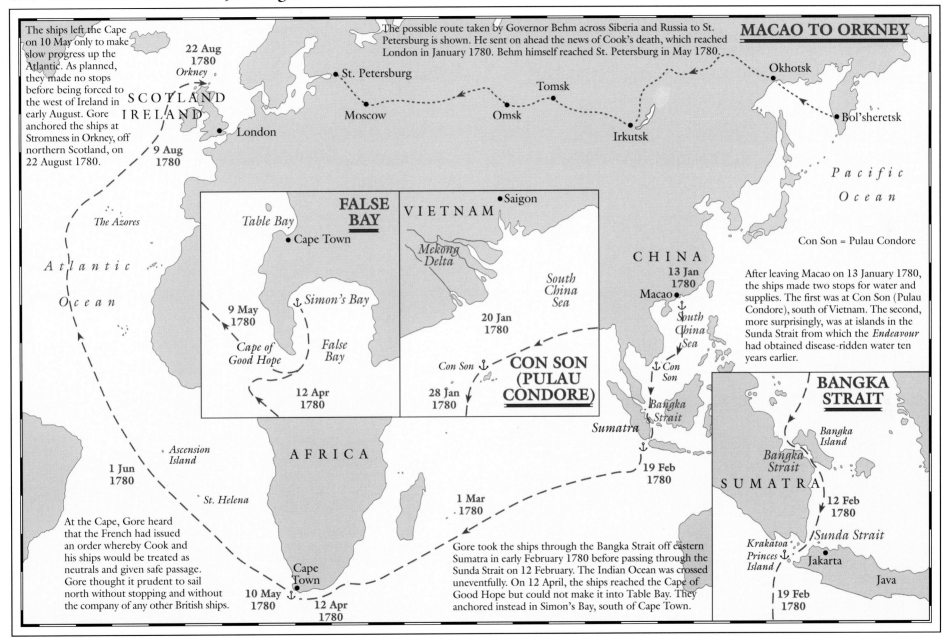

MACAO TO ORKNEY

The ships left the Cape on 10 May only to make slow progress up the Atlantic. As planned, they made no stops before being forced to the west of Ireland in early August. Gore anchored the ships at Stromness in Orkney, off northern Scotland, on 22 August 1780.

The possible route taken by Governor Behm across Siberia and Russia to St. Petersburg is shown. He sent on ahead the news of Cook's death, which reached London in January 1780. Behm himself reached St. Petersburg in May 1780.

Con Son = Pulau Condore

After leaving Macao on 13 January 1780, the ships made two stops for water and supplies. The first was at Con Son (Pulau Condore), south of Vietnam. The second, more surprisingly, was at islands in the Sunda Strait from which the *Endeavour* had obtained disease-ridden water ten years earlier.

At the Cape, Gore heard that the French had issued an order whereby Cook and his ships would be treated as neutrals and given safe passage. Gore thought it prudent to sail north without stopping and without the company of any other British ships.

Gore took the ships through the Bangka Strait off eastern Sumatra in early February 1780 before passing through the Sunda Strait on 12 February. The Indian Ocean was crossed uneventfully. On 12 April, the ships reached the Cape of Good Hope but could not make it into Table Bay. They anchored instead in Simon's Bay, south of Cape Town.

FALSE BAY

BANGKA STRAIT

22 Aug 1780 — Orkney

9 Aug 1780

The Azores

1 Jun 1780

Ascension Island

St. Helena

Cape Town — 10 May 1780 — 12 Apr 1780

9 May 1780 — Simon's Bay — Cape of Good Hope — False Bay — 12 Apr 1780 — Table Bay — Cape Town

VIETNAM — Saigon — Mekong Delta — South China Sea — 20 Jan 1780 — Con Son — 28 Jan 1780 — **CON SON (PULAU CONDORE)**

CHINA — 13 Jan 1780 — Macao — South China Sea — Con Son — Bangka Strait

Sumatra — 19 Feb 1780 — 1 Mar 1780

Bangka Island — Bangka Strait — 12 Feb 1780 — Sunda Strait — Krakatoa — Princes Island — Jakarta — 19 Feb 1780 — Java

St. Petersburg — Moscow — Tomsk — Omsk — Irkutsk — Okhotsk — Bol'sheretsk

London — SCOTLAND — IRELAND

Atlantic Ocean

AFRICA

Pacific Ocean

3.30 ORKNEY TO LONDON Sep–Oct 1780

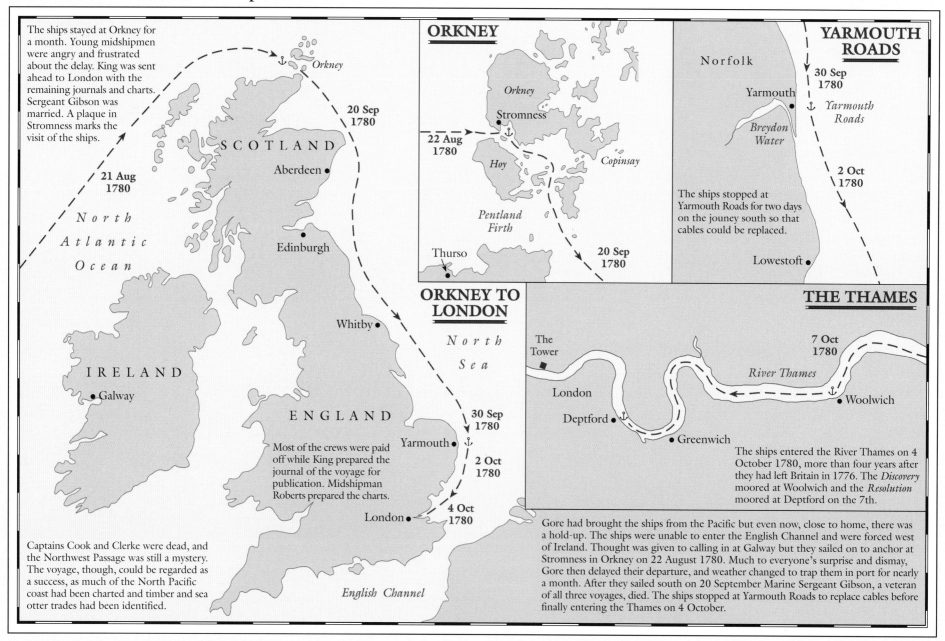

The ships stayed at Orkney for a month. Young midshipmen were angry and frustrated about the delay. King was sent ahead to London with the remaining journals and charts. Sergeant Gibson was married. A plaque in Stromness marks the visit of the ships.

ORKNEY

21 Aug 1780

20 Sep 1780

22 Aug 1780

20 Sep 1780

North Atlantic Ocean

S C O T L A N D

Aberdeen

Edinburgh

Orkney

Stromness

Hoy

Copinsay

Thurso

Pentland Firth

YARMOUTH ROADS

Norfolk

Yarmouth

Yarmouth Roads

Breydon Water

30 Sep 1780

2 Oct 1780

Lowestoft

The ships stopped at Yarmouth Roads for two days on the jouney south so that cables could be replaced.

ORKNEY TO LONDON

North Sea

Whitby

I R E L A N D

Galway

E N G L A N D

Most of the crews were paid off while King prepared the journal of the voyage for publication. Midshipman Roberts prepared the charts.

Yarmouth

London

30 Sep 1780

2 Oct 1780

4 Oct 1780

English Channel

THE THAMES

The Tower

London

Deptford

Greenwich

River Thames

Woolwich

7 Oct 1780

The ships entered the River Thames on 4 October 1780, more than four years after they had left Britain in 1776. The *Discovery* moored at Woolwich and the *Resolution* moored at Deptford on the 7th.

Captains Cook and Clerke were dead, and the Northwest Passage was still a mystery. The voyage, though, could be regarded as a success, as much of the North Pacific coast had been charted and timber and sea otter trades had been identified.

Gore had brought the ships from the Pacific but even now, close to home, there was a hold-up. The ships were unable to enter the English Channel and were forced west of Ireland. Thought was given to calling in at Galway but they sailed on to anchor at Stromness in Orkney on 22 August 1780. Much to everyone's surprise and dismay, Gore then delayed their departure, and weather changed to trap them in port for nearly a month. After they sailed south on 20 September Marine Sergeant Gibson, a veteran of all three voyages, died. The ships stopped at Yarmouth Roads to replace cables before finally entering the Thames on 4 October.

3.31 THIRD VOYAGE 1776–80 SUMMARY

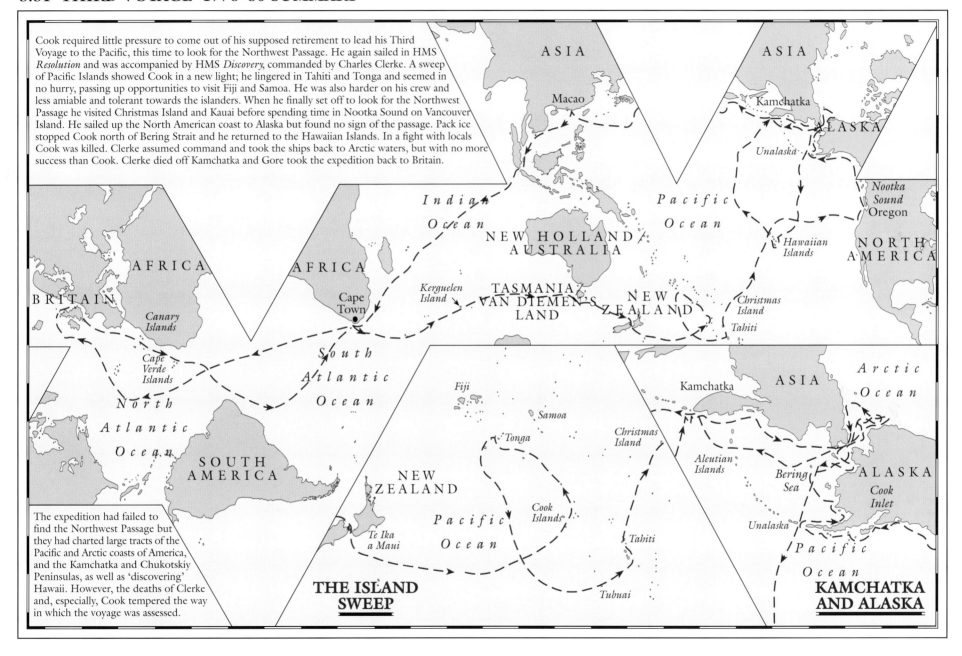

Cook required little pressure to come out of his supposed retirement to lead his Third Voyage to the Pacific, this time to look for the Northwest Passage. He again sailed in HMS *Resolution* and was accompanied by HMS *Discovery*, commanded by Charles Clerke. A sweep of Pacific Islands showed Cook in a new light; he lingered in Tahiti and Tonga and seemed in no hurry, passing up opportunities to visit Fiji and Samoa. He was also harder on his crew and less amiable and tolerant towards the islanders. When he finally set off to look for the Northwest Passage he visited Christmas Island and Kauai before spending time in Nootka Sound on Vancouver Island. He sailed up the North American coast to Alaska but found no sign of the passage. Pack ice stopped Cook north of Bering Strait and he returned to the Hawaiian Islands. In a fight with locals Cook was killed. Clerke assumed command and took the ships back to Arctic waters, but with no more success than Cook. Clerke died off Kamchatka and Gore took the expedition back to Britain.

The expedition had failed to find the Northwest Passage but they had charted large tracts of the Pacific and Arctic coasts of America, and the Kamchatka and Chukotskiy Peninsulas, as well as 'discovering' Hawaii. However, the deaths of Clerke and, especially, Cook tempered the way in which the voyage was assessed.

ASIA

ASIA

Macao

Kamchatka

ALASKA

Unalaska

Nootka Sound Oregon

Indian Ocean

Pacific Ocean

NEW HOLLAND / AUSTRALIA

NORTH AMERICA

AFRICA

AFRICA

Hawaiian Islands

BRITAIN

Canary Islands

Cape Town

Kerguelen Island

TASMANIA / VAN DIEMEN'S LAND

NEW ZEALAND

Christmas Island

Tahiti

Cape Verde Islands

South Atlantic Ocean

North Atlantic Ocean

SOUTH AMERICA

Fiji

Samoa

Tonga

Christmas Island

Arctic Ocean

Kamchatka

ASIA

Aleutian Islands

Bering Sea

ALASKA

Cook Inlet

NEW ZEALAND

Pacific Ocean

Te Ika a Maui

Cook Islands

Tahiti

Tubuai

Unalaska

Pacific Ocean

THE ISLAND SWEEP

KAMCHATKA AND ALASKA

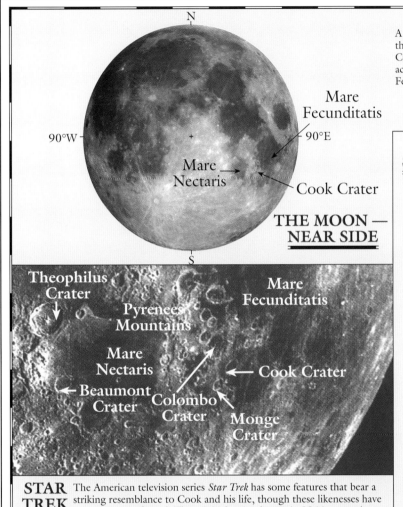

Mare
Fecunditatis

90°W

90°E

Mare
Nectaris

Cook Crater

THE MOON — NEAR SIDE

Theophilus
Crater

Mare
Fecunditatis

Pyrenees
Mountains

Mare
Nectaris

Cook Crater

Beaumont
Crater

Colombo
Crater

Monge
Crater

A small crater in the SE Quarter of the near side of the Moon (18°S, 49°E) is named Cook Crater after Captain James Cook. The crater is about 47 kilometres across. It is situated between Mare Nectaris and Mare Fecunditatis near the Pyrenees Mountains.

SPACE SHUTTLES

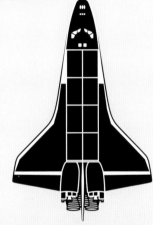

The Space Program of the United States developed the use of Space Shuttle Orbiters in the 1980s. Two of the shuttles, Orbiter Vehicles OV-103 and OV-105, have been named after ships used by Captain Cook on his voyages of exploration. In 1989 President Bush confirmed that, after a competition to choose a name, vehicle OV-105 would be called Endeavour after Cook's first ship. This Endeavour made its first flight in 1992 and has since (as at April 2000) made 14 journeys into space. Cook's *Endeavour* was 368 tons, 100 feet long and 20 feet wide; the Space Shuttle Endeavour is 78 tons, 122 feet long and 78 feet wide. The Discovery, OV-103, was named after the ship that accompanied Cook on his Third Voyage. It made its first flight in 1984 and has since made 27 successful journeys in space.

STAR TREK The American television series *Star Trek* has some features that bear a striking resemblance to Cook and his life, though these likenesses have never been confirmed. The original series, begun in 1966, centred on a spaceship, the USS *Enterprise*, whose commander was Captain James Kirk. These names have strong similarities to *Endeavour* and Captain James Cook. At the beginning of most episodes Captain Kirk would say, 'These are the logs of the Starship *Enterprise* whose mission is to boldly go where no man has gone before.' This is very reminiscent of Cook's statement on his Second Voyage, after just failing to reach Antarctica, where he wrote, 'I who had ambition not only to go farther than any one had done before, but as far as it was possible for man to go.'

UNDERSEA SOUTH PACIFIC

NEW CALEDONIA

Cook
Fracture
Zone

Norfolk
Island

Several undersea features in the South Pacific near New Zealand have been named after Cook, his ships and people on his voyages.

NEW ZEALAND

Cook
Channel

Cook
Canyon

Resolution
Ridge

Pickersgill
Seamount

Solander
Trough

Campbell
Island

Endeavour
Banks

Gazetteer

PLACE	MAP(S)	PLACE	MAP(S)	PLACE	MAP(S)	PLACE	MAP(S)
Bustard Bay; Queensland, Aus.	1.27	Cascade Point; Te Wai Pounamu, N.Z.	1.20	Clerke Peninsula; Vancouver Island, Can.	3.15	Cook, Cape; Vanuatu	2.19
Bustard Head; Queensland, Aus.	1.27	Castle Point; Te Ika a Maui, N.Z.	1.18	Clerke Point; Vancouver Island, Can.	3.14	Cook Channel; Pacific Ocean	4.01
Byron, Cape; New South Wales, Aus.	1.25–26	Cato Point; Bouvet Island	2.03	Clerke, Port; S. America	2.25	Cook Channel; Te Wai Pounamu, N.Z.	2.05
Bystrava River; Kamchatka	3.27	Cavalli Islands; Te Ika a Maui, N.Z.	1.17	Clerkes Island; Bering Sea	3.22	Cook Channel; Vancouver Island, Can.	3.15
		Celery Cove; Te Ika a Maui, N.Z.	1.14	Clerke's Rocks; South Georgia	2.27	Cook Crater; Moon	4.01
Cabot Strait; Canada	**0.21**	Centre Island; Te Ika a Maui, N.Z.	1.14	Cleveland; England	0.01–02, 0.23	Cook Creek; Tasmania, Aus.	3.05
Cairns; Queensland, Aus.	1.28	Chachtoole; W. Alaska	3.22	Cleveland Bay; Queensland, Aus.	1.28	Cook Fracture Zone; Pacific Ocean	4.01
Cairns Reef; Queensland, Aus.	1.29	Chain Island; Tuamotu Islands	1.05	Cleveland, Cape; Queensland, Aus.	1.28	Cook, Glacier; Kerguelen Island	3.03
Caledonia; Scotland	0.12	Chalfont St. Giles; England	0.23	Cloudy Bay; Te Wai Pounamu, N.Z.	1.11,	Cook Glacier; South Georgia	2.27
California; U.S.A.	3.13	Channel Island; Te Ika a Maui, N.Z.	1.15		1.18, 1.20	Cook Hill; Newfoundland, Can.	0.21
Callafanga; Ha'apai Group	3.08	Channel Islands; Britain	0.10; 1.38	Cobras, Ilha das; Brazil	1.02	Cook Inlet; S. Alaska	2.32; 3.18, 3.31
Calm Point; W. Alaska	3.19	Chaplina, Cape; Chukotskiy Peninsula	3.22	Cockburn Islands; Queensland, Aus.	1.31	Cook Island; Christmas Island	3.06
Caloundra; Queensland, Aus.	1.26	Charlotte, Cape; South Georgia	2.27	Codroy Island; Newfoundland, Can.	0.21	Cook Island; New South Wales, Aus.	1.26
Cambridge; England	0.23	Charlotte, Pointe; Kerguelen Island	3.03	Coffs Harbour; New South Wales, Aus.	1.25	Cook Island; South Sandwich Islands	2.28
Camden Head; New South Wales, Aus.	1.25	Chateau; Labrador, Can.	0.19	Coldstream; Scotland	0.01	Cook Islands; Pacific Ocean	2.06, 2.13,
Camel, Mount; Te Ika a Maui, N.Z.	1.16	Chateau Bay; Labrador, Can.	0.19	Collins Point; New South Wales, Aus.	1.23		2.31; 3.06–07, 3.31
Campbell, Cape; Te Wai Pounamu,		Chatham Strait; S.E. Alaska	3.16	Colnett, Cape; New Caledonia	2.21	Cook, Mount; Alaska/Canada	3.17
N.Z.	1.11, 1.18, 1.20; 2.06	Chelsea; England	0.08	Colnett, Mount; New Caledonia	2.21	Cook, Mount (Cooktown); Australia	1.29–30
Campbell Island; New Zealand	4.01	Cherbourg; France	0.10	Coloane; China	3.28	Cook, Mount (Magnetic Is.); Australia	1.28
Campbell, Mount; Kerguelen Island	3.03	Chibukak, Cape; Bering Sea	3.22	Colombo Crater; Moon	4.01	Cook, Mount; Tasmania, Aus.	3.05
Canada; N. America	0.13–22; 3.13–16	Chichagof, Cape; Alaska Peninsula	3.19	Colowan; China	3.28	Cook, Mount; Te Wai Pounamu, N.Z.	1.11,
Canary Islands; Atlantic Ocean	0.13; 1.01,	Chichagof Island; S.E. Alaska	3.16	Colville, Cape; Te Ika a Maui, N.Z.	1.15		1.20
	1.38; 2.01, 2.30; 3.01, 3.31	Chicken Islands; Te Ika a Maui, N.Z.	1.16	Con Son; Vietnam	3.29	Cook Point; Easter Island	2.11
Canberra; Australia	1.22	Chiginigak, Mount; Alaska Peninsula	3.13,	Conception Bay; Newfoundland,		Cook Point; Hawaiian Islands	3.24
Candlemas Island; South Sandwich			3.18–19	Can.	0.17–18	Cook Point; Tongatapu Group	2.09; 3.09
Islands	2.28	China; Asia	3.28–29	Condore, Pulau; Vietnam	3.29	Cook Pond, Big; Newfoundland, Can.	0.22
Cannibal Cove; Te Wai Pounamu, N.Z.	1.19	Chiniak, Cape; S. Alaska	3.18	Connoire Bay; Newfoundland, Can.	0.21	Cook Pond, Little; Newfoundland, Can.	0.22
Canton; China	3.28	Chirikof Island; Alaska Peninsula	3.19	Constantine, Cape; W. Alaska	3.19	Cook, Port; S. America	2.25
Cape Breton Island; Canada	0.14–15	Christchurch; Te Wai Pounamu, N.Z.	1.20	Controller Bay; S. Alaska	3.17	Cook, Recif de; New Caledonia	2.21
Cape Town; South Africa	1.35–37,	Christmas Harbour; Kerguelen Island	3.03	Conway, Cape; Queensland, Aus.	1.28	Cook Reef; New Caledonia	2.20, 2.21
	1.39–40; 2.02, 2.26,	Christmas Island; Pacific Ocean	3.06, 3.31	Cook (Canberra); Australia	1.22	Cook Reef; Torres Strait	1.32
	2.29; 3.02–03, 3.29, 3.31	Christmas Sound; S. America	2.25	Cook, Baie de; (Huahine) Society Islands	1.09;	Cook Reef; Vanuatu	2.18, 2.20
Cape Verde Islands; Atlantic Ocean	1.01,	Chukchi Sea; Arctic Ocean	3.21, 3.26		2.08	Cook Rock; South Sandwich Islands	2.28
	1.38; 2.01, 2.30–31; 3.01, 3.31	Chukotskiy, Cape; Chukotskiy Peninsula	3.22,	Cook, Baie de; (Moorea) Society Islands	3.11	Cook River; Te Wai Pounamu, N.Z.	1.11
Capricorn, Cape; Queensland, Aus.	1.27		3.26	Cook Bay; Easter Island	2.11	Cook Rock; Te Wai Pounamu, N.Z.	1.19
Captain Cook; Hawaii	3.24	Chukotskiy Peninsula; Russia	3.21–22	Cook Bay (Erromango); Vanuatu	2.19	Cook Shoal; Torres Strait	1.32
Captain Cook Heritage Trail; England	0.02	Cid Harbour; Queensland, Aus.	1.28	Cook Bay (Malekula); Vanuatu	2.20	Cook Strait; New Zealand	1.11,
Captain Cook Park; Queensland, Aus.	1.26	Circumcision, Cape; Bouvet Island	2.03, 2.26	Cook Bay; Queensland, Aus.	1.28		1.18–21; 2.04, 2.23; 3.04
Captain Cook Point; Oregon, U.S.A.	3.14	Clapham; England	0.08	Cook Bay; S. America	2.25	Cook Stream; Te Wai Pounamu, N.Z.	2.05
Captain Cook State Recreation;		Clarence, Port; W. Alaska	3.21	Cook Bay; South Georgia	2.27	Cook, Teluk; New Guinea	1.33
S. Alaska	3.18	Clear, Cape; Ireland	0.10	Cook Bluff; Te Ika a Maui, N.Z.	1.14	Cook's Anchorage; Society Islands	2.07; 3.10
Captain Cook's Rock; Vanuatu	2.18	Clerke, Cape; Vancouver Island, Can.	3.14	Cook Calotte; Kerguelen Island	3.03	Cook's Bay; Canada	0.13
Carbonnear; Canada	0.18	Clerke Island; Queensland, Aus.	1.31	Cook Canyon; Pacific Ocean	4.01	Cook's Bay; New Guinea	1.33
Cascade Cove; Te Wai Pounamu, N.Z.	2.05	Clerke, Mount; Te Wai Pounamu, N.Z.	2.05	Cook, Cape; Vancouver Island	3.14	Cook's Bay; Te Ika a Maui, N.Z.	1.14

PLACE	MAP(S)
Endeavour Inlet; Te Wai Pounamu, N.Z.	1.19; 3.04
Endeavour Reef; Queensland, Aus.	1.28–29
Endeavour River; Queensland, Aus.	1.28–31
Endeavour Strait; Queensland, Aus.	1.32
Endeavour Stream; Queensland, Aus.	1.28
England	0.01–07, 0.10, 0.23; 3.30
English Bay; Aleutian Islands	3.20
English Bay; S. Alaska	3.17
English Channel	0.07, 0.10–11, 1.38; 2.30; 3.30
English Roads; Tongatapu Group	2.09; 3.09
English Shore; Newfoundland, Can.	0.17
Entrée, Ile de l'; Canada	0.14
Entry Island; Te Ika a Maui, N.Z.	1.11, 1.18
Entry Island; Te Wai Pounamu, N.Z.	2.05
Epi; Vanuatu	2.18, 2.20
Erroan; Vanuatu	2.19
Erromango; Vanuatu	2.18–19
Esk, River; England	0.02, 0.06
Espiritu Santo; Vanuatu	1.10; 2.17–18, 2.20
Espoir, Bay d'; Newfoundland, Can.	0.20–21
Est, Ile de l'; Canada	0.15
Estevan Point; Vancouver Island, Can.	3.14
'Eua; Tongatapu Group	2.09; 3.09
'Euaiki; Tongatapu Group	3.09
Everard, Cape; Victoria, Aus.	1.22
Everard, Mount; Victoria, Aus.	1.22
Evout Island; S. America	1.04
Faaa; Society Islands	**1.08; 2.15; 3.10**
Faafao, Baie; Society Islands	1.09
Faaroa, Baie; Society Islands	1.09; 2.08; 3.11
Facheux Bay; Newfoundland, Can.	0.20–21
Facile Harbour; Te Wai Pounamu, N.Z.	2.05
Fafa; Tongatapu Group	3.09
Faial; The Azores	2.30
Faial Channel; The Azores	2.30
Fair Isle; Scotland	0.12
Fairway Rock; Bering Strait	3.21
Fairweather, Cape; S.E. Alaska	3.16
Fairweather, Mount; S.E. Alaska	3.16
Falkland Islands; Atlantic Ocean	1.03; 2.26, 2.31
False Bay; South Africa	1.36; 2.02; 3.02, 3.29
False Cape; New Guinea	1.33
Family Islands; Queensland, Aus.	1.28
Fanga 'Uta Lagoon; Tongatapu Group	3.09
Fare; Society Islands	1.09; 2.08, 2.15
Fareone, Motu; Society Islands	1.08
Farerea, Passe; Society Islands	2.08
Farewell, Cape; Te Wai Pounamu, N.Z.	1.11, 1.18, 1.20–21
Farewell Spit; Te Wai Pounamu, N.Z.	1.18, 1.21
Fatu Hiva; Marquesas Islands	2.12
Fatu Huku; Marquesas Islands	2.12
Fayal; The Azores	2.30
Fecunditatis, Mare; Moon	4.01
Feddeya, Cape; Koryakskiy	3.26
Fenua i No, Motu; Society Islands	2.07
Fernando de Noronha; Brazil	1.01, 1.03; 2.29–30; 3.01–02
Ferolle; Newfoundland, Can.	0.19
Ferolle, Point; Newfoundland, Can.	0.19, 0.22
Ferryland; Newfoundland, Can.	0.18
Fidalgo, Port; S. Alaska	3.17
Fiji; Pacific Ocean	2.06, 2.10, 2.13, 2.17, 2.31; 3.06, 3.31
Finch Bay; Queensland, Aus.	1.30
Fingal, Point; New South Wales, Aus.	1.26
Finisterre, Cape; Spain	0.10–11; 1.01; 2.01
Fire Island; S. Alaska	3.18
Fitii; Society Islands	1.09, 2.08
Fitzroy Gardens (Melbourne); Aus.	1.22
Fitzroy Island; Queensland, Aus.	1.28
Five Fingers Peninsula; Te Wai Pounamu, N.Z.	2.05
Five Fingers Point; Te Wai Pounamu, N.Z.	2.05
Fixed Head; Te Wai Pounamu, N.Z.	2.05
Flagstaff Point; New South Wales, Aus.	1.23
Flat Island; Newfoundland, Can.	0.22
Flat Island; Te Ika a Maui, N.Z.	1.13
Flat Point; Te Ika a Maui, N.Z.	1.18
Flattery, Cape; Queensland, Aus.	1.29, 1.31
Flattery, Cape; Washington, U.S.A.	3.14
Flattery Rocks; Washington, U.S.A.	3.14
Fleet Street; London, England	0.08
Flinders Island; Tasmania, Aus.	2.04
Fluted Cape; Tasmania, Aus.	3.05
Foa; Ha'apai Group	2.16; 3.08
Foggy Cape; Alaska Peninsula	3.18–19
Foggy Island; Alaska Peninsula	3.19
Fogo; Cape Verde Islands	3.01
Fonoifua; Ha'apai Group	2.16
Forbes Islands; Queensland, Aus.	1.31
Formosa; Taiwan	3.28
Forster Bay; South Sandwich Islands	2.28
Forster, Lake; Te Wai Pounamu, N.Z.	2.05
Forster, Mount; Te Wai Pounamu, N.Z.	2.05
Forster Passage; South Sandwich Islands	2.28
Fort Venus; Society Islands	1.07
Forth, Firth of; Scotland	0.12
Fortune; Newfoundland, Can.	0.20
Fortune Bay; Newfoundland, Can.	0.18, 0.20
Fotuha'a; Ha'apai Group	3.08
Foulweather, Cape; Oregon, U.S.A.	3.13–14
Foulwind, Cape; Te Wai Pounamu, N.Z.	1.20
Foveaux Strait; Te Wai Pounamu, N.Z.	1.20
Fox Glacier; Te Wai Pounamu, N.Z.	1.11
Fox Islands; Aleutian Islands	3.20
Fox Island Harbour; Newfoundland, Can.	0.21
France	0.10–11
Frankland Islands; Queensland, Aus.	1.28
Fraser Island; Queensland, Aus.	1.27
Frazer, Cape; South Sandwich Islands	2.28
Frederik Hendrik Island; New Guinea	1.33
Freezland Rock; South Sandwich Islands	2.28
Fremantle; Western Australia	1.35
French Pass; Te Wai Pounamu, N.Z.	1.21
French Shore; Newfoundland, Can.	0.17
Friendly Cove; Canada	3.15
Fucusgigantes, Bay of; Kerguelen Island	3.03
Fuerteventura; Canary Islands	3.01
Fujiyama; Japan	3.28
Funchal; Madeira	1.02
Fundy, Bay of; Canada	0.14
Furneaux Isles Group; Tasmania, Aus.	2.04
Futuna; Vanuatu	2.19
Gabarus Bay; Canada	**0.14**
Gallion's Reach; England	0.08
Galway; Ireland	3.30
Gambell; Bering Sea	3.22
Gannet Island; Te Ika a Maui, N.Z.	1.16
Garnish; Newfoundland, Can.	0.20
Gaspe; Canada	0.15
Gaspe, Baie de; Canada	0.15
Gaspe, Cap de; Canada	0.15
Gaspe, Havre de; Canada	0.15
Gaspe Peninsula; Canada	0.15
Gaua; Vanuatu	2.18
George, Cape; Kerguelen Island	3.03
George, Cape; South Georgia	2.27
Georgetown; Ascension Island	2.29
Gilbert Island; Te Wai Pounamu, N.Z.	2.05
Gilbert Islands; S. America	2.25
Gisborne; Te Ika a Maui, N.Z.	1.12, 1.39
Gladstone; Queensland, Aus.	1.27
Glass Houses, The; Queensland, Aus.	1.26
Gloucester, Cape; Queensland, Aus.	1.28
Glubokaya Bay; Koryakskiy	3.26
Goat Island; Vanuatu	2.19
Golden Bay; Te Wai Pounamu, N.Z.	1.18, 1.21
Gomera; Canary Islands	3.01
Good Hope, Cape of; South Africa	1.36; 2.02; 3.02, 3.29
Good Success, Bay of; S. America	1.04; 2.25
Good Success, Cape of; S. America	2.25
Goose Bay; S. America	2.25
Goose Cove; Te Wai Pounamu, N.Z.	2.05
Goose Island; S. Alaska	3.17
Goose Island; S. America	2.25
Gore Island; Queensland, Aus.	1.31
Gore Island; Vancouver Island, Can.	3.15
Gore, Mount; Vancouver Island, Can.	3.15
Gore Point; S. Alaska	3.18
Gore, Port; Te Wai Pounamu, N.Z.	1.19
Gores Island; Bering Sea	3.22
Gough Island; Atlantic Ocean	2.02; 3.02
Graciosa; The Azores	2.30

PLACE	MAP(S)
Lizard Island; Queensland, Aus.	1.28, 1.29, 1.31
Lizard, The; England	1.38; 2.30
Lofanga; Ha'apai Group	3.08
London; England	0.07–11, 0.23; 3.30
London Lagoon; Christmas Island	3.06
Londonderry Island; S. America	2.25
Long Harbour; Newfoundland, Can.	0.20
Long Island; Newfoundland, Can.	0.20
Long Island (Dusky Sound); Te Wai Pounamu, N.Z.	2.05
Long Island; (Queen Charlotte Sound); Te Wai Pounamu, N.Z.	1.19; 2.23
Lookers on; Te Wai Pounamu, N.Z.	1.20
Lookout, Point; Queensland, Aus.	1.26
Lopatka, Cape; Kamchatka	3.26–28
Loranchet, Peninsule; Kerguelen Island	3.03
Louisbourg Harbour; Canada	0.14
Louisbourg; Canada	0.13–15
Low Neck Bay; Te Wai Pounamu, N.Z.	1.21
Low Wooded Island; Queensland, Aus.	1.29
Lowestoft; England	3.30
Loyalty Islands; New Caledonia	2.21–22
Luangahu; Ha'apai Group	3.08
Lucy Wright Beach Park; Hawaiian Islands	3.12
Luncheon Cove; Te Wai Pounamu, N.Z.	2.05
Luzon Island; Philippines	3.28
Lyons Point; Queensland, Aus.	1.28
Lyttelton Harbour; Te Wai Pounamu, N.Z.	1.20
Maalaea Bay; Hawaiian Islands	**3.25**
Maara; Society Islands	3.10
Maatea; Society Islands	3.11
Macao; China	3.28–29, 3.31
Macarira; China	3.28
Mackay; Queensland, Aus.	1.27
Macleay River; New South Wales, Aus.	1.25
MacMasters Beach; New South Wales, Aus.	1.25
Macquarie Island; Southern Ocean	2.04; 3.04
Madagascar; Indian Ocean	1.35
Madeira; Atlantic Ocean	0.13; 1.01–02, 1.38–39; 2.01, 2.30–31; 3.01
Madeleine, Iles de la; Canada	0.14–15
Maewo; Vanuatu	2.18
Magdalen Islands; Canada	0.14–15
Magellan, Strait of; S. America	1.03; 2.25
Magnetic Island; Queensland, Aus.	1.28
Magra Isle; Queensland, Aus.	1.31
Mahaena; Society Islands	1.08
Mahaena, Passe; Society Islands	1.08
Mahaiatea; Society Islands	1.08
Mahamate Beach; New Caledonia	2.21
Mahina; Society Islands	1.07
Maiao; Society Islands	1.06
Maio; Cape Verde Islands	2.01; 3.01
Makaha'a; Tongatapu Group	3.09
Makahauena Point; Hawaiian Islands	3.25
Makapuu Point; Hawaiian Islands	3.25
Makushin Bay; Aleutian Islands	3.20
Mal Baie; Canada	0.15
Malekula; Vanuatu	2.18, 2.20
Mallicollo; Vanuatu	2.18, 2.20
Malo; Vanuatu	2.20
Malokilikili; Vanuatu	2.20
Manawaora Bay; Te Ika a Maui, N.Z.	1.17
Manele Bay; Lanai	3.25
Mangaia; Cook Islands	3.06–07
Mango; Ha'apai Group	2.16; 3.08
Mangrove River; Te Ika a Maui, N.Z.	1.14
Manifold, Cape; Queensland, Aus.	1.27
Manley Isle; Queensland, Aus.	1.31
Manuae; Cook Islands	2.06; 3.07
Many Islands; Te Wai Pounamu, N.Z.	2.05
Marau Point; Te Ika a Maui, N.Z.	1.13
Mare Fecunditatis; Moon	4.01
Mare Nectaris; Moon	4.01
Margaret Bay; Queensland, Aus.	1.31
Maria Island; Tasmania, Aus.	2.04
Maria Van Diemen, Cape; Te Ika a Maui, N.Z.	1.11, 1.16
Marion Island; Prince Edward Islands	3.03
Marmot Bay; S. Alaska	3.18
Marmot Island; S. Alaska	3.18
Maroe, Baie; Society Islands	2.08
Marokau; Tuamotu Islands	1.05
Marquesas Islands; Pacific Ocean	2.10, 2.12–14, 2.31
Marseveen; Atlantic Ocean	2.26
Marske; England	0.02
Marton; England	0.01–03, 0.23
Mary's Peak; Oregon, U.S.A.	3.14
Maskelyne Islands; Vanuatu	2.20
Mataiea; Society Islands	1.08
Mataso; Vanuatu	2.18
Mataura; Austral Islands	3.06
Matavai Bay; Society Islands	1.06–07; 2.07, 2.14, 2.15; 3.10
Maui; Hawaiian Islands	3.23, 3.25
Mauke; Cook Islands	3.07
Mauna Kea; Hawaiian Islands	3.23
Mauna Loa; Hawaiian Islands	3.23
Maupihaa; Society Islands	2.14
Maurice, Port; S. America	1.04
Mauritius; Indian Ocean	1.35
Mauuloa; Hawaiian Islands	3.12
Mayachnyy, Cape; Kamchatka	3.27
Mayfair; England	0.08
Mayor Island; Te Ika a Maui, N.Z.	1.13, 1.15
McCallum; Newfoundland, Can.	0.20–21
Meama; Ha'apai Group	3.08
Mechigmenskaya Inlet; Chukotskiy Peninsula	3.22
Mednyy Island; Bering Sea	3.26
Mehetia; Society Islands	1.05
Mekong Delta; Vietnam	3.29
Melbourne; Victoria, Aus.	1.22
Melville, Cape; Queensland, Aus.	1.31
Mercury Bay; Te Ika a Maui, N.Z.	1.11, 1.13–15
Mercury Islands; Te Ika a Maui, N.Z.	1.15
Meretoto; Te Wai Pounamu, N.Z.	1.19
Mew Stone; England	1.01
Miall; Queensland, Aus.	1.27
Mid-Atlantic Ridge; Atlantic Ocean	2.02
Middelburg; Netherlands	0.07
Middelburg; Tongatapu Group	2.09
Middle Brother; New South Wales, Aus.	1.25
Middlesbrough; England	0.02–03
Mile End; England	0.09
Minami Iwo; Kazan-Retto	3.28
Miquelon; Newfoundland, Can.	0.18
Miquelon, Ile; Newfoundland, Can.	0.15, 0.17, 0.18, 0.20
Mirimiri, Pointe; Society Islands	1.09
Mission Bay; Queensland, Aus.	1.28
Mitiaro; Cook Islands	3.07
Mo'unga'one; Ha'apai Group	3.08
Moa Island; Queensland, Aus.	1.32
Moerai Bay; Austral Islands	1.10
Mohotani; Marquesas Islands	2.12
Mokapu Point; Hawaiian Islands	3.25
Molokai; Hawaiian Islands	3.25
Molokini; Hawaiian Islands	3.23, 3.25
Monge Crater; Moon	4.01
Monkhouse Point; Queensland, Aus.	1.30
Montagu, Cape; South Sandwich Islands	2.28
Montagu Island; South Sandwich Islands	2.28
Montague Island; New South Wales, Aus.	1.22
Montague Island; S. Alaska	3.17
Montague Island; Vanuatu	2.18
Montague Strait; S. Alaska	3.17
Monument, The; Vanuatu	2.18
Moon, the	4.01
Moorea; Society Islands	0.24; 1.06, 1.08; 3.10–11
Moray Firth; Scotland	0.12
Mordvinof, Cape; Aleutian Islands	3.20
Moreton Bay; Queensland, Aus.	1.26
Moreton, Cape; Queensland, Aus.	1.26
Morlaix; France	0.10
Morotoi; Hawaiian Islands	3.25
Morton; England	0.02
Moscow; Russia	3.29
Mosquito Cove; Newfoundland, Can.	0.18
Motane; Marquesas Islands	2.12
Motuara Island; Te Wai Pounamu, N.Z.	1.19; .23; 3.04
Motuarohia Island; Te Ika a Maui, N.Z.	1.17
Motukawanui Island; Te Ika a Maui, N.Z.	1.17
Motukorure; Te Ika a Maui, N.Z.	1.14
Motuoroi Island; Te Ika a Maui, N.Z.	1.13

Select Bibliography

Beaglehole, J.C., *The Life of Captain James Cook*. London: Adam & Charles Black, 1974. 0713613823.

Begg, A. Charles and Neil C. Begg, *James Cook and New Zealand*. Wellington: N.Z. Government Printer, 1969.

Bibliography of Captain James Cook R.N., F.R.S., Circumnavigator, Ed. M.K. Beddie. 2nd ed. Sydney: Council of the Library of New South Wales, 1970. 724099999.

Burnicle, Ada and Rod Fleck, *A Genealogical Study of the Family of Captain James Cook R.N., F.R.S. 1728–1779*. Rev. ed. Middlesbrough: Middlesbrough Borough Council, 1990.

The Charts and Coastal Views of Captain Cook's Voyages, Volume one: The Voyage of the Endeavour 1768–1771. Ed. Andrew David. London: The Hakluyt Society, 1988. 0904180239.

The Charts and Coastal Views of Captain Cook's Voyages, Volume two: The Voyage of the Resolution and Adventure 1772–1775. Ed. Andrew David. London: The Hakluyt Society, 1992. 090418031X.

The Charts and Coastal Views of Captain Cook's Voyages, Volume three: The Voyage of the Resolution and Discovery 1776–1780. Ed. Andrew David. London: The Hakluyt Society, 1997. 0904180557.

Cook, James, *The Journals of Captain Cook*. Ed. J.C. Beaglehole. 5 vols. Woodbridge, UK: Boydell & Brewer, 1999. 0851157440.

Cook, James, *The Journals of Captain James Cook on his Voyages of Discovery, Volume one: The Voyage of the Endeavour 1768–1771*. Ed. J.C. Beaglehole. Cambridge: The Hakluyt Society, 1955.

Cook, James, *The Journals of Captain James Cook on his Voyages of Discovery, Volume two: The Voyage of the Resolution and Adventure 1772–1775*. Ed. J.C. Beaglehole. Cambridge: The Hakluyt Society, 1961.

Cook, James, *Voyages of Captain James Cook*. Facsim. ed. 9 vols. London: Curzon Press, 2000. 070071149X.

Cook, James and James King, *The Journals of Captain James Cook on his Voyages of Discovery, Volume three: The Voyage of the* Resolution *and* Discovery *1776–1780*. Ed. J.C. Beaglehole. 2 vols. Cambridge: The Hakluyt Society, 1967.

James Cook, Surveyor of Newfoundland, Being a collection of charts of the coasts of Newfoundland and Labradore, drawn from original surveys taken by James Cook and Michael Lane. With an introductory essay by R.A. Skelton. San Francisco: David Magee, 1965.

Joppien, Rudiger and Bernard Smith, *The Art of Captain Cook's Voyages. Volume one: The Voyage of the* Endeavour *1768–1771*. Melbourne: Oxford University Press, 1985. 0195544552.

Joppien, Rudiger and Bernard Smith, *The Art of Captain Cook's Voyages. Volume two: The Voyage of the* Resolution *and* Adventure *1772–1775*. Melbourne: Oxford University Press, 1985. 0195544560.

Joppien, Rudiger and Bernard Smith, *The Art of Captain Cook's Voyages. Volume three: The Voyage of the* Resolution *and* Discovery *1776–1780*. Melbourne: Oxford University Press, 1987. 0195547268.

Kippis, Andrew, *The Life of Captain James Cook*. London: G. Nicol, G.G.J. & J. Robinson, 1788.

Parkin, Ray, *H.M. Bark* Endeavour: *Her place in Australian History*. Melbourne: The Miegunyah Press, 1997. 0522847161.

Rae, Julia, *Captain James Cook Endeavours*. London: Stepney Historical Trust, 1997. 0951792415.

Rienits, Rex and Thea Rienits, *The Voyages of Captain Cook*. London: Paul Hamlyn, 1968.

Thornton, Clifford E., *Captain Cook in Cleveland: A study of his early years*. Middlesbrough: Middlesbrough Borough Council, 1978.

Whiteley, William H., *James Cook in Newfoundland 1762–1767*. St. John's, Newfoundland: Newfoundland Historical Society, 1975.